MAGILL'S SURVEY OF AMERICAN LITERATURE

Volume 8

Lorde–Wright

Cumulative Indexes

Edited by

FRANK N. MAGILL

Marshall Cavendish Corporation
New York • London • Toronto • Sydney • Singapore

Published By
Marshall Cavendish Corporation
2415 Jerusalem Avenue
P.O. Box 587
North Bellmore, New York 11710
United States of America

∞ The paper used in these volumes conforms to the American
National Standard for Permanence of Paper for Printed Library
Materials, Z39.48-1984.

Library of Congress Cataloging-in-Publication Data
Magill's survey of American literature. Supplement / edited by Frank
    N. Magill.
    p. cm.
Includes bibliographical references and index.
    1. American literature—Dictionaries. 2. American literature—
Bio-bibliography. 3. Authors, American—Biography—Diction-
aries. I. Magill, Frank Northen, 1907   .
PS21.M34   1994 Suppl.
810.9'0003—dc20
[B]
ISBN 1-85435-734-4 (set)   94-25192
ISBN 1-85435-733-6 (volume 2)   CIP

CONTENTS

MAGILL'S SURVEY OF AMERICAN LITERATURE

MAGILL'S
SURVEY
OF
AMERICAN
LITERATURE

AUDRE LORDE

Born: New York, New York
February 18, 1934
Died: Christiansted, St. Croix, Virgin Islands
November 17, 1992

Principal Literary Achievement

Describing herself as a "black lesbian feminist warrior poet," Audre Lorde used her powerful writing to battle for the rights of all people and helped to legitimize the use of poetry as ethical, moral, and political commentary.

Biography

Audrey Geraldine Lorde was born on February 18, 1934, in New York City, the third child of Linda Gertrude Belmar Lorde and Frederick Byron Lorde. Her parents had immigrated to the United States from Grenada ten years previously. After the births of his three daughters, Lorde's father attended real-estate school and began to manage small rooming houses in Harlem. Lorde later remembered how consistently her parents shared responsibility for the family.

Lorde was an inarticulate child who did not begin to speak until she was approximately five years old. At that time, she was charmed out of a tantrum in a library by a librarian who read several storybooks to her. The young Audre then began to interact with the world, learning to read, then to speak, and then to write. As she was growing up, Lorde communicated through poetry, responding to questions or comments with poems she had memorized. When she was twelve or thirteen, she began to write her own poetry to express feelings that were not reflected in what she had been reading. Initially, Lorde did not write down her poems; rather, she preferred to memorize them.

Even as a child, Lorde exhibited independence in her approach to life. For example, as she recounts in *Zami: A New Spelling of My Name* (1982), when she was first learning to print her name, Lorde disliked the tail of the "y" in "Audrey." Instead, she liked the evenness of "Audre Lorde," a lifelong preference. Part of her unique view of the world may stem from the fact that Lorde was vision-impaired. When she was three years old, she recalled that "the dazzling world of strange lights and fascinating shapes which I inhabited resolved itself in mundane definitions, and I learned another nature of things as seen through eyeglasses."

Lorde progressed through grade school in New York, finally spending four years

at Hunter High School, where poetry became an accepted effort rather than a "rebel-lious vice" and where she was elected literary editor of the school arts magazine. This period in her life was tumultuous and was marked by a strained relationship with her parents, her mother especially; however, her first published poem was accepted during her high school years by *Seventeen* magazine. About her first love affair with a boy, the poem was judged by her English teachers to be "too romantic" to be included in the school paper.

Two weeks after her high-school graduation, Lorde moved out of her parents' home and became self-supporting. After a few years of working as a nurse's aide and at various other jobs, she had saved enough to take her to Mexico, where she attended the National University of Mexico in 1954.

After her return from Mexico, Lorde worked as a librarian while continuing to write poetry and essays. She completed her bachelor of arts degree at Hunter College in 1959 and her master of library science degree at the Columbia University School of Library Science in 1960. In 1962, Lorde married Edwon Ashley Rollins and sub-sequently gave birth to a daughter and a son. She and Rollins divorced in 1970. In 1968, shortly after the publication of her first book of poems, Lorde was offered a position as poet-in-residence at Tougaloo College, an experience she called "pivotal." Her first trip into the South, it was also her first time away from her children and the first time that she had to deal with young black students in a workshop setting. During this time, she realized that writing and teaching were inseparable and that she had found her calling.

Lorde had continued to teach, write, and travel when, in 1978, she discovered a lump in her breast which turned out to be malignant. Though battling breast cancer, Lorde kept writing and, later, collated some of her writings into *The Cancer Journals* (1980), a remarkable story of despair, hope, support, and courage. Such an action was typical of Lorde, whose life experiences and work are inextricably woven together.

Analysis

As a young girl, Lorde expressed nearly all of her daily conversation by quoting poetry she had memorized. As she began to grow up, however, she realized that there were no poems that addressed many of her feelings and experiences as a black feminist lesbian. She felt "totally alienated, disoriented, crazy." Thus, Lorde began writing to fill her own needs. She said that she wrote for herself, for her children, and for those women who do not speak because they have been silenced or because they have been taught to respect fear more than they respect themselves. Lorde wrote, often militantly, always expressively, of racism, sexism, homophobia, love, and pain as well as on political, social, and environmental issues. Critic Jerome Brooks has discerned three central themes in Lorde's work: the issue of power, her quest for love, and her commitment to intellectual and moral clarity about so-called familiar things.

Lorde's discussion of the existence and use of power is not limited to an examination of the power of words, a theme she uses frequently, but includes explorations of black versus white, female versus male, child versus mother, the disadvantaged versus bureaucratic institutions, patients versus the medical establishment, and smaller nations versus the United States.

Lorde's poem "Coal" (1976) is, on the surface, a study of the power of a word, of "how sound comes into a word, colored/ by who pays what for speaking." A closer examination indicates the poet's own power, which, one critic has noted, helps her to "transform rage at racism into triumphant self-assertion." Another example of the theme of power appears in "From the House of Yemanja" (1978), in which Lorde's troubled childhood relationship with her strong mother is painted.

Lorde's love poetry deals not only with romantic love but also with the many different faces of human love: love between parent and child, love between friends, love for one's family, and love for one's art. While she does occasionally use the theme of heterosexual love, it is clear from her work that her sexual preference is for women, that she is "woman-oriented." As the scholar and poet Joan Martin has commented, however, "anyone who has ever been in love can respond to the straightforward passion and pain, sometimes one and the same, in Lorde's poems."

The poem "From the House of Yemanja" also witnesses Lorde recalling a childhood that made her feel imperfect and unloved. She cries, "Mother I need/ mother I need/ . . ./ I am/ the sun and moon and forever hungry" and is left craving the mother-love that she missed. In contrast, "Now That I Am Forever with Child" (1976) is a rapturous song to her new parent-child relationship, which bears no resemblance to her earlier troubled childhood.

While these poems display beauty, and roughness, strength, and emotion, Lorde's writings dealing with mature love include some of the most beautiful poems in her work. For Lorde, there is no such thing as universal love in literature; there is only immediate, particular love, which results in art. The prose work *Zami: A New Spelling of My Name* is a blend of autobiography and fiction that provides accounts of her childhood years and of her coming of age as a lesbian; the book is a celebration of all the women whom she loved and from whom she learned. Many of these formative experiences are referred to or form a base for some of Lorde's poems. For example, in "Fog Report," she writes, "In this misty place where hunger finds us/ seeking direction/ I am too close to you to be useful," a comment about a relationship that is decaying. Another of Lorde's best poems is "Walking Our Boundaries," which was written after a battle with cancer and which honors the wonder of life and love. Lorde's experience with cancer was, like most of her experiences, incorporated into her work. One result was Lorde's first major prose piece, the extraordinarily honest and descriptive *The Cancer Journals*, which describes the course of her battle from the first discovery of a lump in her breast to her post-mastectomy experiences (which include such telling moments as a nurse's informing her that not wearing a prosthesis is bad for the morale of the office and a physician's claiming that no truly happy person gets cancer).

Such experiences evoked the "warrior" in Lorde, which had previously been roused in poems such as "The American Cancer Society: Or, There Is More than One Way to Skin a Coon," in which Lorde vehemently attacks racism in America. Lorde saw social protest as a means of encouraging people to realize the inconsistencies and horror in modern life; for her, the issues of social protest and art were inseparable.

Another example of her artistry, her social commentary, and her talent for making her readers squirm is the poem "The Brown Menace, Or Poem to the Survival of Roaches," in which the pests symbolically represent black Americans, whose destruction will extend to their destroyers. While Lorde's skillful poetry reflects the intensity of her life and feeling, her work's most outstanding characteristics are her complete honesty and her sincere love for the world and the people in it.

POWER

First published: 1974
Type of work: Poem

"Power" is Lorde's enraged response to the acquittal of a white policeman who shot and killed a ten-year-old black boy.

"Power" is based on an actual event and Lorde's personal reaction, which she recorded in her journal. Driving across town, Lorde heard a radio broadcast announcing the acquittal of a white policeman who had shot and killed a black ten-year-old. She was so furious and sickened that she felt that the sky turned red, that she had to park the car before she drove it into a wall. Then and there, she inscribed her feelings of outrage over the decision of the jury of eleven white men and one black woman.

In the unforgettable imagery employed in "Power," the streets of New York become "a desert of raw gunshot wounds," a white desert where the only liquid for miles is the blood of a dead black child. Through this poem, Lorde tries to "make power out of hatred and destruction," to heal her "dying son with kisses." Yet she cannot help expressing her rage at the policeman's comment, offered in his own defense, that "I didn't notice the size or nothing else/ only the color."

While expressing her rage over this story, "Power" also illuminates Lorde's ability to provide what one critic has called a "relentlessly clinical analysis" that "often leads to a perception of human character that is, perhaps, the ultimate justification for art." For example, Lorde writes that the black jurywoman said that she had been convinced, "meaning/ they had dragged her 4'10″ black woman's frame over the hot coals of four centuries of white male approval/ until she let go the first real power she ever had." Lorde's own powerful imagery returns in the following lines, as she compares this surrender to the jurywoman's lining "her own womb with cement/ to make a graveyard for our children."

The final stanza of "Power" begins with the poet unable to deal with the destruction and the rage she feels. As the stanza continues, what she fears and what her audience fears become one: Unless she (representing black youth) can learn from her experience, her rage will corrupt her. She will seem inert—until, one day, she will explode into frenzied violence against an elderly white woman "who is somebody's mother." In this version, Lorde hears "a greek chorus . . . singing in 3/4 time/ 'Poor thing. She never hurt a soul. What beasts they are.'"

The haunting imagery serves to highlight the themes of rage and power that are woven through Lorde's writings. She directs rage not only at the glaring injustice of racism, as characterized in "Power," but also toward sexual oppression and, to a lesser extent, political issues and the slight cruelties of everyday life. Lorde is particularly sympathetic to the anguish of all outsiders, especially the young black population of New York. Despite the intense physical and emotional pain she and all outsiders experience, Lorde manages to transform that rage into a force for change.

WALKING OUR BOUNDARIES

First published: 1978
Type of work: Poem

In this quiet, spiritual poem written after her confrontation with cancer, Lorde and her partner walk together through their garden.

One of Lorde's best poems, "Walking Our Boundaries" was written after she was forced to confront her own mortality in a battle with breast cancer. About a walk she shared in the small garden surrounding the house that she and her partner own, this poem is beautifully narrated and quietly blends symbolism together with deep feeling. The poem begins, "This first bright day has broken/ the back of winter./ We rise from war/ . . . both stunned that sun can shine so brightly/ after all our pain."

As the pair cautiously inspects their "joint holding," they talk of "ordinary articles/ with relief." A sense of delicacy and unexpected peace is conveyed, which implies just how severe was the "last winter's storm." In the midst of the symbolism she employs, Lorde does not lose her sense of perspective, saying that "it does not pay to cherish symbols/ when the substance/ lies so close at hand/ waiting to be held." This thought blends into the next, as her lover's hand "falls off the apple bark/ like casual fire/ along my back," the light affectionate touch breaking the back of her emotional winter as the sun has broken the back of the physical winter.

The calm delicacy of tone and technique in this poem is in startling contrast to the passions and turmoil Lorde expressed in *The Cancer Journals*, reflecting the peace that comes after "war"; the battle is, at least for the time being, over. In *The Cancer Journals*, Lorde wrote that it was very important for her to develop and regain her own sense of power, to be able to view herself as a warrior rather than a victim. Her anger that the medical establishment encourages its patients to behave as victims is expressed in an extremely biting manner, and her writing drips with scorn as she details the ways in which she was encouraged to pretend, during treatment and after her mastectomy, that everything was back to normal. Another theme in *The Cancer Journals*, however, is the strength that Lorde gained through the love and support of her network of friends as well as her partner, who is compared to a sunflower. It is this love that she cherishes so deeply and for which she expresses her gratitude in "Walking Our Boundaries."

The final stanza of "Walking Our Boundaries" continues the moods of delicacy, fragility, and wonder. The voices of the two women "seem too loud for this small yard/ too tentative for women/ so in love." Despite the physical decay that has occurred ("the siding has come loose in spots"), the human spirit is triumphant ("our footsteps hold this place/ together/ as our place"), and the life surrounding and filling the house and garden is made possible by the joint decision of and the love between the partners. The poem ends on a beautiful note of hope: Although Lorde does not know when they will laugh freely again, they are planning to dig up another plot for the spring's seeding.

COAL

First published: 1976
Type of work: Poem

"Coal" is a study of the power and the form of words that represents a declaration of the poet's self-awareness and self-confidence.

In her essay "Poetry Is Not a Luxury," Lorde argues that poetry, as a revelatory distillation of experience, provides the illumination by which people scrutinize their lives and give substance to their unformed ideas. She also believes that each woman's being holds a dark place where her true spirit grows hidden, forming a reservoir of creativity, power, and unexamined and unrecorded feeling. She has written that "the woman's place of power within each of us is neither white nor surface; it is dark, it is ancient, and it is deep." It is not surprising, then, that one of Lorde's most frequently anthologized poems is "Coal," with its final two lines independently declaring "I am Black because I come from the earth's inside/ now take my word for jewel in the open light." This self-assertion and her awareness of the power of words are not merely themes but a necessity and a way of living for Lorde.

In form, "Coal" is a discussion of the many different forms that Lorde's words can take, "colored/ by who pays what for speaking." Lorde's imagery is as skillful as ever, as in such phrases as "singing out within the passing crash of sun," an "ill-pulled tooth with a ragged edge," or "seeking like gypsies over my tongue/ to explode through my lips/ like young sparrows bursting from shell." The words that she analyzes, however, are both servant and served. The phrasing she employs seems to imply that Lorde herself is trapped by her words: "Some words live in my throat/ breeding like adders . . ./ Some words/ bedevil me."

One of Lorde's principal themes concerns her reaction to racist attitudes and acts; her response to racism is, in a word, anger. Lorde lived with that anger for her entire life; and she once remarked that it "has eaten clefts into my living only when it remained unspoken, useless to anyone." For Lorde, the expression and use of anger was not destructive. Rather, as one critic has explained "the poem 'Coal' suggests the strength through which she can transform rage at racism into triumphant self-assertion."

Summary

Audre Lorde is noted for her poems and essays expressing rage at the injustices of modern American society. Her work is distinctly political and her subjects topical. Lorde sought to encourage awareness of and to provide an example for other "outsiders." Nevertheless, she remained a caring individual whose love poems are moving and poignant. In the words of teacher and writer Jerome Brooks, the world is reflected in Lorde's poetry, "mainly through the conflicts and confrontation of her coming to terms with herself or with very private pain."

Bibliography

Evans, Mari, ed. *Black Women Writers (1950-1980)*. Garden City, N.Y.: Anchor Press/Doubleday, 1983.

Gilbert, Sandra M., and Susan Gubar, eds. *The Norton Anthology of Literature by Women*. New York: W. W. Norton, 1985.

Lorde, Audre. *A Burst of Light: Essays*. Ithaca, N.Y.: Firebrand Books, 1988.

_____. *Sister Outsider: Essays and Speeches*. Trumansburg, N.Y.: Crossing Press, 1984.

Tate, Claudia, ed. *Black Women Writers at Work*. New York: Continuum, 1983.

Wall, Cheryl A., ed. *Changing Our Own Words: Essays on Criticism, Theory, and Writing by Black Women*. New Brunswick, N.J.: Rutgers University Press, 1989.

Katherine Socha

TERRY McMILLAN

Born: Port Huron, Michigan
October 18, 1951

Principal Literary Achievement
McMillan's honest, realistic novels dramatize the struggles of African American women in their search for love and commitment.

Biography

Terry McMillan was born on October 18, 1951, in Port Huron, Michigan, a largely working-class town northeast of Detroit. Her father, Edward Lewis McMillan, a sanitation worker, was an alcoholic. Her mother, Madeline Tillman McMillan, a hardworking, determined woman, finally tired of being physically abused by her husband and divorced him. He died three years later, at the age of thirty-nine.

As the oldest of the five McMillan children, Terry had more than her share of responsibility. One of the jobs she took in order to contribute to the family income, however, brought her more than the meager $1.25 an hour she earned. When, at sixteen, she started shelving books at a local library, McMillan learned to love books. At first, seeing the classic works by writers such as the German novelist Thomas Mann and New England essayists Henry Thoreau and Ralph Waldo Emerson, she assumed that all authors were white. Only when she saw the picture of African American writer James Baldwin on the cover of a novel did she realize that blacks, too, could be writers. Even though she as yet had no idea of becoming a novelist herself, McMillan would come to consider this moment a turning point in her life.

At seventeen, McMillan decided that there was no future for her in Port Huron. Leaving her job as a keypunch operator, she headed for Los Angeles, where she found secretarial work and enrolled at Los Angeles City College. There, in a course on African American classics, she learned for the first time about the richness of her own heritage.

For a writer who was to be preoccupied with relationships, it was appropriate that McMillan's own first literary effort, a poem, was the result of an unhappy involvement with a man. Soon, she said, words began "turning into sentences." She decided to major in journalism at the University of California at Berkeley, and she also began writing fiction. In 1976, thanks to the novelist Ishmael Reed, she saw her first short story in print.

It was to be eight years, however, before McMillan's writing career would begin in earnest. First, she had to defeat her alcoholism and her drug habit, which had already begun to dominate her existence. After being graduated from Berkeley in 1979, McMillan moved to New York City and enrolled in a master's program at Columbia University, then dropped out of graduate school and started working as a word processor with a law firm. In her free time, instead of writing, McMillan drank and took drugs with her boyfriend, Leonard Welch. Finally, on the eve of her thirtieth birthday, McMillan decided to change the direction of her life. She gave up cocaine and a few months later joined Alcoholics Anonymous and stopped drinking. In 1984, she had a son, Solomon. Several months later, seeing in her life the same pattern of abuse that she had observed in her own parents, McMillan broke off with Welch, resolving to make a new start for her baby and herself.

At the urging of friends in the Harlem Writers' Guild, McMillan had turned one of her short stories into a novel, *Mama*. After it was accepted by Houghton Mifflin for publication in 1987, the author realized that her publisher intended to promote it only minimally. With characteristic determination, McMillan sent three thousand letters to universities, colleges, book chains, and independent booksellers, set up her own promotional tour, and managed to get the first printing of her book sold before it was even published. Her success at this venture amazed Houghton Mifflin and made McMillan a legend in the publishing world.

In 1987, McMillan took a teaching position at the University of Wyoming in Laramie and began work on her second novel, *Disappearing Acts* (1989). Praised by critics, the book became a bestseller and was optioned for film production. McMillan followed it with a collection, *Breaking Ice: An Anthology of Contemporary African-American Fiction* (1990), composed of fifty-seven selections by both established and relatively unknown black writers.

In August, 1990, a multimillion-dollar lawsuit was filed against McMillan and her publishers by Leonard Welch, who alleged that the character of Franklin Swift in *Disappearing Acts* was actually an unflattering picture of him. The case, however, was decided in McMillan's favor.

In 1990, McMillan had accepted a teaching position at the University of Arizona in Tucson, but in the fall of 1991, taking leave from the university, she moved to Danville, California. Her 1992 novel *Waiting to Exhale* was both a critical and popular success. The paperback rights alone brought the sum of 2.64 million dollars, and Twentieth Century-Fox bought the film rights to the book. In the wake of her enormous success, however, McMillan commented that what is of primary importance to her is not the amount of money she makes but rather the fact that she is happy about her work and her life.

Analysis

It has distressed some African American activists that McMillan does not focus on racism or social inequities. Instead, her primary emphasis is on personal fulfillment, particularly for black women. Except for Mildred in *Mama*, all of McMillan's protagonists are well-educated, upwardly mobile, bright young women like the author. She has defended her focus on such characters by proclaiming that hers is a new generation of black women writers, who are writing about a different world. McMillan frequently points out that her fiction arises out of her own observation and her own experience; it is not tailored to ideological purposes.

This is also McMillan's answer to complaints about her use of profanity. Her characters, she says, speak as they would in real life, and the fact that so many of her fans compare reading a McMillan novel to talking with their girlfriends supports the author's argument. By seeming simply to report her characters' thoughts and conversations, McMillan achieves an effect of immediacy that would be lost if she wrote in chaste, formal prose.

The most vehement criticisms of McMillan, however, concern her attitude toward African American men. A major theme in McMillan's novels is the difficulty that black women have in finding partners who are worthy of them. In contrast to her strong, responsible, independent women, McMillan's black male characters are weak and unreliable. They tend to define manliness in primitive terms of their power to subdue women or to seduce them.

Many of McMillan's men are like Crook Peacock in *Mama*, who makes a habit of getting drunk, breaking whatever fragile objects his wife treasures, and then giving her a thorough beating, which can be halted only by her agreeing to sexual intercourse. Even those male characters who do not descend to physical violence are only too willing to exploit the women who love them. In *Waiting to Exhale*, for example, a man in whom one of McMillan's heroines has invested three thousand dollars is repeatedly unfaithful to her, while the wealthy husband of another not only deserts his wife but also tries to escape with all of their property, heartlessly leaving her and their children in desperate financial straits.

Many of McMillan's male characters truly believe that they are worth supporting merely for their sexual skills. Even the relatively sympathetic Franklin Swift, who eventually reforms, seems through most of *Disappearing Acts* to be much better at talking about improving his lot in life than at doing anything about it. Admittedly, in the segments of the book that are written from Franklin's point of view rather than through the eyes of his long-suffering lover Zora Banks, McMillan makes it clear that not all of Franklin's problems are his own fault. It is difficult for an uneducated black man to get a job, and even when, through the quota systems, Franklin manages to do so, he is before long laid off, sold out by his own representative. Franklin cannot be accused of not trying; his flaw is that he gives up too easily. It is obvious that most of his problems could be solved if he took the trouble to get an education. Unlike the determined Zora, however, Franklin is too weak-willed to do so. It is easier to get drunk and let Zora worry about the bills.

Since the women in her novels are so much more impressive than the men, most of whom impress one as being essentially childish, McMillan is often accused of blatant "male-bashing." Again, her answer is that she is writing about things as they are, not as they ought to be. While her women characters do make some scathing comments about the men in their lives, McMillan does not believe that men cannot change; indeed, as a satirist, she is committed to point out their shortcomings in hope that at least some of them will improve. Nevertheless, she has learned the hard way what the women in her books are forced to discover: that no relationship is worth the sacrifice of one's self-respect. In many cases, one is better off settling for the love of children and the friendship of other women than for a love affair that is ultimately destructive.

MAMA

First published: 1987
Type of work: Novel

Despite personal disappointments and desperate poverty, a strong black woman gives her children a chance for a better future.

Mama, McMillan's first novel, is the story of an uneducated black woman living in the 1960's who possesses the strength to survive and the will to hope. Mildred Peacock, the protagonist of the story, is no saint. She swears, she drinks constantly, and whenever she has a good opportunity, she lets a good-looking man make love to her. Her capacity for violence is established in the much-quoted first sentence of the book, "Mildred hid the ax beneath the mattress of the cot in the dining room." As Mildred recalls the night she has just been through, it is clear that she might almost be justified in killing the man who has been her husband for the last ten years. Once again, her drunken husband has battered her, while the five children he professes to love cowered, terrified, waiting for the sounds of fighting to change to the sound of sexual intercourse. Since it is she who provides the financial and emotional support for the family, and her unfaithful husband comes home only to beat her, make love, and father more children, Mildred finally decides that Crook is not worth keeping. She is going to get a divorce.

The rest of the novel shows how Mildred accomplishes the goal she has set herself: to rear her children so that they will have a better life than hers. It is not an easy task. She has to deal with heartless employers, persistent rent collectors, and suspicious welfare workers, as well as with her own weaknesses, particularly her needs for sex and alcohol. At one point, when her nerve pills are not enough, she has a nervous breakdown; however, she pulls herself together and rejoins the battle. At the end of the book, she sees all of her daughters settled, and she even has hopes for her prodigal son, who has sworn to stay away from the drugs that have caused him to land in prison.

In telling her story, McMillan alternates between two points of view, that of Mildred herself and that of her oldest daughter, Freda Peacock. Even though the two characters are often separated in the second half of the novel, each is always a part of the other's consciousness. Moreover, because mother and daughter share the same strengths, notably intelligence, determination, and an amazing capacity for hope, as well as the same weaknesses, including a susceptibility to addiction and a real talent for deluding themselves about men, the two lives often seem like one. Although it seems straightforward and simple, in fact *Mama* is intricately patterned and carefully choreographed, with the two main characters advancing and retreating until, at the end of the novel, they join in a touching expression of their love for each other.

DISAPPEARING ACTS

First published: 1989
Type of work: Novel

Two urban lovers with little in common except their feelings for each other move toward real commitment.

Disappearing Acts has been called an urban romance because it is in essence simply another New York City love story, as funny as the best works of Neil Simon. Underneath the wisecracks, the idiotic behavior, and the foolish misunderstandings that qualify McMillan's novel as a romantic comedy, however, there is a serious exploration of the nature of human relationships.

It is never easy for one person to love another; when two people differ as much as the lovers in *Disappearing Acts*, it is particularly difficult. Zora Banks is an educated, ambitious black woman, a gifted singer and songwriter who is supporting herself temporarily by teaching music in a junior high school. Franklin Swift is a construction worker with a high school equivalency diploma who for years has been thinking about going to night school and starting his own business but who has as yet done nothing about it. As Zora soon finds out, however, there is more to Franklin than his striking good looks and his talent for lovemaking. He is responsible; he does his best to support the wife from whom he is not yet divorced and the two children he had by her. He is generous; early in their relationship, he surprises Zora with three hundred dollars so that she can get her piano out of layaway. He is intelligent; even though he never finished high school, he can beat Zora at every word game they play. Moreover, in his attitude toward woodworking, Franklin exhibits the same kind of artistic integrity that he so admires in Zora.

Nevertheless, there are problems that the lovers prefer not to face. Franklin is easily discouraged and too easily sinks into apathy. Furthermore, the two are not honest with each other. When he loses his job, Franklin lies to Zora. In turn, she does not warn him about her epilepsy; he learns about it only when she has a seizure. Even more important, when she becomes pregnant with Franklin's child, Zora has an abortion without even consulting him.

Ironically, it is after Zora decides to go through with another pregnancy that the relationship reaches a crisis. Still haunted by the rejection of his own mother, Franklin sees his new son as a rival for Zora's love. Soon he is threatening Zora, and after she makes him move out, he comes back and breaks up their apartment, then gets drunk and takes cocaine. Yet when he has reached rock bottom, it is his love for Zora that motivates Franklin to change. After months of struggle, he returns, bringing Zora as a gift no less than his own life, which he has finally begun to set in order.

Disappearing Acts is written as a series of monologues, some of them voiced by Zora and some by Franklin. The characters are so distinct that after the first two sections, McMillan does not even bother to head her chapters with the name of the speaker. Interestingly, she felt so strongly about this dual point of view that she changed publishers rather than change the structure of her book. When her editors pressured her to tell the entire story through Franklin's eyes, McMillan switched to another publisher. Obviously, she felt that both viewpoints were essential to her story. From the enthusiasm with which critics and readers have received *Disappearing Acts*, it is clear that McMillan's decision was the right one.

WAITING TO EXHALE

First published: 1992
Type of work: Novel

 Four women friends support one another by sharing their uncertainties, their disappointments, their successes, and their dreams.

In several ways, *Waiting to Exhale* is quite different from McMillan's two earlier novels. Instead of two protagonists, there are four. Moreover, each of the twenty-eight chapters in *Waiting to Exhale* has its own provocative title, for example, "Venus in Virgo" and "Interstate Lust," and each also has the kind of beginning, middle, and end that one ordinarily finds in a short story. The novel proceeds from episode to episode, unified by the interaction between McMillan's four heroines, all of whom are successful women in their thirties living in Phoenix, Arizona, who are having trouble finding the right man.

Giving up on finding a man in Denver, Savannah Jackson quits her public-relations job and, with her cat and her art collection, moves to Phoenix, where she hopes to have better luck. From the beginning, however, the cards seem to be stacked against her. The good-looking man who agrees to drive her to Phoenix turns out to be a phony and a drug addict; the doctor out of her past who reappears in her life keeps stalling about the divorce he is supposedly considering; and the romantic San Franciscan she meets at a convention never returns her calls.

Meanwhile, Savannah's best friend, Bernadine Harris, has lost her husband of eleven years to a younger white woman. Although their marriage had long been dead, Bernadine had not expected to see the end of her comfortable lifestyle. She finds, however, that for months her husband has been transferring and concealing his assets so as to reduce the divorce settlement. Nothing makes Bernadine feel much better, not setting fire to her husband's BMW, not selling his restored antique car for a dollar, not even slapping his mistress. With the aid of her friends and the help of a determined lawyer, however, she finally gets a good settlement and even finds a fine man who wants to marry her.

Of all the friends, Robin Stokes is the one who seems most responsible for her own disasters. Good-hearted and generous, she is besotted with a man whose chief talent seems to be as a lover. Even though there is no possibility that this philanderer and parasite will settle down as a husband and father, she keeps taking him back. At the end of the novel, pregnant, Robin finally breaks off with him and decides instead to build her life around her baby.

For seventeen years, the fourth protagonist, Gloria Matthew, has done just what Robin plans to do. Ever since his birth, her son Tarik has been the center of her life. Whenever she feels lonely and empty, Gloria has made a habit of just eating a little more or working a little harder at the Oasis, the beauty shop that she owns. Ironically, not until she has nearly died from a heart attack, the direct result of poor diet and years of stress, does Gloria realize that in fact she is surrounded by people who love her: her three devoted women friends as well as her son, who is showing all the signs of fulfilling her hopes and expectations.

As far as the quest for worthy men is concerned, *Waiting to Exhale* must be said to end with probabilities, not with certainties. Yet there is one thing the protagonists can be sure of: From their friendship, they can draw the strength to face whatever life holds for them.

Summary

In a relatively short time, Terry McMillan has established herself as a spokesperson for a new generation. Although her major characters are black, McMillan's stories of bright, spunky, ambitious women who have almost everything they ever wanted—except the love of a good man—have evoked a warm response from women of all races.

McMillan justifies her use of profanity and her often unflattering portraits of men, as well as her inattention to racial issues, by insisting that she describes life as she sees it. Though she is a realist, however, McMillan is not a pessimist. While her women are often disappointed in the men they love, they do find pleasure in their children and both strength and joy in their friendships with each other.

Bibliography

Isaacs, Susan. "Chilling Out in Phoenix." *The New York Times Book Review*, May 31, 1992, 12.

McMillan, Terry. "Black America's Hottest Novelist: Terry McMillan Exhales and Inhales in a Revealing Interview." Interview by Laura B. Randolph. *Ebony* 48 (May, 1993): 23-28.

Max, Daniel. "McMillan's Millions." *The New York Times Magazine*, August 9, 1992, 20-26.

Sellers, Frances Stead. Review of *Waiting to Exhale*, by Terry McMillan. *Times Literary Supplement*, November 6, 1992, 20.

Smith, Wendy. "Terry McMillan: The Novelist Explores African American Life from the Point of View of a New Generation." *Publishers Weekly* 239 (May 11, 1992): 50-51.

Trescott, Jacqueline. "The Urban Author, Straight to the Point: Terry McMillan, Pulling Together the Urgent Fiction of Black Life." *The Washington Post*, November 17, 1990, p. D1.

Rosemary M. Canfield Reisman

PAULE MARSHALL

Born: Brooklyn, New York
April 9, 1929

Principal Literary Achievement
Marshall introduces a rich West Indian perspective into the body of African American literature, examining cross-cultural conflicts between individuals and their society.

Biography
Paule Marshall was one of three children of Samuel and Ada Burke, West Indian immigrants from the island of Barbados. Her father, whom she dearly loved, was unskilled but dreamed of a better life. Eventually, he left the family to join the "kingdom" of black religious leader Father Divine in Harlem. Her mother worked as a domestic. Marshall credits her early interest in language and stories to "the poets in the kitchen," her mother's Barbadian friends who gathered in the basement kitchen of her brownstone house after work to have a cup of tea or cocoa and discuss their lives.

At the age of nine, Marshall visited Barbados, where she first encountered her maternal grandmother, an impressive figure who appears in many of her works. Her story "To Da-duh, in Memoriam" (1967) is a nearly autobiographical account of this visit. Inspired by the beauty of the island, she began to write poetry, and on her return began a period of intense reading. By accident, she discovered the poetry of Paul Laurence Dunbar, the first African American author she had ever read, and his work gave her the courage to think of becoming a writer.

In 1950, she married Kenneth E. Marshall. Three years later, she was graduated Phi Beta Kappa, cum laude, from Brooklyn College. Her first published story, "The Valley Between" (1954), reflects her own struggle as a wife and mother with her desire for education and a writing career. Marshall worked in New York public libraries and from 1953 to 1956 was the only female staff writer for *Our World* magazine, traveling on assignment to Brazil and the West Indies.

While doing postgraduate work at Hunter College in 1955, Marshall began her autobiographical novel *Brown Girl, Brownstones* (1959), completing it in Barbados. A television adaptation of the novel was presented on the Columbia Broadcasting System (CBS) the following year. At first, the book was treated as a book for juveniles and was largely ignored; since its reissue by the Feminist Press in 1981, however, it

has been considered a classic female *Bildungsroman.*

A Guggenheim Fellowship awarded in 1960 allowed Marshall to complete and publish a collection of four novellas, *Soul Clap Hands and Sing* (1961). This book marked a significant shift in her work: Each novella is written from a male character's perception and bears a political subtext.

In the 1960's, black women writers remained largely unread. Marshall, divorced in 1963, determined to support herself and her son Evan-Keith by writing rather than by teaching, and she was thus dependent on grants. In the eight years it took to complete her ambitious second novel, *The Chosen Place, the Timeless People* (1969), she received the Rosenthal Award from the National Institute of Arts and Letters (1962) and grants from the Ford Foundation (1964) and the National Endowment for the Arts (1967).

In 1970, Marshall entered an "open and innovative marriage" with Nourry Menard, a relationship that allowed her more freedom to write. A journey to West Africa in 1977 gave her a broader perspective and strengthened her awareness of African influences in her own life. Three years later, she traveled to East Africa, where she was welcomed as a native daughter.

Marshall became more widely known in the 1980's. A collection of earlier work, *Reena and Other Stories*, appeared in 1983 and was republished in 1985 as *Merle: A Novella and Other Stories.* The book includes her autobiographical essay "From the Poets in the Kitchen" (1983), initially published in *The New York Times Book Review*, and the novella *Merle.* Adapted and rewritten from *The Chosen Place, the Timeless People*, *Merle* defines Marshall's most fascinating character, the charismatic West Indian Merle Kinbona.

A third novel, *Praisesong for the Widow*, was also published in 1983. Set in the islands of Grenada and Carriacou, it won the Before Columbus American Book Award the following year. In 1991, *Daughters* appeared, a novel that draws strong parallels between the lives of women, past and present, in New York and the West Indies. In addition to her writing career, Marshall has taught and lectured at a number of universities, including Yale, Oxford, Columbia, and Cornell.

Analysis

One of Paule Marshall's unquestioned strengths is her skill with language, especially the colorful West Indian dialects. She has identified herself as trilingual, at ease with the dialect of Barbados, the African American dialect of Harlem, and the "proper" English she spoke at school. She believes that her sense of language is an African characteristic, triggered by listening to her mother's friends, who "did marvelous things with the English language. . . . They brought to bear the few African words and cadences that they remembered and they infused and enriched it." In "From the Poets in the Kitchen," Marshall confesses that she longed to possess the same power with words. Her evocative scene at the beginning of the 1961 novella *Barbados* affirms her mastery of that power:

Dawn, like the night which had preceded it, came from the sea. In a white mist tumbling like spume over the fishing boats leaving the island and the hunched, ghost shapes of the fishermen. In a white, wet wind breathing over the villages scattered amid the tall canes.

Marshall is not a static writer, for each book presents a new challenge. *Reena and Other Stories* demonstrates in one volume her increasing command of language between 1954 and 1983. *Brown Girl, Brownstones* is seen primarily through the viewpoint character of the girl Selina, but the novellas of *Soul Clap Hands and Sing* are perceived through their male protagonists. Her longest novel, *The Chosen Place, the Timeless People*, is lushly overwritten, encompassing the voices of many characters, whereas *Praisesong for the Widow* is taut and compact. *Daughters* employs some experimental techniques—a poetic slash between words to mark direct thought, an occasional shift into present tense.

Marshall's themes include the individual quest for identity and the need for community, as well as a recognition of individual interconnectedness with the past. In her work, the desire to establish an identity is always linked to integration within a larger community, and her concept of community spreads outward from Brooklyn to encompass the entire African world. A character's sense of community is then strengthened by an awareness of communal history.

Discovering her historical past, first in Barbados, later in Africa, gave Marshall that communal view that was so healing, and her characters seek similar discoveries. In *Brown Girl, Brownstones*, Selina Boyce longs to break away from her family to become her own person, but she does so by determining to go to Barbados, her ancestral home. In *The Chosen Place, the Timeless People*, the American Jew Saul Amron finds himself embraced by the community of Bournehills and is then better able to come to terms with his own history. In *Daughters*, Ursa Mackenzie breaks away from her father's influence only to become aware of the community of daughters to which she, her mother, and every other woman belong.

All of Marshall's major characters find they must explore their collective as well as their personal history. One way to connect with the past is through ritual, especially dance, and Marshall uses it often. Examples include the social rituals of the Barbadian Association in Brown Girl, Brownstones, the pigsticking ritual of the cane workers and the Carnival reenactment of Cuffee Ned's revolt in *The Chosen Place, the Timeless People*, and the collective ritual of the Carriacou Big Drum in *Praisesong for the Widow*.

Another major concern of Marshall's work is the need for social change. Perhaps her most political novel is *The Chosen Place, the Timeless People*, which examines the social and economic problems of Bournehills, a hard-luck section of a small Caribbean island where the shadows of slave and master have not been fully obliterated. A number of references are made to thirty pounds sterling, the former price of a slave. Merle Kinbona reminds her American guests that nine million Africans died on their journey to the New World, and the raging sea below her Cassia House will never forget them. Yet the major tension now is between the oppressive British owner of the sugarcane mill and the exploited native workers, known locally as the "Little Fella."

Marshall questions not only British capitalism, as seen in Bournehills, but American materialism. *Brown Girl, Brownstones'* Silla Boyce succumbs to the American Dream of ownership, sacrificing her husband, her daughters, and much of her humanity. Mr. Watford of *Barbados* loses his human tenderness in his pride of possession.

Marshall also addressed the control that society has over women. In her own world, men were the ones who held power. In a 1979 interview, she stated, "I wanted to turn that around. I wanted women to be the centers of power." Elsewhere, she notes the triple invisibility of her mother's Barbadian friends, her mentors in America, who were black, female, and foreign. By emphasizing the role of the black woman in her community, Marshall anticipated popular culture by twenty years. She believes that her role as a writer is to tell the truth about her community, to counteract negative stereotypes of African Americans, and to offer a model for young black women.

BROWN GIRL, BROWNSTONES

First published: 1959
Type of work: Novel

A young girl of West Indian ancestry comes of age in 1940's Brooklyn, discovering her identity to be apart from yet defined by her parents and her culture.

Brown Girl, Brownstones, Marshall's first novel, is the story of Selina Boyce, the daughter of Barbadian immigrants, and her journey to womanhood. At ten, Selina resists her awkwardly changing body, uncomfortable yet fascinated by a dawning sexual awareness. Marshall writes candidly about women's bodies, menstruation, and sexuality at a time when writers, especially women, were not encouraged to be so frank.

Yet this initiation novel brings Selina into much more than physical womanhood. She must also develop emotionally and mentally; she must learn humiliation, grief, understanding, and the courage to be herself. Many characters guide Selina through her approaching womanhood: the voluptuous boarder Suggie; Miss Thompson, an elderly Southern hairdresser who serves as comforter and surrogate mother and whose foot bears an ulcerous "life-sore" as a direct result of racism; Selina's schoolmate Beryl; and, of course, her parents. A final guide is Clive, a sometime artist whose major lesson for her is to learn to leave him.

Selina's real and ongoing conflict is with her mother, a blank, formidable woman. Eventually, Selina learns to understand her mother better, but she never completely overcomes her anger at her mother's treatment of her father. Selina also recognizes that a part of her is determined and ruthless too. She is her mother's daughter as well as her father's.

A second plot line follows the complex struggle between Selina's parents. Deighton, her charming yet doomed father, was a cosseted child who was sent to college in

Barbados to become a teacher. His proud refusal to be treated as second-class, his insistence that the white world must see him as an equal, leads him to grandiose, ill-fated schemes. Silla, her mother, comes from a background of rural poverty and is determined to survive in "this man country" by acquiring property and renting to tenants. Her strength allows the family to survive as she moves from domestic work into a wartime job as a lathe operator. Silla, however, is weakened by her unquestioning embrace of American materialism. When she realizes that her husband's dreams will never allow him to share her practical goals, she betrays him by acts that devastate the family.

The faded elegance of the Brooklyn brownstone that the Boyce family shares with other tenants symbolizes the changing neighborhood of the 1940's. Upstairs lies the invalid Miss Mary, the death-in-life white servant of the building's former owners, whispering of her dead lover and the vanished poet. Next to her lives good-time Suggie, who lures a succession of strange men to her room on weekends to obliterate the loneliness and frustration of her life as a maid to a white family.

Marshall's West Indian characters are, as always, her strength. Their rich dialect leaps off the page. They add an extra dimension to the novel by virtue of their customs, idioms, and intense desire for a better life.

SOUL CLAP HANDS AND SING

First published: 1961
Type of work: Four novellas

Four aging men, each in a different country, face mortality and their incomplete lives.

The title and thematic center of *Soul Clap Hands and Sing* are taken from William Butler Yeats's poem "Sailing to Byzantium": "An aged man is but a paltry thing,/ A tattered coat upon a stick, unless/ Soul clap its hands and sing." The male protagonists of these novellas are not singing. Each is middle-aged or older and has lived a life essentially empty of commitment; each reaches out tentatively and too late to another person.

In this collection, Marshall moves the setting beyond the United States to the Caribbean and South America, deliberately shifting to a male perspective. These stories concern not so much the age of the men but the parched condition of their souls.

Barbados is the first and shortest novella. Mr. Watford, thin, spare, and comfortably retired from his job in America, spends his days tending his coconut trees and scoffing at the young people and their political slogan, "The Old Order Shall Pass." A local shopkeeper urges Mr. Watford to support the unsteady economy by hiring a servant, but the girl he sends disturbs Mr. Watford, who is grudging and harsh with her, though he allows her to stay. Only when he sees her dancing with a young man does he begin to realize how jealous he is of her, and how lonely. He tries to approach the girl, but she spurns him, and he realizes that in his life "it had been love, terrible in its demand, which he had always fled."

In *Brooklyn*, Max Berman, a middle-aged Jewish professor undone by the Communist-baiting of the 1950's and his self-imposed isolation, is physically attracted to his young African American student and suggests she visit his country home. She reluctantly agrees. He fantasizes a romantic idyll based upon his power over her, but she, who has always quietly sidestepped life, determines to face her fear of him head on. Refusing his advances, she becomes aware of her own strength, and he is humiliated.

The appropriately named Gerald Motley, of British, Hindu, and African ancestry, is the protagonist of *British Guiana*. Educated in England and privileged because of his light skin, he is the first man of color to become program director for British Guiana Broadcasting. Now in his sixties, he has allowed himself to become a figurehead, spending most of his time in a hotel bar. Ironically, Motley fails to recognize his reflection in the mirror, and thus himself. He too has rejected love—for the angry young man who has become his protégé and for Sybil, the woman who tries to save him.

Finally, *Brazil* introduces the small, dark figure of comic O Grande Caliban, who with his foil, tall blonde Miranda, has been a fixture of Rio de Janeiro's night life for thirty-five years. Caliban, preparing to retire, is shocked to learn that his real identity has been absorbed by his comic persona. Even his new young wife does not know his true name. A symbolic search leads him from his former mentor Nacimento, who cannot recognize him, to his gaudy and aging mistress Miranda, who knows him only as Caliban. His real self unrecognized by present, past, or future, Caliban destroys Miranda's apartment in despairing fury.

PRAISESONG FOR THE WIDOW

First published: 1983
Type of work: Novel

A middle-class African American widow rediscovers her personal and ancestral past through her visit to a small Caribbean island.

In *Praisesong for the Widow*, Avey Johnson and two friends are in the midst of a Caribbean cruise, which her friends have urged upon her, when Avey suddenly feels that she cannot continue. Without explanation, she disembarks at Granada, knowing only that she must get back to her immaculate home in North White Plains, New York. Instead, she finds herself walking too far down the beach in the heat and seeks refuge in a small bar. Lebert Joseph, the lame and ancient owner, urges her to stay for an extra day to join the annual excursion to his native island of Carriacou. There, the Big Drum celebration is held to honor the Old Parents, the Long-time People: "Each year this time they does look for us to come and give them their remembrance."

The novel reiterates Marshall's concern with "the need for black people to make the psychological and spiritual journey back through their past." On her journey, Avey Johnson recalls the hard but rewarding years with her husband Jay on Halsey Street in Brooklyn, before they moved to the respectability of White Plains. She remembers her childhood visits to her father's great-aunt in South Carolina and the old woman's thrilling story of Ibo Landing, of slaves who turned their backs on the New World and walked home across the sea. Lebert Joseph also reminds her of her heritage by pointedly asking her, "And what you is?" He does not mean American, but rather wants to know her African tribal heritage.

A dual vision of reality is particularly evident here. The great-aunt tells Avey that "those pure-born Africans was peoples my gran' said could see in more ways than one." Modest Avey is also Avatara (incarnation), named for and by the great-aunt's grandmother in a vision. Her passionate husband Jay becomes the severe businessman Jerome Johnson, almost a stranger. When she looks at Jerome's face in his coffin, Avey to her horror sees another pale, thin-lipped face superimposed on his—the face of some white ancestor. Even the polished splendor of her White Plains dining room reminds her of the museum of the dead at the foot of Mount Pelee on Martinique.

On her sea journey to Carriacou, Avey is violently and symbolically purged. She is placed in the deckhouse, reminiscent of a slave ship's hold, and senses she is not alone; she must remember and reenact the journey of her African ancestors.

After Avey is ceremonially purified, the enigmatic Lebert Joseph guides her through the rituals of the Big Drum, the Beg Pardon, the Nations Dance. One critic identifies him as "the incarnation of the African deity Legba—trickster, guardian of the cross-roads where all ways meet." This beloved figure served as a link between humans and gods and was vital to many rituals. Thus the Big Drum is real but mythic, the Nations Dance is contemporary but timeless. When Avey joins the final dance, she recognizes it as one performed by her great-aunt's people in South Carolina, and she remembers the steps. *Praisesong for the Widow* connects Avey Johnson, a modern black American, with her worldwide African heritage, her present life with an ancient past, so that she is finally made whole.

Summary

Paule Marshall has incorporated into her work her personal struggle as a black woman and black writer living in a society that undercut her sense of self and her concern for social change. Her books explore the individual search for identity as well as the simultaneous need for integration within a larger community and a deeper awareness of the past. Her vivid portrayal of West Indian-American life contributes to a better understanding of the multiple aspects of African American experience.

Bibliography

Bone, Robert. "Merle Kinbona Was Part Saint, Part Revolutionary, Part Obeah-Woman." *The New York Times Book Review*, November 30, 1969, 4, 54.

Brathwaite, Edward. "West Indian History and Society in the Art of Paule Marshall's Novel." *Journal of Black Studies* 1, no. 2 (December, 1970): 225-238.

Busia, Abene P. A. "What Is Your Nation?: Reconnecting Africa and Her Diaspora Through Paule Marshall's *Praisesong for the Widow*." In *Changing Our Own Words: Essays on Criticism, Theory, and Writing by Black Women*, edited by Cheryl A. Wall. New Brunswick, N.J.: Rutgers University Press, 1989.

Evans, Mari, ed. *Black Women Writers (1950-1980): A Critical Evaluation*. Garden City, N.Y.: Anchor Press/Doubleday, 1984.

Kapai, Leela. "Dominant Themes and Technique in Paule Marshall's Fiction." *College Language Association Journal* 16, no. 1 (September, 1972): 49-59.

Nazareth, Peter. "Paule Marshall's Timeless People." *New Letters* 40 (October, 1973): 113-131.

Schaeffer, Susan Fromberg. "Cutting Herself Free." *The New York Times Book Review*, October 27, 1991, 3, 29.

Waniek, Marilyn Nelson. "Paltry Things: Immigrants and Marginal Men in Paule Marshall's Short Fiction." *Callaloo* 6, no. 2 (Spring-Summer, 1983): 46-56.

Washington, Mary Helen. Afterword to *Brown Girl, Brownstones*, by Paule Marshall. Old Westbury, N.Y.: Feminist Press, 1981.

Joanne McCarthy

W. S. MERWIN

Born: New York, New York
September 30, 1927

Principal Literary Achievement

One of the leading American poets of his generation, Merwin has won most of the major honors for poetry and translation.

Biography

William Stanley Merwin, the son of a Presbyterian clergyman, was reared and educated in Union City, New Jersey, and Scranton, Pennsylvania. After high school, he attended Princeton University (A.B., 1947), and did graduate work in modern languages. Thereafter, he worked as a tutor for two years, spending 1950 on Majorca as tutor to the sons of the poet Robert Graves, who influenced him considerably. He was quite successful in placing his early work, publishing his first volume, *A Mask for Janus*, in 1952. From 1951 to 1955 he lived in London, supporting himself by writing for British radio and television and translating Spanish and French classics. He brought out his second volume, *The Dancing Bears*, in 1954.

After 1954, he supplemented his income through a series of literary fellowships. In 1956, he returned to the United States for a number of years. For a time, he wrote plays for the Poets' Theatre in Cambridge, Massachusetts. *Green with Beasts* came out in 1956, and four years later he published *The Drunk in the Furnace*. By 1966, he was able to issue his first *Collected Poems*.

This first collection marks the first phase of his career, during which he worked mainly with traditional forms, heavily symbolic imagery, conventional rhetoric, and literary allusions characteristic of mainstream poetry. This phase is usually described as heavily influenced by T. S. Eliot and Ezra Pound, though the hand of the Irish poet W. B. Yeats can also be detected. Merwin's work in these years is formidably intellectual, typical of these models. He is also attracted to themes related to the disintegration of personality in the face of modern stresses and to the loss of traditional order. Yet he manages a charming recasting of a fairy tale as a ballad in "East of the Sun and West of the Moon," from *The Dancing Bears*, and several poems, conspicuously "Leviathan," in *Green with Beasts*, show him simply reveling in language.

The first collection also disclosed a change in direction, primarily in *The Drunk in the Furnace*. Several striking poems track his reactions to the aging of his grandparents

and to his impending sense of loss of all that they represent. The title poem consolidates several of his preoccupations: Both individual and environment are castoffs of the world that humans have made, and both stand as criticisms of it. Merwin developed these patterns further in *The Moving Target* (1963). Here the forms were flexed almost to the breaking point, and the language became at best personal and at extreme elliptical. Yet his characteristic themes—loss, death, disorientation, disintegration— remained constant. What changed was the manner; Merwin was speaking with a different, more evasive, perhaps more subtle voice.

Still, although this volume signals change, it did little to prepare readers for *The Lice*, easily Merwin's most celebrated book, which appeared in 1967. In it, the poet appeared to have completely abandoned the former starting points of his poetry, substituting for them mental attitudes from an altogether alien tradition, almost as if an orthodox priest should suddenly embrace Shintoism. Careful reading, however, shows that the divergence is more apparent than real. What has happened is that the disintegration—of values, of traditions, of cultural unity—has carried over to the medium of language itself. What recourse does a poet have in the collapse of communication? If language itself fails, then poetry becomes an exercise in solipsism, and the poet seems to be speaking to himself. If the poet still persists in poetry, it can only mean that some hope remains of eventually making a connection. Merwin persists, his words now often sounding like voices heard vaguely in dreams, but bearing all the freight of dreams at the same time.

Subsequent volumes—*The Carrier of Ladders* (1970; awarded the Pulitzer Prize), *Writings to an Unfinished Accompaniment* (1973), *The Compass Flower* (1977), *Feathers from the Hill* (1978), *Opening the Hand* (1983), and *The Rain in the Trees* (1988)—primarily follow the leads established in the 1960's, although in the later works Merwin seems to be returning to earlier, temporarily abandoned forms and traditions, or experimenting with classical oriental forms. In the late 1970's he settled in Hawaii, where he has continued to work.

Analysis

The poetry of W. S. Merwin covers such a range that it is difficult to generalize about it; yet he has been recognized as in the first rank from the beginning, with publication of *A Mask for Janus*. The title identifies his early orientation as a traditionalist-formalist in the mold of Eliot and Pound. The poems are in regular formal measures and employ conventional rhetorical devices; the tone is distant and sophisticated; the voice is cultivated. Even more popular patterns, such as ballad measure in "Ballad of John Cable and Three Gentlemen," are formalized: this is a literary ballad, alluding to medieval folk-song tradition and requiring that reference for interpretation.

His second volume, *The Dancing Bears*, mainly follows the line of the first. Its touchstone poem, "East of the Sun and West of the Moon," recasts the traditional folk tale of the same title, dealing with a peasant's daughter given in marriage to a white bear who lives at the end of time and visits her only after dark. Merwin transforms this into a triple allegory of the nature of love, the responsibility of man to the past and his heritage, and the function of literature. Other poems in the volume expand a recurring theme of life as continual self-proving and obligation to the past.

Green with Beasts contains further exercises with formal structures. These are all deftly turned, fashioned by the hands of a master—but a master who paradoxically seems less assured of the permanence of his work. Merwin repeatedly turns in this book to images of incompleteness, of frustrated energies. "The Master" laments the lot of those doomed to work in the shadow of genius, especially when that genius is not humanly admirable. "Saint Sebastian" likewise is a delicately wrought sonnet; but its subject is a Christian martyr cut down before his prime, shown in the act of entering death. The subject contradicts the artistic premise of the style.

The Drunk in the Furnace looks like further expansion. The formal structures are similar to those used earlier, though simpler, and the same is true of the themes. The voice, however, has changed. Early in the book, the poem "Odysseus" sets the tone. This voice is quiet, reflective, showing an Odysseus musing over his restlessness, an Odysseus so perplexed between undifferentiated choices that he can hardly make up his mind. The plaint informs the book, appearing over and over in various guises. In a series of poems on his aging and dying grandparents, for example, Merwin repeatedly attempts to come to terms with the part his life plays in the pattern of theirs—and then with whether there is any pattern in theirs at all. The book closes with "The Drunk in the Furnace"; the image of a vagrant howling in a makeshift shelter parallels that of the hesitant Odysseus.

In *The Moving Target*, Merwin almost completely drops the public voice and turns introspective, as if he has despaired of open discourse. The poems themselves turn bleak, once their protective shells are breached. "Lemuel's Blessing" is based on an eighteenth century poem by a madman in which Lemuel "blesses" his readers with the wolf—that is, with a curse. Merwin feels that the only appropriate blessing for a race bent on destroying itself is cursing. Similarly, "The Saint of the Upland" laments that his worshippers have learned nothing from him. *The Lice*, probably the most praised book of Merwin's career, extends this approach; in fact, it carries the poetry of hopelessness about as far as it can go and reduces Merwin's formal patterns to the level of contextless, broken mutterings. Everything here is fragmented, indrawn, muted. "The Gods," for example, addresses nonexistent beings, for men have developed into things no god would have the patience to endure. There are a few moments of relief, as when the song of birds at dawn in "How We Are Spared" raises the light in the sky, which can only be a sign of hope; but there is no clue to hope of what. The visions of this book cleanse the eyes and mind, though only by searing.

The Carrier of Ladders brought the poet the Pulitzer Prize and celebrity. It continues the difficult vein opened in the two previous books, though with some tempering. Some of the poems even show a partial return to his earlier, more straightforward style. "The Judgment of Paris" presents a relatively direct account of a standard myth, even if it does slant it negatively. One group of poems dealing with the American West acts almost like a nucleus for the book. In them, the speakers show awareness both of the beauty of the landscape and of the ugliness that humans have brought in their migration. This divided reaction almost paralyzes the will; it probes the depth of the pain that the poet is both registering and disguising. "The Removal" attests this, in its dedication "to the endless tribe." The poet himself is one of them, in speaking to them, though, he cannot help recalling the destruction they bring, nor can he help reminding them of that.

Writings to an Unfinished Accompaniment contains further examinations of internal states of awareness and further attempts at frustrated communication. In these poems, however, Merwin seems less desperate, more accepting than he had been, even if still far from reconciled. Some of them even seem playful; "Tool" and "The Unwritten" show a zest in wordplay long absent from his work. More significant is the fact that other figures appear here, breaking into the void previous poems had spun around the isolated individual. At this point, the turn is slight, hardly noticeable. "Finding a Teacher" is elliptical, almost impersonal, but the poem's speaker does end in staying for a meal. "The Search" carries the process further, describing how the speaker's world grows silent when he suddenly becomes aware of the absence of the other. The book ends with "Gift," in which the speaker acknowledges the existence of hope and the possibility of giving oneself to another.

This slight turning becomes more definite in subsequent books. *The Compass Flower*, *Feathers from the Hill*, and *Finding the Islands* all mark both a reacceptance— or at least a reacknowledgment—of others and the external world, and a return to poems as made objects rather than the expression of emotional states. The two latter books, in fact, contain explicit love poetry, quite distinct from anything else the poet has done; in *Finding the Islands*, Merwin composes exclusively in stripped-to-the-bone unpunctuated triplets. Yet he includes nothing from these books in his *Selected Poems*, which could indicate that he intends to discard them. Nevertheless, the change in direction seems clear. *Opening the Hand* makes it definite: "Sheridan" is a reanimation of the Civil War general's consciousness during the Battle of Cedar Creek; "Questions to Tourists Stopped by a Pineapple Field" is a marvelous send-up of typically inane tourist-guide conversation; and "Black Jewel" recaptures the timeless timekeeping of crickets. *The Rain in the Trees* includes a number of fine lyrics that have won the admiration of critics.

THE DRUNK IN THE FURNACE

First published: 1960
Type of work: Poems

In a series of dramatic portraits and monologues, Merwin shows human failures as stemming primarily from internal deficiencies.

With *The Drunk in the Furnace*, Merwin intensified and expanded his earlier position that human beings had become increasingly subject to divorce from their environment and from their integrating spiritual centers. The book is enclosed by two defining figures, a Greek warrior-hero and a street person, who reflect for Merwin the typical human situation. The first is the title character in "Odysseus," the epic wandering hero of the Homeric poems, about whom Alfred, Lord Tennyson had written two poems in the high Victorian mode projecting Odysseus' role as the model male hero, the man whose will admits no obstacles to his quest. Merwin interprets him differently. His character is trapped in a self-perpetuating dilemma, one that refuses to be resolved regardless of what choice the hero makes. Ultimately, Merwin suggests, the role is itself a trap, one foisted on people by their culture. Once humans value decision making as leadership, then making the decision becomes the hallmark of the hero. Yet what, Merwin asks, if the quality of life depends on completely different issues?

"One Eye" considers the probable consequences of the proverb, "In the country of the blind the one-eyed man is king." Commonly this saying is taken to summarize folk wisdom, the idea being that one can capitalize on one's advantages by choosing one's objective audience carefully. Things do not work out this way in Merwin's world. Although One-Eye at first finds immediate acceptance, his situation quickly begins to pall. As king, he discovers his subjects rich in goods he cannot profit from, like their intricate music; worse, he learns that he cannot share his gift, his advantage, with them: No matter what he does, they will never see. In the end, he cannot save them from their common human fate. He is powerless to change the fundamental conditions of their lives—and death.

Merwin uses the image of the singing derelict from the title poem to close the volume. The poem actually begins with the image of the abandoned furnace, cast off to add its litter of decay to an already poisonous creek. This illustrates Merwin's view of what humans do to themselves, progressively contaminating their environment until it can no longer support life. The drunk, equally cast out by society, appropriately houses himself in this pile of junk, from which he serenades the community. The good people ignore him, for good or evil, but their children cannot keep from gaping at him and, the poet says, studying him. What they learn is the human way: casting out and refusing, even to their own harm. Merwin at this point holds out little hope.

THE MOVING TARGET

First published: 1963
Type of work: Poems

   In more personal and less formal poems, Merwin examines the bleak options left for humans in a world they have desolated.

The Moving Target catalogs Merwin's ventures into the dark void of possibility available to humans. As before, Merwin finds little hope. "Noah's Raven," for example, explains why that bird did not return to the ark with the message that the deluge had passed, that God would once again establish his covenant with humans. On leaving, it realized it had nothing more in common with humans; their kinds would henceforth be alienated. By refusing to bring back empty promises, the raven signifies that it sees little hope. Similarly, "Dead Hand" illustrates in two lines that this most human of organs continues to clutch even after death; its only value to anyone resides in the metal and mineral of its rings.

"Lemuel's Blessing" develops from an allusion to Christopher Smart, an eighteenth century poet who suffered from religious mania and was considered insane. Merwin suggests that only madmen can see accurately in a world that has chosen madness as a way of life. Smart prayed that Lemuel "bless with the wolf," the traditional and mythical enemy of humans—arguing, that is, that releasing wolves on humans would paradoxically purge them of their own beastliness. He goes on to call the wolf a "dog without a master," hinting that humans are destroying themselves by failing to practice the mastery for which they were created. Finally, he notes that the Lord will care for the wolves of the desert, implying that humans who have chosen to abandon nature deserve no such care. All these points tally with Merwin's theme. The poem goes on to show humans reveling in the dogginess of their lives.

In "The Saint of the Uplands," the saint laments that his message has fallen on deaf ears, in two ways. He is no more than his followers, hence undeserving of being considered a saint, and he has no more to give them than they can find for themselves. Yet instead of learning that simple point, they persist in building a shrine to him, in which they perpetuate their ignorance. Perhaps the most striking poem in the book is "The Crossways of the World etc.," which certainly prefigures the next turn in Merwin's development. Totally unlike his earlier work in its broken lines, stanzas, and phrases, it looks like abbreviated, interrupted, and unpatterned musings. The imagery is entirely of loss, of failed connections—which perfectly reflects the overwhelming sense of devastation in Merwin's vision of human reality.

THE CARRIER OF LADDERS

First published: 1970
Type of work: Poems

Still working with broken forms, Merwin begins to find some evidence of human significance.

The metaphor implicit in the title of *The Carrier of Ladders* signals a change, however slight, in Merwin's orientation and attitudes: Only humans carry ladders, and their object in so doing is to rise, to climb to a new level, even if they do not know exactly what they will find there. The poems in the volume mostly build on this premise. The opening poem, "Teachers," sets the pattern. The speaker is not clear about much, and his surroundings witness mostly pain. But he finds some solace in sleep, and sleep brings dreams in which he remembers learning from books of voyages, "sure tellings" that taught him. Where they led or may lead is dark; but the speaker values these teachers, and that can only bear hope—not much, maybe, but some.

"The Judgment of Paris" re-creates the ancient Greek myth in which three goddesses compete for mastery before Paris; the decision he makes brings on the Trojan War. Classically, this was interpreted as showing the connection between man's pursuit of female beauty and its consummation in war. Merwin does not reject this version, but he expands it by suggesting that the contest was rigged: Any decision Paris, being human, made would have led to destruction. Human beings, Merwin suggests, are so defective that they cannot avoid self-destructive behavior. Yet he adds here a note lacking earlier: that this may be what makes them interesting, possibly even significant. The note is appropriate to its subject; one of Homer's themes, picked up by the Greek dramatists afterwards, is that humans bring suffering down on themselves, but that this suffering engenders compassion, which promotes unity. Merwin ends the poem with an image of Helen picking a flower with roots that allay pain, recalling that it is human to relieve suffering.

One section of this volume consists of poems dealing with the westward movement in American history. Merwin certainly does not see this as a glorious episode in the nation's history. While admitting the intoxication of the quest, the poet is fully aware of how much past and present destruction was implicit in it. In "Other Travellers to this River," he conjures up the early travel writer William Bartram—who popularized the notion of "conquering" the new land—to draw the contrast between the intensity of his vision and the damage done to the land. "Western Country" carries this further by suggesting that the conquest itself is illusory as well as wrongsighted: The land is not to be conquered but revered. In attempting this wrong, humans are also discrediting and damaging themselves. Still, Merwin's voice here is less strident than saddened, as if he has learned to accept as inevitable the loss that is the human experience.

Summary

At no point in his career has W. S. Merwin been a particularly accessible writer, but he has everywhere won praise for high craftsmanship and searing vision. These are evident in every stage of his poetry, which has evolved through an extremely wide range. Of the poets of his generation, he is most remarkable perhaps for his insights into the spiritual desolation of postindustrial human society, into the cost in spirit of technological gains. He is often difficult of expression and uncompromising in his assessment of human pride, but his great poems finally acknowledge something worth saving.

Bibliography

Byers, Thomas G. *What I Cannot Say: Self, Word, and World in Whitman, Stevens, and Merwin*. Urbana: University of Illinois Press, 1989.

Christhilf, Mark. *W. S. Merwin, the Mythmaker*. Columbia: University of Missouri Press, 1986.

Merwin, W. S. *Unframed Originals*. New York: Atheneum, 1982.

Nelson, Cary, and Ed Folsom, eds. *W. S. Merwin: Essays on the Poetry*. Urbana: University of Illinois Press, 1987.

Shaw, Robert B., ed. *American Poetry Since 1960: Some Critical Perspectives*. Chester Springs, Pa.: Dufour, 1974.

James Livingston

BRIAN MOORE

Born: Belfast, Northern Ireland
August 25, 1921

Principal Literary Achievement
Moore has used his Roman Catholic background to examine spiritual, ethical, and social issues in what has become a quietly impressive canon of novels.

Biography

Brian Moore was born in Belfast as the fourth child in a family of nine. His father, James Bernard Moore, had made his way through medical school on scholarships to become a prominent surgeon. He had not married until he was fifty, and he died when Brian was eighteen. Moore recalls his father as an exacting man, impatient with failure, who put great pressure on his children to excel in their schooling. The son's response has been to focus on failed or marginal characters in his fiction; he has said that he regards failure as "a more intense distillation [than success] of that self you are."

Moore was educated at Newington Elementary School and St. Malachy's Diocesan College, both in Belfast. He bitterly recalls his formal education as old-fashioned, rigid, and harshly disciplinary, with canings for the slightest infractions. In *The Feast of Lupercal* (1957), he draws an acrid portrait of St. Malachy's in his Ardath College, were clerical masters prevent students from developing independent minds. His feelings about his Jesuit education are related to the ambivalence he has about religious belief.

The Moore family had originally been Protestant, but Brian's paternal grandfather converted late in life to Catholicism. Brian was reared a Catholic, only to be stunned when his mother confessed her unbelief on her deathbed. From this youth, he has been an unbeliever, yet all his life he has remained fascinated by the role faith plays in people's lives. In most of his novels, he has dramatized what he regards as the suffocating weight of Irish Catholicism's moral flaws.

After having failed in mathematics, Moore left college in 1938 without taking a degree. For a year he took courses at the University of London's Belfast branch. In 1940, he joined Belfast's Air Raid Precautions Unit and National Fire Service—experiences he would delineate in *The Emperor of Ice-Cream* (1965). In 1943, he joined the British Ministry of War Transport and accompanied the Allied Occupation Forces into North Africa, France, Italy, and Germany. In 1945, he worked for the

UNRRA Economic Mission in Warsaw, then traveled as a freelance reporter in Scandinavia and France.

Moore returned to England in 1947 but emigrated to Canada the following year. From 1948 to 1952, he reported for the *Montreal Gazette* and also had several pulp novels published under an assumed name. In 1953, he became a Canadian citizen, and he retained his Canadian citizenship even after moving to the United States in 1959. In 1955, Moore issued his first serious—and perhaps still best—novel, *The Lonely Passion of Judith Hearne*. The book won him Britain's Authors' Club First Novel Award.

From 1959 to 1962, Moore resided in New York City, living partly on a Guggenheim Fellowship while writing *The Luck of Ginger Coffey* (1960, set in Montreal) and *An Answer from Limbo* (1962, set in New York). In 1963, he moved to Los Angeles to do the screenplay for *The Luck of Ginger Coffey*, then to write *Torn Curtain* for Alfred Hitchcock. In 1964, he settled in Malibu with his second wife, Jean Denney. The first marriage, to Jacqueline Sirois, lasted from 1951 to 1957. In Southern California, Moore has written occasional film scripts and travel articles and has taught as an adjunct professor at the University of California at Los Angeles, but he has devoted the bulk of his time to his novels. He is essentially a loner who gives few interviews and enjoys his international status, living in restless California yet retaining his Canadian citizenship while writing, more often than not, about Ireland's tabooridden, backward society.   .

Analysis

Even though Brian Moore has written many highly praised novels, he has rarely been considered in books or essays dealing with contemporary fiction. Such British peers as John Fowles, Doris Lessing, Iris Murdoch, Kingsley Amis, Anthony Burgess, Anthony Powell, William Golding, Muriel Spark, and Julian Barnes have received far more attention. Moore's limitations have been noted: His canvas is often small, his subject matter is usually restricted, he seldom breaks new ground in either theme or technique, he sometimes yields to temptation by writing slick melodramas, and he has seemed unable to create a masterwork that would show his powers at their highest level.

Granting all this, a powerful case can be made for the view that Moore, while not a major novelist, belongs in the front row of the distinguished second-rank authors of contemporary fiction. His prose is clear, spare, taut, apparently flat yet cumulatively lyrical, with a rare metaphor producing a powerful impact. His highly accessible books teem with convincing details and are populated by characters who speak and act vividly. His tonal command can mix the poignant with the droll, the sardonic with the tragic. He masters a matrix of substantial themes that include failure, loneliness, loss, exile, and meaninglessness. Moore excels in dramatizing crisis points in which people are compelled to confront the core of their lives, which are often led in quiet desperation.

Moore is not a popular writer, since his subject matter is unexciting and his treatment of it pessimistic and never sensational. Except for sexual affection, emotional intimacy between men and women does not engage his imagination. Over and over again, he strikes his deepest notes in the chords of parental relationships, risking sentimentality to arrive at ordinary truths of behavior in such novels as *The Luck of Ginger Coffey, An Answer from Limbo, The Emperor of Ice-Cream*, and *Fergus* (1970). Whereas other modern writers fizz, soar, and flash on stylistic sprees, Moore's voice remains quiet and sober. His consistently high artistry has earned him a solid reputation among other writers—Graham Greene called Moore his favorite living novelist—but his preoccupation with personal defeat, renunciation, and unhappiness has cost him the wide readership his talent deserves.

On the literary horizon, Moore casts himself as a shadowy presence, since his fiction cannot be conveniently classified. He chooses to reject what he acidly termed, in an interview, "Barthian byways . . . Borgesian mazes . . . Beckett's crossroads." He is averse to such symbolic fiction as Saul Bellow's *Henderson the Rain King* (1959) and such philosophic narratives as Bellow's *Herzog* (1964). He has also expressed his distaste for the school of the New Novel inspired by Nathalie Sarraute and Alain Robbe-Grillet, and he has dismissed the postmodern works of such writers as Vladimir Nabokov, Italo Calvino, and Thomas Pynchon as lacking a sense of real life.

Real life is what Moore's fiction focuses on: the ordinary, frequently dull, always recognizable world in which parents and relatives, friends and enemies, all live. His fictive mode is that of such realistic probers of the ethical life as George Eliot, Henry James, and E. M. Forster. By far the leading influence on his work, however, is the example of James Joyce.

Like Joyce, Moore has chosen to write about Ireland from the perspective of exile. Joyce's obsession with Irish paralysis and death is comparable to Moore's preoccupation with Belfast's stagnation and decay. Moore's first two novels, *The Lonely Passion of Judith Hearne* and *The Feast of Lupercal*, are directly indebted to Joyce's great collection of his stories, *Dubliners* (1914). The protagonists of both books are "outcast from life's feast," like Maria in "Clay" or Mr. Duffy in "A Painful Case." In several interviews, Moore has stated that he found the experimental Joyce of *Ulysses* (1922) and *Finnegan's Wake* (1939) to be "inimitable," but the Joyce who celebrates life's commonplaces was his prime mentor.

In 1993, Moore surprised many of his readers by issuing, for his first time, a political novel, *No Other Life*. The book deals with a messianic Catholic priest's rise and fall from power on a corrupt, poverty-stricken Caribbean island; the parallels to Jean-Bertrand Aristide's career are numerous. Yet the work is only superficially a *roman à clef*. It focuses on the relationship between a French Canadian missionary, Father Paul, and his brilliant black protégé, Jeannot. Father Paul nourishes Jeannot's soul and promotes his career until Jeannot becomes the leader of the island's dispossessed, only to be forced into exile. The book becomes a meditation on the struggle between religious and temporal faith, spiritual doctrine and public deeds. Moore finds himself, after all, once more in his familiar domain.

THE LONELY PASSION OF JUDITH HEARNE

First published: 1955
Type of work: Novel

A fortyish Irish spinster loses her last hope for a husband, her faith, and her mind.

In *The Lonely Passion of Judith Hearne*, Moore's first novel, he introduces all the themes that will flower in his distinguished career. He takes a large risk by making his protagonist an unmarried, plain, narrow-minded woman over forty who is impoverished, lonely, conventionally pious, and secretly alcoholic. He is tender with her, even inviting the reader to like her as he describes in impressive detail her confused interior life. Honoré de Balzac would have made her a villain, as he did the brooding title character in *La Cousine Bette* (1846; *Cousin Bette*); Flannery O'Connor would have mocked her with gothic glee; Eudora Welty would have drawn her comically; F. Scott Fitzgerald, Ernest Hemingway, and William Faulkner would not have imagined her; Vladimir Nabokov would have disdained her.

Joyce, though, would have joined Moore in empathizing with Judith Hearne as a loser whose fate is determined by the suffocating weight of Irish banality, hypocrisy, and empty religiosity. Hearne is an aging, long-faced Belfast music teacher with barely one hundred pounds a year to her name, in a land where a good man is almost impossible to find. Yet she longs for such a husband, and the merciless way in which her hope is broken makes for the action of Moore's most moving novel.

Before the book's present time, Judith has spent years caring for her aunt, a selfish, domineering woman whose life, like that of Eveline's mother in the *Dubliners* tale, lays a crazy spell on her. In dour, drab, and dreadful Belfast, spinster Judith has been evicted from a series of boarding homes because of her drinking. She ends up in a house run by a malicious, slimy-voiced woman whose son is a Machiavellian lout. The landlady's vulgar brother, James Patrick Madden, has returned from New York and is rumored to be rich; it turns out that the only fortune he ever made was a small sum compensating him for having been run down by a city bus. His American occupation was that of a doorman.

Madden is equally deluded about Judith: Her air of high breeding and an expensive wristwatch given her by her aunt lead him to hope that she is wealthy and might finance his scheme to open a hamburger joint for Yankee tourists. As their mutual illusions crumble, Judith locks herself in her room and opens her secreted cache of whisky. Later, she beseeches her God in a dark, empty church; God gives her no sign. In despair, Judith withdraws her meager savings from the bank, checks into Belfast's best hotel, and goes on a bitter binge.

Moore has skillfully balanced Judith's understandable drive to fulfill her sexual and social needs with the repressive institutional forces in Belfast that deny and taunt, humiliate and defeat her. He superbly chronicles her movement from hope to despair to nihilism. Knowing the grim truth leaves her emotionally and spiritually bankrupt, hopelessly tangled in the net of her lace-curtain destiny. Judith's passion mounts to unrelieved suffering, too pathetic even for tragedy.

AN ANSWER FROM LIMBO

First published: 1962
Type of work: Novel

An examination of an ambitious writer's commitment to his career at the price of destroying his family.

In *An Answer from Limbo*, Brendan Tierney, a thirty-year-old Irishman who has emigrated to New York City, is supporting himself, his wife, and their two bratty children by working for a magazine while also trying to write his first novel. Moved to competitive action by a younger friend's announcement that his own novel will soon be published, Brendan hits on what he regards as a great solution to speeding his creative career: He brings his mother from Belfast to look after the children, encourages his wife Jane to take a job, quits his own, and devotes himself unreservedly to his novel.

Brendan's maneuvers prove as simplistic as they are selfish. Mother Tierney turns out not to be the simple, stalwart person she appears to be. Her dreams and fantasies reveal a troubled heart and mind as she, with her unquestioning Catholic faith, comes to live among pagans as an unpaid, overworked servant, made to feel like an exploited intruder. Jane Tierney looks on religion as a vulgar superstition while employing psychoanalytic jargon as her dogma. Hers is a spiritual emptiness that she seeks to fill by having a humiliating affair with the office creep.

As for Brendan, his ruthless ambition to become a successful writer—rich, socially prominent, sexually magnetic—permits him to rationalize his sacrifice of his family to his work; he is certain that he is offering himself on the altar of art, as such authors as Gustave Flaubert and Thomas Mann have done. When he tells his mother that he has made art his religion, she only laughs at him. Moore is careful not to inform the reader whether or not Brendan has literary talent, saying only that a publisher does accept his novel. Brendan refuses to acknowledge his responsibility for the circumstances of his mother's death (she suffers a broken hip and a stroke and experiences two days of agonizing pain in an impersonal, unfeeling environment). At her funeral, he has an unusual crisis of self-understanding:

Is my belief in my talent any less of an act of superstitious faith than my mother's belief in the power of indulgences? And, as for the ethics of my creed, how do I know that my talent justifies the sacrifices I have asked of others in its name?

On the book's final pages, Brendan admits to himself that more powerful than his grief over his mother's death is his author's drive to observe the graveside scene carefully so he can write about it someday. He confesses, "I have altered beyond all self-recognition. I have lost and sacrificed myself."

An Answer from Limbo is Moore's most disturbing as well as one of his finest novels. The book is about cultural alienation, as Mrs. Tierney finds herself uprooted from her Irish Catholic norms in the secular wasteland of North America. It is about the emotional limbo in which Jane is cast, as she realizes that her husband and children do not love her, nor she them. It is, above all, about the consequences of a dehumanizing obsession, a private ambition that ends up ruining the writer as well as those around him.

THE DOCTOR'S WIFE

First published: 1976
Type of work: Novel

An Irish doctor's wife has a liaison with a young American and ends up leaving both men.

The temptation is powerful to compare *The Doctor's Wife* to Flaubert's *Madame Bovary* (1857): The protagonists of both novels are married to provincial doctors, have convulsively passionate affairs with younger lovers, and engage in the subterfuges and stratagems that adulterous relationships necessitate. Yet the differences between the heroines are important: Emma Bovary was bored and unhappy in her incompatible marriage long before she encountered Rodolphe and Léon; Moore's Sheila is seemingly satisfied to be married to Dr. Kevin Redden and looks forward to a second honeymoon, when they plan to revisit Villefranche in the French Riviera.

Sheila's overworked husband is unable to join her for medical reasons, however, and when she visits her good friend Peg in Paris, she soon finds herself involved, emotionally and, in a few days, sexually, with a wholesome, handsome, charming American graduate student, Tom Lowry, who is eleven years the junior of thirty-seven-year-old Sheila. It turns out that Kevin is rigid, anti-intellectual, unadventurous, unimaginative, and just plain unable to understand her. Moore links Dr. Redden with his native Belfast: bleak, rainy, repressive, bitter, bombed, and barricaded. Villefranche stands, in stark contrast, for a lover's paradise: sunny, sexual, self-indulgent, beautiful, uncomplicated, a world away from the blight of Ireland. Tom follows Sheila there, she discourages her husband from joining her, and soon she and Tom are joyously united.

Kevin Redden's suspicions darken to irrational rage as he finally confronts his candid wife in her hotel room and ends up raping her. Their marriage is over, but Sheila decides not to accompany the adoring Tom to America. She is a person of moral integrity who feels, in a Jamesian mode of moral renunciation, that she must not derive personal profit from her decision to abandon her husband. Moore dramatizes Sheila's psychological crisis in spiritual terms: She has attained a state of grace during the Villefranche episode, but, according to her Catholic outlook, she must enter purgatory to expiate her venial sins. She chooses an uncertain new life in London, where she can shed her past yet continue her penance for having betrayed both her husband and her lover. Moore, with his sober artistry, has created in Sheila Redden a heroine of a depth, intensity, and subtlety rare in contemporary fiction.

Summary

Brian Moore is a writer who may never attract a wide public, but he is admired by discerning readers for his intelligent and sensitive command of such dark aspects of human nature as guilt, disillusionment, unfulfillment, loneliness, betrayal, and misunderstanding. He tenderly yet unsparingly creates characters who are outcast from life's usual joys and who forlornly seek a spiritual beatitude they will find unattainable. Himself a lapsed Catholic and self-exile from Ireland, Moore nevertheless revisits the struggles of people who are religiously tormented and morally baffled, either as victims of a puritan, taboo-ridden, benighted Belfast or as strangers to a hedonistic, dehumanizing, aimless United States. His quietly impressive body of work has earned him a place among the English-speaking world's best writers of minor rank.

Bibliography

Dahlie, Hallvard. *Brian Moore*. Boston: Twayne, 1981.

Flood, Jeanne. *Brian Moore*. Lewisburg, Pa.: Bucknell University Press, 1974.

Foster, John Wilson. *Forces and Themes in Ulster Fiction*. Totowa, N.J.: Rowan and Littlefield, 1974.

McSweeney, Kerry. *Four Contemporary Novelists*. Kingston, Canada: McGill-Queen's University Press, 1983.

O'Donoghue, Jo. *Brian Moore: A Critical Study*. Montreal: McGill-Queen's University Press, 1991.

Ricks, Christopher. "The Simple Excellence of Brian Moore." *New Statesman* 71 (February 18, 1966): 227-228.

Gerhard Brand

Principal Literary Achievement

Blending the hard-boiled detective novel with themes drawn from African American literature, Mosley has produced mysteries that explore important racial themes.

Biography

Walter Mosley was born on January 12, 1952, in Los Angeles, California, to an African American father and a white Jewish mother. Mosley's father had moved from Texas to California and had been largely on his own from the age of eight. Both of Mosley's parents worked in the field of education, and they provided Mosley with a fine formal schooling. His father also shared stories of the migration of many African Americans to California from the South during the 1930's and 1940's. Mosley thus grew up steeped in the history that would provide the distinctive foundation for his novels featuring Easy Rawlins, an African American who migrates to Los Angeles after World War II.

In 1970, Mosley left home to attend Goddard College in Vermont. He soon left Goddard, but he stayed in Vermont, holding various jobs until he enrolled in Johnson State College, also in Vermont. Mosley was graduated from Johnson State in 1975 with a degree in political science. After graduation, Mosley worked as a potter, a caterer, and a computer programmer. Moving to New York City in 1981, he continued to work as a computer programmer but eventually decided to become a writer. Enrolling in the City College of New York's writing program in the mid-1980's, he achieved success with relative rapidity. His first novel, *Devil in a Blue Dress* (1990), was nominated for an Edgar Award by the Mystery Writers of America and received a Shamus Award from the Private Eye Writers of America. *A Red Death* (1991) and *White Butterfly* (1992) also achieved critical acclaim and commercial success.

Analysis

Mosley's novels fall into the category of hard-boiled detective stories. This genre is associated most often with Dashiell Hammett, Raymond Chandler, and Ross Macdonald, pioneers who transformed a popular form of entertainment into world-

recognized literature. By the time Mosley started writing, there were dozens of successful authors working within the genre. In addition, the once exclusively white male enclave of the private eye had included several female and African American detectives.

Easy Rawlins is not a licensed private investigator, but the unlicensed operative has a long lineage. The detective in Hammett's *The Glass Key* (1930), for example, is a friend of the primary suspect, and John D. MacDonald's Travis McGee and Lawrence Block's Matt Scudder are unlicensed agents who, like Easy Rawlins, do "favors" for people. There is also a related genre of hard-boiled novels that are stylistically similar to hard-boiled detective stories, only without a detective as protagonist. Prominent writers within this genre have included James Cain, Jim Thompson, David Goodis, and Harry Whittingham. Easy's first-person narrative and continual struggles with his inner self are reminiscent of many works in this latter genre, though Mosley's novels are definitely "whodunits" as well.

In both of its forms, the hard-boiled genre features a lean, hard style of language, suspense, fast-paced action, and psychological as well as social realism. As Raymond Chandler pointed out in his 1950 essay "The Simple Art of Murder," hard-boiled literature differs from the classical British detective story in its focus on the "mean streets" of America's cities and the real motives behind human behavior. Rather than inventing and unraveling puzzling crimes (for example, locked-door mysteries), hard-boiled writers explore the puzzles of the human heart.

The detective in hard-boiled literature is usually a lonely "knight," full of human flaws yet devoted to truth and justice. Unlike police officers, hard-boiled detectives are not limited by their bureaucratic positions or by the law. They are, however, limited. They often fail, and though they may note the world's injustices, they usually end up coping with them rather than bringing about instantaneous reform.

Mosley's series fits well into this genre. His style is lean and true to the streets. He presents Los Angeles in a conspicuously unidealized way. In addition, Easy is a loner who, despite his personal flaws, takes risks and bends rules to make the world more just. He also has a hunger for truth, though he is willing to lie if it serves his purpose.

What distinguishes Mosley's work, in addition to depth of characterization and sheer storytelling ability, is that he deals with issues of race, which pose many vexing problems of social justice. (Note the theme of color in Mosley's titles, as well as the fact that he begins his series with references to the colors of the American flag.) Following the lead of such prominent African American authors as Richard Wright, Ralph Ellison, and Chester Himes, Mosley explores problems of discrimination, black identity, and black alienation.

Mosley also treats the theme of violence. Easy Rawlins hesitates to use violence except in self-defense, yet he is saved more than once by his friend Mouse's willingness to use violence freely. Indeed, Easy seems to be incomplete without Mouse. Mouse's violence, however, also does not provide an answer. Left to himself, Mouse would merely drink, chase women, and occasionally shoot people.

Mosley's work has notable predecessors. Hammett explored the issue of race briefly in his short story "Nightshade" (anthologized in 1944), and Whittingham's 1961 novel *Journey into Violence* explores Southern racism in a political context. Mosley's closest precursor, though, is Chester Himes. Himes's first novel, *If He Hollers, Let Him Go* (1945), takes place in Los Angeles and uses a hard-boiled prose style to explore issues of racial justice and black alienation. Himes's novel ends with the main character, Bob Jones, about to enter the Army in 1943. Mosley's Easy Rawlins is a World War II veteran who starts his tales just after the war. Moreover, Himes later made a name for himself by writing suspense novels featuring two black Harlem detectives who often play by their own rules.

What Mosley has fully demonstrated is the compatibility of two essentially radical literary perspectives. Although African American literature has been more overtly critical, the best hard-boiled work also challenges accepted beliefs about the justness of American society. With the successful marriage of these two literary perspectives, Mosley has produced eminently readable novels that resonate with meaning.

DEVIL IN A BLUE DRESS

First published: 1990
Type of work: Novel

A black World War II veteran turns to the dangerous world of detective work when he loses his job in a factory.

Devil in a Blue Dress introduces readers to Ezekiel "Easy" Rawlins, the principal character in Mosley's detective novels. Easy is not a licensed detective; in fact, he is not a detective at all at the outset of the novel. It is 1948, and he is a young black veteran of World War II who has moved to the largely black Watts section of Los Angeles after growing up in a tough Houston neighborhood.

Circumstances conspire to put Easy in the detective business. He has lost his job at an aircraft factory after standing up to his white supervisor. Easy likens the plant to a plantation, but without his job there, he has no way to make the mortgage payments on his small house in Watts.

A solution arises when a bartender and former fighter named Joppy, also from Houston, introduces Easy to a menacing white man named Albright. Albright is searching for a white woman named Daphne Monet, who has been seen in Watts. According to Albright, Daphne's former lover merely wants to get in touch with her. Despite misgivings, Easy takes on the job of finding Daphne.

Soon a string of murders convinces Easy that he has gotten himself into something more dangerous than he imagined. The police also rough him up. Desperate, Easy summons his friend Mouse from Houston to help. Mouse is Easy's best friend, but he is also the reason Easy left Houston. Mouse is a killer who, on one occasion, made Easy an accessory to murder. Easy leaves a message for Mouse. Not knowing what to expect, he then tries to handle the situation himself.

Daphne has been linked to a black gangster named Frank Johnson, whom Easy wants to avoid. He gets a break when Daphne calls and asks for his help. Instead of turning her over to Albright, Easy grants her request. When Daphne bolts again, Easy is sure that Albright means to harm her, even if his client does not. Easy believes that Albright is principally interested in thirty thousand dollars Daphne took when she disappeared.

In order to help Daphne, Easy tries to locate Frank Johnson. Instead, he returns home one day to find Johnson waiting for him. Suspicious about Easy's interest in his affairs, Johnson is about to kill Easy when Mouse appears and scares Johnson out of the house.

Daphne calls again, and Easy takes her to what he thinks is a safe haven, a motel owned by his Mexican American friend Primo. Daphne and Easy become lovers. Coming back from a meal, they find that Albright and two henchmen have tracked them down. Easy is knocked out, but when he comes to, he manages to find out Albright's address. He pursues Albright, leaving word for Mouse.

Easy finds that Daphne is being held by Albright and Joppy. They are trying to persuade her to tell them where the money is hidden. Easy tries to free Daphne, but he is once again about to be killed when Mouse comes to the rescue. Mouse mortally wounds Albright, kills Joppy, and makes Daphne (who, it turns out, is Frank Johnson's half-sister) tell the whereabouts of the money. Mouse, Easy, and Daphne split the money three ways. Daphne leaves Easy because he now knows that she is not white. Indeed, she left her lover partly because a blackmailer threatened to expose her lineage.

Easy is left to square things with the police. He implicates Joppy, Albright, and another murderer. Easy leaves Mouse out of his story; he also protects Daphne, who has killed the blackmailer.

Easy also has his compassionate side. He rescues a boy, Jesus, who has been sexually abused by the blackmailer. He finds the boy a home with Primo and his wife. Easy cannot change the world, but he can make it better for one child.

A RED DEATH

First published: 1991
Type of work: Novel

Easy Rawlins is drawn into a case involving Communists, a rogue federal agent, and the FBI.

In *A Red Death*, it is now 1953, during the period of McCarthyism. Easy has used the money he made in *Devil in a Blue Dress* to buy rental properties, which he owns secretly; he pretends to work for Mofass, his manager and rent collector. Trouble looms, however, when an Internal Revenue Service (IRS) agent named Lawrence targets Easy for investigation. Easy is soon facing the possibility of prison.

As if this is not enough, Etta Mae and LaMarque, Mouse's wife and son, come up from Houston. Etta Mae is estranged from Mouse and wants to live with Easy. Easy desires Etta Mae, but he knows that living with her might put him on a collision course with Mouse. Sure enough, Mouse appears in Watts, though he spends a night partying before looking Easy up. The delay gives Easy a chance to find an apartment for Etta Mae and LaMarque.

The situation with the IRS takes a twist during Easy's meeting with Lawrence. Desperate enough to respond violently, Easy is saved from drastic action when a Federal Bureau of Investigation (FBI) agent named Craxton offers to help. Craxton says that he will patch up Easy's problems with the IRS in return for help in nailing a union organizer and suspected communist named Chaim Wenzler. Wenzler, a Jew, is also active in several black churches, including one in Easy's neighborhood. Easy agrees to cooperate.

Easy meets Mouse in a bar. He tells Mouse the truth about Etta Mae and LaMarque, but he honors Etta Mae's request and refuses to tell Mouse her address. Mouse does not push the matter, but warns that he will not wait forever to hear from Etta Mae.

The following morning, Easy finds the body of Poinsettia Jackson, one of his tenants, in her apartment. She appears to have hung herself, which seems plausible in light of her poor health and lack of money to pay rent. Easy, in fact, had been on the verge of letting Mofass evict her.

Easy takes Etta Mae to church the following Sunday morning. He hears an avid sermon against the waste of black youths in the Korean War, perhaps direct evidence of Chaim Wenzel's influence. Easy is introduced to Chaim. Despite himself, Easy likes the man.

Easy accompanies Etta Mae home. Displaying her divorce papers, she seduces him, and the two become lovers.

Easy begins to work with Chaim. The two become friendly; the only group that Chaim seems to be linked to is the National Association for the Advancement of Colored People (NAACP), which Craxton quickly brands as "communist." Easy does learn from one of Chaim's former associates that Chaim has, quite by chance, come into possession of some classified documents. Easy now has enough on Chaim to satisfy the FBI.

Meanwhile, Lawrence refuses to go along with the FBI bargain and seals Easy's home. Easy is outraged, but he is restrained by sympathetic federal marshals. A call to Craxton gets the FBI agent to work directly with Lawrence's boss, who orders Lawrence not to bother Easy; Easy moves back into his house.

Two problems remain. Easy is Etta Mae's lover, and the threat of Mouse looms over him. Moreover, he has become close friends with Chaim, whom he has to betray if he is to keep Craxton happy and escape his tax problems. Together with the guilt he feels over Poinsettia's death, this situation drives Easy to drink one night while he is working at the church. Chaim and his daughter take Easy to the daughter's house to sleep off his drunk.

The next day, Easy again confronts death when the minister and his lover are found shot to death at the church. Easy calls the police, who seem suspicious of him now that he has been involved with two deaths.

Easy is picked up by the police, who now have evidence that Poinsettia was murdered; they have also learned that Easy owns the buildings run by Mofass. The presence of a black policeman, Quinten Naylor, does not keep Easy from being roughed up, but it does allow him to make a phone call to Craxton's office. Craxton gets him out of the lockup and puts him back on Chaim's case.

Chaim himself is then killed, however, and a shot is taken at Easy as he brings Chaim's daughter to his house to spend the night. Easy now thinks he knows the killer—Mofass, who has mysteriously disappeared. Enlisting the help of Mouse, Easy locates Mofass and is about to kill him. When, to Mouse's disgust, Easy hesitates, Mofass reveals that it is Lawrence who has done the killings in an attempt to get Easy's property. Mofass has helped because Lawrence has previously nailed him on a tax charge.

Working alone now, Easy locates the stolen classified documents and puts them into Lawrence's possession in order to save Chaim's reputation. He then arranges a meeting with Lawrence to check out Mofass' story. When Lawrence jumps him, Easy is once again saved by Mouse, who shoots Lawrence dead.

. In the end, Etta Mae dumps Easy for Mouse. Easy is left with the orphan Jesus, who has come back to live with him. He forgives Mofass in light of his own partial betrayals of Mouse, Chaim, and Poinsettia.

WHITE BUTTERFLY

First published: 1992
Type of work: Novel

Easy Rawlins investigates a series of brutal murders in Watts.

White Butterfly takes place in 1956. Easy is married and rearing two children, an infant from his new marriage and Jesus, the orphan from the earlier books. This life is not idyllic, however; Easy has not told Regina, his wife, about his secret business holdings or about his detective work. Moreover, there are other important instances of miscommunication between the two that cloud the future of their marriage. On the other hand, Easy is staying away from bars and living a cleaner, healthier life.

The situation worsens when Easy is approached—first by black policeman Quinten Naylor and then by a slew of high city officials—for help in tracing a serial murderer loose in Watts. This burst of attention is brought about by the appearance of a white victim. Up until this time, the victims have been black prostitutes and exotic dancers; the white victim, though, is a college student from a respectable family. Easy is bullied into helping when officials threaten to pin the crimes on Mouse.

Easy goes to work, frequenting bars and asking questions that lead him to a suspect but also to a surprising revelation: The white coed led a double life, coming to Watts to work as the "White Butterfly." When Easy reports this, he is told to discontinue his line of inquiry, partly because the girl's father is a former district attorney. Curiosity, though, gets the better of Easy. He speaks to the girl's mother, who is quite upset. The police chastise Easy and penalize him by arresting Mouse. Easy talks the police into releasing Mouse, and the two of them track the suspect, a black man, to San Francisco. They locate him just in time to witness his death in a bar fight staged by the local police. They learn that San Francisco has had a chain of similar murders about which the black population was never informed. The suspect's death becomes the final step in a massive coverup.

Frustrated, Easy returns to Los Angeles; there, he learns that the white victim had had a baby. When he puts the girl's parents in touch with the woman who is keeping the baby, he is arrested for extortion and appears to be hopelessly framed. Mouse comes up with bail money, and Easy reveals that the white coed was killed by her father.

Easy decides to be more open with Regina and to stop keeping secrets from her, but it is too late; Regina has run off with another man, taking Easy's daughter with her. Easy is left heartbroken, and he drinks heavily until Mouse and Jesus bring him back from the brink of self-destruction.

A subplot involves Mofass, who gets into trouble with white developers from whom he receives a bribe. While Easy will not bail Mofass out of trouble, the two do work together to get the upper hand over the white businessmen. Thus, while Easy's marriage fails, he is able to solidify his finances and, therefore, his independence.

Summary

Walter Mosley has joined two worthy literary traditions in a fruitful partnership. He employs the form of the hard-boiled detective story to explore important racial themes in a suspenseful and eminently readable manner. His Easy Rawlins series also provides an accessible introduction to the history of Watts and of postwar America in general.

Mosley presents a realistic look at poverty and violence, but he also projects a profound idealism. Mosley also does a good job of exposing forms of racism, yet he rejects the temptation to brand all white people as bigots. The strength of his work lies in his refusal to offer simple solutions to the complex issues he raises.

Bibliography

Baker, Robert A., and Michael T. Nietzel. *Private Eyes—One Hundred and One Knights: A Survey of American Detective Fiction, 1922-1984.* Bowling Green, Ohio: Bowling Green University Popular Press, 1985.

Chandler, Raymond. *The Simple Art of Murder.* Boston: Houghton, 1950.

Geherin, David. *The American Private Eye: The Image in Fiction*. New York: Frederick Ungar, 1985.

Hitchens, Christopher. "The Tribes of Walter Mosley." *Vanity Fair* 56 (February, 1993): 46-50.

Lomax, Sara M. "Double Agent Easy Rawlins: The Development of a Cultural Detective." *American Visions* 7 (April-May, 1992): 32-34.

Mason, Theodore O., Jr. "Walter Mosley's Easy Rawlins: The Detective and Afro-American Fiction." *Kenyon Review* 14 (Fall, 1992): 173-183.

Ira Smolensky

FRANK O'HARA

Born: Baltimore, Maryland
June 27, 1926
Died: Mastic Beach, New York
July 25, 1966

Principal Literary Achievement

O'Hara renewed American poetry by his use of direct language, surreal imagery, humor, and personal subject matter.

Biography

Francis Russell O'Hara was born in Baltimore, Maryland, on June 27, 1926. He grew up, however, in central Massachusetts in Grafton, a suburb of Worcester. He attended local Catholic schools and was graduated from St. John's High School in Worcester in 1944. After graduation he enlisted in the Navy and served as a sonar operator on a destroyer until his discharge in 1946. He did not see combat, although he was in the Pacific theater.

After military service, O'Hara entered Harvard University as an undergraduate majoring first in music and later in English. He was graduated from Harvard in 1950. At Harvard, O'Hara was already writing poetry, and he was one of the founders of the Poet's Theatre in Cambridge. O'Hara's play *Try! Try!* was produced at the Poets' Theatre in 1951. During the Harvard years, he met John Ashbery and Kenneth Koch, who were to become lifelong friends and subjects of a number of his poems. In 1950, O'Hara entered Michigan University to do graduate work in English, and in 1951, he was awarded the prestigious Avery Hopwood Major Award in Poetry. After a year at Michigan, he moved to New York City, which was to become his home until his death in 1966.

O'Hara was deeply involved in the New York art world during these years; he worked as an editor of *Art News* and as a special assistant and later as an associate curator of the Museum of Modern Art. Painting is very often the subject of his poems, and his technique has often been compared to that of modern painting. O'Hara was a friend of many of the most important modern painters, including Jasper Johns, Willem de Kooning, and Larry Rivers. They respected him as a fellow artist and appreciated his immediate and intelligent response to their paintings. O'Hara put together a number of exhibitions of such painters as Robert Motherwell, Franz Kline, and Arshile

Gorky for the Museum of Modern Art, and in 1959 he published *Jackson Pollock*, one of the earliest important studies of the painter. O'Hara was also well informed about modern music and wrote poems about Sergei Rachmaninoff and John Cage. For O'Hara, the arts were truly one and indivisible.

O'Hara wrote poetry at odd moments while he worked at the Museum of Modern Art. Some of these were circulated to friends or appeared in letters. He saw his poems as works designed to please friends or for special occasions rather than as monuments. Later, some of these poems were collected and published with the help of such friends as Ashbery, Koch, and James Schuyler. O'Hara did, however, publish several volumes during his life. His first book of poems, *A City Winter, and Other Poems*, was published in 1952,and was followed by *Oranges* in 1953. *Meditations in an Emergency* appeared in 1957, and many of his poems were included in *The New American Poetry 1945-1960*. One of his most typical volumes was *Lunch Poems*, which was published in 1964. Another important volume, *Love Poems (Tentative Title)*, was published in 1965. *The Collected Poems of Frank O'Hara* was published posthumously in 1971; many were amazed that the casual and occasional poems of O'Hara filled a volume of more than five hundred pages.

O'Hara was a homosexual, and his life was marked by intense friendships and love affairs, many of which became subjects for his poetry. There is a strong sense of the shared perspective of a small group in the poems. The intensity of the most casual experience and the significance of personal relationships is captured forcefully in O'Hara's poems, especially *Lunch Poems* and *Love Poems*. In July of 1966, O'Hara was fatally injured on Fire Island when a jeep struck him as he was waiting for a beach taxi. He died a few days later in Bayview Hospital at Mastic Beach, New York.

Analysis

O'Hara's style and subject matter are very different from the dominant poetic tradition of the period. O'Hara disliked the complex modernism of T. S. Eliot, and he was displeased about Eliot's influence upon the most important critical school of the period, the New Criticism. He described Eliot's influence on modern poetry as "deadening." In contrast, he called his critical view "Personism"; this was a rejection of nearly all the formal aspects of poetry—such as rhyme, meter, assonance, even logical structure—while substituting for these elements the immediacy and presence of the individual speaking voice. Often, in some of O'Hara's most interesting and amusing poems, that personal voice is captured in conversation with friends about the seemingly trivial events of the day. There is no attempt to create symbolic or mythic depth out of these ordinary events; the emphasis is on the intensity and wit revealed in these exchanges and descriptions.

O'Hara did not, however, reject all poetic influence. He preferred the simplicity of diction of William Carlos Williams and the surrealistic imagery of the French Symbolists, especially Arthur Rimbaud, to the high modernism of poets who followed the lead of Eliot. Another important influence was the poetry of the Russian Formalist Vladimir Mayakovsky, whose riddling lines concentrated on making the literary device reveal itself. O'Hara never seeks to hide the fact that what he is creating is a work of art.

O'Hara also has a Walt Whitman-like openness to experience that is manifested in lists of people and places. The long list in "Second Avenue" is a good example of the technique. "And must I express the science of legendary elegies/ consummate on the Clarissas of puma and gnu, and wildebeest?" There is an exuberance in the production of witty lists. O'Hara has the same inclusiveness as Whitman, although O'Hara does not usually reach out to embrace all America. His world is bounded by Manhattan and the Hamptons. It is a particularly urban art that has little use for nature or the rural world.

Proper names, especially the names of friends, appear in nearly every one of the poems, and names dominate some of them. "At the Old Place" is a good example of O'Hara's insistence on naming. "Through the street we skip like swallows./ Howard malingers. (Come on Howard.) Ashes/ malingers. (Come on, J.A.) Dick malingers./ (Come on, Dick.) Alvin darts ahead. (Wait up,/ Alvin.) Jack, Earl, and Someone don't come." Naming seems to have a special value for O'Hara, although O'Hara's poetry seems, at times, to be addressed to those who know or can recognize the names that are invoked. Yet it is not necessary to know the names of places to which O'Hara refers, since the effect is to reveal the delight the speaker has about the world in which he lives.

O'Hara often mixes the real with the surreal in his poems to create what John Ashbery has called "home-grown surrealism." A typical example can be found in the first stanza of "Je Voudrais Voir."

> an immense plain full of nudes
> and roses falling on them from the green air
> a smile of utter simplicity speaking to the soldiers
> of the camel corps, so brief and smelly

The effect is created by the precision of the detail and the strange mixture of roses and nudes, of a smile and the camel corps. O'Hara's version of Surrealism involves the connection of a conventional poetic image—the rose—to some esoteric imagery.

O'Hara once described some of his work as his "I do this, I do that poems." The most random and trivial events are related with a breathless excitement. Such a description can be found in "John Button Birthday":

> And in 1984 I trust we'll still
> be high together. I'll say "Let's go to a bar"
> and you'll say "Let's go to a movie" and we'll go to both;
> like two old Chinese drunkards arguing about their
> favorite mountain and the million reasons for them both.

For O'Hara, every experience, even the most trivial, can become a poetic element. Poetry for O'Hara was made up not of grand moments but of small ones, especially those with friends, which the poet's voice singles out and exults over. Critic Marjorie

Perloff has noted that O'Hara's "poetic world is one of immanence rather than transcendence."

Painters and painting were often the subjects of O'Hara's poems, and at times, he used the structure of modern art in this poems. "Why I Am Not a Painter," paradoxically, is a good example of O'Hara's use of painting as subject and form. He describes a painter's process of inclusion and exclusion and contrasts it to his own method. Both the poet's and the painter's methods, however, are strikingly similar, as are the results. Both works are generated by an early impulse that may not exist in the completed work except as a remnant in the title. Neither art relies on logical form but rather on the path the work itself seems to take. Above all, the creation of a work of art—a painting or a poem—is something that cannot be consciously explained, but some mystery about how it is brought about remains.

O'Hara's word choice is interesting. One of his favorite techniques is the use of exotic and strange words, which are often strung together: "Oh! kangaroos, sequins, chocolate sodas!/ You really are beautiful! Pearls,/ harmonicas, jujubes, aspirins!" O'Hara loves the sound of words for their own sake and for their strangeness. There is no attempt to transform such an amusing pattern of words into symbolic meaning; the pattern exists for its own sake.

O'Hara uses meter or rhyme only for effect, as in such lines as "At night Chinamen jump/ on Asia with a thump." The effect is comic rather than formal. The poetic line, however, is an important structural unit in O'Hara's poetry. Most of the lines run on, creating the effect of breathless conversation or suggesting the exuberance of a speaker as exulting over the wonder of life in all of its variety. O'Hara makes no attempt to keep his lines to similar metrical lengths, although he does attempt at times to create a visual design out of a series of lines.

TO THE FILM INDUSTRY IN CRISIS

First published: 1957
Type of work: Poem

A humorous celebration of the populist and mythic values of American films.

"To the Film Industry in Crisis" is a love letter from Frank O'Hara to the most popular and accessible of the arts: the motion pictures. The poem begins by excluding serious and pompous arts such as "experimental theatre" and "Grand Opera." The speaker rejects also "lean quarterlies and swarthy periodicals," since they too are for the elite, not the masses. The speaker does not merely approve of the "Motion Picture Industry" but declares his love and devotion to it. The title's emphasis on Hollywood as an industry effectively distinguishes the filmmaking world from the realm of art by defining it as a factory producing for the masses.

The second verse paragraph places O'Hara's preferences in a context. "In time of crisis, we must all decide again and again whom we love./ And give credit where it's due. . . ." O'Hara never makes clear what the "crisis" is, and the reference seems to be used as a provocation to comically inflate the reader's response to the subject.

The speaker rejects a few more candidates for his affection, such as the Catholic Church and the American Legion, and finally begins to discuss his true love: "glorious Silver Screen, tragic Technicolor, amorous Cinemascope,/ stretching Vistavision and startling Stereophonic Sound, with all/ your heavenly dimensions and reverberations and iconoclasms!" The technical innovations of the "industry" are greeted with the same hyperbole that went into their advertisement and promotion. Each of these has its own adjective; some of the adjectives are wildly inappropriate, such as "tragic Technicolor." The ironic point that O'Hara is making is that there can be no tragedy in the gaudy world of Technicolor.

The next section of the poem contains an even longer list of actors and their famous roles. The list ends with a reaffirmation of the devotion of the speaker: "yes, to you/ and to all you others, the great, the near-great, the featured, the extras/ . . . / my love!"

O'Hara often refers to the popular arts in his poems, and "To the Film Industry in Crisis" is his fullest and wittiest attempt to account for the power that motion pictures have over the public imagination. The poem first shows what films are not—high art—and then shows what they really are—magic. O'Hara does echo the hyperbole of his subject in his own style and reveal its essential function as providing myths by which to live.

THE DAY LADY DIED

First published: 1964
Type of work: Poem

The news of blues singer Billie Holiday's death turns the poet's trivial world into a tragic one.

"The Day Lady Died" is one of O'Hara's "I do this, I do that" poems, until the sudden reversal of the last few lines. The poem begins with the O'Hara speaker recording the details of the day. "It is 12:20 in New York a Friday/ three days after Bastille day, yes/ it is 1959. . . ." The casual description is an effective way of establishing the date and time in which a surprising and momentous event will be recognized.

The speaker now switches to describing his own activities, which include getting a shoeshine and planning a train itinerary. He eats, and he buys "an ugly NEW WORLD WRITING to see what the poets/ in Ghana are doing these days." The preparations for the journey continue, as the speaker gets money at the bank and buys gifts for the people he is going to visit. There is a humorous aside about the bank teller, "Miss Stillwagon," who for once does not look up the poet's bank balance; the poet also records his agitation about selecting the proper gifts.

Suddenly, in the midst of these mundane activities, the speaker experiences a moment of deep personal significance. The speaker buys a newspaper and sees "her" face on it. The poem's title, which refers to Holiday by her nickname, indicates who "her" is, although Holiday is not explicitly named in the poem. The news changes the poet's physical being ("I am sweating a lot by now," he remarks). He is then taken from the present moment back to a time when he had heard Holiday sing; he remembers "leaning on the john door in the 5 SPOT/ while she whispered a song along the keyboard/ to Mal Waldron and everyone and I stopped breathing."

The poem sets up its literally breathless moment by its cataloging of the trivial activities of the day. At other times, O'Hara seems to be using lists and names for their own sake, but in this poem, there is a clear utility to these techniques, as the revelation transforms the ordinary into something memorable. It is interesting to note that the art of Billie Holiday is seen here as turning a public moment into a private one (she "whispers" a song in public), while O'Hara's art is to make private moments and experiences public.

IN MEMORY OF MY FEELINGS

First published: 1956
Type of work: Poem

The poem explores some of the different selves that live in the poet in order to sort out his authentic self, the artist.

"In Memory of My Feelings" is a surreal poem that attempts to find an authentic self amidst the many selves that can be discerned within the speaker. The poet seems to relate these selves to the different feelings he has. For example, in the first section of the poem, he identifies both a "transparent" self that "carries me quietly, like a gondola, through the streets" as well as a number of "naked selves" that use "pistols" to protect themselves. The division continues as "One of me rushes/ to window #13 and one of me raises his whip. . . ." The speaker is also being hunted by some malign force. The only unifying element in these contrasting selves is "love of the serpent." At first, this seems to be a phallic symbol; in the context of the poem, however, the serpent image operates as a symbol for the artist self, which the poet must acknowledge and privilege over all of his other selves. At the end of the poem's first section, the "transparent selves" are together "like vipers in a pail, writhing and hissing/ without panic, with a certain justice of response. . . ." The section's final line, in which "the aquiline serpent comes to resemble the Medusa," unites the various selves by the central symbol of the serpent. The Medusa, therefore, is not a threatening but a positive image.

The second section is a regressive movement dominated by references to those who have sacrificed their lives for the poet. "My father, my uncle,/ my grand-uncle and the several aunts. My/ grand-aunt dying for me. . . ." While this carnage of sacrifice is going on, the speaker is in a suite "in the Grand Hotel/ where mail arrives for my incognito." The cool façade is sometimes amusing in O'Hara's poems, but this one is clearly selfish, cruel, and isolated.

The next section begins to reverse the negatives, as the poet writes, "The most arid stretch is often richest." The speaker adopts the role of a war hero during the French Revolution or under Lord Nelson; however, he "wraps himself" in memories now "against the heat of life." The hero pose, finally, cannot be sustained, since it is an avoidance of life.

The next section deals with a real incident, a visit to Chicago. The poet begins to see some positive value in multiple selves: "Grace/ to be born and live as variously as possible. The conception/ of the masque barely suggests the sordid identifications." There is, in contrast to section three, an acceptance of life in its diversity that includes multiple selves. He then becomes a Hittite, a Chinaman, and an Indian who has "just caught sight of the *Niña*, the *Pinta*, and the *Santa Maria*." He then asks "What land is this? so free?" That freedom consists of accepting the "whitemen" and their gift of "the horse I fell in love with on the frieze." The horse he is given is, as Marjorie Perloff suggests, a work of art. That acceptance of art as central to his existence serves as a transition to the last section of the poem.

The last section of the poem returns to the serpent, which is "coiled around the central figure." After briefly summarizing the different roles that have been assayed in the poem, the poet realizes what is needed. All the selves "I myself and singly must now kill/ and save the serpent in their midst." His essential being is as a serpent-artist, so the loss of the other selves becomes a gain that will enable him to live the fullest and truest life.

Summary

Frank O'Hara's poetry altered the range and possibilities of poetry in the middle of the twentieth century. He rejected complex modernism for a poetry of direct speech that dealt with everyday events. O'Hara showed other poets that a poem could be about any subject. It could be a description of the poet's daily actions or his changing relationships. There was no need for poetry to be profound; it needed only to delight. That delight and wit can be found in the details of nearly all O'Hara's poems. O'Hara also expanded the range of poetic structures and subjects by his references to modern painting and French Surrealism. His poetry was at first criticized for being incoherent or trivial; however, later critics have confirmed that his poetry is grounded in an American literary tradition that includes such major figures as Walt Whitman and William Carlos Williams.

Bibliography

Altieri, Charles. "The Significance of Frank O'Hara." *Iowa Review* 4 (Winter, 1973): 90-104.

Feldman, Alan. *Frank O'Hara*. Boston: Twayne, 1979.

Gooch, Brad. *City Poet: The Life and Times of Frank O'Hara*. New York: Alfred A. Knopf, 1993.

Perloff, Marjorie. *Frank O'Hara: Poet Among Painters*. New York: George Braziller, 1977.

Vendler, Helen. "The Virtues of the Alterable." *Parnassus: Poetry in Review* 1 (Fall/Winter, 1972): 5-20.

James Sullivan

SHARON OLDS

Born: San Francisco, California
November 19, 1942

Principal Literary Achievement
Olds's accessibility and her concern with family and human relationships give her work a general appeal.

Biography
Sharon Olds was born in San Francisco, California, on November 19, 1942. She has said that her literal-minded approach to the world surfaced when, at the age of two, she tried to eat a book of ration stamps, having being told that they were to be the family's source of food during the war.

The family lived near a school for the blind, and Olds sang in an Episcopal church choir with some of the blind girls, an experience that became the subject for a later poem, "The Indispensability of the Eyes," in which she recalls her fear of the blind eyes and the unearthly things they saw. She also recalls that, as a child at Girl Scout camp, she began to recite her homemade verses aloud, hidden behind a tree. During that time, she also began to sense a relationship between her physical self and the earth, a perception that appears in her poetry.

She grew up in a troubled household; her poems refer to her grandfather's cruelties toward her and her sister, to her grandmother's anger, to her father's alcoholism, which led to her parents' divorce, and to her abusive sister. When Olds was fifteen, she was sent to a boarding school near Boston. There, she came to love Eastern landscapes and New York City. A poem from her adulthood ("Infinite Bliss") records her desire never to live where it does not snow.

Also during that time, she began to read a substantial amount of poetry and to write it as well, using conventional poetic forms for most of her early work. She has stated that it took her a long time to learn to balance a poem's need for exceptional language with the need to establish a voice of her own. She has said that she accomplished that discovery partly through dance, once more underscoring the relationship between her physical world and her writing.

Olds received a B.A. with distinction from Stanford University in 1964. She studied languages (French, Italian, German, Greek, and Middle English) as an undergraduate. In 1972, she received a Ph.D. in American literature from Columbia University; her

dissertation examined the prosody of Ralph Waldo Emerson.

Her first collection of poems, *Satan Says*, was published in 1980. Reviews were mixed but generally positive; reviewers attributed some of the collection's faults to Olds's inexperience. *Satan Says* was followed by *The Dead and the Living* (1984), which won the Lamont Poetry Prize and the National Book Critics Circle award. *The Gold Cell* was published in 1987 and *The Father* (a series of poems about her father's death from cancer) appeared in 1992.

Olds has spent her adult life living in New York City. Although family life forms a major theme in her writing (she has described herself as a full-time mother and full-time poet), she has also made an active career of teaching and lecturing. She has taught at Sarah Lawrence, the Theodor Herzl Institute, Columbia University, New York University, and Brandeis University. She has also conducted a poetry workshop at Goldwater Hospital for the severely physically handicapped and has worked with the PEN Freedom-to-Write committee. Olds's social concerns can also be recognized in her work with PEN's Silenced Voices subcommittee (which deals with censorship) and Helsinki Watch. In 1989, she became director of New York University's Graduate School of Arts and Science Creative Writing Program.

Analysis

Olds has said that poetry has several wellsprings. It functions as the artist's release for personal emotion and satisfies the human desire to create beauty. It also establishes human interconnectedness by revealing writer to reader in an especially intimate way, and it bears witness for life and for the parts of the world that have no voice. That statement serves well as an introduction to Olds's work, for it implies much about her subjects, her themes, and her language.

Olds's poetry is, first of all, accessible. Without sacrificing poetic power, she nevertheless is careful to ground her reader in the poems. (Some early reviewers faulted her, in fact, for being too explicit, for explaining too much.) Settings and characters are from daily life—men, women, lovers, children. Her topics range from Chinese food to the atrocities recorded in the newspapers to the death of her estranged father.

Olds's language is as accessible as her subject matter; her syntax is usually composed of the direct structures of the speaking voice. Her diction is from daily life as well, with a strong presence of blunt sexual words. Commenting on her first book, *Satan Says*, some reviewers condemned her for overusing vulgarities and suggested that she was merely trying for shock effects. Yet sexual awareness is a significant element of Olds's work, and clinical euphemisms would seem out of place in her diction and her often angry tone. In the title poem of *Satan Says*, for example, the speaker makes quite clear that the curses Satan encourages her to utter against her parents are only part of her "freedom"; the other part is her admission that she loves them, too, with a love that both traps and warms her.

Sexuality holds an important place in Olds's view of the world. She writes unflinchingly about her sexual experiences, and she is strongly conscious of others' sexuality, including that of her parents and children. It is part of how she understands herself and them.

Anger and violence are also elements in this understanding. The abuses of her childhood join with her awareness of the world as a place where the weak and helpless are routinely tortured and brutalized. The nature of Olds's imagery is such that violence and sexuality often merge in her poems in a way that some reviews have labeled sensationalism. The images of blood, the violent overtone of the sexual act, the vulnerability of sexuality all seem to allow such connections, however, and Olds makes full use of those relationships. In "Monarchs," for example, she links the red wings of the monarch butterfly with the blood she shed during her first sexual experience and the dark red of her lover's "butcher's hands."

That Olds's poems offer the reader an intimate view of their creator is almost understatement, so willing is she to refuse readers nothing in her experience. She describes sitting out a family fight, crouched beside her sister in an upstairs hall; she records her sudden perception of her father as a potential killer while he is driving drunk; she pictures her five-year-old son abstractedly urinating on the front door, his mind on other things. She details the agonizing events of her father's death. The anger that some of these events call up in her has led some readers to compare Olds with Sylvia Plath, but Olds's work has themes that counterbalance her anger.

The most powerful of these themes is her insistent emphasis on nurturing and caregiving. Those themes appear in her first volume and continue to appear steadily in her later poems as well, recording her awareness of to what her gender seems to have committed her—the fostering of life and growth wherever it seems possible.

The series of poems called "Young Mothers" from *Satan Says* makes a good example of the complex relationship between a mother and her infant. To Olds, nurture is far from a sentimental picturing of parental love. The infant is part of the mother herself; it depends on her for everything it receives. She loves and protects it more fiercely than anything else in her life, and at the same time she feels trapped by its dependence, its demands and vulnerability.

The Father, Olds's volume of poems about her father's death, demonstrates clearly the ironic tension that such nurture can create. In these poems, the reader at first sees a grown daughter returning home to help nurse her dying father. Typically, Olds spares the reader nothing in describing the mouth tumor that is devouring the old man; she pictures his daughter helping him drink, helping him spit and wipe his mouth. Gradually, the reader recognizes the special pain that attends this relationship. This is the cold, rejecting alcoholic father who made the daughter's life hell and who finally left his family. The wife in the poems is his second wife, not the daughter's mother. Yet during the horrors of tending him (as well as in the months that follow his death), Olds comes to terms with the hurt he has caused her and at last is freed to state her love for him and to recognize his for her, damaged though those loves must be.

One other quality of Olds's work demands notice: Her ironic wit, which often helps to mitigate the pain of her subjects. In "The Indispensability of the Eyes," for example, she describes the discomfort she feels in the presence of blind girls; she cites as part of the reason for this discomfort the fact that the girls cannot tell when others are looking at them. She laughs at the sexual stereotyping done by an assistant fire commissioner on a television talk show ("The Housewives Watching Morning TV"). She describes her small children as puppies tangled around her ankles ("Seventh Birthday of the First Child"). Even Olds's angriest and most powerful poems retain her ability to see similarities, to recognize irony and to use it to soften the harsh realities about which she often writes.

TIME-TRAVEL

First published: 1980
Type of work: Poem

The speaker journeys back in time to find her childhood self in her troubled family.

"Time-Travel" is a good introduction to Olds's use of themes concerning her painful past. The title and the poem's first sentence explain what is happening. The speaker says she has learned to return to the past in order to find doors and windows. The meaning of those apertures is made clear at the poem's end, but the reader recognizes them already as typical means of enlarging one's view or of escaping.

The next lines place the poem in time—a hot summer day in 1955. The setting seems to be a lake house, perhaps a vacation cabin, for it has pine walls and a splintery pine floor. The speaker says that she is looking for her father in this time travel, and her slow, deliberate tracing of her steps from small room to big (she even notes the doorway she passes through) suggests the elaborate care, perhaps because of fear or uncertainty, which she is using in this search. When she finds him, it is as if she stumbles over something inert lying on a chair.

The second stanza explains that the father is asleep, sleeping off a drinking bout. Once again, Olds leads the reader carefully through the picture, suggesting reasons for her care. She can somehow own her father, possess him, in this state. She shows him as he sleeps, newspaper comics on his stomach, plaid shirt, hands folded across his body. He looks almost dead. She describes his looks in some detail, but all of his physical characteristics are dependent on the central thing she has explained—that this "solid secret body" is "where he puts the bourbon." The care with which she has searched for him is partly caused by fear of waking him. The stanza ends with the information that this is the family's last summer together and that the speaker has learned to walk very quietly that summer, so that no one will be aware of her. The second stanza is enjambed into the third so that a stanza break occurs in the middle of the sentence after the word "walk," which hangs at the line's end like a careful footstep.

The third stanza locates the other members of this unhappy family. The mother is weeping upstairs. The brother, like the other children in the family, has escaped to the outdoors. He is in a tent, reading the speaker's diary. The older sister is "changing boyfriends somewhere in a car." Only the father seems really at peace; ironically, he is described as a baby, suggesting a sort of infantile quality in his relationship with his family.

The stanza ends with a reference to a twelve-year-old girl who is down by the lake, watching its waves. The speaker approaches her and the girl turns to face her; the child is the speaker's young self, who looks up toward the house as if she does not see the speaker but must concentrate on the pain going on in her family. The adult speaker identifies her as the one she was seeking. She looks into the girl's eyes and sees waves that are somehow a cross between the lake's water and the air of hell. The poem concludes by explaining what the young girl cannot know: that this pain will have an end and that, of all of her family, she will be the survivor. Once again at the poem's end, Olds makes special use of a line break, ending the next-to-last line after "one" so that "survivor" rests all alone—like the girl herself—in its line. The line break also creates a sort of pun in the next-to-last line, which says that the girl does not know that "she is the one"—as if, in addition to being the "one" survivor, she has been singled out for some other special gift, a gift she will not recognize until much later.

THE ONE GIRL AT THE BOYS PARTY

First published: 1984
Type of work: Poem

The mother sees her daughter's imminent sexual maturity, even though the girl is still surrounded by childhood's images.

In the slender action of the twenty-one lines that make up "The One Girl at the Boys Party," Olds combines three patterns of imagery that underscore the speaker's recognition of her daughter's approaching maturity. In the poem, the speaker (that this is the mother is never explicitly stated) takes the girl, a superior math student, to a swimming party where boys immediately surround her. The speaker sees the young people dive into the pool and imagines her daughter working math problems in her head to calculate her relationship to the diving board and the gallons of water in the pool. The girl's suit has a pattern of hamburgers and french fries printed on it, and when she climbs from the pool, her ponytail will hang wet down her back. The speaker knows that as the girl looks at the boys, she will be recognizing the appeal of their masculinity.

One element of the poem's language concerns the childishness of the young girl. The speaker calls her "my girl," as if she is a small child, and places her at the pool party as if she were an infant. Although she will soon become a woman, her appearance is childish, too. The hamburger-and-fries pattern of her bathing suit, her ponytail, and the sweetness of her face all suggest a very young child.

Yet this girl is no fool, as her mother knows. Humorously, the speaker imagines the girl's math scores unfolding around her in the air, and mathematics makes up the second significant element of the poem's language. Not only do her math scores follow her to the party, but her quick mind can also make calculations about the pool at the same time she is diving into it. Moreover, she can calculate the interesting qualities of the young men around her. At this point, the poem's mathematical diction merges with the sexual.

Early in the poem, the speaker compared the girl's sleek, hard body to a prime number. Now she sees the girl's face as a factor of one, as the girl evaluates the boys in numerical terms—eyes and legs, two each; the "curves of their sexes, one each." The speaker knows that this recognition will lead the girl to more interesting calculations, "wild multiplying."

The language of male and female has been present from the poem's start. The boys are early described as "bristling"; the girl is "sleek." So it is no surprise that the end of the poem reveals the girl's latent sexual power, which is about to appear. It will be considerable, as the concluding image suggests: Many droplets of water, which seem sexually energized by their contact with the girl's body, fall "to the power of a thousand."

The tone of the poem is both amused and admiring. Clearly, the speaker respects the girl's intellect as well as her right to grow into sexual maturity.

THE LIFTING

First published: 1992
Type of work: Poem

The sight of her dying father's naked body makes the daughter aware of the depth of their relationship.

The collection from which this poem comes concerns the death of Olds's father from cancer, and it details her evolving relationship with the cold, alcoholic man who so hurt her and her family when she was a child. The father's death occurs about halfway through the collection; the poems following his death describe how their relationship continues to grow and deepen even after he has died. "The Lifting" is set not long before he dies, and it incorporates elements that are typical of Olds's work, particularly in her awareness of her father's sexuality and her linkage of that awareness to her own being and that of her daughter.

The poem begins with the shocking statement that her father suddenly lifts his nightgown, exposing himself to her. In this action, he violates a powerful taboo between fathers and daughters, and the tension of that taboo permeates the entire poem. The action is made still more complex by the poet's use of the word "nightie," a word for a woman's garment, and a rather playful word at that. Soon, the reader realizes that the setting is a hospital and the nightie a hospital gown.

The speaker looks away when her father lifts the gown, but he calls her name to make her look. He wants to show her how much weight he has lost. The folds of loose skin tell her how near he is to death. Immediately, she goes beyond the shock of his gesture to notice that his hips look like hers and that his pelvis resembles her daughter's. When she looks at the smile on his face, she recognizes that he had done this not to offend her but because he knows she will be interested. In a strange way, perhaps because, despite the "thick bud of his penis," he resembles her and her daughter, he expects her to find him appealing. Despite the strangeness of the situation, she does, and she feels affection as well as "uneasy wonder." The mystery he seems to evoke is the mystery of generation; the sexual organs she is viewing caused her to exist, and her sex has in turn created another person. The three of them are related in a way that somehow transcends the awful pain of their relationship (that pain plays little part in this poem and is not referred to explicitly).

The poem concludes with another reference to the title, this time extending its meaning. Olds describes the hospital gown lifting, rising as if on its own, as if it were the father's soul itself rising at death to approach the final mysteries.

Summary

Sharon Olds's use of her family's past, her willingness to discuss delicate and painful subjects, and her lack of squeamishness about sex all place her in the tradition of confessional poetry. Additionally, her subjects are those that have often been associated with feminist writers. Her language, her ferocious honesty, and her equally fierce maternalism, which demands recognition of the rights of all living things to grow into what they were meant to be, constitute her special contribution to this sort of poetry.

Bibliography

Behrendt, Stephen. Review of *The Dead and the Living*, by Sharon Olds. *Prairie Schooner* 59 (Spring, 1985): 100.

Kinzie, Mary. Review of *The Dead and the Living*, by Sharon Olds. *The American Poetry Review* 13 (September, 1984): 38.

Lesser, Rika. "Knows Father Best." *The Nation* 255 (December 14, 1992): 748-750.

Tillinghast, Richard. "Blunt Instruments." *The Nation* 239 (October 13, 1984): 361-363.

Zeider, Lisa. Review of *The Father*, by Sharon Olds. *The New York Times Book Review*, March 21, 1993, 14.

Ann Davison Garbett

GEORGE OPPEN

Born: New Rochelle, New York
April 24, 1908
Died: Sunnyvale, California
July 7, 1984

Principal Literary Achievement

Oppen was one of the central figures in defining and developing the poetry movement known as Objectivism.

Biography

George Oppen was born in New Rochelle, New York, on April 24, 1908, the son of George August Oppenheimer (who changed the family name in 1927) and Elsie Rothfeld. When Oppen was four and his older sister Elizabeth was seven, their mother had a nervous breakdown and committed suicide, an unsettling event compounded by his father's marriage in March, 1917, to Seville Shainwald, a woman from a very wealthy family whose relationship with Oppen was difficult and abusive. Oppen developed a warm, supportive relationship with his half-sister June Frances, who was born in 1918, the year the family moved to San Francisco.

In accordance with his family's social expectations, Oppen attended a military academy, but he was expelled six weeks before graduation for his drunken involvement in a fatal automobile accident. After traveling in the British Isles, he completed his secondary education at a small preparatory school and followed a friend to Corvallis to enroll at Oregon State College (later Oregon State University). There he met Mary Colby, an independent, literate young woman, and fell deeply in love. When they were punished for violating a curfew, the couple left school in 1926, pledging to form a pact to live together as artists. Oppen and Colby hitchhiked across the West in 1927, marrying in Dallas, Texas. The couple drove to the Great Lakes in 1928, sailed down the Erie Canal to New York City, and settled there when Oppen took a position as a switchboard operator in a brokerage house. Oppen had been writing poetry during their travels, and in New York, he met Louis Zukovsky, a young poet and teacher, and Charles Reznikoff, a lawyer and friend of Zukovsky.

When Oppen turned twenty-one, he received a substantial legacy. He and Mary moved to France in 1929, and he began the composition of *Discrete Series* (1934), his first collection of poems. In 1931, he and Zukovsky, who functioned as editor, began

the press To Publishers, which issued important modernist texts by William Carlos Williams, Ezra Pound, and Zukovsky. The Oppens returned to the United States in 1933, and Oppen was instrumental in establishing the cooperative The Objectivist Press. The Oppens joined the Communist Party in 1935 to work for social change. In response to the controlled, propagandistic manipulation of artists by the Party, and in response to the realization that he had no real experience from which to write, Oppen began an almost quarter-century of poetic silence. Oppen describes this period as "a poetic exploration at the same time it was an act of conscience."

Oppen maintained an active membership in Party activities from 1936 to 1941. In 1942, after the birth of his daughter Linda Jean, he gave up a military exemption to provoke his induction into the armed services. He was driven by anger at the Adolf Hitler-Joseph Stalin pact, which nearly forced him out of the Party, and perhaps by guilt that he had not volunteered to fight against facisim in the Spanish Civil War. Oppen saw active duty in Europe in 1944 and 1945 in an antitank company, fighting in the Battle of the Bulge and later suffering a severe wound. He won numerous decorations, including the Purple Heart and two Bronze Stars. After the war, the Oppens settled in California, where George worked as a carpenter. Following four years of federal harassment during the Joseph McCarthy era, the Oppens moved into exile in Mexico in 1950; there, Oppen worked briefly for General Electric and did no writing.

In 1958, Oppen was granted a U.S. passport, signaling the end of McCarthy's persecution. Following a session with a therapist, Oppen had a revelatory dream that, in a sense, unblocked his artistic inclinations. In May, 1958, he wrote the poem "Blood from the Stone" to initiate his new writing life. For the next two decades, Oppen worked diligently at both poetry and an extensive literary correspondence.

The Oppens returned to the United States in 1960; that same year, Oppen's sister Elizabeth committed suicide. In 1961, he worked closely with Reznikoff on a volume of selected poems, and in 1962 he published *The Materials*, his first book of poetry in thirty years. That volume was followed by *This in Which* (1965) and *Of Being Numerous* (1968), which won him a Pulitzer Prize in 1969. His *Collected Poems* was published in England in 1972, and an American edition followed in 1975.

In 1977, Oppen completed his final book, *Primitive* (1978), but he required his wife's assistance, as his health had begun to decline. He accumulated further honors in the early 1980's (including the PEN/West Rediscovery Award in 1982), but when he was diagnosed with Alzheimer's disease, he entered a nursing home in January, 1984. He died in July of that year.

Analysis

George Oppen's decision to stop writing poetry—literally in midpoem, as he wrote in a letter in 1972—stemmed from his belief that he was not prepared, either experimentally or technically, to satisfy his vision of what a poem could be. As the critic Rachel Blau De Plessis has pointed out, however, this act was not a negation of his career as a poet but a self-chosen silence that helped Oppen to prepare himself for the moment when he would feel ready to begin again. He was able to recommence his craft with such verve in 1958 because of changing factors in his life, but he was still essentially dependent on the solid conception of a poem that he had developed during the relatively brief but intense time from 1928 to 1934, when he was in close association with Zukovsky, Williams, Reznikoff, and Pound.

The term "Objectivist" has been applied to this group—with Pound regarded as an allied member and mentor and Carl Rakosi and Lorine Niedecker as a part of the loose affiliation—but the association was never a conscious movement or a part of a strategy for gaining attention. What these poets shared was a group of assumptions held—with individual variations—in common. What drew them together was a mutual interest in a poetics that was at a distinct remove from many of the conventional or traditional ideas about what constituted a poem. The Objectivists were working in a near void as far as a general audience was concerned, and they needed one another's responses as well as a strong sense of their craft to work at all. Even the most prominent figures, Pound and Williams, were almost invisible for the early decades of the twentieth century. Oppen and the others wrote sporadically, with great gaps between volumes, and relied on their personal visions to sustain them.

As Oppen saw it, the term "Objectivist" had nothing to do with an objective viewpoint but expressed the idea that the poem itself was an important object—an entity recording not merely reality but a distinct and separate aspect of reality. For Oppen, the act of writing was not primarily a means of ordering the world (as critic Paul Auster has put it) but a discovery of it. As Oppen remarked, one has to "write one's perceptions, not argue one's beliefs," and the process of composition was one way to engage the perceptual apparatus.

This led Oppen to the revolutionary position that familiar poetic forms were not the only ways to arrange a poem. Oppen contended that the poet "learns from the poem, his poem: the poem's structure, image, language." This is one of the first statements of the distinction between "closed" (or traditional) and "open" (or original) form, and Oppen argued that "the danger is that as the poem forms, the doors close." In other words, as Robert Creeley, one of Oppen's most accomplished poetic successors, has phrased it, "there is an appropriate way of saying something inherent in the thing to be said." Or, as Oppen observed, "the poet does not write what he already knows."

The effect of these striking and radically new assertions was to make Oppen's poetry, even his work from the early 1930's, so unusual that it was not dated at all; in fact, the tremendous changes in poetry initiated by Oppen and his colleagues have made his work more accessible in the decades since. On the other hand, this treatment of poetry as a record of the poet's mind in action tends to make poetry narrowly specific, so that Oppen's style still may not be immediately accessible for a reader who has not moved beyond more conventional approaches to poetry.

Although there are interesting rhythmic patterns in Oppen's work, he has essentially eschewed the most magnetic kind of song that often makes poetry initially compelling. His use of elliptic, often austere word groupings and suggestions of images tends to produce a compression that is resistant to immediate emotional responses. As Oppen pointed out, "the weakest work . . . occurs where the poet attempts to drive his mind in pursuit of emotion for its own sake . . . I would hold that the mere autonomy of the mind or the emotions is mendacity." Oppen is not suggesting that emotion or feeling is inappropriate but rather that an easy evocation of an emotional response will prevent the more significant and hard-won kind of deep feeling he hopes to achieve. Therefore, the position of the poet with respect to the world is a function, in Oppen's work, of the totality of the poem rather than of any particularly dynamic line or image, and the effect of the poem depends on the entire piece, or in some cases on a grouping of poems that are linked, if not directly interconnected.

Hugh Kenner has called Oppen a "geometer of minima" and has rightly pointed out how effectively Oppen has used Williams' oft-quoted dictum "no ideas but in things." While this makes Oppen's poetry almost "unanthologizable" (as critic John Taggart has remarked), the difficulties of his style may eventually yield to an understanding of and appreciation for an original conception of how a poem works to connect a person and the world.

THE BUILDING OF THE SKYSCRAPER

First published: 1965
Type of work: Poem

The creative artist is compared to a steelworker on a girder, and the process of creation is considered in terms of a person's life.

Oppen's fascination with the meaning latent in an individual word, and his interest in the manner in which meaning is established and explored through the arrangement or construction of the words in a poem, led him in many works to compare the artist to an artisan or builder. In "The Building of the Skyscraper," Oppen begins with a rather specific image, a steelworker who has "learned not to look down," suggesting a kind of focus or concentration on the task at hand. Then, in a characteristic shift in vision, Oppen moves directly to his philosophic position, extending the poem beyond the steelworker by saying, "And there are words we have learned/ Not to look at,/ Not to look for substance/ Below them." He thus opens the poem to include a broader human reliance on the materials available for building an artifice of understanding—materials that might not bear the weight of too much close scrutiny.

In a letter, Oppen explained that, for him, the word "building" carried connotations of creation and "the building of one's life." He explained further that he felt the word "skyscraper" had a kind of "homeliness" that grounded the poem in the fundamental flow of life. This grounding permits a turn toward the reflective that brings the poet to "the verge/ Of vertigo." The balance between the skills required to continue a person's daily tasks and the curiosity that draws a person to inquire into areas that reveal no real or final answer carries the poem onward into the second stanza, in which the question of words is directly addressed.

After asserting that "there are words that mean nothing," Oppen states one of his basic tenets: "But there is something to mean." It is "the business of the poet" to struggle amid the "things of the world" and "to speak them and himself out." This is Oppen's central goal as a poet. He explained that "to speak them out" conveys both a sense of exhausting the possibilities of meaning in a situation and the ambition of the poet to speak "*out*-wards," or toward a greater meaning or larger audience.

The final stanza introduces the natural world in a heartfelt paen: "O, the tree, growing from the sidewalk," Oppen declares, contrasting its "green buds" with the manmade, perplexing uncertainty of "the culture of the streets." He concludes by reintroducing the vertigo of the initial stanza in a final image of a nation stretching back three hundred years toward an origin that is so open to construction—its "bare land" like a blank page—that the importance of finding amid the vastness "a thing/ Which is" offers ample compensation for the vertigo, the suffering, that the poet/builder must experience.

O WESTERN WIND

First published: 1962
Type of work: Poem

    The poet regards the woman he loves, and his reflections on her beauty are deepened by his sense of her vital place in his life.

Oppen's determination to avoid what he considered a sort of easy emotionalism or cheap sentimentality restricted his production of poems that reached for a mood of intense feeling. Yet the absence of conventional protestations of desire and the austerity that is a signature of his style made his lyric moments glow with a special quality that he called "emotional clarity." He hoped to capture the moment "when the world stops, but lights up," as he put it.

The importance of love for his wife Mary is evident in his frequent comments in his letters. When she was the energizing figure for a poem, he wrote, "You will see that I have not exaggerated Mary's beauty, total beauty, confidence, strength of beauty." These attributes presented a challenge for Oppen, who did not want to resort to familiar styles of praise but who was aware of the power of the literature of romance. "O Western Wind" is an attempt to evoke the impact of the myriad moments when he looked at his wife and felt, afresh but with the memory of similar instances, the mystery and pleasures of her being. The poem begins with an image that is construed in metaphysical terms. "A world around her like a shadow" is Oppen's first statement, suggesting both the tangible and the evanescent. The woman is presented in motion ("She moves a chair"), and her action implies a purposeful or useful endeavor ("Something is being made—/ Prepared/ Clear in front of her as open air"). There is no punctuation at the end of the first stanza, carrying the poem toward Oppen's familiar shift to a reflective mode. "The space a woman makes and fills," he says, reemphasizing the tangible and the theoretical. He then assumes an unusually direct position, his typically distant, sharply observant poetic consciousness transformed by the very personal phrase "I write again." The poet is fully involved, "Naturally," because he is concentrating on what is most familiar, his wife's face.

The third stanza is a direct continuance of the previous one. "Beautiful and wide/ Blue eyes/ Across all my vision," Oppen observes. He once explained that "the noun 'eyes' directly above 'across all my vision' gives immediacy to the poem—gives reality to the poem." In this stanza, the lyric impulse charges the poem with an indelible impression of a profound love that remains undiminished by custom and routine, alive still in the power of the poet's vision.

OF BEING NUMEROUS—14

First published: 1968
Type of work: Poem

The poet recollects his experiences in World War II and tries to reconcile his wartime feelings with his present ones.

Oppen thought of his fourth collection of poems, *Of Being Numerous*, as poetry written from the perspective of "the language of New York"—an expression of the forces and energies available in a huge city. He described the poems as "intellectual and philosophic," in contrast to those of his next collection, *Seascape: Needle's Eye* (1972), which concentrated on the terrain around San Francisco and which he thought of as "atmospheric." Consequently, the poems in *Of Being Numerous* tend to be introspective, probing the poet's responses to various phenomena. The poem that begins, "I cannot even now/ Altogether disengage myself," characteristically is set in the poet's mind, the opening "I" and the reinforcing "myself" locating the poem in the realm of immediate consciousness.

Oppen's meditations here have been triggered by recurring thoughts of his experiences on the battlefields of World War II. Yet the nature of combat is less his subject than are his comrades, people he knew only briefly but with the emotional fusion possible under very intense experiences. The most vivid image of the poem follows Oppen's declaration of his condition of mind, as he recalls men in "emplacements, in mess tents,/ In hospitals and sheds" who "hid in the gullies/ Of blasted roads in a ruined country."

In the second section of the poem, Oppen considers the philosophic consequences of the action he has recalled. Placing his thoughts in an interrogatory mode to show how he has been permanently shaped by his participation and by his continuing reflection on it, Oppen asks "How forget that?" and moves into the present. His eye on the streets of the city has led him to group the anonymous crowds into something distant he calls "The People." His curiosity about individuals prohibits him from distancing himself from humanity, even when he is confronted with a mass of cars moving down "walled avenues." The crucial issue is that it is the individual whose actions "echo like history," but the nature of anonymous singularity—only rarely broken by some intense circumstance—places the poet in a position, as the last line states, "In which one cannot speak." The lack of resolution, the open-ended quality of the conclusion, carries the poem onward into time, its queries unresolved but ever-present.

Summary

In his time, George Oppen was largely ignored except by those poets who knew and valued his distinct and original approach. While he still remains largely unknown, his work has not become dated and will reward the serious student of literature who is prepared to look beyond the familiar.

Bibliography

Cuddihy, Michael, ed. "An Adequate Vision: A George Oppen Daybook." *Ironwood* 13 (Fall, 1985): 5-31.

Freeman, John, ed. *Not Comforts/But Vision: Essays on the Poetry of George Oppen.* Budleigh Salterton, England: Interim Press, 1984.

Hatlen, Burton, ed. *George Oppen: Man and Poet.* Orono, Maine: National Poetry Foundation, 1981.

Heller, Michael. *Conviction's Net of Branches: Essays on the Objectivist Poets and Poetry.* Carbondale: Southern Illinois University Press, 1985.

Oppen, George. *The Selected Letters of George Oppen.* Edited by Rachel Blau Du Plessis. Durham, N.C.: Duke University Press, 1990.

Oppen, Mary. *Meaning a Life: An Autobiography.* Santa Barbara, Calif.: Black Sparrow Press, 1978.

Leon Lewis

ANN PETRY

Born: Old Saybook, Connecticut
October 12, 1908

Principal Literary Achievement

Petry's fiction broke new ground for African American women writers by exploring the deterministic impact of race, gender, and class.

Biography

Ann Lane Petry was born to Peter Clarke Lane and Bertha James Lane on October 12, 1908, joining a family that had lived for several generations as the only African American citizens of Old Saybook, Connecticut. The descendant of a runaway Virginian slave, Petry never felt herself to be a true New Englander; her cultural legacy was not that of the typical Yankee, and as a small child she came to know the isolating effects of racism upon being stoned by white children on her first day of school. Nevertheless, her family distinguished itself within the community and boasted numerous professionals: Her grandfather became a licensed chemist, her father, aunt, and uncle became pharmacists, and her mother became a chiropodist. Inspired by the example of independent female relatives, Ann pursued a degree in pharmacology from the University of Connecticut and was graduated as the only black student in the class of 1931. She worked in family-owned pharmacies until 1938, when she married George D. Petry and moved to New York City.

There, Petry began her writing career and quickly secured jobs with various newspapers. Participation in a creative writing seminar at Columbia University greatly influenced her during this period. Her first published short story, "On Saturday the Siren Sounds at Noon," appeared in a 1943 issue of *The Crisis* and led to Petry's receipt of the 1945 Houghton Mifflin Literary Fellowship. With that financial support, she completed *The Street* (1946), which was to earn her widespread critical acclaim and make her the first African American woman to sell more than a million copies of her fiction. Over the next thirty years, she published stories and essays in numerous magazines, wrote two more adult novels, *Country Place* (1947) and *The Narrows* (1953), and issued a collection of her short fiction, *Miss Muriel and Other Stories* (1971). Petry also began writing for children and produced such classics as *The Drugstore Cat* (1949), *Harriet Tubman: Conductor on the Underground Railroad* (1955), and *Tituba of Salem Village* (1964); the latter two books deal with African

American historical figures and reflect Petry's desire to give the nation an honest picture of its racial history.

Disconcerted by the fame brought by the success of *The Street*, in 1948 Petry returned with her husband to the obscurity of Old Saybook, where the couple reared a daughter, Elizabeth Ann. Petry held a visiting professorship at the University of Hawaii in 1974-1975, and in 1977 she received a National Endowment for the Arts grant. Boston's Suffolk University awarded her a D. Litt. degree in 1983.

Analysis

While Ann Petry's fiction typically involves African Americans struggling against the crippling impact of racism, her overarching theme involves a more broadly defined notion of prejudice that targets class and gender as well as race. That vision explains what might otherwise seem to be inconsistencies of direction in Petry's career: her decision, for example, following the potent racial protest of *The Street*, to focus her next novel, *Country Place* (1947), on a white community's postwar crises of adjustment, or her movement into the realm of children's literature. Uniting these diverse efforts is Petry's critique of oppressive social hierarchies and her admiration for those whose moral epiphanies lead them to more inclusive, life-affirming conceptions of human community.

Petry's dissection of cultural hypocrisies exists alongside her willingness to allow her characters their own moments of narrative self-revelation through alternating interior monologues. The chorus of voices thus created avoids privileging any single character and infuses her fiction with compassion. Petry delineates time and again how the American society has proven cruelly adept at building walls that deny some of its citizens real participation in its prosperity.

Rather than celebrating the American ideal of self-making with which her native New England is so closely associated, Petry exposes the illusions it has fostered and depicts their graphics costs to those relegated to the periphery of American possibility. Racism invites Petry's most scathing attacks, not only for the material hardship it forces upon people of color but also for the psychological and cultural distortions it produces. At her most biting, Petry lampoons the absurdist systems of human classification into which racist societies ultimately fall. Generally, her perspective is more tragic than comic, however, and includes the recognition that confronting racism necessitates confronting history itself.

That class distinctions pervade American culture becomes one of Petry's most insistent indictments of the egalitarian myths of American opportunity. In quest of the material security, comfort, and status that propel middle-class striving, Americans, she suggests, acquiesce to a soul-numbing view of labor and retreat into a moral inflexibility that blindly sanctions aggressive self-interest. A novel such as *Country Place* shares with Petry's other work an interest in how the American class structure produces venal, grasping have-nots at the bottom whose ambitions mimic the ruthless acquisitiveness of those at the top.

Petry's most important characters are those who reject the fallacy of the self-made individual existing independent of the world or the continuing legacy of the past. Though that perspective assumes certain mechanistic dimensions in her work, she does not concede full authority to deterministic necessity; the dice may be loaded against her protagonists, but the game is not inexorably mandated to play itself out to any single predetermined end. Her characters sometimes prove capable of personal growth that moves them toward a common humanity. At its most compelling, such discovery may fuel real and far-reaching change in the social order itself. Petry's narratives often grow from characters' chance movements across rigid cultural boundaries; the resulting crises test the spiritual flexibility of many others besides her protagonists.

Overlooked by academic critics, Petry's children's books offer tantalizing clues to her larger agenda as a writer. Their emphasis upon personal fearlessness in rethinking entrenched assumptions and disengaging from unjust systems invites comparison to figures from her adult fiction such as Abbie Crunch of *The Narrows* or Mrs. Gramby of *Country Place*, both of whom ultimately escape the prejudices that have constrained their humanity. Moreover, in applying their new insights, these characters take subtly revolutionary actions that defy the cultural boundaries that have previously defined their lives. It takes a saint, perhaps, to challenge a predatory universe with an alternative vision of love, but having told children in *Legends of the Saints* (1970) that true sanctity is a function of bravery, Petry seems willing to evaluate her "serious" fictional characters on their receptivity to grace as an antidote to hate.

THE STREET

First published: 1946
Type of work: Novel

Inspired by the American Dream, a young black mother discovers the inhibiting power of racism, sexism, and poverty.

When *The Street* appeared in 1946, earning Alain Locke's praise as "the artistic success" of the year, it was immediately identified with the literature of social protest that had become the primary vehicle for African American fiction of the period. Petry's novel tells the story of a young African American mother in New York City whose ambitions have been fed by her early reading of Benjamin Franklin and her domestic service in the household of wealthy white suburbanites. Lutie Johnson's goals are the stuff of the American Dream itself and on the surface appear eminently worthy: Although recently abandoned by her husband, she eschews defeat and is convinced that she will obtain a white-collar job that will foster her personal dignity and provide a comfortable life, a good education, and promising social opportunities for her eight-year-old son, Bub. As Petry makes grimly evident, however, Lutie fails to recognize the incongruity of applying the credo of upward mobility to her own circumstances, which reflect a social system organized to benefit the dominant white community and dismiss the claims of the marginal. Nor has she registered the spiritual bankruptcy that accompanies the success she so covets.

Lutie pays dearly for her unexamined adherence to white bourgeois myths. While emphasizing the crippling impact of poverty, sexuality, and race upon individual striving, *The Street* is also a thoughtful examination of a complex character whose education and class aspiration lead to self-conscious choices and allegiances that demand as much scrutiny as the sociological obstacles she confronts.

Not that those obstacles are minimized. Lutie's circumstances reveal the interplay between the economic disenfranchisement of black men, the exploitative employment options imposed on black women, the fragmentation of the black family, and the terrifying vulnerability of black youth. To offset his humiliation at being unable to support his family, Jim Johnson takes up with another woman. Forced by her restricted means to move in with her father and his string of mistresses, Lutie chafes at having to leave Bub each day among the vulgar underclass she so desperately seeks to escape. She painstakingly masters secretarial skills to secure a civil-service appointment with better pay, only to find that her access to better neighborhoods is still constrained by the exorbitant rents charged the poor. Lutie reluctantly takes an apartment on morally dissolute 116th Street, the kind of area she describes as "the North's lynch mobs" and "the method the big cities used to keep Negroes in their place." For all her concern about Bub, she cannot alter the fact that at the end of a school day soured by the bigotry of his white teacher, Bub must manage alone for hours until his mother returns home. Finally, Lutie discovers that as a black female she is made most vulnerable by her sexuality, which arouses virulent male passions that she can neither predict nor control.

Ironically, Lutie's own beauty baits the trap that crushes her dreams when it sparks the lust of three men, each of whom attempts to deflect her life to his own ends. Jones, the janitor of her apartment building, is a man psychologically deformed by years of diminishment in grinding jobs. Lutie's appearance in his life crystallizes his dissatisfactions, making him determined to possess her from the moment he meets her. He makes a devious alliance with the lonely Bub that later allows him to dupe the boy into criminal activity when Jones's rape attempt against Lutie fails. Boots Smith, although far more glamorous a figure than Jones, proves just as venal: A jazz-band leader who discovers Lutie's singing ability, he cynically tries to turn her ambition to his own sexual benefit. The most far-reaching figure of male control in the novel, however, is Junto, the white entrepreneur whose businesses dominate the neighborhood. Not coincidentally, he employs the two black men and sees to it that his desire for Lutie effectively cancels out theirs. He is responsible for rescuing her from Jones's stalking, only to preserve her for himself; he insists that Boots deny Lutie a real salary for singing with his band, so as to ensure the economic vulnerability on which he will prey.

As Lutie discovers that she has become a pawn in a larger sexual competition among these men, she becomes increasingly frantic and self-destructive. When Jones's vengeful scheme against Bub lands the boy in jail and threatens him with reform school, Lutie desperately seeks an attorney, unaware that she could handle the legal proceedings herself. The quest for money that has defined her character from the first thus assumes a heightened urgency that leads her back to Boots, who in turn plays procurer for Junto. Lutie resists explicitly selling herself for personal gain, although she does attempt to manipulate Boots's interest to her own advantage. She learns how unskilled she is at such games when Boots tries to beat and rape her; in retaliation, she kills him with a candlestick. Convinced that the white justice systems does not believe in black female virtue, she boards a Chicago-bound train and becomes a fugitive. The novel ends with Lutie's having implicitly consigned her son to a reformatory and herself to the life of moral degradation she had resisted for so long.

In *The Street*, Petry conveys the monstrous distortions of the human spirit effected by racism and privation, but she does so through interior monologues that illuminate the complex psychological history explaining each monster. Similarly, the rich musicality of the text, with its insistent evocation of blues and jazz, offers yet another measure of the interior struggles between dehumanization and survival waged in the souls of the oppressed. Petry's first novel remains her most potent enunciation of the tragedies wrought by urban blight even in the lives of those determined to transcend it.

THE NARROWS

First published: 1953
Type of work: Novel

An interracial love affair exposes the murderous hostilities that lie beneath the surface of a New England town.

The Narrows combines the racial protest of *The Street* with the exposé of small-town America in *Country Place*. It depicts the steady march toward disaster of the Dartmouth-educated veteran Lincoln Williams (or "Link"), who has returned from four years at war with little faith in the opportunities for a satisfying life he has theoretically earned by his various accomplishments. Link grew up as the foster son of a black middle-class couple living on a street now overtaken by the rougher elements of African American urban life. Throughout the novel, he functions as a bridge figure connecting radically alien worlds whose citizens abjure contact with one another. Link's attraction to antithetical worlds deprives him of a true home anywhere, while his boundary-jumping earns him an enmity on all sides that eventually assumes lethal proportions. Link is also full of a misogynistic rage; such suspicion of women fills Petry's fiction and suggests the deadliness of the gender dialectic operating within a patriarchal power structure.

Link's gender biases are complicated by race when chance introduces him to Camilo Treadway Sheffield, a beautiful Barnard graduate whose boredom prompts her to take a late-night walk on the African American side of town. Fleeing in dense fog from a grotesque street figure, she is rescued by Link, who does not realize that Camilo is white until he later takes her into a bar (when she, too, discovers with a jolt that he is black). Not until much later does he learn that she is both married and the heir to the Treadway family fortune, a fortune derived from the munitions works that is the town's major employer. The animus aroused by their pairing erupts first within the black community. Abbie Crunch, Link's prim adoptive mother, and Bill Hod, his earthy street-life mentor, find themselves unlikely partners in sabotaging the couple. Abbie throws Camilo into the street as a trollop, and Bill humiliates Link by exposing Camilo's deceits.

Nor are the lovers themselves free from prejudice. Camilo reveals a tendency to see Link as something of an exotic toy on whom she lavishes her money and affection in return for sexual and intellectual excitement. Link's fascination stems in no little part from Camilo's iconographic status as the proverbial white goddess, an obsession that reveals its sinister underside when he feels emasculated by the news of her betrayal. With both psyches deteriorating under the pressure of their thwarted desire for one another, the accusations become more virulent, until Camilo finally uses the most deadly charge at her command to punish Link for repudiating her. She accuses him of rape and thereby sets in motion the machinery of the larger social order, which will not tolerate Link's iconoclastic threat.

If the black community proves resistant to Link's attempted move across boundaries, the white power structure responds with even more malice. No one believes the rape charge, but that does not exonerate Link, since the truth is in fact far more dangerous: The white woman has actually fallen in love with the black man. To the powers that be, Camilo's mental breakdown embodies the damage to family reputation and social hierarchies she has wreaked, and the man responsible for her lapse must be eliminated. The old order, though, is beyond recovery, a point made through Petry's grim version of the lynch mob to whom she subjects her hero: Link's murderers are a genteel dowager and her effete son-in-law, who pursue their victim in a limousine. More important, their insular privilege is shattered forever as the retributive power of the justice system now turns against them.

The novel comes to rest, finally, with Link's adoptive mother, Abbie Crunch. Over the course of the novel, Abbie moves beyond the internal class divisions that have guided her life, preparing her for the even more startling decision to challenge the racial antimonies that kill her son. Given evidence that Bill Hod is plotting against Camilo to avenge Link, Abbie chooses to free herself from the expanding waves of hatred and she warns the police of the threat. Abbie's quiet gesture is at heart a revolutionary one, for it bespeaks her attentiveness to the real lesson of Link's martyrdom—his effort, however flawed, to move beyond the crippling polarities of race and class.

MISS MURIEL AND OTHER STORIES

First published: 1971
Type of work: Short stories

The wide-ranging consequences of a cultural obsession with racial difference create a community of lost souls seeking some clearer vision of human relationship.

The pieces in this volume range over several decades of Petry's career and provide a compact introduction to her imaginative concerns, chief among them racism's psychological consequences. In the prize-winning story "Like a Winding Sheet," a husband's impotence before the racist assaults he sees all around him makes him respond to his wife's affectionate teasing with the beating he is forbidden to direct at his real oppressors. His actions lay bare the starkness of the struggle between male and female in Petry's world and the sobering betrayals that occur in it. "In Darkness and Confusion," a meditation on the harlem riot of 1943, fictionalizes an historical event. The story's protagonist, William Jones, a man who has worked hard to secure a better world for his son, witnesses the killing of a black soldier and erupts into a violence that expresses his grief and rage; Petry assigns Jones responsibility for leading the first mobs. In "Miss Muriel" and "The New Mirror," Petry creates a black family much like her own—the Layens are professionals who own the pharmacy in a small New England town. The adolescent girl who narrates these tales speaks of "the training in issues of race" she has received over the years, not only through casual bigotries but also through the painful self-consciousness of respectable people like her parents, whose behavior is a continual refutation of cultural stereotypes. The child learns to use the codes by which the black middle class shields itself from white contempt, and she learns as well the burden of always acting with an eye on the reputation of "the Race": "all of us people with this dark skin must help hold the black island inviolate."

Against the most aggressive forms of white hatred, however, there is no defense except a temporary erasure of one's humanity. "The Witness" presents the case of a retired black college professor who takes a high-school teaching position in a Northern white community. Called upon to assist the local pastor in counseling delinquent adolescents, he finds himself their prey out in the world as they kidnap him and force him to watch their sexual abuse of a young white woman. Having at one point coerced him to place his hand on the girl, they effectively blackmail him into complicit silence about their crime. His exemplary life and professional stature cannot protect him, and he bitterly describes himself as "another poor scared black bastard who was a witness." In "The Necessary Knocking on the Door," a participant at a conference about Christianity finds herself unable to master her dislike for a white woman dying in the hotel room across the hall from hers—a woman who had earlier in the day refused to be seated next to a "nigger." In these stories, Petry vividly captures the spiritual anguish of discovering that one's own grievances can weaken rather than strengthen one's moral courage.

Her handling of white perspectives on racism is more unyielding. For example, the absurdities into which segregationist practices lead multiracial societies are lampooned in "The Bones of Louella Brown," wherein the most prestigious family in Massachusetts finds its plans to build a chapel for its deceased members compromised when an undertaker's assistant confuses the bones of an African American maid and the sole noblewoman in the clan.

Other stories in the collection evoke the mysterious private centers of grief hidden in the human heart: "Olaf and His Girl Friend" and "Solo on the Drums" show Petry's interest in African American music as an exquisite, untranslatable evocation of pain. "Mother Africa" introduces Emanuel Turner, a junk dealer who acquires the huge sculpture of a female nude that a wealthy white woman is discarding. Convinced that the figure is a mythic evocation of Africa itself, he resents the prudish efforts of others to clothe it, just as missionaries had once insulted his ancestors. Thus he is stunned to learn that this dark madonna is not a black woman at all but a white woman—the oxidation of the metal had misled him. By parodying the assumed black male obsession with white women, Petry implies that the real hunger at work in the story is for authentic enunciation of the African American experience, a hunger left unmet as Turner hurriedly rushes to sell the piece for scrap.

Summary

Ann Petry analyzes the American scene from a variety of angles, always exposing the debilitating impact of its hierarchical social systems and capitalistic materialism. Like her contemporaries, she recorded the daunting obstacles to human fulfillment facing those on the margins of American prosperity, and yet hers is finally a Christian existentialist vision celebrating the individual's potential for spiritual liberation through which an entire culture might relinquish its crippling prejudices. Her examination of gender as another locus of oppression laid important groundwork for the writings of African American women since the 1960's.

Bibliography

Christian, Barbara. *Black Women Novelists: The Development of a Tradition, 1892-1976*. Westport, Conn.: Greenwood Press, 1980.

Clark, Keith. "A Distaff Dream Deferred? Ann Petry and the Art of Subversion." *African American Review* 26 (Fall, 1992): 495-505.

Gross, Theodore. "Ann Petry: The Novelist as Social Critic." In *Black Fiction: New Studies in the Afro-American Novel Since 1945*, edited by A. Robert Lee. New York: Barnes & Noble, 1980.

Hernton, Calvin C. *The Sexual Mountain and Black Women Writers: Adventurers in Sex, Literature, and Real Life*. New York: Anchor Press, 1987.

McKay, Nellie. "Ann Petry's *The Street* and *The Narrows*." In *Women and War: The Changing Status of American Women from the 1930s to the 1950s*, edited by Maria Diedrich and Dorothea Fischer-Hornung. New York: Berg, 1990.

Petry, Ann. "A *MELUS* Interview: Ann Petry—The New England Connection." Interview by Mark Wilson. *MELUS* 15 (Summer, 1988): 71-84.

Washington, Mary Helen, ed. *Invented Lives: Narratives of Black Women, 1860-1960*. New York: Doubleday, 1987.

Barbara Kitt Seidman

RICHARD POWERS

Born: Evanston, Illinois
June 18, 1957

Principal Literary Achievement

Functioning on a uniquely high intellectual plane, Powers' stylistically complex novels intermix science, music, photography, history, and human psychology in strikingly original ways.

Biography

Richard Powers has been called reclusive, but the term is misleading. Although he struggles to maintain a low profile, fearing that publicity will make inordinate demands on the time he needs to write, he is outgoing, if not notably gregarious. Interviewers find him cooperative but firm in his refusal to share the personal information around which interviews with celebrities often revolve.

This reluctance is not a pose Powers has adopted to project some calculated public persona. He firmly believes, rather, that one's writing must stand on its merits, that details about the life of an author or an author's autograph on the flyleaf of a book should affect neither the public perception of what authors produce nor the value of their books.

Powers' novels display an easy command of information about an amazing range of subjects, from literature to art to photography to science to music to history to astronomy to folklore. His knowledge in this daunting array of subjects is not superficial: He has a thorough understanding of the subjects he chooses to explore.

An encompassing influence on Powers' literary structure is the music of Johann Sebastian Bach, stemming from his exposure as a cellist to Bach's music. Elements of Bach's harmony and, particularly, Bach's counterpoint underlie the structure of *Three Farmers on Their Way to a Dance* (1985) and *Prisoner's Dilemma* (1988). *The Gold Bug Variations* (1991) draws its title in part from Bach's *The Goldberg Variations*; its structure stems from Powers' comprehensive understanding of Bach's inventions.

There are thirty Goldberg variations; Powers' novel has thirty chapters. Bach's *Variations* were based upon four notes or musical phrases; the number four, a controlling element in Powers' novel, is fundamental to an understanding of deoxyribonucleic acid (DNA), the mysteries of which play a central role in *The Gold Bug*

Variations. Powers' title alludes both to Bach's musical masterpiece and to Edgar Allan Poe's short story "The Gold Bug." The latter correspondence alerts readers to the cryptograms and veiled allusions that pervade the novel.

An interchapter toward the end of *Prisoner's Dilemma* provides a rare bit of autographical information about Powers. Major elements of *Prisoner's Dilemma* are autobiographical, although not dependably so. In the autobiographical interchapter, for example, Powers reveals that although his fictional family consists of the Hobsons and their four children, his actual family consisted of his parents and five children. Major elements of this book, set in De Kalb, Illinois, where Powers lived during his high school years, draw upon details surrounding his father's final illness.

Much of *Operation Wandering Soul* (1993) is based upon experiences the author's older brother, a surgeon, had when he completed a rotation as a resident in pediatric surgery in a large California hospital. In this novel, the protagonist is named Richard Kraft. *Kraft* is German for *power*, the plural form of which is the author's name. In his other novels, Powers plays with his surname, dedicating *Prisoner's Dilemma* to "the powers."

Powers, a physics major for his first two years at the University of Illinois at Urbana-Champaign, was graduated in 1978 with a bachelor's degree in rhetoric, completing his university studies with a perfect A average. The following fall, he entered Illinois' master's degree program in English, receiving the M.A. in 1980. For three semesters, he held teaching assistantships in composition and literature. Upon completing the master's degree, Powers lived for nearly three years in the Boston area before returning to Champaign in 1983.

From 1987 until 1992, Powers lived in Heerlen, a coal-mining town in the southern tip of the Netherlands, within biking distance of Germany and Belgium. In the spring of 1992, he was artist-in-residence at Sidney Sussex College at the University of Cambridge in England. After he returned to the United States, he was appointed writer-in-residence in the department of English at the University of Illinois at Urbana-Champaign.

Powers, honored in 1986 by the American Academy of Arts and Sciences, was named a MacArthur Fellow in 1989. *Three Farmers on Their Way to a Dance* and *The Gold Bug Variations* were both among the five finalists for the National Book Critics Circle Award; *The Gold Bug Variations* was *Time*'s 1991 book of the year. *Operation Wandering Soul* was among five finalists for the 1993 National Book Award in Fiction.

Analysis

Richard Powers has a consuming need to understand his world. He has been driven by the necessity to define—for himself and for those who read his novels—his own century, its shift from agrarianism to industrialism to modernism. His books, demonstrating the unique range of his knowledge and reflecting his experimentation with literary style and structure, consistently pose barbed questions that lead readers to serious contemplation and eventually, perhaps, to deepened understandings.

Powers' first-published novel, *Three Farmers on Their Way to a Dance*, illustrates the complexity of his literary structure. The book's twenty-seven chapters are arranged in triplets. One chapter of each triplet carries and sustains the story lines of the book. Another chapter is essentially a philosophical essay relating to the times and their intellectual and historical underpinnings. Yet another chapter presents a historical vignette that helps to relate the basic story to a broader sociopolitical perspective, enabling readers to understand each interlocking plot in its historical context.

Three Farmers on Their Way to a Dance, a multiplot novel, ambitiously—and deftly—sustains the three basic stories developing outside the interchapters while simultaneously interweaving them ingeniously into the whole. The first-person narration, introduced in the first chapter and used elsewhere, lends immediacy and credibility to the stories Powers unfolds.

His subsequent novels use interchapters to place their stories outside the confined milieux within which most storytelling occurs and to key the stories to their broader reference points in Western culture. Powers' ability to relate the plot structure of his novels to what philosophers have called the "Great Chain of Being" distinguishes his work and enhances its artistic impact.

For Powers, such historical events as Henry Ford's organization of a "Peace Ship" to convey well-known Americans to Europe at the height of World War I in his effort to negotiate a peace, or the World War II internment of Japanese Americans, or the evacuation of children from London to Canterbury during World War II are secondary but telling dollops of history that help to explain the confounding century upon which he focuses. They also enable Powers to relate his stories to the broader contexts in which they occur.

Some of Powers' historical vignettes reach to the thirteenth century (the children's Army of the Crusades, to which a chapter of *Operation Wandering Soul* is devoted); others extend beyond a single chapter to create a fuller impression of their subjects than could be gleaned from a single chapter (the Henry Ford vignettes in *Three Farmers on Their Way to a Dance*, for example).

Prisoner's Dilemma's vignette about the internment of Japanese Americans during World War II enables Powers to develop a continuing subplot. From this vignette emerges the fanciful story of an interned Walt Disney, who is released, spirited off to De Kalb, Illinois, and there commissioned by the U.S. government to build a scale model of the entire United States along the lines of a theme park. Powers invents a Japanese mother for Disney to justify his internment.

Interchapters are the underlying mechanisms that allow Powers to construct his complex, multitext narratives; the interchapters provide much of the intricate counterpoint underlying the structure of his novels. This counterpoint distinguishes Powers' writing and permits the author to employ the closely interconnected intellectual crosscurrents that mark his work.

Richard Powers' novels are novels of ideas. They rely on a carefully crafted and extremely calculated style to deliver the essence of what their author seeks to communicate. Powers' chief concerns are philosophical; characters concern him secondarily, even though he has created some touching and memorable ones.

For example, the beguiling Joy Stepaneevong in *Operation Wandering Soul*, who remains innocent and trusting in the face of the severe dislocations she has experienced throughout her twelve years of existence, both touches the hearts and engages the emotions of those who encounter her. Joy quickly becomes a burr in readers' social consciences.

Anyone approaching Powers' work for the first time will be dismayed by the broad range of vocabulary upon which it draws. Technical words and terms from many fields of science and other specialized areas proliferate as the complexity of each novel grows. The scientific background of a book such as *The Gold Bug Variations* is extensive and reflects Powers' scientific training, but the author reveals a sufficient understanding of the mysteries of the DNA molecule to enable him to relate the unraveling of its mysteries to such other intellectual currents as Bach's counterpoint.

In his search for answers to the questions of existence, Powers uncovers suggestions of the interconnectedness of many human accomplishments and events. This author's artistic quest is, simply put, to understand the universe, to try to unlock the meaning of human existence—indeed, of all existence.

Having plotted this ambitious course for himself, Richard Powers works steadily, resolutely, eyes fixed unflinchingly on achieving his intellectually ambitious ends. These ends, still much clearer to him than to some of his critics, determine the direction his work takes. He permits himself no detours, no time-outs to write the occasional potboilers or television scripts that some authors use to replenish their shrinking coffers. Instead he remains in the shadows, always focused on his far-reaching, long-term, self-imposed artistic and philosophical ends.

Judging from asides Powers makes in all of his books, he views authors as artists who create situations that will entice readers into interacting with ideas, dredging up from within themselves memories of experiences that will shape their interpretations of what they read. His obeisance to readers aligns Powers with reader-response enthusiasts.

THREE FARMERS ON THEIR WAY TO A DANCE

First published: 1985
Type of work: Novel

This novel uses the lives of three peasants who are captured in a photograph to present a striking exploration into twentieth century modernism.

In the first chapter of *Three Farmers on Their Way to a Dance*, the first-person narrator happens upon a haunting August Sander photograph in the Detroit Institute of Arts while passing some hours between trains. The photograph captures three youthful peasants resplendent in weekend finery. The picture, bearing the same title as Powers' book, is dated 1914. Given that date, the narrator reads his own meaning into the title: The dance these peasants are destined for is World War I.

The first narrative frame of the novel recounts the narrator's search for basic information about the picture and, once he has gained it, about the people Sander's lenses captured. It turns out that all three—Hubert, Adolphe, and Peter—died in the war.

Yet *Three Farmers on Their Way to a Dance* is about much more than three peasants united in an obscure photograph. The book recounts in some detail the birth of twentieth century modernism and the virtually unbelievable interconnectedness of all human events. In order to fix the story historically, Powers provides readers with recurring interchapters all related in some way to his skillful development of the book's three major plots.

Several historical interchapters deal with the impact Henry Ford had upon American life and culture. Powers includes an interchapter on Ford's unofficial diplomatic efforts to end World War I by chartering an ocean liner and sailing it to Norway with as many prominent people as he could cudgel into joining his midwinter voyage, hoping that this cadre of celebrities might negotiate a peace treaty. Other historical chapters treat such figures as the renowned nineteenth century actress Sarah Bernhardt, the essayist Walter Benjamin, and others whose lives impinge upon the three main stories.

The narrator's account of his quest for information about the photograph constitutes the first narrative frame, which is related closely to the other two narrative frames and to the interchapters. The second frame is concerned with the three subjects in the picture and their simultaneously independent and historically interdependent existences. The third frame, a modern romance, concerns Peter Mays, a computer editor in Boston who pursues a haunting redheaded woman on the street only to discover that she is an actress playing Sarah Bernhardt in a one-woman show.

Peter Mays, it turns out, has immigrated to the United States from the area that was home to Sander's three farmers. Peter, indeed, is the son of the brightest of these, also named Peter. When the younger Peter gave his full name—Peter Hubertus Kinder Schreck Langerson van Maasricht—to immigration officials at Ellis Island, he became "Peter Mays," the name he subsequently carries.

Sarah Bernhardt is subtly woven into each plot. Henry Ford figures in the Peter Mays story because Peter, scavenging in his mother's attic, discovers a picture that leads him to the discovery that he might be due a $250,000 legacy from Ford's estate. He also discovers among his mother's possessions a print of Sander's photograph of the three farmers, one of whom is Peter's father.

The narrator is last seen at an office Christmas party, where he talks with Mrs. Schreck, the aging immigrant who cleans his office. She has a motherly interest in him, regularly leaving chocolate bonbons on his desk.

Mrs. Schreck knows Sander's picture and something about its subjects. She does not, however, have the answers the narrator seeks. A clandestine meeting with her in her home reveals only that the three subjects in the Sander picture "had led lives as verifiable, if not as well documented, as any of those Great Personalities I had poured over."

THE GOLD BUG VARIATIONS

First published: 1991
Type of work: Novel

A double love story provides Powers' pretext for this novel about genetics, DNA, music, computers, information theory, metaphysics—and, ultimately, the meaning of life.

On the surface, *The Gold Bug Variations* consists of two intertwined love stories, those of former DNA scientist Stuart Ressler and Jeanette Koss, Ressler's married lover, and of reference librarian Jan O'Deigh, thirty-four, and art historian Franklin Todd, thirty.

Powers' title gives readers the initial wink. This book has something to do with Johann Sebastian Bach, the eighteenth century composer of the *The Goldberg Variations*, and with Edgar Allan Poe, the nineteenth century author of "The Gold Bug." Poe's short story is cryptic; from the outset, Powers' novel is similarly cryptic.

Arcane meanings lurk in unexpected places throughout *The Gold Bug Variations*, making rereading the book perhaps more pleasurable than the initial reading. The novel overflows with word games and puzzles relating to numbers and to science; this is the sort of book that makes for challenging group reading and discussion.

Stuart Ressler, once a member of the University of Illinois team that cracked the code of the DNA molecule, has faded from public view. Franklin Todd knows him, however; Ressler works with Todd, a part-time computer hacker working nights. He fascinates Franklin. It is clear that Ressler, who now—apparently by choice—lives at the subsistence level, once experienced a little more than the fifteen minutes of public recognition that Andy Warhol suggested was every American's due.

Eager to know more about Ressler, Todd enlists the aid of Jan O'Deigh, the reference librarian at the Brooklyn branch of the New York public library. Tracking down information about Ressler (including his picture in a back issue of *Life*), Jan and Franklin become romantically entangled.

The plot of *The Gold Bug Variations* is told largely through Jan's eyes, in a flood of recollection set loose when, during her lunch hour one day, she finds in her mail a brief note from Franklin announcing Ressler's death. Through Franklin, Jan had met and come to know Ressler. Memories consume her. She quits her library job so that she can devote herself fully to ferreting out the meaning of Ressler's life and, more broadly, of life in general.

Ressler's work on DNA contained so many mysteries about the origins of existence that he, the accomplished scientist, suspected that anything able to create consciousness (life) was too complex for that consciousness to fathom. This suspicion caused Ressler to become an adult dropout from society, to live obscurely and ascetically, working of his own volition at a level considerably below his potential.

OPERATION WANDERING SOUL

First published: 1993
Type of work: Novel

Set in a large California hospital's pediatric surgical ward, *Operation Wandering Soul* explores the evil that society visits upon children.

As in all of Powers' writing, the plot is not the novel. The novel plays with ideas so profound and so complex that they defy brief or simplified presentation. *The Gold Bug Variations* richly rewards frequent rereading, spirited discussion, and imaginative interpretation.

The most pessimistic of Powers' novels, *Operation Wandering Soul* uses a pediatric surgical ward as the microcosm that exposes what contemporary American society does to its children. At the same time, the book provides Powers the opportunity to discuss the status of children in society through the ages and to highlight many of the societal dangers of the late twentieth century. Carver Hospital is located in California, near Los Angeles, where many contemporary social and ecological problems are so exaggerated that they erupt there before middle America notices them.

Richard Kraft, thirty-three, is serving a rotation at Carver as part of his surgical residency. A former musician who, at twenty, traded the conservatory for college and then medical school, Kraft passed a peripatetic youth as his family followed its father from one overseas assignment to another.

Readers encounter the sensitive youth as he is turning into a ward-savvy physician. He struggles against his deepest human instincts to insulate himself from the horrors he witnesses in his patients. He strives consciously to wall off his emotions so that they will not be torn to shreds by the medical realities that daily assail him.

The children on Kraft's surgical ward are a badly afflicted lot: Joy, a twelve-year-old Asian girl with a malignant growth above her right ankle, will lose her leg; Nicolino suffers from progeria and, at puberty, is already an old man; Chuck, a preadolescent, has no face; Tony the Tuff, an adolescent, had his ear lopped off; Ben, also an adolescent, is a double amputee. Visiting this ward is not calculated to lift the spirits.

Into this mix, Powers brings Linda Espera, part physical therapist, mostly saint. She loves these children and learns as much about each of them as she can. Kraft remains aloof. Linda, however, will not countenance his professional detachment. After Kraft snares Linda sexually, she changes his outlook, adding him to her list of those she must save.

Linda plans to compose a year's worth of historical tales relating to the lives of children through the ages; 365 tales in all. Some of these tales provide the fodder for Powers' riveting interchapters, which deal with such stories as the Children's Army during the Crusades, the Peter Pan story, Herod's slaughter of the Innocents, and, as the artistic high point of the novel, the story of the Pied Piper of Hamlin.

These stories add to Powers' contemporary tale the historical perspective that makes his story frightening. They ask, "Has humankind learned anything from history?," while Powers' contemporary account inquires, "Will humankind ever learn anything from history?" The answers readers inevitably reach are bound to be discouraging, which makes *Operation Wandering Soul* essentially pessimistic, although Powers suggests, however faintly, that hope ultimately may reside in one-on-one human relationships, in human understanding and perseverance.

Summary

Richard Powers is among the most intellectually complex novelists to appear on the literary front since James Joyce and Thomas Pynchon. His novels are the fruits of a Renaissance mentality. Powers' encompassing grasp of abstract ideas is impressive; more impressive still is his ability to link them to a central reference point.

Bibliography

Baker, John F. "Richard Powers." *Publishers Weekly* 238 (August 16, 1991): 37-38.
Dudar, Helen. "The Powers Parfait." *Wall Street Journal* (August 14, 1991): A-6.
Gray, Paul. "What Is the Meaning of Life" *Time* 138 (September 22, 1991): 68.
Howard, Maureen. "Facing the Footage." *The Nation* 251 (May 14, 1988): 680-684.
——————. "Semi-Samizdat and Other Matters." *Yale Review* 77 (Winter, 1988): 243-258.
Jones, Louis B. "Bach Would've Liked This Molecule." *The New York Times Book Review* 96 (August 25, 1991): 9-10.
LeClair, Tom. "The Systems Novel." *The New Republic* 198 (April 25, 1988): 40-42.
Powers, Richard. "State and Vine." *Yale Review* 79 (Summer, 1990): 690-698.
Stites, Janet. "Bordercrossings: A Conversation in Cyberspace." *Omni* 16 (November, 1993): 38-48, 105-113.

R. Baird Shuman

MURIEL RUKEYSER

Born: December 15, 1913
New York, N.Y.
Died: February 12, 1980
New York, N.Y.

Principal Literary Achievement

Rukeyser, primarily noted for her poems of social protest, also wrote some of the twentieth century's most moving and lyrical love poetry.

Biography

Muriel Rukeyser was born on December 15, 1913, in New York City to Lawrence B. and Myra (Lyons) Rukeyser. Her father was from Milwaukee, Wisconsin, and cofounded a building business. Her mother, from Yonkers, New York, spent some years struggling as a bookkeeper. Muriel Rukeyser was brought up as the sheltered daughter of her affluent parents, spending time at yacht clubs, camps, and symphonies. Despite her privileged childhood, her toddler years were spent during World War I, and she was a teenager when the stock market crashed in 1929. The activism of Muriel Rukeyser's adult years was a complete rejection of her former protected existence.

Even as a child, Rukeyser wrote poems, although the only people she knew who read any poetry were servants. Rukeyser continued writing poetry during her high-school years, attempting to reconcile her normal adolescent troubles with her feelings about the outrages in the newspaper headlines. The executions of Nicola Sacco and Bartolomeo Vanzetti (two Italian immigrant anarchists convicted of murder and theft) in August, 1927, even after worldwide protest on their behalf, made a powerful impression on the adolescent Rukeyser.

After high school, Rukeyser attended Vassar College, Columbia University, and Roosevelt Aviation School. As she wrote in *The Life of Poetry* (1949), her "first day at college ended childhood." She began to write the poems that would be published in her first book while cofounding (with Elizabeth Bishop, Mary McCarthy, and Eleanor Clark) a literary magazine called *Student Review* to protest the policies of the established *Vassar Review*. Rukeyser frequently contributed to *Student Review*; as part of this work, she drove to Alabama in 1932 to report on the trial of the Scottsboro Boys, nine young black men who were accused of raping two white girls during the spring of 1931. Rukeyser viewed the resulting death sentence as evidence of a dual

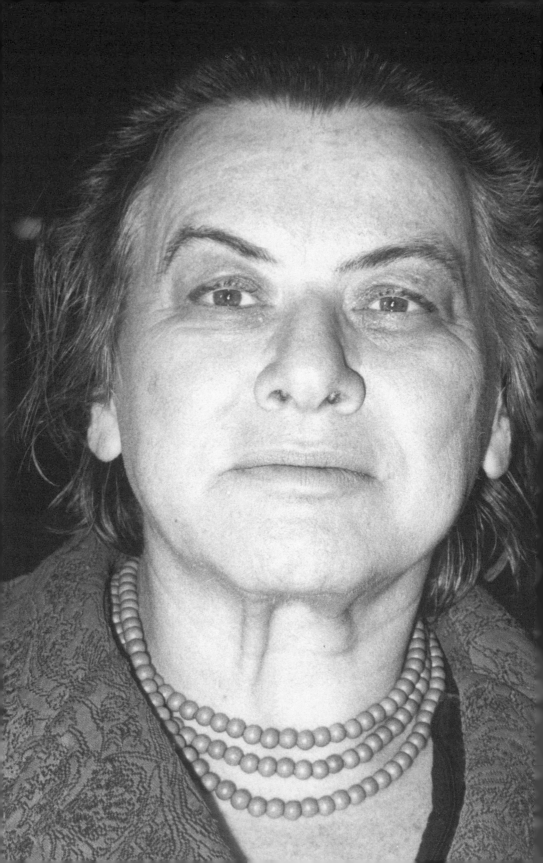

system of American justice, which discriminated against the poor and the nonwhite. While in Alabama, Rukeyser was arrested by police after she and her friends were discovered talking to black reporters; she was carrying thirty posters advertising a black student conference at Columbia University. In the Alabama jail, Rukeyser contracted typhoid.

In 1935, Rukeyser's first book of poetry, *Theory of Flight*, was published and won the Yale Younger Poets Prize. In 1936, Rukeyser traveled to Barcelona, Spain, to cover the Anti-Fascist Olympics for *Life and Letters Today*. While there, she witnessed the outbreak and first fighting of the Spanish Civil War. Rukeyser lobbied for the cause of the Spanish Loyalists and incorporated the images she witnessed into her poetic work.

Rukeyser's second volume of poems, *U.S. 1* (1938), was based on her investigation into the death by silicosis of miners in West Virginia, a notorious scandal of the mid-1930's. Her next three volumes, *Mediterranean* (1938), *A Turning Wind: Poems* (1939), and *The Soul and Body of John Brown* (1940), continued Rukeyser's emphasis on social injustice in America. Upon the outbreak of World War II, Rukeyser became passionately involved in portraying the atrocities visited upon the Jewish people by the Nazis, a subject of great personal interest because of her Jewish heritage and her earlier opposition to fascism in the Spanish Civil War.

In 1945, Rukeyser moved to California, where she was briefly married to painter Glynn Collins. A few years later, she gave birth to an illegitimate son, for which her father disowned her. She incorporated these experiences into her later work, often using the image of giving birth to combat the horrors of the modern world. During this time, Rukeyser was helped by an anonymous benefactor (later known to be the wealthy Californian Henriette Durham) who provided funds to support Rukeyser until her return to New York in 1954, when she began teaching part-time at Sarah Lawrence College.

For the rest of her life, Rukeyser continued to write, to teach part-time (leading poetry workshops at various institutions), and to protest against injustice. In 1972, she flew to Hanoi to participate in a peace demonstration, and later that year she was arrested on the steps of the U.S. Capitol in Washington, D.C., for protesting the Vietnam War. In 1974, as president of the international writers organization PEN, she traveled to South Korea to protest the imprisonment and death sentence of the radical Catholic poet Kim Chi-Ha.

Though Rukeyser was often characterized as a poet of political or social protest, many of her poems were very personal, exploring her experiences as a mother and a daughter, discussing her opinions on creativity and sexuality, and describing her slow recovery after a debilitating stroke. Rukeyser's work is often compared to Walt Whitman's in its imagery and optimism. Yet her work was distinctly individual and always created strong impressions in the minds of her readers. As the writer and poet Kenneth Rexroth wrote, "Muriel Rukeyser is not a poet of Marxism, but a poet who has written directly about the tragedies of the working class. She is a poet of liberty, civil liberty, woman's liberty, and all the other liberties that so many people think they themselves just invented. . . ." Muriel Rukeyser died in New York on February 12, 1980.

Analysis

While writing *The Life of Poetry*, Rukeyser was able to look back at her childhood and pinpoint moments that opened her eyes to the world. Once she began really to see the world, she wrote, she never stopped paying attention to and writing about what she saw.

"Breathe-in experience, breathe-out poetry." So begins "Poem out of Childhood," the first poem in Muriel Rukeyser's first book, *Theory of Flight*. The phrase expresses Rukeyser's fundamental belief that poetry is based on experience: Life, feelings, and reactions are the source of poetry. Further, for Rukeyser, the personal, the political, and the poetical are inextricably woven together. Since she frequently acted on this belief, some critics have called her the poet of the downtrodden. Her poetry, however, contains more than social commentary, slogans, or expressions of outrage over injustice. Rukeyser's poems embody optimism, a belief in the noble aspirations of humanity, and a sense of wonder at the beauty of the world, all expressed in a powerfully lyrical voice. Rukeyser used her lyrical writing to express her social and political awareness and to encourage (even, at times, to exhort) the reader to action or, at least, to awareness. For example, in "Poem out of Childhood," she expresses astonishment at being taught about the ancient Greeks in high school while being taught nothing about current events: "Not Sappho, Sacco," she complains.

Rukeyser's poem "Theory of Flight" is representative of her early work. It is written as a cluster of short verses under seven subheadings; the first section, "Preamble," begins with an appeal to the opposites of the Earth and the sky: "Earth, bind us close, and time   ;   nor, sky, deride/ how violate we experiment again." Near the section's end, the poet writes that the sky is the "meeting of sky and no-sky" and that "flight, thus, is meeting of flight and non-flight." These images present one of Rukeyser's themes, the reconciliation of opposites. As the critic David Barber has noted, Rukeyser's goal was to resolve the conflicts in herself; her means was "to deal completely with the self," and her specific tool was poetry. One aspect of this reconciliation is found in her later work, which included poems exploring her relations with her parents, making peace with her dead mother, and dealing with her failing health. Another aspect of the reconciliation Rukeyser desired was the resolution of conflict between the upper, middle, and lower classes.

Rukeyser's concern with themes of class oppression, death, and justice in America is most clearly visible in "The Trial," a part of "Theory of Flight" that discusses the trial of the Scottsboro Boys in Alabama. This section could have been written with bitterness and anger, but, although it describes lynchings and other terrible injustices, the passage ends with a powerful affirmation of life and human striving as represented by an airplane. The last phrase of the section is the shout "FLY," expressing precisely the sort of optimism in the midst of horrors that led critics to view Rukeyser's work in the same light as Whitman's. This aspect of her work, however, has often been ignored by scholars more interested in her frequently strident social commentary and philosophizing.

While Rukeyser was primarily known for being outspoken and courageous, her language changed over the course of her early career. She moved from an oratorical, prophetic tone to a meditative, spiritual one based more directly on her immediate experience; she also moved away from forming most of her poems out of clusters of verses and toward a more compact style. These changes in form did not, however, affect her passion or lyricism. To the end of her career, Rukeyser remained bardic, romantic, and compassionate.

POEM OUT OF CHILDHOOD

First published: 1935
Type of work: Poem

The poet presents contrasting images of her sheltered youth and societal injustices, which she eventually resolves.

Part 1 of "Poem out of Childhood" opens with Rukeyser's famous declaration "Breathe-in experience, breathe-out poetry" and continues with images of high-school students being affected by the outside world: a girl whose father and brother have just died, for example, and the image of the "mouldered face" of a "syphilitic woman" that intrudes upon a school orchestra's playing. The poet is hit with image after image that, like bandages, wrap her head: "when I put my hand up I hardly feel the wounds."

The poet continues, protesting against those "who manipulated and misused our youth,/ smearing those centuries upon our hands," by focusing the students' attention on the past and ignoring present-day horrors. Part 1 ends with the proclamation, "Rebellion pioneered among our lives,/ viewing from far-off many-branching deltas,/ innumerable seas."

During part 2 of "Poem out of Childhood," Rukeyser is still thinking about world events: "Prinzip's year bore us : see us turning at breast/ quietly while the air throbs over Sarajevo/ after the mechanic laugh of that bullet." The reference is to Gavrilo Princip, the Serbian student whose assassination of the Austrian Archduke Ferdinand at Sarajevo on June 28, 1914, triggered World War I. The aftermath of the assassination is the throbbing pain accompanying the birth of Rukeyser's modern world, and the children born into that world are shown as innocent and ineffective. The early days of the modern world are viewed through a kaleidoscope of Rukeyser's memories, including an abandoned factory at which "the kids throw stones." The empty factory seems to represent the old social structures, abandoned during the war.

Part 3 begins with the poet's decision to

> Organize the full results of that rich past
> open the windows : potent catalyst,

harsh theory of knowledge, running down the aisles
crying out in the classrooms, March ravening on the plain,
inexorable sun and wind and natural thought.

As critic Louise Kertesz has explained, this is how Rukeyser will deal with her memories of suffering and conflict, by creating "an organizing vision which is intensely personal and hard-won." The youth now will not throw stones at the abandoned factory but will knock at its walls, questioning its meaning and determining its place in her life. Here is Rukeyser's reconciliation of the opposites of her innocent, sheltered youth and her memories of the awful events that took place during that youth. Part 3 of "Poem out of Childhood" ends with the positive image of young people trying on different roles and exploring their significance by "summoning fact from abandoned machines of trade," ready "for the affirmative clap of truth."

AJANTA

First published: 1944
Type of work: Poem

"Ajanta" chronicles Rukeyser's inner journey to free herself from the bonds of society and to resolve her conflict between personal and political values.

"Ajanta" has been hailed as the finest poem of Rukeyser's first decade of work and is one of her most famous writings. The name "Ajanta" refers to a number of ancient cave temples and monasteries in India that are famous for their wall paintings. The poem is written in Rukeyser's characteristic cluster form and is made up of five parts entitled "The Journey," "The Cave," "Les Tendresses Bestiales," "Black Blood," and "Broken World."

"The Journey" explains the significance of "Ajanta": The poem will describe Rukeyser's solitary youthful journey through the stormy world to that moment of peace that is the cave. Although she blessed her heart's ability to suffer (and to empathize), she was torn between youth's natural desire to cherish the values it had been taught and the activism that her conscience demanded at the sight of injustice. In other words, "Ajanta" will tell the story of her synthesis of personal and political concerns.

"The Cave" represents the peacefulness the poet will feel when she finally accepts the reality of the world's condition and her place in that world. In this section, Rukeyser describes the nature of the cave: It is both a space in the mind and a space in the body, yet it "is not a womb," for "nothing but good emerges" from the cave. (This contrasts with the mixture of good and evil in all humans.) Rukeyser's journey, then, is to be internal. In the cave, "the walls are the world," and "the space of these walls is the body's living space." She senses that the "spaces of the body/ Are suddenly limitless," that once she reconciles her inner conflicts she will have her freedom.

In the third section of "Ajanta," "Les Tendresses Bestiales," it becomes apparent that Rukeyser has not yet reached the cave but is still held in the outside world. This world suddenly changes from a world of beauty into a world of savagery and tumult, paralleling the change in Rukeyser from a peaceful, sheltered child into a torn, lost being. She writes, "I am plunged deep. Must find the midnight cave."

"Black Blood," the fourth section of "Ajanta," conveys all the anger, fear, greed, and turmoil of real life. As the poet runs, lost in this welter of blood and viciousness, she is found by a bit of hope: "—As I ran I heard/ A black voice beating among all that blood:/ 'Try to live as if there were a God.' "

In the fifth section, "The Broken World," Rukeyser has reached the Ajanta cave, "The real world where everything is complete./ There are no shadows, the forms of incompleteness." Here, the conflicts within her have been resolved, and she has no doubts. She experiences not merely freedom from conflict but also happiness, and she writes, "Here all may stand/ On summer earth."

Even as she has achieved unity and contentment, however, "Crawls from the door,/ Black at my two feet/ The shadow of the world." This shadow reminds Rukeyser of the disunity and trouble in the world outside the cave and will not let her withdraw into herself. By writing "Ajanta," she has not only united the differences within herself but also accepted the task of speaking out against worldly injustices.

SEARCHING/NOT SEARCHING

First published: 1972
Type of work: Poem

The poet bears witness to truth while in the midst of social crises and tries to transcend the barriers between people.

The poem "Searching/Not Searching" carries an epigraph attributed to the poet Robert Duncan: "Responsibility is to use the power to respond." This might almost be taken as Rukeyser's motto, since her entire adult life and most of her poems responded sharply to the world events that she witnessed.

The first of the fourteen sections of "Searching/Not Searching" asks, "What kind of woman goes searching and searching?/ . . . for what man? for what magic?" The answer is that Rukeyser's kind does. Throughout the world, she "searched for that Elizabethan man,/ the lost discoverer, the servant of time." This reference is to the latter part of the sixteenth century, when classical humanism (providing a noble vision of the dignity of humanity) and the medieval tragic sense of life (providing an awareness of death) were united into a heroic picture of humanity that was circumscribed by the sense of human mortality. This unification parallels Rukeyser's own unification of the personal and the political; in light of her unflagging optimism and her sense of reality, Rukeyser herself might almost be called Elizabethan.

Rukeyser's commitment to speaking out (or bearing witness) is renewed in the poem's second section, "Miriam : The Red Sea." The section's title refers to a prophet of the Old Testament, the elder sister of Moses and Aaron who led the celebration of the Hebrew women after the crossing of the Red Sea. Rukeyser, as Miriam, says "I along stand here/ ankle-deep/ and I sing, I sing,/ until the lands/ sing to each other."

As the critic Louise Kertesz explains, each section of "Searching/Not Searching" is "another witness to wholeness and unity, despite the discouragement of silence and unresponsiveness." Further, each section provides a particular image, either of inspiration or of outrage, which gives the poet strength to continue her quest. For example, in the third section, "For Dolci," in Kertesz's words, "the direct vision and speech of children will help the poet in her search to speak the truth." In section 4, "Concrete," Rukeyser's poems are poured down as concrete is poured, both forming the foundation for the future, helping to alleviate the poet's sense of futility. Inspiration also comes from a Vietnamese epic heroine who sells herself to save her father, from the Sistine Chapel, and from Rukeyser's dying friend Hallie Flanagan (the director of the Works Progress Administration Federal Theatre Project), who taught Rukeyser the most important element of a theatrical production: "The audience   the response." Outrage is felt in the tenth section, "The President and the Laser Bomb," in which a politician's proclamation of peace is juxtaposed with an image of destructive technology.

Yet the poem closes with a declaration of hope in the power of communication. What the poet has found in her quest for truth is that communication between people "was the truth." Through their words and deeds, everyone is "trying to make, to let our closeness be made,/ not torn apart tonight by our dead skills."

Summary

Muriel Rukeyser merged her personal vision with her political vision and wrote poems of remarkable intensity. Her work was so linked to current events that one critic claimed that the whole of twentieth century history could be learned by reading Rukeyser's work. Though noted for her poems of social protest, Rukeyser also wrote deeply personal poems, incorporating such diverse elements as scientific language and mysticism, all in a unique lyrical, demanding style. One of her most unique traits was her optimism: While describing the injustices and the horrors of her times, Rukeyser usually was able to express faith in the potential of civilization, wonder at the beauty of the world, and love for humanity.

Bibliography

Barber, David S. "Finding Her Voice: Muriel Rukeyser's Poetic Development." *Modern Poetry Studies* II, no. 1-2 (1982): 127-138.

Gardinnier, Suzanne. "'A World That Will Hold All the People': On Muriel Rukeyser." *The Kenyon Review* 14, no. 3 (Summer, 1992): 88.

Kalaidjian, Walter. "Muriel Rukeyser and the Poetics of Specific Critique: Rereading 'The Book of the Dead.'" *Cultural Critique* 20 (Winter, 1991): 65.

Kertesz, Louise. *The Poetic Vision of Muriel Rukeyser.* Baton Rouge: Louisiana State University Press, 1980.

Rukeyser, Muriel. *The Life of Poetry.* New York: Current Books, Inc., 1949.

Katherine Socha

MAY SARTON

Born: Wondelgem, Belgium
May 3, 1912

Principal Literary Achievement
Sarton has integrated aspects of her life and art through a variety of artistic forms and served as a role model to generations of readers.

Biography

May Sarton was born Elèanore Marie Sarton, the daughter of George Sarton, an eminent philosopher and author of a four-volume history of science, and Mabel Sarton, an artist and designer. Because she was born on May 3, she was called May. During World War I, the Sartons emigrated to America and settled in Cambridge, Massachusetts, where George taught part-time at Harvard University.

May was a precocious child; she wrote poetry from the age of nine, and some of her poems were published when she was seventeen. She attended an innovative high school in Cambridge known as Shady Hill School. Her future path appeared set: She would attend college and then marry a prominent man. After seeing the renowned actress Eva La Gallienne star in a production of Henrik Ibsen's *Hedda Gabler* in 1928, however, May became devoted to the theater. She became a member of the Civic Repertory Theater in New York City and then the founder and director of the Apprentices Theater in New York from 1933 to 1935. After another year of productions, her company failed, partly as a result of the effects of the Depression. May was twenty-four and seemingly without direction; she fell back on one of her many strengths and became a writer.

Her first book was a collection of poems, *Encounter in April* (1937), which explored themes related to the differences between physical passion and love. In order to support her career as a writer, Sarton began a cycle of almost forty years devoted to teaching, lecturing, and reading from her works. She taught creative writing, was a poet-in-residence, and lectured at several colleges and universities, including Harvard University and Bryn Mawr College, and at the prestigious Bread Loaf Writers' Conference. Although she published dozens of books, Sarton was not able to support herself on her writings alone until she was in her sixties.

Her first novel, *The Single Hound*, was published in 1938, and her second book of poetry, *Inner Landscape*, in 1939. After World War II, Sarton continued to write

novels and poems. She was unusually close to her parents; she was an only child, and she never married. Her mother died in 1950, and her father died in 1956. Her move to Nelson, New Hampshire, in 1958 marked a turning point in her life. The memoir *I Knew a Phoenix: Sketches for an Autobiography* (1959), based upon her move, examined her life from her childhood to the age of twenty-five. Sarton settled into her middle age as a woman who lived alone, who no longer had family ties, and who had no part in the traditional roles of wife and mother.

Her record of her life from the ages of forty-five to fifty-five is found in *Plant Dreaming Deep* (1968), a book that has inspired numerous readers because it showed the possibilities of the solitary working woman's life. She balanced this enthusiastic response to her life alone in rural New England with the 1973 volume *Journal of a Solitude*, which drew upon her frustrations with celebrity. By then she was a world-famous author and literary personality, and she often felt confounded by the pressures of fame.

As We Are Now, a novel about an old woman who suffers harsh treatment after she is placed in a rural nursing home, appeared in 1973. That year Sarton moved to York, Maine. Her *Collected Poems, 1930-1973*, appeared in 1974 and a journal about her new home, *The House by the Sea*, appeared in 1977. Although she had reached retirement age, she gave little consideration to retiring from her writing. Twice she made use of experiences related to illness or disability and found a means of resolving her traumas through the process of writing journals. In 1980, she published *Recovering: A Journal* after suffering from breast cancer, and in 1988 she published *After the Stroke: A Journal*, about her recovery from a debilitating stroke. Her achievements were recognized by honorary degrees from eight colleges and universities—a remarkable accomplishment for a woman who never attended a college or university.

She continued to be productive through her seventies, publishing the novels *Anger* (1982), *The Magnificent Spinster* (1985), and *The Education of Harriet Hatfield* (1989); the poetry volumes *Letters from Maine* (1984) and *The Silence Now* (1989); and two journals that explored her experiences as an older adult, *At Seventy: A Journal* (1984) and *Endgame: A Journal of the Seventy-Ninth Year* (1992). In the latter book, Sarton shares the emotional and psychological pain associated with chronic illness and physical disabilities. Although she realizes that she may never "get well," she faces the task of recording her moods and thoughts with equanimity, courage, and, always, hope.

Analysis

Although she has written novels, journals, memoirs, and literary criticism, May Sarton considers poetry to be the primary means by which she expresses her creativity and identity. She wrote poetry as a child, and it was to poetry that she turned when she left the theater. Many themes are apparent in her poetry, including love relationships, passion for the natural world, devotion to art and music, aging and death, the dynamics of growth and change, solitude, travel, and contemporary social issues.

Although she has written in free verse, the majority of her poems use stricter formal structures such as the sonnet. Four of her major works are collections of sonnets. The sonnets in *Encounter in April*, her first collection, portray the depth of passion between two lovers and their inevitable separation and sense of loss. This pattern of love found and love failed dominates in two other sonnet sequences, "A Divorce of Lovers" (1961), which recounts an emotionally painful separation, and "The Autumn Sonnets" (1972), in which the agony of lost love leads to a healing process and acceptance of a renewal and growth. In *Letters from Maine*, the poet affirms the desire for love that exists in late life.

Despite her lifelong devotion to writing poetry, most of Sarton's readers return to her work because of her memoirs and journals. In *I Knew a Phoenix*, Sarton recalled her childhood, the influence of her parents, and her experiences in the theater. In effect, this memoir ended at the point where her career as a writer began, in 1937. As in her journals, Sarton recounted significant friendships that provided mentoring, inspiration, and education for the young woman. *Plant Dreaming Deep* opened Sarton's works to a wider audience. Sarton wrote about her middle age, when she began to live alone in rural New England. Many readers responded positively to her depiction of the life of a working woman living alone. Sarton's life alone enabled her to engage in a struggle with solitude and find the means through which she could experience self-renewal and creativity.

Sarton continued to explore that struggle in journals. If *Plant Dreaming Deep* depicted the joys of solitude, then *Journal of a Solitude* provided a corrective by noting the negative effects of the solitary life. In all of her journals, Sarton has taken great risks to expose her fears and insecurities, her bouts with depression, her ambivalence toward fame. Another risk has been to write about events that are part of the round of daily living, such as preparing meals, visiting the doctor, feeding the birds, or planting bulbs. Yet readers have embraced Sarton's journals because she is able to maintain a freshness and originality even when writing about mundane events. She maintains sufficient distance between the emotion of the moment and the creative act of recounting the effects of that emotion. Self-discipline, honesty, and objectivity are her strengths when it comes to this form. In two of her journals, *Recovering* and *After the Stroke*, Sarton has shared her struggles with disease and physical disability. *Endgame* exposes her feelings of vulnerability and hopelessness in the face of physical disabilities and chronic pain.

The title of her novel *Crucial Conversations* (1975) provides a clue to a basic organizing principle Sarton employs in most of her fiction. The dominant internal structure within each of her novels is the conversation between two characters. In fact, extended dialogue between characters is emphasized far more than conventional use of external action and plot construction. In some respects, this technique may reflect Sarton's theatrical aptitude and skills. Perhaps, however, Sarton employs conversations because the action of most of the novels is internal rather than external. What matters is how the characters change, not what the characters experience. The subject matter of her novels is the process of women (more often than men) coming to an understanding of their identity and values, the significance of relationships in their lives, the possibilities for change in their lives, and their strengths and independence. Unfortunately, the attendant thinness of plot distracts from the repeated use of the conversational structure.

Sarton has used the novel form to celebrate important women in her own life (a character in *The Single Hound* is based on a teacher Sarton had in Belgium, and the main character in *The Magnificent Spinster* is modeled after her teacher Anne Thorp). *Mrs. Stevens Hears the Mermaids Calling* (1965) and *The Education of Harriet Hatfield* explore issues related to androgyny and homosexuality.

In all of Sarton's work the integration of the self, and particularly the self of women, is of primary value. Working inward to discover self-knowledge, balance, wholeness, and creativity are the tasks of the individual.

JOURNAL OF A SOLITUDE

First published: 1973
Type of work: Journal

Sarton records and reflects upon her experiences, ever-changing moods, and significant relationships and on the strains in her personal and creative life.

In *Journal of a Solitude*, May Sarton explores significant issues in her life through the creative form of the journal. To Sarton, the journal is not to be confused with the diary. In the journal, the writer reflects upon experiences and analyzes the details of daily living. To Sarton, writing a journal means examining her life, putting herself in touch with priorities in her life (friends, work, gardening), reflecting upon the imbalances in her personal and creative life, and, most important, clarifying and resolving aspects of her sense of self.

Entries in *Journal of a Solitude* begin September, 1970, and end September, 1971. At the beginning of the journal, she examines a dominant theme in her life: the conflict between the opposing forces of solitude and society. She acknowledges the strains of public appearances and social engagements and recalls the times she yielded to the onslaught of personal inquiries and unwanted visits. These, she declares, are not part of her "real life." For Sarton, who has always lived alone as an adult, real life means engaging in a process of reclaiming the self and finding a creative center from which new life can spring. In many respects she welcomes solitude, because in spite of its recurring loneliness, depression, and rage, solitude provides a source of energy and vitality to stimulate her creativity.

Sarton settles down in the fall of the year to renew herself in solitude. She realizes that after publication of *Plant Dreaming Deep* in 1968, she was "discovered" by many who viewed her as a seer or sage, someone who seemed "above" emotional frailty. She wrote *Journal of a Solitude* to reveal a May Sarton who faces daily the struggles between solitude and society, joy and despair, companionship and loneliness.

Love and creativity are closely allied in Sarton's life. She comments several times on the rejuvenating power of love in an affair with someone she refers to only as "X." This relationship spurs a creative breakthrough in her writing of poetry. Other high points in the year include the publication of her latest novel, *Kinds of Love* (1970); reunions with friends; several poetry readings; and her plans to publish a new book of poems, *A Durable Fire: New Poems*, to mark her sixtieth birthday in 1972. Low points include the death of a handyman, Perley Cole, who was the inspiration for a character in her 1973 novel *As We Are Now*; the death of one of her pets, a parrot named Punch; and the eventual ending of the relationship with her lover.

After a year of entries, she realizes it is time to end her journal. She marks the transition in her life with the decision to move away from Nelson, New Hampshire, to live in a house by the sea in Maine. For Sarton, writing the journal has been a process. She examines moods as they come, charts the high and low points of her days, and measures the gradual changes that occur within her sense of self. In this way, the changes in her life unfold, like the changes of the seasons. At the end of the journal, she is a different person, but that difference is not based upon one event or encounter. She has been changed through the process of living, thinking, interacting, surviving, and creating.

AS WE ARE NOW

First published: 1973
Type of work: Novel

An old woman, oppressed and abused by her caregivers after moving to a nursing home, strikes back with a desperate act.

The plot of *As We Are Now* is simple: An old woman, Caro Spencer, is placed in a rural nursing home, finds little stimulation in her relationships with other residents, experiences hostile and abusive treatment from the administrator and head nurse, communicates her distress to helpful acquaintances from the outside world, is frustrated and ridiculed by the head nurse after repeated attempts to improve conditions in the home, and decides finally to set fire to the nursing home and kill everyone inside, including herself.

Sarton tells this tragic story from Caro's point of view by means of a journal that she begins to write shortly after entering the nursing home. The journal reveals Caro as an intelligent, articulate, and sensitive older woman who is definitely out of place in this inadequate rural facility. Few residents share her intellectual background. Only one, Standish Flint, befriends her. He is a tough-minded old farmer who appreciates Caro's clarity of mind and sense of humor. He seems a potential ally of Caro's, but his untimely death hastens the development of her desperate state of mind.

Sarton wants readers to feel the physical, psychological, and spiritual degradation the elderly experience at the hands of insensitive, controlling caretakers who treat them as invisible and useless. The journal format invites readers to empathize with Caro's feelings of helplessness and vulnerability and to appreciate the individuality and complexity of older adults. Caro begins her journal with the reference to the nursing home as "a concentration camp for the old, a place where people dump their parents or relatives exactly as though it were an ash can." Sarton aims to show that individuals (the old included) may strike back when they are made to feel unproductive, worthless, and abandoned. The only escape may be a cleansing holocaust that occurs when the old person, her identity and sense of well-being crushed by cruel and abusive treatment, believes there are no other options available to her.

Caro does meet others who understand the complexity of her character and the beauty of her spirit. A minister who visits residents befriends her, and his daughter joins him and soon comes to love and appreciate Caro. They do their best to assist Caro in her attempt to alleviate the degrading conditions in the nursing home, but their actions are undermined by the oppressive hand of Harriet Hatfield, the administrator. When Harriet goes on vacation, Caro experiences a brief respite from this woman's harsh treatment. Anna Close replaces Harriet and treates Caro as an individual. Anna's warmth and affection rejuvenate Caro, but when Harriet returns to work and Anna leaves, Caro becomes desperate and feels trapped.

Caro's last act before setting the fire is to place her journal inside an old refrigerator so that it will be spared and others can read about her experiences. Caro's creative act of writing the journal represents a victory over her oppressive caregivers and suggests a view of old age as a time of creativity and growth.

GESTALT AT SIXTY

First published: 1972
Type of work: Poem

To mark her sixtieth birthday, Sarton reviews the forces that have contributed to her identity and to the meaning of her life.

"Gestalt at Sixty," from *A Durable Fire*, repeats many of the themes found in Sarton's earlier poems, journals, and novels. The poet reviews her ten years of living in Nelson, New Hampshire, celebrates her sixtieth birthday, and explores the fabric of her life and the significance of her experiences. The "gestalt" of the title refers to the wholeness or totality of life experiences. In gestalt psychology, the overall meaning of one's experience is greater than the sum of its parts (such as individual experiences, events, interactions). Thus, when Sarton analyzes her life on her sixtieth birthday, she tries to make sense of the underlying patterns that are the basis of her experiences. She examines the various forces that have contributed to the formation of her identity, her values, her philosophy of life.

What does it mean to be sixty? Sarton divides her response to that question into three parts. In part 1, she affirms the importance of the natural world in her life. She refers to lakes, mountains, flowers, and trees, all of which nurture her soul and stimulate her creativity. She addresses an important theme of the relationship between solitude and creativity. She maintains, "Solitude exposes the nerve." Solitude provides the greatest test for the artist, who has to face the limitations, fears, and shortcomings within herself in order to create. The pressures of solitude provoke passionate responses to life. Sarton admits to fits of weeping, loneliness, and panic, all of which constrain her and diminish her sense of well-being. In the face of these trials, she draws upon an inner resolve of courage and fortitude in order to find a sense of wholeness. She survives by creating a world for herself in the same way that her garden grows; in order for creativity to bloom, she must clear away inner constraints and renew herself.

In part 2, she admits that she is sometimes overwhelmed by of her fame. She feels oppressed when contacts with others become collisions, when there is the pressure of unwanted interactions. In this context, solitude is a restorative; she can be nourished by the joys of music and poetry and aloneness. For Sarton, there must be a balance between the forces of solitude and society. When she finds that balance, she is able to participate fully in human relationships and open herself to growth and change.

In part 3, Sarton integrates her response toward her aging with a synthesis of a variety of religious and philosophical perspectives, including Taoism, a Chinese philosophy; Buddhism, an Eastern religion; and Christianity. She portrays herself with images reminiscent of the Taoist sage, the wise person who embraces change as the basis of all life. Her acceptance of her impending old age and her mortality reflects Buddhist thought in her references to "detachment" and "learning to let go." She ends the poem with a Christian prayer in which she accepts a God who is at once merciful and demanding. She acknowledges that on these various spiritual levels, creativity flows from the dynamic tension between life and death, youth and old age, light and dark, just as her creativity has flowed from the tension between solitude and society.

Summary

May Sarton's public and private lives are not separate and distinct. Through a lifetime of writing memoirs, journals, novels, and poems, Sarton has shared the details of her childhood, her relationships to her parents, her significant friendships, her love affairs, and her daily life. She has triumphed as a writer because she as maintained freshness and originality and avoided repeating narrow formulas. In her journals, she has striven to discern a synthesis of her overall experience by devoting herself to an examination of who she is "now," what her moods and experiences mean to her on a particular day. Readers—particularly women—have identified with her struggles to adapt to a life of solitude. In effect, she has distilled the meaning of her own life through her writings and, in the process, uncovered universal themes.

Bibliography

Blouin, Lenora P. *May Sarton: A Bibliography*. Metuchen, N.J.: Scarecrow Press, 1978.

Evans, Elizabeth. *May Sarton*. Rev. ed. Boston: Twayne, 1989.

Hunting, Constance, ed. *May Sarton: Woman and Poet*. Orono, Me.: National Poetry Foundation, 1982.

Ingersol, Earl, ed. *Conversations with May Sarton*. Jackson: University Press of Mississippi, 1991.

Sibley, Agnes. *May Sarton*. New York: Twayne, 1972.

Woodward, Kathleen. "May Sarton and the Fictions of Old Age." In *Gender and Literary Voice*, edited by Janet Todd. New York: Holmes & Meier, 1980.

Robert E. Yahnke

ANNE SEXTON

Born: Newton, Massachusetts
November 9, 1928
Died: Weston, Massachusetts
October 4, 1974

Principal Literary Achievement
One of the most widely read and imitated of the confessional poets, Sexton wrote memorable poems exposing the most intimate aspects of her painful personal life.

Biography
Anne Sexton was born Anne Gray Harvey on November 9, 1928, in Newton, Massachusetts. The third child of wealthy wool manufacturer Ralph Churchill Harvey and his wife Mary Gray Staples, Anne was surrounded by luxury; the four-story Harvey house contained living quarters for maids, a cook, and a butler. Yet Anne felt overlooked and unwanted, and even as a child she developed a reputation for doing daring and drastic things just to be noticed. Later, she would write of her economically comfortable childhood with bitterness rather than nostalgia.

Her years in the public schools of Wellesley, Massachusetts, and then at the boarding school Rogers Hall were marked by episodes of rebelliousness. After graduation, she enrolled in the Garland School, a Boston finishing school. In 1948, before her twentieth birthday, she eloped with Alfred Muller Sexton II, a sophomore at Colgate University.

Anne and "Kayo," as she called him, then led such a difficult life for five years or so that she must have at least at that time looked back with regret at her privileged childhood. The couple moved to Hamilton, New York, where Kayo attempted to finish his education, but financial pressures were extreme. Then Kayo joined the Naval Reserve and shipped out; Anne lived sometimes with her parents and sometimes with his, while she used her dazzling good looks to support herself by working as a model between his leaves.

In 1953, she gave birth to Linda Gray Sexton, her first child; she found this experience shocking and devastating. It now became apparent that Anne suffered from serious emotional troubles. Her illness was triggered by the birth of her first child, but it continued to plague her for the rest of her life. She was treated for depression and

attempted suicide; she seemed to be making a recovery when she became pregnant again. The second daughter, Joyce Ladd Sexton, was born in August, 1955; six months later, Anne was admitted to a mental hospital for several months, and the second child was sent to live with Kayo's parents. Her discharge from the hospital was followed by another suicide attempt, but this time she found a new psychiatrist, Dr. Martin Orne, who told her to write about her problems as part of her therapy. Thus Anne Sexton became a poet.

Sexton's realization that she could exorcise her own demons and provide a moving experience for others through poetry prompted her to enroll in John Holmes's poetry seminar at Boston University. There she met Maxine Kumin, a fellow poet who would inspire and encourage her and who would eventually coauthor children's stories with her. She also learned much from W. D. Snodgrass and Robert Lowell, whose work was beginning to popularize the confessional mode of poetry. In 1960, her first collection of poetry, *To Bedlam and Part Way Back*, was published by Houghton Mifflin. These poems chart her experiences through the crisis of mental illness and back toward health.

Her work caught the eye of the poetry establishment instantly; although some critics panned it, no one ignored it. Her second book, *All My Pretty Ones*, appeared in 1962, again describing the mental illness but also focusing on the many personal losses Sexton had suffered. The book was followed by prestigious awards and grants. Travel grants allowed Sexton to visit Europe and Africa, although her travels never seemed to provide satisfaction but instead left her depressed. Her third book, *Live or Die* (1966), won for her the Pulitzer Prize in poetry in 1967. She received honorary degrees from a number of prestigious universities and a Guggenheim Fellowship; the woman who had dropped out of finishing school taught at Harvard and Radcliffe. Houghton Mifflin published *Love Poems* in 1969 and *Transformations* in 1971, and these books were widely reviewed. By then, it was clear that Sexton's career was an unqualified success.

Yet she did not find peace within herself. She wrote several more books and prepared them for publication during the last four years of her life, and all these show a struggle between despair and religious belief. *The Book of Folly* appeared in 1972. *The Death Notebooks* came out in 1974, the last year of her life. *The Awful Rowing Toward God* (1975) and a play, *45 Mercy Street* (1976), were published posthumously, as was *Words for Dr. Y: Uncollected Poems with Three Stories* (1978). In these last books, Sexton's earlier themes are recapitulated, but the element of personal turmoil is often represented by a battle between herself and a dimly understood God. During these last few years, Sexton became more difficult to live with, and it became harder for her to live with others. In 1973, she withdrew from her marriage, against her husband's will; she entered a hospital once more to be treated for depression. She refused most invitations, and her lifelong friendships dwindled. This time no new outlet presented itself as poetry had through the agency of Dr. Orne in 1956. On October 4, 1974, Anne Sexton committed suicide by poisoning herself with carbon monoxide.

Analysis

Anne Sexton believed and frequently asserted that poetry should hurt. Her poetry deals with the most painful incidents in her life in a direct and uncompromising way; it is often excruciating to read. Although her style changed considerably over the approximately twenty years of her writing life, her subjects remained basically the same: madness, death, and God's silence. Although she wrote some poetry as a student, she did not really begin her career as a poet until after her first mental breakdown, when her psychiatrist directed her to write her feelings down. Thus her work begins on a basis of breakdown and chaos. Her various books show her attempt to work back to some sense of wholeness.

The first collection, *To Bedlam and Part Way Back*, focuses on her madness and conveys to the reader the impressions of a patient in a mental ward. Written after the crisis that followed the birth of her first child, it shows Sexton's slow steps back to the rational world. Poems of her experiences in the asylum are interspersed with elegies for people she has known. Her second book, *All My Pretty Ones*, deals with the loss of her parents and other loved ones, as well as with other losses—lovers, faith, identity. In an interview, she explained that the first book described the nature of madness and the second explored the causes of it. Sexton felt constantly aware of death and loss, and this awareness overwhelmed any other, more positive feelings. In the first two collections, Sexton often uses formal patterns to contain and control her materials. This formality often distances the material somewhat and gives the work the tone of a dignified elegy. Patterns are part of the effect of "Elizabeth Gone" and "Some Foreign Letters," two poems in which Sexton commemorated the life and death of her aunt, Anna Ladd Dingley, who had lived with her. These poems are restrained but moving in their effort to show through particulars of the woman's life how much the speaker has lost through her death.

The fear of death and the sadness of loss are replaced to a certain extent in the Pulitzer Prize-winning *Live or Die* by a deep longing for death. When she hears of the death of sister poet Sylvia Plath, according to "Sylvia's Death," she is envious of Plath. In "Wanting to Die," she explains how the desire to end her life obsesses her, addressing those who are not afflicted by this visceral urge and do not understand it. Her tone is ironic, almost playfully so:

> But suicides have a special language.
> Like carpenters they want to know *which tools*.
> They never ask *why build*.

The collection ends with the poem "Live," which describes her decision not to kill the unwanted puppies her dog bore, and her choice to allow herself to live also. Yet although the book ends with this positive poem, darker tones outweigh any glimmers of hope throughout the collection.

The later Sexton is more unrestrained, wilder in her outpourings and yet not always directly confessional. *Transformations* is something of a diversion from her usual concerns. She puts her anger at the world's injustices into retellings of Grimm's fairy tales. *Transformations* consists of feminist poetry that bears the mark of the 1970's. The fairy tales Sexton has twisted and retold are in themselves frightening; they are tales of Rapunzels and Cinderellas and Snow Whites, women who are abused and imprisoned but who are finally able to overcome all obstacles to win the ultimate joy of the happy-ever-after marriage with the prince. The 1970's feminist interrogated the fairy tales of her childhood to ask whether this desired ending was, after all, the ultimate joy—or if it was not, in fact, just more imprisonment and abuse.

Sexton retells these stories with dark humor and wicked irony, so that the reader can share her doubts about the tales and the values they imply. She stresses the unreality of the Cinderella ending, for example, when she concludes her tale that Cinderella and the prince lived "happily ever after,/ like two dolls in a museum case/ never bothered by diapers or dust,/ . . . their darling smiles pasted on for eternity./ Regular Bobbsey Twins." (The Bobbsey Twins are two sets of unrealistically upbeat twins in a popular children's series from Sexton's childhood.) The *Transformations* tales show a different Anne Sexton; they sparkle with wicked humor. In this one collection, she substitutes women's issues for her own torments, at least in part.

Sexton's later work, however, returns to her earlier preoccupations, this time without the use of form to shape them. The last few years of her life resulted in several books that express her desperate struggles to escape despair and find a reason for living. The search for God became an obsession, as the poet tried to find some way of approaching the deity that would make her feel validated and forgiven. "Rowing," a frequently anthologized poem from The Awful Rowing Toward God, shows the intensity of her desire for God and her energetic pursuit of grace. She begins the poem with a quick summary of her emotional life, presented as a tale: "A story, a story!/ (Let it go. Let it come.)" Rowing is her metaphor for her search: "God was there like an island I had not rowed to." The rest of the poem takes her on an exhausting trip toward this island: "I am rowing, I am rowing/ though the oarlocks stick and are rusty/ and the sea blinks and rolls/ like a worried eyeball. . . . When she arrives, she says, God will "get rid of the rat inside"—the "gnawing pestilential rat" that has been eating her all of her life. "God will take it with his two hands/ and embrace it." The rat is a presence throughout Sexton's poetry, and she even wanted to have it in her epitaph. She desired to have the sentence "RATS LIVE ON NO EVIL STAR," which she claimed to have found in an Irish churchyard, engraved on her tombstone. According to her daughter, the statement—which reads the same forward and backward—gave Sexton an odd kind of comfort. Yet if the last collections are not unremittingly grim, anything positive in them tends to be set in a hypothetical future—when she arrives at the island of God, when He plays cards with her. The present action in the poetry depicts only the ongoing struggle to arrive at a distant place of peace and forgiveness.

Anne Sexton's poetry provides an unforgettable vision of one woman's search for healing. Moreover, it carries the reader along on his or her own quest.

THE STARRY NIGHT

First published: 1962
Type of work: Poem

The speaker reflects on Vincent van Gogh's well-known painting and on her desire to dissolve into the infinite.

"The Starry Night" shows Anne Sexton's identification with another tortured and suicidal artist, Vincent van Gogh. The short free-verse poem begins with an epigraph from one of van Gogh's letters to his brother. "That does not keep me from having a terrible need of—shall I say the word—religion," van Gogh wrote. "Then I go out at night to paint the stars." Anne Sexton used epigraphs from a variety of works to begin her poems, and the epigraphs are often of major importance, pointing to a main theme of the poem that might otherwise be overlooked. Here she is indicating that she shares not only the mental imbalance, suicidal tendencies, and artistic nature of the Dutch artist, but also his unsatisfied desire for the spiritual.

When van Gogh wrote the letter to his brother, he was painting the masterpiece *Starry Night on the Rhone*, which is described in the poem. The painting captures the night sky in blues and blacks, with a swirl of violent orange representing the moon, and burning yellow-white stars. One would expect a peaceful scene from the title, but this painting is intensely disquieting. The movement seems to be a great rush skyward, the sleeping town beneath the sky unconscious of this spiraling of all nature toward infinity. Sexton sees this painting as a reflection of her own death wish. The dark tree at the edge of the painting is described as "black-haired"—Sexton was a brunette—and it "slips/ up like a drowned woman into the hot sky." To make her meaning clearer, she continues, "This is how/ I want to die."

The poem interprets the painting as presenting a nature that is animate and hostile. Nevertheless, the picture attracts the speaker, because nature's brute force promises death, release from the burden of self. Sexton sees the central moon image in the painting as a great dragon that will suck her up into its being. She desires, she says, "to split/ from my life with no flag,/ no belly,/ no cry"—to merge silently and painlessly with the infinite. The images may suggest not a rediscovery of religion, but a terrifying substitute for it. Part of the appeal of this poem lies in the vivid interpretation of the painting and in the kinship the reader sees between Sexton and van Gogh.

ALL MY PRETTY ONES

First published: 1962
Type of work: Poem

A daughter sorts through her father's belongings after his death and reviews their difficult relationship.

"All My Pretty Ones," the title poem of Sexton's second collection, expresses the grief and loss that characterizes the volume in which it appears. In this poem, Sexton uses formal, rhymed verse to reflect upon the shock and sorrow of losing both parents within a few months. The title itself recalls the grief of William Shakespeare's Macduff, when he is told that Macbeth has had his wife and children killed. Sexton quotes the relevant passage as an epigraph to the poem.

Sexton's poetry closely reflects her life and appears to represent her own voice. "All My Pretty Ones" follows Sexton's efforts to go through her father's effects after his death, which occurred shortly after her mother's. His business fortunes had suffered a reversal. Addressing the father directly, she tells of her attempts to "disencumber/ you from the residence you could not afford" and get rid of mementos that were meaningful to him but not to her: "boxes of pictures of people I do not know./ I touch their cardboard faces. They must go." The father's life is woven into the dead reminders of him that are of another time period. The daughter finds news clippings in an old album and is taken back through the country's history and through her father's. The clippings describe the destruction of the *Hindenburg* and the election of President Herbert Hoover. The father's personal history is chronicled in photographs of formal dances speedboat races, and horse shows, reflecting the wealth and luxury of the life he led.

As the poem progresses, however, it becomes clear that this is no ordinary elegy. The problems in the family become evident: The daughter calls the father "my drunkard, my navigator" and tells of the diary her mother kept, in which she did not speak of the father's alcoholism but only said that he "overslept." The daughter wonders if the alcoholic tendency has been passed on to her with the rest of her dubious inheritance: "each Christmas Day/ with your blood, will I drink down your glass/ of wine?" At the poem's conclusion, the daughter reflects on how brief a space love and memory endure.

The poem is often anthologized with "The Truth the Dead Know," another poem about her parents' deaths, written at approximately the same time. Both poems express a sense of loss complicated by resentment and feelings of isolation. "All My Pretty Ones" gives a memorable portrayal of a survivor who, not having resolved the difficulties with her father during his life, is forced to cope with his death.

WITH MERCY FOR THE GREEDY

First published: 1962
Type of work: Poem

The speaker considers a crucifix that a friend has sent to her and concludes that for her, poetry must serve as confession.

"With Mercy for the Greedy" shows Sexton's need for religious faith and her inability to find it. The poem also provides Sexton's explanation of how her art functions as therapy and, to some degree, takes the place of the religion that she cannot comfortably accept. Addressed to a friend "who urges me to make an appointment for the Sacrament of Confession," the poem explores the speaker's attempt to grasp faith. The friend, identified as "Ruth," has sent her a cross, which she has been wearing "hung with package string" around her neck; this cross, though, has nothing to say to her. It remains unresponsive to her desperate need. "I detest my sins and I try to believe/ in The Cross," she says. Yet she must conclude, finally, that "need is not quite belief."

Having determined that she cannot approach traditional religion through her friend's gift, she tells her friend what she does do: She writes poems, and these are her confession, her way of dealing with her sense of guilt. "I was born/ doing reference work in sin, and born/ confessing it. This is what poems are," she explains. Poems are the struggle with the self and the world that provide "mercy for the greedy"—they are "the tongue's wrangle,/ the world's pottage, the rat's star." Only through the difficult and painful process of creating poetry can she aspire to any kind of peace. The phrase "tongue's wrangle" suggests the awkwardness and difficulty of setting oneself straight through words.

The rat is Sexton's inner turmoil and torment. Later, in "Rowing," she would imagine the rat transformed and accepted. In "With Mercy for the Greedy," however, Sexton does not go so far as to imagine this acceptance, this forgiveness. The only means of confession for her is the poetry, the "rat's star." This poem is anthologized frequently, perhaps because it shows how literally the term "the confessional poet" may be understood when it is applied to Sexton. She is not only sharing intimate and painful experiences with her readers, but also making a confession to her God.

Summary

Anne Sexton's direct and personal poetry forcefully imparts her obsession with loss, suicide, and the authoritarian male figure. Her recurrent images, the bones and rats and other reminders of death and psychic torment, retain their ability to surprise and shock the reader despite their repetitiousness. She always has an original twist that violates expectations and leads the reader to question his or her assumptions. It is true that in her poetry Sexton seems to skim over experience like a magnet attracting iron filings, seeking out suicidal soulmates in literature, history, folklore, and her daily life; however, the intensity of Sexton's poetry makes up for the narrowness of its range. Her work serves to define and illustrate confessional poetry.

Bibliography

Bixler, Frances, ed. *Original Essays on the Poetry of Anne Sexton.* Conway: University of Central Arkansas Press, 1988.

Colburn, Steven E., ed. *Anne Sexton: Telling the Tale.* Ann Arbor: University of Michigan Press, 1988.

George, Diana Hume. *Oedipus Anne: The Poetry of Anne Sexton.* Urbana: University of Illinois Press, 1987.

——————, ed. *Sexton: Selected Criticism.* Urbana: University of Illinois Press, 1988.

Hall, Caroline King Barnard. *Anne Sexton.* Boston: Twayne, 1989.

McClatchy, J. D., ed. *Anne Sexton: The Artist and Her Critic.* Bloomington: Indiana University Press, 1978.

Middlebrook, Diane Wood. *Anne Sexton: A Biography.* Boston: Houghton Mifflin, 1991.

Wagner-Martin, Linda, ed. *Critical Essays on Anne Sexton.* Boston: G. K. Hall, 1989.

Janet McCann

JANE SMILEY

Born: Los Angeles, California
September 26, 1949

Principal Literary Achievement
Smiley depicts the tragic impact of desire and egotism upon American middle-class domesticity and exposes the contradictoriness of human personality.

Biography
Jane Graves Smiley was born September 26, 1949 during her father's military service in Los Angeles, California. Members of long-established Midwestern families, her parents, James La Verne Smiley and Frances Graves Nuelle, soon returned to that region, and although Jane never lived on a working farm, she claims deep "roots in rural country." After a childhood spent in St. Louis, Missouri, she attended Vassar College and in 1971 received a B.A. in English, writing her first novel as a senior thesis. Subsequent graduate studies earned her a master of fine arts degree in 1976 and an M.A. and Ph.D. in medieval literature in 1978, all from the University of Iowa. In 1981 she began teaching literature and creative writing at Iowa State University in Ames, becoming a full professor in 1989. She has been a visiting professor at the University of Iowa in 1981 and 1987. A Fulbright Fellowship to Iceland in 1976 and 1977 enabled Smiley to transform her study of Norse sagas into *The Greenlanders* (1988), an epic novel of fourteenth century Scandinavian pioneers. Grants from the National Endowment for the Arts supported her writing in 1978 and 1987.

Having begun her publishing career in 1980 with *Barn Blind*, Smiley had seen two more novels to press (*At Paradise Gate* in 1981 and *Duplicate Keys* in 1984) by the time critical praise for her work intensified with the appearance of *The Age of Grief* (1987), a collection of short fiction that was nominated for the National Book Critics Circle Award. It was followed by an acclaimed pair of novellas published together as *Ordinary Love and Good Will* in 1989. With the novel *A Thousand Acres* (1991), Smiley won the 1991 National Book Critics Circle Award and the 1992 Pulitzer Prize in fiction.

Smiley suggests that her two key themes—"sex and apocalypse"—derive from a childhood shadowed by the atomic bomb and an adolescence informed by "the Pill." Her personal history reflects the complications of family life that are the subjects of her fiction. A first marriage to John Whiston in 1970 ended in 1975. With second

husband William Silag, whom she married in 1978, she bore two daughters, Phoebe and Lucy. A third marriage, to Stephen Mark Mortensen, began in 1987. Smiley regards her experiences as woman and mother as important influences on her imagination. Having begun her career as a "devoted modernist" infatuated with the nihilistic vision of early twentieth century literature, she found herself losing that alienated edge during her first pregnancy. She consciously challenges the Western literary prejudices embedded in the question, "Can mothers think and write?" Smiley proudly joins those contemporary women writers who document recesses of female subjectivity—including maternity—that have until recently been ignored in creative literature.

Analysis

The scope of Jane Smiley's fictional universe is ostensibly small. Even when she is re-creating medieval Norse frontier settlements in *The Greenlanders* or reworking William Shakespeare's *King Lear* (c. 1605) in *A Thousand Acres*, her dramatic focus remains on the domestic space that characters painstakingly articulate for themselves as a refuge from the chaos of existence. Yet the coherence sought in those spaces does not hold up under the pressure of individual desire, with its perverse and irrational will toward satisfaction and its disruptive impact upon the emotional rhythms of family life. Smiley's typical subject is the contemporary American middle-class family, and her preferred landscape is the Midwest farm belt, a canvas on which she draws scenes of a universal existential loneliness for which there is minimal remedy. In addition to demonstrating a finely tuned ear for the speech of family life, she deftly captures the hunger for connection and empathy that the nuclear family promises to gratify. In capturing this seductive dream of family, however, Smiley also reveals its heartbreakingly predictable insufficiency. Loyalties abruptly give way to shattering betrayals, and love fails repeatedly to transcend the imperatives of sexual longing or personal doubt. Family members and childhood friends face the challenge of finding ways to survive their tortured devotions.

Smiley is especially awed by the psychological power that parents wield over children and by the lifelong contortions such influence can assume. Parental tyrants of both genders surface in her fiction: the matriarchal rigidities of Kate Karlson in *Barn Blind* prove as catastrophic as the patriarchal violations of Larry Cook in *A Thousand Acres*. Such parents assume the right to full ownership of their offspring, a will to power that is the primal transgression in Smiley's world and that prompts usurpation in other areas of life beyond the personal. By linking the subordination of children and the conquest of nature, for example, Smiley details the ecological as well as human costs of overweening egotism and the lust for dominance it promotes.

Although Smiley's protagonists range broadly in age (from the adolescent boys whose perspectives appear in *Barn Blind* to the Vietnam veteran who offers his story in *Good Will* to the septuagenarian grandmother whose consciousness dominates *In Paradise Gate*), the sensibility that most consistently colors her fiction is the middle-aged voice of adult experience ruefully taking stock of its shattered illusions and discovering its potential for compromise and negotiation. It is the absolutist who appears most shallow in Smiley's work, for refusing to admit that maturity demands a willingness to settle for less than one once imagined as one's due. At the end of Smiley's murder mystery *Duplicate Keys*, protagonist Alice Ellis romanticizes the elderly parents and grandparents she has left behind in Minnesota for a life in New York City, speculating that "Her relatives seemed actually to have learned something in their long existences. . . . They had not been battered by random events into numbness. . . ." Yet Rachel Kinsella, the fifty-two-year-old Iowa accountant who narrates *Ordinary Love*, emphasizes a far less confident discovery: "I have learned over the last twenty years to embrace the possible and not mourn the rest." After decades of self-scrutiny, Rachel cannot explain why her life has taken its particular shape: "However my life looks to others, what it looks like to me is a child's tower of blocks, built in ignorance and without a plan."

In that sense, Smiley's medieval studies, given fictional expression in *The Greenlanders*, provide an illuminating gloss on her rendering of the human condition, for hers is a tragic and incomprehensible universe. Nothing is surer than the steady turn of the wheel of fortune that insistently exposes the transitoriness of all earthly pursuits; prosperity, power, fame, and pleasure all prove ephemeral under the yoke of human mortality. Within that context, the misery that human beings inflict upon themselves and others through weaknesses they cannot conquer proves enormous: Violence, sexual betrayal, greed, and envy continually disrupt the most strenuous efforts to create social harmony, and even love proves as likely to destroy as to create. In confronting such a world, however, Smiley eschews the absurdist self-mockery associated with the high modernism she once hoped to emulate. Her most admirable characters are those who, despite their limitations and failures, stumble toward a personal vision of moral responsibility and communal obligation that both enables their survival and dignifies their self-awareness. The medieval and the existential thus fuse in Smiley's imagination to create characters who stoically confront their griefs. Her perspective draws her, philosophically as well as temperamentally, to Midwesterners and medieval Scandinavians as peoples remarkably similar in their ability to absorb disaster, commit themselves to the burdens of daily labor, and engage in serious moral examination of their lives.

Smiley's feminism explains her attention to the nature of power and the hierarchical valuations it encourages within social structures ranging from the family to the state. Her novels capture the inner lives of women whose subjectivity has often been assumed nonexistent simply because it has been hidden or obscured. In giving these women voice, Smiley dissects the platitudes about women's nature that obstruct their ability to see themselves clearly and live authentically. She also challenges sentimental equations of sexual desire and romantic love, creating decent women who learn to their dismay how easily the two may be separated.

Smiley's most significant feminist insight lies in her insistence that women take themselves seriously as moral beings responsible for their own self-definition. She exposes the attitudes and social structures that encourage women toward economic, emotional and societal dependency and critiques the wider consequences of patriarchal assumptions: "Women, just like nature or the land, have been seen as something to be used. . . . Feminists insist that women have intrinsic value, just as environmentalists believe that nature has its own worth, independent of its use to man." Yet she does not create idealized feminist saints; her women include shrews, tyrants, wallflowers, apologists, and airheads along with solid matriarchal earth mothers. The result is as rich a collection of female personalities as exists in contemporary fiction.

THE AGE OF GRIEF

First published: 1987
Type of work: Short stories

Young adults, confronting the impossible expectations surrounding love, marriage, and family, discover the compromises necessary to sustain those relationships.

The Age of Grief, a collection of short fiction, presents a wide array of characters battling for and against emotional commitment as adults shocked to find themselves inhabiting their parents' roles. The five stories examine family life through characters on the periphery of domesticity. Because the female protagonists in "Lily" and "The Pleasure of Her Company," admire a marital realm they observe only from a distance, both prove unprepared for the disruptions that ensue. Their limited insight into the potential for upheaval within human relationships results in part from the absence of such entanglements in their own lives. Lily's emotional "virginity" permits her the freedom to write but also leads her to meddle unwittingly in a marriage whose compromises she has overlooked. Florence, in "The Pleasure of Her Company," witnesses the dissolution of an "ideal" marriage but finally rejects the cynic's conclusion that love is a delusion, pursuing her own blossoming love affair with the realist's admonition that "it's worth finding out for yourself."

Smiley also caricatures those who orchestrate their emotional lives with the same professional calculation they apply to their stock portfolios, as with the female letter-writer of "Jeffrey, Believe Me." The protagonist is so intent on bearing a child before she is too old that she seduces a gay male friend and willfully resists personal responsibility for the other human beings she is exploiting. The male protagonist of "Long Distance" offers an alternative response to such narcissism: His Christmas odyssey to join his brothers for the holidays prompts a reassessment of his callousness toward a Japanese woman with whom he has had an affair. Never having acknowledged the continual negotiations at the heart of family life, he now sees the moral bankruptcy in his self-serving behavior.

In "Dynamite," a woman in early middle age is torn by conflicting impulses about integrating her past lives. A radical political activist in the 1960's, Sandy has lived underground for the past twenty years. Even as she yearns to recover ties with a mother she has never truly known, she restlessly yearns "to do the most unthought-of thing, the itch to destroy what is made—the firm shape of life, whether unhappy, as it was, or happy, as it is now." Memory and fantasy weave an elaborate web of longing in her that prompts wild behavior swings and punctures the bourgeois stability that she seems, superficially, to covet. Sandy's paradoxes defy taming and make her representative of the struggle against self that is typical of Smiley's protagonists.

The volume's title novella depicts a family crisis in which a laboriously constructed normality is upset from within its own preserves. The story is told in the first person by David Hurst, guardian of that normality: Father of three young daughters and a successful dentist, he sees his carefully balanced world collapse when his wife and professional partner Dana falls suddenly in love with another man. David struggles with how to handle his knowledge of the affair and chooses to remain silent even as it intrudes into every facet of his life. The family moves to the edge of dissolution as Dana's obsession keeps her away from home for twenty-four hours. When she finally reappears, she and David agree not to discuss what has led her to relinquish her lover and cautiously resume their marriage. With a generosity of spirit—or failure of will—steeped in profound sadness, David describes his midlife experiences as "the same cup of pain that every mortal drinks from."

ORDINARY LOVE AND GOOD WILL

First published: 1989
Type of work: Novellas

The loss of parental illusions about one's control over the family circle sparks the dubious consolation of witnessing one's children fall from innocence—and into humanity.

By placing a mother's story alongside a father's story in this volume, Smiley experiments with the differing narrative rhythms she associates with gender. The first-person narrator of *Ordinary Love*, a fifty-two-year-old Iowan who is the divorced mother of five grown children, typifies Smiley's clear-eyed defiance of sentimental pieties about the heartland matriarch. Rachel Kinsella's story, matter-of-factly told in a voice at once stoic and unrepentant, involves the jarring incompatibility of having proudly borne five babies in five years while married to a doting, ambitious doctor, then initiating an adulterous love affair that ruptured the family idyll so completely that even her identical twin sons were separated in ensuing custody battles. Rachel's history, an arc of emotional devastation and recovery, leads her in middle age to a maturity brought into being out of wildness, grief, and tenacity.

The novella's more immediate drama involves Rachel's effort to manage the return of one twin son, Michael, from a two-year stint in India as a teacher. In a family in which each separation reprises the traumatic earlier severance of mother from child, sibling from sibling, Michael's personal transformation overseas again exposes the instability of even the most basic human ties. Within this charged atmosphere, a series of confidences unfolds. Rachel tells her children for the first time about the love affair that disrupted their lives; her elder daughter Ellen retaliates with a description of their subsequent neglect by an irresponsible father; Michael reveals his destructive liaison with a married woman. Meditating on these secrets, Rachel concedes that the real fruit of such knowledge lies not simply in one's own suffering but in learning one's potential to inflict suffering on others, especially those one holds most dear. Rachel confronts the fact that she cannot spare her children the heart's perverse and unrelenting hunger for what it cannot have, a lesson she herself taught them years ago.

Good Will also demonstrates Smiley's talent for capturing the daily struggles for psychological control underlying the surfaces of family life. The first-person narrator is Bob Miller, a Vietnam veteran who has systematically created a world for his nuclear family that seems to exist virtually independent of mainstream American society. The novella opens eighteen years into his counterculture experiment, just as the rearing of the son he and his wife Liz thought had completed their idyll begins instead to destroy their insularity.

Bob's considerable talents with his hands provide the means to craft an economic self-sufficiency that is grounded in a moral code repudiating the empty materialism of American culture. Yet his virtues slip over into dogmatism, as he uses his ingenuity to keep his loved ones within the range of his own imagination and authority. Ironically, the discord within Bob's self-willed paradise comes from the very people he believes to be his allies. In joining a fundamentalist religious congregation, Liz betrays a spiritual longing that she cannot satisfy through marriage. More sinister, and ultimately more disastrous, is the racist hostility conceived by their seven-year-old son Tommy for an African American schoolmate whose affluent home life focuses the boy's rage at his own marginality. His destructiveness forces his parents to confront their arrogance in assuming the right, much less the power, to control Tommy's responses to the world. To his surprise, Bob finds himself mimicking his son's emotional conflicts; Lydia Harris, the mother of Tommy's victim, proves a similar challenge to his professed allegiances, with her university professorship, her elegant decorating sense, and her acceptance of life's ambiguities (her field of study is, suggestively, probability). Like Tommy, Bob struggles with the shock of seeing the limitations of his own meager existence so baldly exposed.

Miller is equally humbled by his inability to curtail the steadily escalating violence of Tommy's behavior, and his failure compels ever tighter relationships with the community from which he has so aggressively sought to distance himself. The real target of Tommy's hostility, of course, is the father who has isolated him from the world of his peers and has refused him his own choices, and the boy sets in motion a grim social services machinery that slowly strips the Millers of their hard-won autonomy. Insurance demands for reparations force the sale of their homestead and convert both adults into wage-earners struggling to keep up with the expenses of apartment living. All three family members enter therapy, and the adults face the threat of further legal action for the "recklessness" that led them to cut themselves off from the networks that might have intervened to save Tommy. As the story ends, Bob concedes the futility of his effort to build a world that would keep the incoherence of human life at bay: "Let us have fragments, I say . . . and remember the vast, inhuman peace of the stars pouring across the night sky above the valley. . . ." Whether Bob will find the inner resources to withstand the life before him is unclear, but he will no longer evade the grinding truth of Eden's evanescence or his own role as the worm at the heart of that dream.

A THOUSAND ACRES

First published: 1991
Type of work: Novel

The vagaries of a Midwestern patriarch upend a tenuous familial equilibrium to destroy its material and spiritual moorings.

If Bob Miller must come to terms with his desire for control and the damage it wreaks, Larry Cook, the patriarch who sets in motion the tragedy of *A Thousand Acres*, reflects his opposite number: a man whose stunted interior life crashes in upon him as his family grapples with the emotional devastation he has unleashed, past and present. The third-generation heir to a homestead begun in 1890 and steadily expanded to the largest farm in the area, Cook decides suddenly to retire and to form a corporation of his land, with his three daughters and sons-in-law as stockholders. The parallels to Shakespeare's *King Lear* are obvious, with an important difference: While the play explores the failure of filial responsibility in the face of its protagonist's moral blindness and aligns itself ultimately with the sufferings of Lear and his youngest child Cordelia, Smiley emphasizes the parental betrayal of children and tells the tale through the first-person perspective of the eldest daughter, Ginny. (The names of the Cook family principals echo those of the characters in the play: Larry/Lear; Ginny/Goneril; Rose/Regan; Caroline/Cordelia.) As Smiley explains, "I never bought the conventional interpretation that Goneril and Regan were completely evil. Unconsciously at first, I had reservations: this is not the whole story."

True to form, she sets her revisionist *King Lear* in the Midwest, a transposition allowing her to complement medieval notions of the rise and fall of kings with American assumptions of prosperity as the just reward for lifelong diligence and skill. The wheel of fortune thus meets the American Dream to produce a forceful indictment of the hubris informing American privilege. Larry's willful acquisition of the land (in some cases through the business failures of neighbors) is an extension of the frontier mission of conquering the wilderness and nature itself, a mission furthered by aggressive farming methods meant to manage nature's force. Patriarchal egotism prompts a domination of children and landscape against which the narrative's violent backlash occurs. Ginny's retrospective commentary expresses her desire to learn exactly how the spring of tragic machinery has been released, as well as what role she herself has played in the ensuing disaster.

Larry's decision about the farm elicits mixed responses from the extended family. For questioning his wisdom in the matter, Caroline is abruptly cut out of the picture, while her sisters' husbands leap at the chance to move into the forefront of the farm's management, and Rose sees herself as finally rewarded for years of inarticulated grievance. Ginny is initially torn among these responses, her usual efforts to placate and mediate eroded by her husband Ty's excitement and her own surfacing resentments. For his part, Larry does not foresee the deflation of purpose he will suffer upon relinquishing his primacy within the household, and in the disorientation that overtakes him, he becomes increasingly eccentric and difficult. Following a confrontation with Rose and Ginny in which he speaks his sexually charged loathing for both, he rushes off into a violent summer storm. Larry's deterioration galvanizes Caroline to return to his side, but her self-serving righteousness and dismissal of her sisters' perspective makes her appear far less noble than Shakespeare's Cordelia—at least through Ginny's eyes.

Within Rose and Ginny's households, each marriage also deteriorates, in part because of the disequilibrium introduced into their lives by Larry's action, but also because of the sexually charged intrusion of a returning neighbor, Jess Clark. Based on the Gloucester subplot within *King Lear*, Harold Clark manipulates the filial loyalties of his two sons, one dutiful and dull, the other a daring rebel. Returning home to make his peace with his father and seduced by the possibility of applying his organic farming ideas to the family homestead, the prodigal son not only threatens his brother's expected patrimony but also exploits the emotional hungers of Ginny and Rose, becoming the lover of first one and then the other sister. Like *King Lear*'s Edmund, Jess exacerbates the disorder set in motion by patriarchal tyranny and provides yet another locus of male exploitation within the novel. Jess's distrust of his father hardens when Harold publicly repudiates his younger son and mocks his ambitions, which he has cynically manipulated. He is in turn punished for his arrogance and cruelty with a blinding as gruesome as its Shakespearean model. Jess proves as destructive a presence as Larry himself, for he undermines both sisters' marriages, fuels the suicidal despair that kills one husband, and ruptures the bond between Ginny and Rose that has sustained each through a lifetime of crisis.

Rose eventually explains that her hatred of her father derives from his repeated incestual bedding of her years earlier; Ginny, too, unearths memories of her own violation and is flooded with crushing and conflicted emotion. Ironically, it is Rose's determination to see Larry confront the magnitude of his sin that feeds her vindictiveness toward him, a vindictiveness that only accelerates the spectacle of his descent— and escape—into madness. Forgiveness lies outside Rose's ken—grace evades her as it did her father, and before the book ends her previous cancer has recurred; she dies a wasting death and leaves two more motherless daughters for Ginny to raise. The homestead disappears, cannibalized by debt, the family enterprise played out.

Smiley does not, however, privilege the supposedly faithful daughter. Caroline's suit to restore her father's legal control of the farm fails, and the judge sternly rebukes her for bringing a case without legal merit. Having been preserved from the knowledge of her father's transgressions, her ignorance precludes her claims to wisdom. Nor can Caroline take comfort in her father's doting upon her; the whimsy of a madman, it exposes his confused inability to distinguish his three children from one another. He dies without even being able to recognize them.

Ginny is accorded the last word. She ends the novel living an almost anonymous life as a waitress in St. Paul and responding to the teenage angst of the nieces who now live with her—motherhood at last, but with its burdens far more real than its joys. Trying to heal and achieve some measure of self-respect, she hones a keener self-awareness than had been hers in the past. In this tragedy, then, it is not the patriarch who comes to wisdom but his orphaned eldest child, who finds herself not exactly capable of forgiveness but willing to imagine herself into the psyche of her victimizer. Such a leap of understanding appears the best that grace allows in a fallen world.

Summary

Jane Smiley's true subject as a writer involves the adult crises produced by the destructive nature of human desire and the enormous emotional power, for good and ill, of each member within the family network. In making the American family her focus, she illustrates how that bedrock institution of middle-class faith in the future actually encompasses its own antithesis: the paralyzing grip of the past; the capacities for selflessness, self-love, and betrayal within the same individual; and the terrible grief attendant upon all experiences of love.

Bibliography

Bernays, Anne. "Toward More Perfect Unions." Review of *The Age of Grief*, by Jane Smiley. *The New York Times Book Review*, September 6, 1987, 12.

Carlson, Ron. "King Lear in Zebulon County." Review of *A Thousand Acres*, by Jane Smiley. *The New York Times Book Review*, November 3, 1991, 12.

Humphreys, Josephine. "Perfect Family Self-Destructs." Review of *Ordinary Love and Good Will*, by Jane Smiley. *The New York Times Book Review*, November 5, 1989, 1, 45.

Klinkenborg, Verlyn. "News from the Norse." Review of *The Greenlanders*, by Jane Smiley. *The New Republic* 198 (May 16, 1988): 36-39.

Leavitt, David. "Of Harm's Way and Farm Ways." *Mother Jones* 14 (December, 1989): 44-45.

Smiley, Jane. "Fiction in Review." *The Yale Review* 81 (January, 1993): 148-161.

———. "Imposing Values." *The New York Times Magazine*, September 20, 1992, 28-29.

Barbara Kitt Seidman

CATHY SONG

Born: Honolulu, Hawaii
1955

Principal Literary Achievement
The winner of the prestigious Yale Series of Younger Poets Award in 1982, Song has made a major breakthrough for Asian American poetry.

Biography

Cathy Song was born in 1955 to a Korean American father and a Chinese American mother in Honolulu, Hawaii. She grew up in Wahiawa, a small town on the island of Oahu that serves as the setting for many of her poems. Because her ancestral roots can be traced to both China and Korea—the two countries where her maternal and paternal grandparents originated—and because she as spent most of her life in Hawaii, Song has at times been identified as a Hawaiian poet; at other times, she has been called either a Korean American or Chinese American poet, though in fact the three aspects of her heritage are essentially indivisible.

As a child, Song exercised her creative energy in what she later called the "pure fantasy" and "dream wishes" of fiction (her first story, written at the age of eleven, is a spy novel), romance (short stories about "beautiful blonde heroines on summer vacations"), and make-believe journalism ("imaginary interviews with movie stars"). After her schooling in Hawaii, when Song had left the University of Hawaii for Wellesley College in Massachusetts, her talent in poetry began to blossom. While attending Wellesley, she came across the book *Georgia O'Keeffe* (1976), written by O'Keeffe herself, which so deeply impressed Song that it inspired her to write an entire sequence of poems (loosely known as the "O'Keeffe poems").

After receiving her B.A. from Wellesley in 1977, Song went on to study creative writing at Boston University, where she received an M.A. in 1981. She also attended the Advanced Poetry Workshop conducted by Kathleen Spivak, who offered suggestions on the divisions and subtitles of her first book manuscript. The manuscript, *Picture Bride*, which collects poems formerly published in journals and anthologies such as *Bamboo Ridge*, *The Greenfield Review* and *Hawaii Review*, was selected by the poet Richard Hugo from among 625 manuscripts as the winner of the 1982 Yale Series of Younger Poets competition, and was published by Yale University Press as Volume 78 of the series in 1983. The series, which had once featured poets such as

Adrienne Rich and John Ashbery, brought Song to prominence. The book was nominated for the National Book Critics Circle Award. Song's second collection of poems, *Frameless Windows, Squares of Light*, was published by W. W. Norton in 1988. Since then, she has also published a number of uncollected poems in *Poetry* magazine, which awarded her the Frederick Bock Prize. Song's poetry has been widely anthologized in such volumes as *Breaking the Silence: An Anthology of Contemporary American Poets* (1983), *The Norton Anthology of Modern Poetry* (2d edition, 1988), *The Norton Anthology of American Literature* (3d edition, 1989), *The Heath Anthology of American Literature* (1990), and *The Open Boat: Poems from Asian America* (1993). She is also the coeditor (with Juliet S. Kono) of *Sister Stew: Fiction and Poetry by Women* (1991).

Song has taught creative writing at various universities on the U.S. mainland and in Hawaii, where she maintains a permanent home. She is married to Douglass Davenport, a doctor, and has a son and a daughter.

Analysis

Cathy Song's poetry general deals with her personal experience as a woman with family roots in Hawaii and with ancestral and kinship ties to Korea and China. Although her subject matters revolve around regional, ethnic, and private experiences, they are expressed in idioms evidently inseparable from her formal training in Western culture. Her interest in art also comes through unmistakably in the visual qualities of her poems, especially in those inspired by family photographs, paintings by O'Keeffe, and eighteenth century Japanese artist Kitagawa Utamaro's prints. In her poetry, Song often affectionately thematizes about family ties by providing portraits of and stories about family members in language that is both contemplative and dramatic and retrospective and prospective, moving freely between past and present and between observation and speculation. Because her memory of the past often merges with the reality of the present as if the two were indivisible, there is a lively immediacy to her poems. Many of her poems employ the second-person pronoun, thus simulating a conversational style, which in turn is characterized by frequent understatements. Deceptively prosaic at times, her language has in store delightful surprises of images and a variety of emotions ranging from sadness to humor. Initially, readers such as Richard Hugo tended to see Song's poems as "flowers—colorful, sensual and quiet— offered almost shyly as bouquets." In his 1986 review of *Picture Bride*, however, Stephen Sumida cautioned that "Song's poems seem especially liable to being appreciated or criticized for the wrong reasons" and suggested that her work deserves an alternative approach.

Although Cathy Song is one of the most visible of Asian American poets, her poetry, curiously, has not generated critical attention and acclaim proportionate to her phenomenal emergence as a member of the Yale Series of Younger Poets and her inclusion in prestigious anthologies. *Picture Bride* attracted a handful of reviews, and her second book, *Frameless Windows, Squares of Light*, though published by a commercial publisher, received hardly more than a couple. Furthermore, the few reviews that did appear, though positive, are somewhat reserved about the merits of Song's work. The mixed reception of her poetry may have resulted from the small readership of poetry in general and of Asian American poetry in particular, or from the fact that Song's output has been rather modest. A significant factor affecting her reception, however, appears to be that Song, despite (and because of) her initial success, has been faced with the same predicament by which most Asian American writers are plagued: to explore their ethnicity explicitly often subjects them to risks of exoticism (if the ethnic experience is noticed) or marginality (when such experience is assumed to be beneath notice). As Song warily put it in a 1983 interview, "I'll have to try not to write about the Asian-American theme," although such a focus is "a way of exploring the past." Song's statement is essentially a reflection on the artificial dilemma, between ethnicity ("Asian") and the mainstream ("American") culture, that is deeply ingrained in the literature of the United States. As a poet, Song deserves special attention for her struggle to bridge the hiatus—not so much by circumventing ethnicity as by concentrating on her personal experience as a woman. This effort is reflected in the introduction to *Sister Stew*, where she and coeditor Juliet S. Kono proclaim the primacy of women's experience and assert the plenitude of women's voices. This introduction, in retrospect, could also serve as an introduction to Song as "a poet who happens to be Asian American."

The effort to bridge the hiatus discussed above is already evident in the textual history of Song's *Picture Bride*, a collection of thirty-one poems covering a range of topics including family history, life in Hawaii, childhood memories, sibling relationships, love, art, character studies, ethnic experience, and the quest of the self. The book is organized according to two interrelated frameworks or principles. To take the title poem as the focal text, the book is apparently a collection of poems structured around the immigration and assimilation experience of the Song family, beginning with the arrival of her Korean grandparents—the grandmother in particular. Seen from this perspective, the book is essentially autobiographical in nature, with the poems serving as miniature memoirs and chronicles of the family's history and as memories of parents, relatives, and siblings. It is important to note, however, that such an ethnicized principle of organization was not Song's idea but her publishers'.

Even as it stands, the book, which Song originally intended to be entitled *From the White Place*, also incorporates another framework of organization. This framework is derived from a five-part sequence, "Blue and White Lines After O'Keeffe," a poem placed at the center of the collection. The subtitles of the volume's five divisions ("Black Iris," "Sunflower," "Orchids," "Red Poppy," and "The White Trumpet"), which were suggested to Song by Kathleen Spivak, in fact come from this strategically positioned text. Used as a structuring device, these subtitles imply that the book can be perceived as a poet's attempt, by way of visual art (the work of O'Keeffe and Kitagawa Utamaro), to fashion personal experience into esthetic experience and thereby define her vision as an artistic one. Reading the book according to this framework tends to deemphasize the ethnic elements of the poems, but the risk of viewing the book as an ethnographic document is also reduced. Such an artist's framework is not without its problems, since it poses the danger of diminishing the peculiarity of Song's experience and her voice. Taken alone, neither of the two frameworks is entirely satisfactory, but as Fujita-Sato explains, "What results . . . from the interlocked frameworks provided by the book's title and sections titles, is a structure embodying synthesis." Corresponding to this synthesis, Fujita-Sato proposes, is the technique of "singing shapes" derived from O'Keeffe's paintings, by which two often dissimilar objects are juxtaposed and become mutually illuminated and transformed into "a fluid shaping and reshaping of energy."

The motivation toward synthesis in *Picture Bride* is further developed in *Frameless Windows, Squares of Light* in which Song concentrates on personal experiences in various stages of her life as a daughter, sister, wife, mother, and Hawaiian and Asian American woman. In this collection, her voice as a poet who is not only a woman but also an artist also matures. The volume consists of twenty-six poems and is divided into four parts ("The Window and the Field," "A Small Light," "Shadow Figures," and "Frameless Windows, Squares of Light") that are named after the title poems of each section. The organization recalls but transcends that of *Picture Bride*; the esthetic rendition of personal experience no longer relies on the appeal of ethnic elements or the authority of another artist, but rather disseminates from the play and interplay of framed and frameless blocks and touches of light and shadow—vignettes of life as lived. The higher level of unity in this second collection also stems from Song's rather unique technique—related to that of "singing shapes"—of juxtaposing and transposing (or compressing) different segments of time, in the manner a telescope is collapsed or expanded, so that memories of the past and realities of the present merge into one another. For example, she shows how what happened to herself and her brother as children in the past would recur, with variations, in the present when she looks upon her son and daughter growing up. This unique approach to experience, by which the personal is merged with the familial and the mundane is elevated to the esthetic, suggests that Song's attempt to bridge the hiatus, and hence resolve the dilemma confronting Asian American writers, is in fact feasible.

PICTURE BRIDE

First published: 1983
Type of work: Poems

A young woman leaves Korea to marry a sugarcane field laborer in Hawaii.

"Picture Bride," the title poem with which Song's volume of the same title begins, serves as the seminal text of the collection, in a way defining the thematic direction of the book. In this poem, the poetic persona, aged twenty-four, attempts to imagine what it was like for her maternal grandmother, at the age of twenty-three, to leave Korea for Hawaii to marry a laborer thirteen years her senior, a man she has never seen before. The entire poem, except for the first three lines, consists of a series of questions intended to re-create not only the scenes of the departure, the journey, and the arrival, but also the psychology and emotions of the picture bride throughout the process. The concluding question, which speculates on how willing she might have been with regard to her conjugal obligation ("did she politely untie/ the silk bow of her jacket,/ her tent-shaped dress"), focuses an entire economic and sociohistorical phenomenon onto the question of sexuality, making the poem linger on a moment of truth in human terms. This ability to crystalize the general into the personal is characteristic of Song's poetry.

The figure of the picture bride serves as a muse of sorts for the poet, in part because the questions raised in "Picture Bride" are either answered or contextualized in the volume's other poems. For example, in "Untouched Photograph of Passenger," Song contemplates the picture of a man dressed in a poorly tailored suit who is gazing into the camera; she observes, "Rinsing through his eyes/ and dissolving all around him/ is sunlight on water." The portrait is likely of the bride's grandfather, and the poem captures the optimism with which the emigrant embraces the promise of a foreign land. The other poems in the volume, which loosely chronicle the proliferation of the first generation through two more generations, can be regarded as indirect answers to the question of sexuality raised in "Picture Bride." As an older woman the bride jokes about her extraordinarily big breasts, which the poet describes as being like "walruses" and imagines to have been sucked by "six children and an old man"; the breasts are symbols of the bride's fecundity. Always keeping her focus on the personal dimension, when Song finally writes about the death of the grandmother in "Blue Lantern," she makes it clear that what matters in the picture bride phenomenon is, ultimately, the human element. Prearranged marriages and love are not mutually exclusive under certain circumstances, as is evident from the grandfather's mourning: "He played for her each night;/ her absence,/ the shape of his grief/ funneled through the bamboo flute."

A PALE ARRANGEMENT OF HANDS

First published: 1983
Type of work: Poem

The poet pays tribute to her mother by way of recollections of childhood.

"A Pale Arrangement of Hands," also from *Picture Bride*, begins with the poet sitting at the kitchen table listening to the all-night rain. Seeing her own hands on the table, she remembers her mother's hands, which always seemed nervous "except when they were busy cooking": "Her hands would assume a certain confidence/ then, as she rubbed and patted butter/ all over a turkey as though/ she were soaping and scrubbing up a baby." The poet further recalls that her mother used to describe the rain in Hawaii as "liquid sunshine" to her three children. Further associations bring back memories of the mother applying lipstick; the poet remembers the mother using her discarded tissues for a surprising purpose during rainy afternoons when the children were idle: She shows them "how to make artificial carnations . . . with a couple of hairpins." As the memory unfolds, many more mundane but fond episodes emerge. By detours, the poet's memories begin to reel back to the present, concluding with one more memory—of the children's habitual refusal to take a nap in the afternoon, which for the mother was the longest part of the day: "Sleep meant pretending. Lying still/ but alert, I listened from the next room/ as my mother slipped out of her damp dress./ The cloth crumpling onto the bathroom floor/ made a light, sad sound."

Although the poem appears to be unstructured and plain, and although the moments captured are mundane, Song's ability to re-create the vivid and even noisy scenes of childhood is unmistakable. The poem also exemplifies Song's favorite device of bringing the past and the present together. More important, however, "A Pale Arrangement of Hands" is a good example of what Song and Juliet S. Kono have characterized as women writers' voices. The mother in the poem is not deified, but the poet, through negotiations between her subjectivity and her subject matter, has given an ordinary mother a voice—a tribute to women who have most of the time been silent. The poem "The Seamstress," from the same book, can also be interpreted from a similar perspective, as can "Humble Jar" from *Frameless Windows, Squares of Light*, a poem occasioned by the memory of an assortment of buttons that the mother kept in a jar.

HEAVEN

First published: 1988
Type of work: Poem

A mother ponders the significance of her son's childish ideas about an afterlife.

"Heaven" appears toward the end of *Frameless Windows, Squares of Light*. By this time, the poet has already married and is the mother of a son and a daughter. The son, who has blond hair (which comes from his father), "thinks when we die we'll go to China," causing the mother to pause at the thought of "a Chinese heaven." The poet further imagines how her son's hand "must span like a bridge/ to reach it." She continues to wonder how such an idea could occur to her son, since even she herself has never seen China. As the question of identity and ethnicity is pressed, the poet's thoughts are rerouted to a historical time when a boy in Southern China started his long journey to America to make a living at the gold mines and the railroad, indefinitely prolonging his stay. Switching back to the present, the poet muses that "It must be in the blood,/ this notion of returning./ It skipped two generations, lay fallow,/ the garden an unmarked grave." This realization, triggered by the innocent thoughts of a child, leads the poet to call to the children to look to where "we can see the mountains/ shimmering blue above the air."

Although one of the themes in "Heaven" is innocence, this poem obviously contradicts Song's earlier statement that she would try not to write on the Asian American theme. Her observation that "it must be in the blood" can be seen as a bold correction of that earlier declaration. The question of returning to China is a symbolic rather than a practical concern, especially after an entire generation of Asian American writers has worked furiously to establish the legitimacy of Asian Americans as Americans. Yet the poem raises a fundamental issue about the nature of Song's poetry in particular and American literature in general: To what extent is it possible, or desirable, to purge the American experience of ethnicity? Song's return to this issue is an important signal because, unlike her earlier, mostly retrospective treatments of the Asian American experience, "Heaven" involves a future generation and is forward-looking. The fact that Song can raise such a controversial issue at all intimates the arrival of another stage in the Asian American writer's search for identity.

Summary

Cathy Song's struggle to be heard as a poet is tied to her experience as a woman with multiple cultural backgrounds. Her exploration of subject matters related to immigrants, family history, generational ties, Hawaiian culture, and personal visions of life and art is an integral part of the American experience. Confronted with the gulf between ethnic and mainstream cultures, Song has worked toward bridging the gap with creative means informed by her artistic sensibility. Her unfaltering interest in the primacy of the human and the personal, especially from the perspective of women without voices, is a distinct and dominant trait of her poetry.

Bibliography

Fujita-Sato, Gayle K. "'Third World' as Place and Paradigm in Cathy Song's *Picture Bride*." *MELUS* 15, no. 1 (Spring, 1988): 49-72.

Hugo, Richard. Foreword to *Picture Bride*, by Cathy Song. New Haven, Conn.: Yale University Press, 1983.

Lim, Shirley. Review of *Picture Bride*, by Cathy Song. *MELUS* 10, no. 3 (Fall, 1983): 95-99.

Song, Cathy, and Juliet S. Kono. Introduction to *Sister Stew: Fiction and Poetry by Women*. Honolulu: Bamboo Ridge Press, 1991.

Wallace, Patricia. "Divided Loyalties: Literal and Literary in the Poetry of Lorna Dee Cervantes, Cathy Song, and Rita Dove." *MELUS* 18, no. 3 (Fall, 1993): 3-19.

Balance Chow

GARY SOTO

Born: Fresno, California
April 12, 1952

Principal Literary Achievement
Soto was one of the first writers to capture the life and labor of the impoverished Chicanos in the streets and fields of California.

Biography

Gary Soto was born on April 12, 1952, in Fresno, California. His parents were Mexican American, and Soto was born into not only a Chicano culture but also a culture of poverty. His father died in 1957, when Gary was only five years old; this created economic hardship for a family that was already having difficulties.

Soto went to school in the Fresno area, and he worked in the fields as an agricultural laborer and as a low-paid factory worker, the inevitable lot of so many in his situation. He entered Fresno City College in 1970; when he started college, he was a geography major, but he switched to English when he entered California State University at Fresno. At that institution, he studied under Philip Levine, a noted American poet. Levine taught him how to read a poem, and he helped Soto to form a style and develop his craft as a poet. Soto was graduated magna cum laude from Fresno State in 1974, and he spent the next two years as a graduate student at the University of California at Irvine. He received an MFA in creative writing from Irvine in 1976. He also published a number of poems in important journals and began making his reputation as a poet. A poet needs to make a living, however, and Soto began to teach in the English and Chicano Studies departments at the University of California at Berkeley. In 1975, he married Carolyn Oda, whose father owned a small farm in the Fresno area. The couple had one daughter and settled in Northern California near the Berkeley campus, where Soto became an associate professor.

In 1974, Soto published his first book of poetry, *The Elements of San Joaquin*. It is an ambitious book that attempts to describe and classify the harsh world of migrant workers and other poor people in Central California. Those workers are portrayed as stoically enduring the hostility or indifference of the Anglo establishment and the apparently malign power of a fierce nature. In 1975, Soto was awarded the Academy of American Poets Prize. In 1977, *Poetry* magazine, the most prestigious journal in the field of poetry, awarded Soto the Bess Hopkins Prize.

Soto's second book of poetry, *The Tale of Sunlight* (1978), represented an expansion of his subject matter and vision. In 1979, he received a Guggenheim Fellowship, and he spent 1979 and 1980 in Mexico City observing the culture and writing.

In 1981, Soto published *Where Sparrows Work Hard*. These poems are, for the most part, autobiographical pieces that give some distance to pure memoir by the use of irony, especially in the resolution of the poems' structure.

Soto was granted a National Education Association Fellowship in 1981, and in 1984 he received the Levinson Award from *Poetry* Magazine. Soto had become one of the most prolific and honored of the young poets of the period. In 1985, another book of his poems, *Black Hair*, was published. It again dealt with childhood experiences and male friendship, but it is filled with forebodings of death.

In 1988, Soto was named Elliston Poet at the University of Cincinnati, and he spent a year in residence there. In 1990, he published his fifth book of poetry, *A Fire in My Hands*, a compilation of poems from the earlier collections. *Who Will Know Us* (1990) represents a new direction. Soto counterpoints his current life as a professor with a wife and daughter in Northern California to his early life as a poor Mexican American child and worker. There are also a number of poems that deal with death, an important and recurrent theme in Soto's work.

Soto wrote three collections of prose that portray the world of his childhood and adolescence. He won the American Book Award in 1985 for *Living Up the Street: Narrative Recollections*. *Small Faces* is a book of short narratives that explore the world of the San Joaquin Valley in a less individual way than Soto's poems do; it focuses on community and friendship as well as on adolescence. *Lesser Evils* (1987), Soto's third collection of prose narratives, also deals with Soto's early experiences. Soto saw his prose as having some of the same concentration and imagery as his poetry, but he said that his real achievement as a writer must be in poetry.

Analysis

Gary Soto is one of the most important voices in Chicano literature. He has memorably portrayed the life, work and joys of the Mexican American agricultural laborer. Furthermore, he has done this with great poetic skill. He has an eye for the telling image in his poetry and prose, and he has the ability to create startling and structurally effective metaphors. Each of his poems has a design. One aspect of that design is his frequent use of an ironic reversal to resolve the poetic structure. His style is concrete and rooted in the language of the fields and the barrio.

There are many significant themes in Soto's poetry. One of the earliest and most persistent is his view of the natural world as a wasteland. Although he uses natural imagery, nature is never benign or pastoral. It is, instead, harsh and unrelenting. It scars those who are nakedly exposed to it from dawn to nightfall. A related theme is Soto's refusal to yield to the temptation to evoke a transcendental view of nature. His heroes are obliterated from that world; they cannot and do not transcend it.

Soto does, however, modulate his bleak view of the human condition when he writes about childhood. That state is filled with a quest for knowledge and experience. In the poem "Chuy," the young speaker may be naïve or mistaken in his idealized love; however, he does manage to pass through his experiences and gain some wisdom, and he does not give in to cynicism. In the later poems, he contrasts the bleak conditions of his childhood with the innocence and privilege of his own daughter. In "Small Town with One Street," for example, he shows his daughter a young boy in Fresno whom he says is an image of himself as a child. The daughter is shocked to see that poor and troubled image of her apparently powerful father. Soto did not alter his pessimistic view of the world as he grew older and prospered. In "The Way Things Work," the speaker inventories the expenses of the day and worries about meeting them. The culture of poverty cannot be overcome by relative affluence; it continues to mark Soto's view of the world, as the wind and dirt marked the workers in the field.

Soto's poetic style is marked by the use of short free-verse lines. There are seldom more than three stresses to a line, and the lines often run on, creating the effect of a rapid flow of images hurrying to reach a final resolving line. He uses occasional metaphors, but his primary poetic device is imagery. The poems are packed with images that follow one another, often creating a structural design. Since the poems deal with the Chicano experience in the field or in the street, the language is always concrete and dense in detail. Soto does not write any long poems; nearly all are short lyrics. If he does expand a poem, he does so by creating a longer poem that has many separate sections.

Soto uses irony consistently in his poems. He seems chary of ending a poem with a positive statement or image. The last few lines often reverse or sardonically comment on what went before. These ironic structures convey his bleak view of a world in which everything passes away, including any sign of the poor inhabitants. Soto is concerned not only with the fact of death but also with whether individuals can leave any sign of their presence on an indifferent universe.

Soto is the poet of the Chicano experience, but his view of that people is not hopeful. He shows their condition to be one of hard work with few rewards. There may be a few isolated moments of joy on the street or in the privacy of the home, but difficult economic conditions make such happiness short-lived. The one positive element in Soto's poetry is his portrayal of his own family, which has escaped the confined and limiting world of manual labor Soto had experienced in Fresno. That family is also a composite, since Soto's wife is a Japanese American. The family scenes he creates are tender and hopeful.

Soto's prose has many similarities with his poetry. His subject in his prose books is primarily childhood and adolescence. He does not, of course, use the formal devices of poetry in these books, but he does use the same concrete detail and imagery. He often uses the same ironic reversal in many of the short pieces that make up each book. The prose narratives do have more humor than the poems, and they tend to deal more fully with relationships within the Chicano community than the poems do.

THE ELEMENTS OF SAN JOAQUIN

First published: 1977
Type of work: Poem

A catalog of the fierce natural forces that make the lives of workers difficult and unfruitful.

"The Elements of San Joaquin" is a long poem divided into seven sections that together make up the "Elements" of this agricultural workers' world. "Elements" is an interesting word choice, since it has connotations of scientific, objective discourse while the poem is a direct personal statement. "Elements" may also refer to the four classical elements of the universe: earth, air, fire, and water.

The first section of the poem is entitled "Field." The field is described in harsh, naturalistic terms; forces of nature impose their presence and will upon the impoverished workers who work the field. One of these forces, the wind, "sprays dirt into my mouth/ The small, almost invisible scars/ On my hands." The speaker is literally marked by these natural forces; this is not a pastoral communion but a painful union. In the second stanza, there are some positive suggestions, as the speaker's pores "have taken in a seed of dirt of their own." Yet the seed image is ironic, since it is not a seed that will flower or produce anything that will sustain life.

The forces in the field continue making marks upon the speaker as they create "lines/ On my wrists and palms." The last stanza brings together the separate parts of the poem. The speaker is "becoming the valley"; man and nature are, apparently, united. That unity, however, is ironically reversed in the last two lines, when the speaker realizes that the soil "sprouts nothing/ For any of us." The perspective has now widened to include all those who work this land. For them, there is no sustenance to be wrought from the land that they work.

The third section, "Wind," deals with the power of this natural force. The poem presents a human figure waking in the morning beneath a blazing sun. The sky darkens, and a cold wind begins "moving under your skin and already far/ From the small hives of your lungs." Once more, nature is a destructive force. It can burrow under the skin, but it will not bring its life-giving breath to the lungs that need it.

The last section of the poem, "Daybreak," portrays the workers entering an onion field at dawn. They are contrasted to the distant consumer who will literally feed on their labor: "And tears the onions raise/ Do not begin in your eyes but ours," the poet notes. The consumers will not know or see that other world, but the laborers "won't forget what you failed to see, / And nothing will heal / Under the rain's broken fingers." The rain does not give life but only shatters those who are vulnerable to its power. The poem ends with an image of rain that first suggests a flourishing world and then denies it. Soto's poems are rooted in actual experience and not in transcendence.

CHUY

First published: 1979
Type of work: Poem

A portrait of a poor boy who passes from early experiences through the exploration of his world to his oblivion.

"Chuy" is an autobiographical poem that portrays the earliest formative experiences of the speaker. The poem is divided into separate sections and moves from youthful initiation to oblivion.

The first section of "Chuy" presents the young speaker alone in the landscape announcing his presence and causing changes in his environment. For example, both birds' nests and "pocked fruit" drop into his arms. Such fruitfulness, however, contrasts with his poverty. His lunch bag contains only air from his lungs. Chuy then observes the stars, and a voice announces that he is "blessed/ In the name/ Of a violin. . . ." At the end, however, what transforms him is not nature; it is, instead, a sexual initiation with his first "touch of breast." The fullness of this image reverses the emptiness of his impoverished life and the distance of the stars. He has been acted on by nature in the poem, but the touch is both a conscious act and a transforming one.

The fourth section of the poem further deals with a young man's experience with women. This time, however, it is not an actual sexual experience but an idealistic longing that is released by his vision of a "girl/ On a can of peas." He pictures her as the object of a knightly quest; in contrast, he portrays himself as a poor squire whose wrists are "shackled in sores." At the end of this section, Chuy gains what solace he can by using his knife to pop a pea into his mouth. The section thus ends with an ironic reversal: The ideal is driven out, and all that remains are the actual, all-too-literal peas and not the vision.

In the next section, Chuy is seen as an explorer who wonders about the nature of electricity. He unscrews the flashlight to search for answers; he notices that "light bends." He writes in his journal, "Light/ Is only so strong." For a moment, he is portrayed as a hero who seems to be developing into a scientific genius. The ending, however, brings him back to a reduced world: "Chuy wondered what/ He could do after lunch." The discovery that light bends is not sufficient to fill the emptiness of his days. It seems, instead, an isolated experience. There is no outlet to develop that curiosity about the world into the discipline of scientific inquiry.

In the last section, Chuy attempts to discover not only the nature of things but also "why/ He was there." He now sees nature in a poetic rather than a scientific manner; he sees the moon as "a lozenge/ Sucked before sleep." Both light and the moon are seen as natural elements that are vulnerable to change and decay. This foreshadows the end of the poem, in which Chuy buries a leaf and other signs of this existence on the Earth so that extraterrestrial explorers will discover a sign of his presence among the ruins. The poem moves from the emergence of the hero to his destruction; in that destruction, Chuy attempts to leave some sign of his creative search for meaning.

BLACK HAIR

First published: 1985
Type of work: Short story

A tale of a young man's early experiences as a laborer and his attempts to come to terms with that life.

"Black Hair" is a brief autobiographical story that deals with Soto's working experiences. The narrator introduces that theme in the first sentence: "There are two kinds of work: One uses the mind and the other uses muscle." The work that uses muscle is degrading, but it is the only choice the narrator has during the troubled period he is going through. Muscle work is also the only alternative for both the small group of workers with whom Soto comes into contact and the larger group who are condemned to such labor by their race or birth.

The main character is a seventeen-year-old runaway. He takes a romantic swim in the ocean at a Southern California beach, but he must then confront the world of work to survive. He sleeps in abandoned cars and houses and walks miles to Glendale to apply for a job in a tire factory.

The work is exhausting and dirty, and the character has no place to live until he receives his first paycheck. At the tire factory, he is isolated from the black workers by race and the Mexican workers because of his poor Spanish. He is alienated from everyone, without the support that a home supplies, and he must survive with his muscle and what wits he has.

In one scene, the narrator is united with the poor Mexican workers who had spurned him earlier. When immigration authorities make a raid, his boss thinks he is an alien, so he runs with the others. Afterward, those who fled make up outrageous stories about their exploits. For the only time, there is both joy and unity at work. The telling of tales suddenly changes the atmosphere of the factory; it seems to bring the world of the street into the world of work. The spinning of stories also points to the path that Soto was to later take. The work of writing would use, of course, not muscle but mind; that type of work would be joyful and meaningful.

Soto portrays the life of menial labor at the tire factory as dismal and joyless. The work is monotonous and dirty and makes the workers' home life just as empty. Soto asks why they had all arrived at this place, but supplies no answer. He merely gives an image that defines this life: "When you picked up a tire, you were amazed at the black it could give off." The menial and unending work literally marks those caught in it, as the dirt of the San Joaquin Valley marks the farmworkers there. An alternative is suggested by the first sentence of the story: work that "uses the mind." Soto was to take that way, although he continues to write of the life of manual labor that he has escaped. He does not, however, describe mental labor as an alternative in the story. He shows little solidarity with the poor working men; he asks only why these people have reached such a hopeless and degrading state. There is, of course, an understanding of their condition and an implicit sympathy, but Soto does not provide an answer to his own question.

Summary

Gary Soto has chosen as his subject the culture of poverty. He portrays that world without sentimentality; it is a hard and, at times, an inhuman one. Soto has described this world in detailed and memorable images and complex poetic structures. Of special importance to Soto is childhood and adolescence; In Soto's view, childhood shapes people for good or ill. People who develop their imaginations may find a way out of a life of monotonous manual labor and find "the work that uses the mind," which may make for a fuller life.

Bibliography

Addiego, John. "Chicano Poetry: Five New Books." *Northwest Review* 21, no. 1 (1983): 147-158.

Bruce-Novoa, Juan. "Patricide and Resurrection: Gary Soto." In *Chicano Poetry: A Response to Chaos*. Austin: University of Texas Press, 1982.

Candelaria, Cordelia. *Chicano Poetry*. Westport, Conn.: Greenwood Press, 1986.

Cheuse, Alan. "The Voice of the Chicano." *The New York Times Book Review*, October 11, 1981, 15.

Cooley, Peter. "I Can Hear You Now." *Parnassus* 8, no. 1 (1979): 297-311.

De la Fuentes, Patricia. "Mutability and Stasis: Images of Time in Gary Soto's *Black Hair*." *American Review* 16 (1988): 188-197.

Williamson, Alan. "In a Middle Style." *Poetry* 135 (March, 1980): 348-354.

James Sullivan

JEAN STAFFORD

Born: Covina, California
July 1, 1915
Died: White Plains, New York
March 26, 1979

Principal Literary Achievement

The beautifully crafted fiction of Stafford contains sensitive portraits of characters, especially young women and children, who feel alienated from their worlds.

Biography

Jean Wilson Stafford was born in Covina, California, on July 1, 1915, to Ethel McKillop Stafford and John Richard Stafford, a writer of Westerns who had just three years before moved out from Missouri. Unfortunately, in 1920, John sold his ranch, moved to San Diego, and began to play the stock exchange. Within a year, he had lost all the money he had accumulated during his lifetime, including a substantial inheritance from his wealthy father. Stafford next took his family to Colorado, first settling in Colorado Springs, then in Boulder, only to find that the frontier he had imagined, with its limitless opportunities, was gone forever. Although John Stafford did occasionally sell a story, he was never again able to support his family. As she saw her beloved father retreating further and further into bitterness and eccentricity, and her mother seemingly becoming indifferent to everything except her money-making ventures, Jean Stafford developed the sense of alienation that permeates her work.

Although the small university town of "Adams," or Boulder, is shown in Stafford's fiction as a dull, provincial, and intellectually stifling place, it did at least provide Ethel with the economic opportunity she had so desperately sought. She kept the family afloat by running a boardinghouse for students, and though they were poor, her children could live at home, work, and get a college education.

After she entered the University of Colorado in 1932, the beautiful and brilliant Jean found friends both among the professors and the student "barbarians," a group of intellectuals who, like Jean, were too impoverished to join Greek-letter organizations. She also won her first recognition as a writer when her play about the German composer Ludwig van Beethoven won first place in a contest and was performed on campus. Nevertheless, Jean's college years were not untroubled. A medical student

broke off his engagement to her because he needed a wife with better social credentials. More important, when her flamboyant friend Lucy McKee committed suicide, Jean was suspected of being somehow responsible. The resulting scandal probably cost her a Phi Beta Kappa key and caused the elder Staffords to leave Boulder for Oregon.

In 1936, after she was awarded both her bachelor's and her master's degrees, Jean spent a fellowship year at the University of Heidelberg. When she returned to the United States, she went to a writers' conference in Boulder, where she met the young poet Robert Lowell, a member of the famous and wealthy Massachusetts family, who was obviously attracted to her. After a miserable year teaching at a girls' school, Stephens College in Missouri, which she satirized effectively in "Caveat Emptor" (1956), Stafford went to Cambridge, Massachusetts, to be near James Robert Hightower, a longtime friend to whom she had become engaged.

Lowell, however, continued to pursue her, and Stafford continued to find him fascinating. In several ways, their relationship was to prove disastrous. In December, 1938, Lowell, who was drunk, caused a car accident in which Stafford was badly injured. Despite a long hospital stay and excruciatingly painful operations like that which is graphically described in her short story "The Interior Castle" (1946), Stafford was never to look or feel the same again. During her recuperation, she formed the habit of turning to alcohol to alleviate her sufferings; eventually, of course, this addiction would further damage her health and imperil her relationships. The marriage of Lowell and Stafford in 1940 produced still more problems. Stafford submitted to Lowell's religious obsessions and to his emotional and physical abuse; she also remained loyal to him when he was imprisoned for refusing to serve in the armed forces.

Yet she must have been annoyed by the fact that in the academic circles they frequented, she was expected to take a subordinate role because of her gender. Moreover, from the first, the poor girl from the West, who had her own distinguished ancestors, was infuriated by the snobbishness of the Lowell family. The great success of Stafford's first novel, *Boston Adventure* (1944), which satirized the society of which her husband was a part, must have been immensely satisfying to her.

By 1946, the marriage was over. During the next several years, Stafford drank heavily, threatened suicide, and spent time in mental hospitals. Nevertheless, in 1947, she published one of her best novels, *The Mountain Lion*, which was based on her memories of the West. During this period, too, she got to know Katherine White, the fiction editor of *The New Yorker*, who became her friend, her adviser, and her mentor. As a result of this association, over the next thirty years Stafford was to publish some twenty-two short stories in the highly respected magazine.

Although the early 1950's saw Stafford into and out of another marriage, this time to *Life* staff writer Oliver Jensen, they proved to be her most productive years. In 1952, she published an impressive novel, *The Catherine Wheel*, and in 1953 she brought out two collections of her fiction. What ended this creative spurt has been much debated. Certainly, there were problems with alcoholism. Stafford, however, may simply have been too contented to write. At last she had found the perfect man for her, the writer Abbott Joseph ("A.J." or "Joe") Liebling, whom she met in 1956, married in 1959, and lived with happily until his death in 1963. During those years, Stafford published only two children's books and a great many book and film reviews.

After Liebling's death, Stafford was again short of money, and although she disliked teaching, she was forced to accept visiting lectureships and speaking engagements. She also wrote feature articles, reviews, and book introductions. In 1970, she was awarded a Pulitzer Prize for *The Collected Stories of Jean Stafford*, published the preceding year. Yet she was never able to finish a projected autobiographical novel, to be entitled *The Parliament of Women*. During her final years, Stafford waspishly alienated members of her family and even her most devoted friends. In 1976, after a stroke left her unable to talk or to write, she seems to have turned to her housekeeper for solace. When her final will was read, it was found that Stafford had made this uneducated woman her literary executor and had left her the bulk of her estate.

Analysis

Stafford's fictional world is one of loneliness, isolation, and alienation. For one reason or another, her protagonists are separated from other individuals or from their society as a whole. Even though they are often powerless to transcend their situation, their detachment makes these characters excellent observers. It is through their eyes that Stafford tells her stories.

Some of Stafford's most appealing protagonists are imaginative, rebellious children. In "Bad Characters" (1954), Emily Vanderpool becomes fascinated by a young thief and with her embarks on a brief but exciting crime spree. In "A Reading Problem" (1956), the same protagonist gets involved with a traveling evangelist, again with hilarious results. In such stories, however, the protagonists face nothing worse than a scolding from their parents. There is no danger that society will actually expel them.

Some of Stafford's adults, too, manage to transcend the problem of alienation from society. In "Maggie Meriwether's Rich Experience" (1955), for example, an American girl who has been humiliated by a group of sophisticates at a French country house transcends her embarrassment by dramatizing it for American friends, thus making it truly "rich," or funny. Similarly, in "Polite Conversation" (1949), Margaret Heath and her husband, both of whom are working writers, risk losing only their time and their privacy when local organizers try to incorporate them into summer activities. One suspects that the Heaths can find appropriate excuses.

In such comic and satirical stories, the protagonist-observer emerges triumphant. Stafford's tone, however, can be far gloomier. In "A Modest Proposal" (1949), for example, a dinner guest is confronted at once with the prevalence and the horror of colonial racism. On a more personal level, in "A Country Love Story" (1950), a wife comes to realize that what she had thought was a temporary estrangement between herself and her husband is in fact the kind of separate life that he desires. Sometimes, too, Stafford blends sadness with satire, as in the novel *Boston Adventure*, in which Stafford ridicules Boston society and yet sympathizes with the outsider who has exposed herself to it. A similar mixture is evident in the autobiographical story "The Tea Time of Stouthearted Ladies" (1964), in which struggling boardinghouse keepers, like Stafford's own mother, engage in transparent attempts to convince themselves and each other that their daughters have wonderful lives, both as "Barbarians" excluded from college social life and as summertime waitresses serving the affluent. In this story, the eavesdropping daughter pities and yet despises the "ladies" while recognizing that their efforts will enable girls like her to escape.

Interestingly, the patterns and preoccupations of Stafford's works did not change in the course of her writing career, although her style did. While it had many virtues, the worst fault of *Boston Adventure* was its Victorian wordiness. By the publication of *The Mountain Lion* just three years later, however, Stafford had transformed her style; her prose had become precise, economical, and colloquial.

The new style is particularly effective in recording the thoughts of the young, such as the brother and sister in *The Mountain Lion*; the inexperienced, such as Maggie Meriwether; or the intellectually limited, such as the woman in "The End of a Career" (1956) who has devoted her life to being beautiful. Although much of the renewed attention to Stafford's fiction concerns its emphasis on the inner lives of girls and young women, it is not only her vision but also the uniqueness of her voice that assure her place in literary history.

BOSTON ADVENTURE

First published: 1944
Type of work: Novel

A poor girl, the daughter of immigrants, realizes her dream of penetrating Boston society, only to discover its falseness and its cruelty.

Boston Adventure, Stafford's first novel, was also her most popular work. Although critics do not consider it her best novel, they do point out how effectively Stafford presents the inner life of the protagonist, much in the manner of the nineteenth century novelists Henry James and Marcel Proust.

The story is divided into two parts, each of which has been given the title of a place. Book 1 is called "Hotel Barstow," after the summer place on the North Shore across from Boston, where the poverty-stricken protagonist sees the wealthy Bostonians whose lives she yearns to imitate. Book 2 is entitled "Pinckney Street," after the exclusive area in Beacon Hill to which the protagonist is taken by a benefactor.

Sonia ("Sonie") Marburg, the protagonist of *Boston Adventure*, has good reason to want to escape from the place of her birth. The daughter of two immigrants who have failed to achieve the American Dream, she spends her childhood in a drafty shack, listening to her parents' quarrels, which are interrupted only by their bouts of drunkenness. Her beautiful but bad-tempered Russian mother, who works as a chambermaid at Hotel Barstow, hates her husband, a German shoemaker she met on the boat trip to America, because he cannot give her the luxury he promised. From her earliest consciousness, Sonia feels unwanted; indeed, her father tells her that she should never have been born.

Sonia cannot help contrasting the chaotic atmosphere of her own home with the order of the Hotel Barstow room occupied by an aristocratic Boston spinster, Lucy Pride. Because of her tranquil demeanor and her self-possession, Miss Pride becomes a symbol of an ideal way of life. When her father asks Sonia what she would like to be, she replies simply that she would like to live on Pinckney Street.

Ironically, it is the disintegration of Sonia's family that makes her dream a possibility. Her father walks out; the little brother who is born shortly afterward wanders away from home and dies in a snowstorm; and Sonia's mother, who has gradually declined into insanity, has to be institutionalized. At this point, Miss Pride, who has always taken an interest in Sonia, offers her a position as a secretary, tuition for the training she needs, and, most important, her own room in the mansion on Pinckney Street. The final sentence of this section has a significance that at the time Sonia docs not grasp. Dropping in unexpectedly, Miss Pride has found her protégé reading the newspaper comic strips. Politely, she suggests that she does not expect to find such reading in her home. This comment should alert Sonia to the fact that whatever she gains by moving to Pinckney Street will be at the loss of her own identity.

In book 2, Sonia becomes the person Miss Pride wishes her to be, tailoring not only her reading habits but also her clothes and her conversation to her employer's pattern. Even though she is half in love with a young doctor, Philip McAllister, Sonia accepts the fact that Miss Pride has reserved him for her niece, the lovely, independent Hopestill ("Hope") Mather, whom Philip adores. Sonia soon becomes privy to this subtle society's secret codes, understanding what may be inferred from a word, a gesture, or a casual reference. This skill leads her to a shocking discovery: Hope is pregnant by a notorious philanderer and intends to maintain her respectability by marrying Philip. After the wedding, when it becomes evident that Philip, now undeceived, is taking a subtle revenge upon her, Hope deliberately causes her horse to throw her, losing both her baby and her own life. Now aware of the real viciousness beneath the surface of Beacon Hill society, Sonia sadly realizes that by promising to remain with Miss Pride until her death, she, too, has sold herself into bondage.

THE CATHERINE WHEEL

First published: 1952
Type of work: Novel

A middle-aged spinster and a twelve-year-old boy separately do battle with their selfish impulses.

As the epigraph indicates, the title of *The Catherine Wheel* was taken from a passage in *Murder in the Cathedral* (1935), a play by the Anglo-Catholic writer T.S. Eliot that compares the things of this world to children's pleasures, as ephemeral as firework displays. In her final novel, Stafford again shows the tragic results that occur when individuals become so intoxicated with their own imagined needs that they are willing to sacrifice other people, as well as their own integrity, in order to fulfill them.

The story is told alternately by two protagonists, Katharine Congreve, a wealthy, unmarried woman from Boston, and Andrew Shipley, a twelve-year-old boy, the son of the man whom Katherine loved and lost twenty years before. For years, Andrew and his older twin sisters have spent their summers at Katharine's country house in northern New England, never dreaming that their hostess is anything more than the longtime friend of both their parents and the first cousin of their mother, Maeve Maxwell Shipley. To the children, Katharine is the ultimate aunt, an understanding friend and confidante as well as a magician who can always suggest an exciting remedy for boredom.

This summer, however, both Andrew and Katharine are experiencing serious inner conflicts. After a difficult year at home, Andrew has looked forward to spending the summer with his best friend, Victor Smithwick, a fascinating local boy. This year, however, Victor is acting as nurse for his ailing older brother Charles, and he has no time for Andrew. Andrew feels betrayed, and out of hurt and anger he begins to pray for Charles's death. Meanwhile, Katharine is seriously considering betraying the children who trust her. Discovering in his middle years that he has done nothing with his talents, John Shipley has convinced himself that if he divorces his wife and marries Katharine, he can have a new beginning. Although she has lost her respect for John, Katharine is tempted to take him, not out of love but out of a desire for revenge.

Because both of these essentially decent and sensitive protagonists feel so deeply guilty about their thoughts, each of them mistakenly thinks that the other knows his secret. Since they are extremely fond of each other, the result is an intensification of their misery. Even Stafford admitted that the tragic ending of *The Catharine Wheel* was rather contrived. At a party modeled on that disastrous one of twenty years before, Katharine insists on a display of the spinning firework displays that bear her name. When one of them sets Charles's clothing on fire, Katharine saves him, sacrificing her own life and, of course, begging the question of her love affair. At the end of the book, however, there is a moving scene in which Stafford has her protagonists realize, too late, that they have taken the wrong direction in their lives. The emotions that Katharine and Andrew should have cherished and nurtured were their deep feelings for each other.

THE HEALTHIEST GIRL IN TOWN

First published: 1951
Type of work: Short story

An eight-year-old girl triumphs over a pair of sickly playmates who have made her believe that being healthy is somehow disgraceful.

"The Healthiest Girl in Town" is one of the stories based on Stafford's years in Colorado. It is set in 1924 in a Western town whose principal industry is "tuberculars," that is, people who have come there hoping for a cure for tuberculosis or at least for an extension of their lives. Naturally, the town is dominated by anecdotes of sickness and death. In this atmosphere, Jessie, the eight-year-old narrator, feels like an outsider. Blessed with a strong constitution and sensibly reared by her widowed mother, a practical nurse, Jessie cannot manage to get interestingly ill.

This problem becomes acute when she is thrown into the society of two spoiled, sickly girls, Laura and Ada Butler. Although she despises them on sight, Jessie is forced to play with them because her mother has a new position nursing the senile grandmother of the family.

The Butler girls seem to want Jessie at their home merely so that they can have someone to torment. They comment on her mother's inferior position and suggest that Jessie's own low status in society is proven by the fact that she has no ailments. Finally, they inquire into the death of Jessie's father. Although in fact it was gangrene that killed him, Jessie is inspired to say that the cause of his death was leprosy. Immediately, she realizes that she is trapped. If she admits that she lied, the girls will never let her forget it, but if she sticks to her story, she is firmly convinced that both her mother and Jessie herself will be exiled to the Fiji Islands.

Following up their advantage, the Butler girls summon Jessie to take their nauseating "cure" for leprosy. She, however, has had enough. Defiantly, she insists that her father was shot, that he was as tall as the room they are standing in, and—the only truth in her tirade—that she has been called "the healthiest girl in town." She now has as much pride, or "vanity," in her health as the Butler girls do in their illness. Never again, in her visits to their home, does Jessie let them make her feel inferior.

Because it moves toward a discovery, in this case that health is not to be despised, "The Healthiest Girl in Town" is typical of Stafford's short stories. Not all of her stories, however, have the comic tone that is here evident. When she did choose to use comic irony, Stafford won high praise from critics, who did not hesitate to compare her to Mark Twain, America's greatest humorist.

Summary

In her fiction, Jean Stafford shows how the world looks from the perspective of those who feel alienated from it. Although Stafford's works range in tone from rollicking comedy and social satire to profound tragedy, they all move toward a revelation, knowledge that may bring new hope to the protagonist, who is usually female in gender, but that more often destroys her peace of mind or even her life.

The rediscovery of Stafford's work has stemmed in part from her insights into the feelings of those who are so often victims of society, children and young women in particular. It is her superb style, however, that makes her voice so unmistakable and her fiction so effective.

Bibliography

Auchincloss, Louis. *Pioneers and Caretakers*. Boston: G. K. Hall, 1985.

Goodman, Charlotte Margolis. *Jean Stafford: The Savage Heart*. Austin: University of Texas Press, 1990.

McConahay, Mary Davidson. "'Heidelberry Braids' and Yankee Politesse: Jean Stafford and Robert Lowell Reconsidered." *Virginia Quarterly Review* 62 (Spring, 1986): 213-236.

Oates, Joyce Carol. "The Interior Castle: The Art of Jean Stafford's Short Fiction." *Shenandoah* 30 (Autumn, 1979): 61-64.

Roberts, David. *Jean Stafford: A Biography*. Boston: Little, Brown, 1988.

Ryan, Maureen. *Innocence and Estrangement in the Fiction of Jean Stafford*. Baton Rouge: Louisiana State University Press, 1987.

Walsh, Mary Ellen Williams. *Jean Stafford*. Boston: Twayne, 1985.

Rosemary M. Canfield Reisman

WILLIAM STAFFORD

Born: Hutchinson, Kansas
January 17, 1914
Died: Lake Oswego, Oregon
August 28, 1993

Principal Literary Achievement
One of the most prolific and imaginative poets of his time, Stafford produced many poems of enduring value and greatly contributed to his readers' understanding of the creative process.

Biography
William Edgar Stafford was born in Hutchinson, Kansas, on January 17, 1914, the eldest of three children of Earl Ingersoll and Ruby Mayer Stafford. Though the family was relatively poor and had to move from town to town for the father to find work, Stafford's childhood seems to have been a happy one. His parents were enthusiastic readers and talkers, providing young William with a wealth of shared stories, poems, songs, gossip, and, especially in the case of his mother, a receptive listener to his own stories.

During their frequent moves during the Depression of the 1930's, Stafford took on odd jobs to help support the family: delivering papers, raising vegetables and selling them door to door, harvesting sugar beets, and working as an electrician's mate in an oil refinery. Even so, Stafford found time to roam the countryside, fishing and hunting with his father or camping alone. He developed a love of nature that was to sustain him in the years ahead.

After graduating from high school, he attended junior colleges briefly before enrolling at the University of Kansas, where he devoted himself more seriously to writing. While at the university, his lifelong political convictions also began to take shape. Stafford joined a protest against segregation of the student cafeteria, defying campus rules by sitting with black students. It was at this time that Stafford took a further step that was to change the course of his life forever: He declared himself a pacifist opposed to U.S. involvement in World War II.

When the U.S. entered the war, Stafford applied for conscientious objector status and served four years in alternative service camps in Arkansas, Illinois, and California. Because the war was popular, maintaining pacifist principles required great courage.

Few people could sympathize with conscientious objectors, and the experience for Stafford was isolating. (He describes this time in his first published work, 1947's *Down in My Heart*, a fictionalized memoir that he submitted for his master's thesis at the University of Kansas). Stafford, though, enjoyed the work—firefighting, soil conservation, and other Forest Service tasks—and, if anything, this experience strengthened his belief in the pacifism and in the gentle, receptive, "listening" attitude that characterizes his best poetry. Moreover, the years in camp made Stafford more sharply attuned to the tensions between the demands of the external, social world and the distinctive inner life from which his poetry flowed.

In 1943, while still in the camps in California, Stafford met and married Dorothy Frantz, a public-school teacher and the daughter of a minister. After his release, Stafford taught high school briefly with his wife in San Francisco and then worked for Church World Service, a relief agency. In 1948, he accepted a position at the Lewis and Clark College in Portland, Oregon. During this time, Stafford wrote steadily and began to publish in important literary journals. From 1950 to 1952, he attended the University of Iowa, where he studied with some of the most significant writers of his generation, including Robert Penn Warren, Paul Engle, Randall Jarrell, and Karl Shapiro. After receiving his Ph.D., he returned to Portland and began a prolific and distinguished career as a poet, teacher, and lecturer.

Stafford's first volume of poetry, *West of Your City* (1960), did not appear until the poet was forty-six, an unusually late start. The book, though, met with immediate critical success, and thereafter the volumes followed in rapid succession; including *Traveling Through the Dark* (1962, winner of the National Book Award), *The Rescued Year* (1966), *Allegiances* (1970), *Someday, Maybe* (1973), *Stories That Could Be True: New and Collected Poems* (1977), *A Glass Face in the Rain: New Poems* (1982), *An Oregon Message* (1987), and *Passwords* (1991). Stafford also published two books of essays and interviews on the art of poetry, as well as children's books and correspondence with the poet Marvin Bell. In addition, Stafford published more than twenty small-press books and chapbooks.

Stafford has been highly honored. In addition to the National Book Award, he won the Award in Literature of the American Academy of Arts and Letters, a Guggenheim Fellowship, and the Shelley Memorial Award. He served as a Consultant in Poetry for the Library of Congress and on the Literature Commission of the National Council of Teachers of English. He also lectured widely for the U.S. Information Service in Egypt, India, Pakistan, Iran, Nepal, Bangladesh, Singapore, and Thailand.

Analysis

When once asked what made him start writing poetry, Stafford replied, "What made you stop?" This rather cagey answer reveals several of Stafford's most basic assumptions about poetry. First, for Stafford, poetry is not a specialized endeavor limited to an elite few. It is a natural activity available to anyone. Second, the value of poetry lies not in the success of the final product—which is no doubt why most people do stop writing—but rather in the creative process.

In *You Must Revise Your Life* (1986), Stafford speaks eloquently about trusting the creative process: "At times in my thinking I take my hands off the handlebars and see what happens. In a poem I do that all the time. I let the total momentum of the experience dictate the direction the poem goes." Relinquishing control of the poem, letting it find its own direction, engenders a process of discovery that Stafford finds most valuable. Indeed, this openness to surprises is central to his poetry. To begin with a plan and then execute it would, in Stafford's view, kill the poem. Poetry comes alive in the readiness to accept whatever the imagination, the world, the language itself might offer.

Stafford's own poems offer ample evidence of the worth of this approach. His work is full of surprises for writer and reader alike; when a Stafford poem begins one can never be sure where it might end. Nor is Stafford reluctant to break conventions. For example, nature is often humanized in his poetry: "The green of leaves calls out," "Trees hunch their shoulders," and "a bird says 'Hi!'," for example. Stafford ignores the strict modern censure of the pathetic fallacy with a childlike delight not to be found in other poets of his generation. That his work is so varied and unpredictable makes it difficult to generalize about him. His poetry does contain certain recurring themes, however, such as memory and the passing of time, concern about nuclear annihilation, the evocative power of the wilderness and its potential destruction and, most prominently, a desire to be at home in the world, attentive and receptive both to the inner life and the outer environment, which Stafford once called the "two rivers of my life." Broadly stated, Stafford's most inclusive concern is, simply, "learning how to live."

For Stafford, learning how to live consists primarily of learning how to be receptive to the world and how to interpret its messages. Like William Wordsworth, Stafford views the world as charged with meaning. The poem "Sophocles Says" (1966) begins: "History is a story God is telling/ by means of hidden meanings written closely/ inside the skins of things. . . ." The poet's task is to penetrate the surfaces of things to discover their underlying meanings. In this sense, Stafford rejects the modernist view that nature is simply a nonhuman otherness with nothing to tell humans about themselves. Instead, he insists, "everything that happens is the message." In such a world, "everything counts," whether it is a nuclear bomb test, a snowstorm, or a cocktail party. The crucial point is to see the reality beneath the experience. Such "seeing" allows one to learn how to live in harmony with the world and, by implication, with God.

Stafford often expresses this harmony in images of home. Yet home for Stafford is not a specific place but an attitude of mind, a passive welcoming of process. Just as he believes that poems should unfold as they wish, without too much pressure from the poet, so too does he suggest that to live rightly is to let life unfold without trying to control or manipulate it. Images of wind and rivers, of going with rather than against their motions, embody the value he places on passive receptiveness.

The antithesis to this receptive, passive stance Stafford locates in its exact opposite: war. War is active, aggressive, and most often an attempt to manipulate the world rather than understand it. Fears of war, nuclear holocaust, and encroaching destruction of the wilderness appear throughout his poems. In "Cover Up" (1991), he writes: "don't worry about the mountains;/ and some trees even might survive, looking/ over a shoulder from places too cold for us." Because Stafford sees all life as having spirit—"there is a spirit abiding in everything"—destruction of the natural world, through war or development, appears as the most grotesque consequence of having failed to learn how to live harmoniously.

Still Stafford's poetry as a whole is hopeful, playful, generous, sympathetic, and filled with a kind of wisdom rarely achieved and even more rarely so beautifully expressed. His style is colloquial but tight and quirky, full of sudden turns. His poems are always accessible and, indeed, inviting to the reader; he wishes to be understood. Clearly, too, Stafford's faith in the creative process led him to many discoveries, and he is not reluctant to share those discoveries, or even, at times, to offer friendly advice. In "Freedom" (1973), he writes: "If you are oppressed, wake up about/ four in the morning: most places,/ you can usually be free some of the time/ if you wake up before other people." In "The Little Ways That Encourage Good Fortune" (1973), he warns: "If you have things right in your life/ but do not know why,/ you are just lucky, and you will not move/ in the little ways that encourage good fortune." Readers of William Stafford will find themselves fortunate to follow the path of a poet who learned so well how to live.

TRAVELING THROUGH THE DARK

First published: 1962
Type of work: Poem

Stafford finds a dead deer on a mountain road and confronts a painful dilemma

"Traveling Through the Dark" is Stafford's most famous, most often anthologized poem. It is somewhat atypical, since it tells a story about a real experience in a fairly straightforward way. Yet in its underlying concern with nature—in this case, a deer found dead in the road—with man's invasion of the wilderness, and with the individual's responsibility to do what is right "for us all," the poem reveals some of Stafford's abiding themes.

"Traveling Through the Dark" achieves its power by subtly blending the symbolic and to the real and by seeing underneath the surface event to its larger consequences. The title suggests not so much a drive on a mountain road as a spiritual journey through unknown territory. At the same time, something quite real has happened. Stafford has "found a deer/ dead on the edge of the Wilson River road." That he names the road specifically gives the poem the feel of authentic experience.

Roads and paths for Stafford often symbolize the ongoing process of life, and here he must confront a dilemma that involves his deepest relation to all of life. At first, he realizes that he should roll the deer into the canyon to protect other drivers who come after him; he notes that "to swerve might make more dead." When he examines the deer, however, he discovers that it is a pregnant doe; its fawn is still alive, waiting to be born. Suddenly, the choices are much more complicated. Should he try to save the fawn, or do as he originally intended?

He must act quickly, but the poem does allow the suspense to build. Where other writers might have treated this crisis sentimentally, Stafford shifts the focus from what he is feeling to a vivid, pulsing description of the scene:

> The car aimed ahead its lowered parking lights;
> under the hood purred the steady engine.
> I stood in the glare of the warm exhaust turning red;
> around our group I could hear the wilderness listen.

The car lights point the way ahead, and the engine purrs as if it too were alive, waiting. The warm exhaust fumes "turning red" in the glow of the tail lights suggest the blood that must now be flowing on the ground and cast a ghastly coloring over the whole scene. Most important, the poet can "hear the wilderness listen." To hear something listen is to listen carefully indeed. That it is the wilderness that is listening attributes an awareness to nature that is characteristic of Stafford's poetry; it also implies that his decision matters not only to the fawn and to the speaker but also to the whole of life, which waits to see what he will do.

The decision is not easy, nor does the speaker say how he arrives at it. He simply says that he "thought hard for us all—my only swerving—, / then pushed her over the edge into the river." "For us all" here can mean the poet, the doe, the fawn, the wilderness, and, by implication, all living things. His thought swerves, as a car would have done, but he acts as he feels he must. By deliberately leaving out the precise nature of that thought, Stafford forces the reader to imagine the difficulty of the choice and thus puts the reader, retrospectively, into his dilemma.

THINGS I LEARNED LAST WEEK

First published: 1982
Type of work: Poem

A collection of random observations leads to an ominous reminder of death.

"Things I Learned Last Week" is a wonderfully odd, apparently random poem that illustrates a central element of Stafford's poetics. The poem at first seems remarkably offhand and unambitious, a simple disconnected listing of tidbits Stafford happened across during the week. Such an approach, lacking any grand intentions, reveals Stafford's willingness to follow his impulses wherever they might lead him.

The first two stanzas record observations that one would not usually expect to find in a poem: "Ants, when they meet each other,/ usually pass on the right," and

"Sometimes you can open a sticky/ door with your elbow." Hardly stunning discoveries, these facts amuse partly because Stafford has put them in the poem. They are some of the things he learned last week and so must be included. Perhaps they imply that everyone learns something by paying attention to the small, daily events that are usually ignored.

The next stanza humorously depicts a "man in Boston" who "has dedicated himself/ to telling about injustice." It seems that the poem is about to take a more serious turn, but Stafford adds an element of irony to his description of the man by saying: "For three thousand dollars he will/ come to your town and tell you about it." Stafford gently obliterates the man's dedication simply by mentioning his lecture fees. The man has obviously dedicated himself to making a handsome profit from injustice, making a career out of it, and so he himself commits a kind of injustice and a glaring hypocrisy. There is injustice in the world, no doubt, but Stafford sees that its opponents often participate in it, much as opponents of war often resort to violent protests.

Stafford has also learned some things about writers during the week, and he treats them, too, with a bemused irony. "Yeats, Pound, and Eliot saw art as/ growing from other art. They studied that." Here, Stafford implicitly rejects the poetics of three towering figures of modern literature. Because they believed that art grew from other art, they studied art, forming a closed, elitist circle and cutting themselves off from the soil of daily experience—the soil out of which Stafford's own poem grows.

The final two stanzas introduce a darker subject—death—but it is treated playfully at first. "If I ever die, I'd like it to be/ in the evening. That way, I'll have/ all the dark to go with me, and no one/ will see how I begin to hobble along." The use of the conditional "if" in reference to the one certain fact of existence, the preference for evening, and the hint of embarrassment at being seen hobbling along all make death seem hardly more than a clumsy problem of decorum. The final stanza, however, pushes the poem to a larger consciousness of death that is no joke:

> In The Pentagon one person's job is to
> take pins out towns, hills, and fields,
> and then save the pins for later.

It is one of the grim absurdities of modern life that one person's job would consist of taking pins, indicating targets, out of maps. That he saves the pins "for later" is an ominous reminder that there will be more wars, that death on a large scale will come again, without regard to the poet's preference for evening.

The poem begun so lightly thus leads to the inescapable knowledge of humanity's destructive power and the constant readiness for war that hovers over human existence. Everything that precedes the final stanza, however humorous, takes on a poignancy when seen in light of the threat of nuclear annihilation. A poem that seems pointless and harmless at first thus sharpens itself at the end by reminding the reader of the dark current running beneath daily life.

IT'S ALL RIGHT

First published: 1991
Type of work: Poem

Stafford sees that the natural world can console people for the difficulties they encounter in the social world

"It's All Right" is one of Stafford's most charming poems. It is an example of his characteristic impulse to include the reader in the collaborative process of the poem's meaning. The poem's language and tone are simple and reassuring; it is as if the reader is being cheered up by an old friend, or given some helpful counsel by a wise grandfather.

The poem speaks to the reader directly, as many Stafford poems do, addressing the reader as "you" throughout. Stafford is concerned not only with the events of his own life but with the events of others' lives as well. The experiences he describes are ones that anyone can recognize. "Someone you trusted has treated you bad./ Someone has used you to vent their ill temper." Surely, all readers encountered such treatment. Yet Stafford knows that these difficulties are an inevitable consequence of social life: "Did you expect anything different?"

Stafford goes on to list, with sympathetic understanding, the failures and frustrations that, expected or not, can wear people down. "Your work—better than some others'— has languished,/ neglected. Or a job you tried was too hard,/ and you failed. Maybe weather or bad luck/ spoiled what you did." Stafford takes care to imagine types of disappointments in work that could apply to a wide variety of readers, from writers, who often feel unfairly overlooked, to farmers, whose best efforts may be ruined by the caprice of the weather.

Stafford knows, too, that personal relationships often cause pain. "That grudge, held against you/ for years after you patched up, has flared,/ and you've lost a friend for a time. Things/ at home aren't so good." In only ten lines, the poem has covered many of the sources of unhappiness that people experience in their daily encounters with the world, and the cumulative weight of the poem has become indeed heavy.

Having reached its low point, however, the poem suddenly turns. "But just when the worst bears down/ you find a pretty bubble in your soup at noon,/ and outside at work a bird says, 'Hi!'/ Slowly the sun creeps along the floor; it is coming your way. It touches your shoe." After such large disappointments, what can bring back happiness are the small things not usually noticed—"a pretty bubble"—and the steady, dependable forces of nature. If the social world is inevitably the source of frustration and disillusionment, the poem seems to say, the natural world is just as surely the source of contentment, consolation, and beauty.

Summary

In a preface to *An Oregon Message*, William Stafford said of his poetry that he must allow himself to be "willingly fallible" to deserve a place in the realm where "miracles happen." Whether his poems deal with home, memory, wilderness, fear of war, ordinary daily events, or the creative process itself, this quality of trust in the imagination and his ability to make, or let, miracles happen make Stafford so consistently engaging. Stafford's poems may not be perfect, but they do offer many surprises and provide a vivid picture of one man's quest to learn "how to live."

Bibliography

Holden, Jonathan. *The Mark to Turn: A Reading of William Stafford's Poetry.* Lawrence: University Press of Kansas, 1976.

Kitchen, Judith. *Understanding William Stafford.* Columbia: University of South Carolina Press, 1989.

Lensing, George S., and Ronald Moran. *Four Poets and the Emotive Imagination: Robert Bly, James Wright, Louis Simpson, and William Stafford.* Baton Rouge: Louisiana State University Press, 1976.

Pinsker, Sanford. *Three Pacific Northwest Poets: William Stafford, Richard Hugo, and David Wagoner.* Boston: Twayne, 1987.

Stitt, Peter. *The World's Hieroglyphic Beauty: Five American Poets.* Athens: University of Georgia Press, 1985.

John Brehm

WALLACE STEGNER

Born: Lake Mills, Iowa
February 18, 1909
Died: Santa Fe, New Mexico
April 13, 1993

Principal Literary Achievement

Often called "the Dean of Western Letters," Stegner devoted his life to depicting the true West, as opposed to the "Wild West" sensationalized in popular fiction and motion pictures.

Biography

Wallace Stegner was born in Lake Mills, Iowa, on February 18, 1909, the son of George and Hilda Paulson Stegner. His father was a dynamic but unstable dreamer who was always coming up with schemes to strike it rich in some new part of the West. Stegner's mother cherished culture, tradition, polite manners, and all the values of established civilization. She was mismated to the rowdy, uncouth George Stegner but remained faithful to him until her death from cancer in 1933.

Wallace was so impressed by his own family history that he wrote about it in thinly disguised versions in many novels and stories. Stegner was attracted to his father's adventurous spirit and his mother's high moral principles; he spent the rest of his life trying to reconcile these conflicting elements in his own nature through his writing.

Stegner had an unstable childhood, because his father was always leading the family to a different part of the West. They lived in Iowa, North Dakota, Saskatchewan, Montana, and Utah. This is the vast area that Stegner wrote about for the rest of his life. He worshipped his mother but had mixed feelings about his improvident father, who sometimes provided the family with luxuries and sometimes led them to the brink of starvation.

Wallace was a sickly and timid boy who buried himself in books. He did so well in school that he was able to enter the University of Utah at the age of sixteen. During this time he began to conceive the possibility of becoming a professional writer, but he wisely continued with his academic work and remained a scholar and teacher throughout his life. He taught at a number of different colleges and universities, gradually building a reputation and achieving financial security. His salary as a professor enabled him to devote time to writing without financial anxiety, and his

growing number of publication credits made it easier for him to advance in the academic world. He became known as a distinguished American writer and one of the leading authorities on the American West.

Stegner projected his own psychological conflicts onto his fictitious characters. His mismatched parents had left him with problems about his personal identity. Part of him identified with his likable but uncouth father; part of him identified with his refined, idealistic mother. His fiction can often be read as a struggle to reconcile these contradictory traits within himself. Perhaps his father's recklessness influenced him to select the risky career of a freelance writer, while his mother's conservative influence may have caused him to seek security by becoming a tenured college professor.

The combination was good for Stegner, who became a famous author and a revered teacher. He established one of the world's best creative writing programs at Stanford University in California and remained associated with it from 1945 until his retirement in 1971. He received many honors and awards during his lifetime, including election to the American Academy of Arts and Sciences and the National Academy of Arts and Letters.

Readers who first become acquainted with Stegner through his fiction often go on to read some of his equally well-written nonfiction, which includes such fine works as *Beyond the Hundredth Meridian: John Wesley Powell and the Second Opening of the West* (1954) and *The Gathering of Zion: The Story of the Mormon Trail* (1964). He was also a distinguished essayist as well as a biographer and historian. Many of his best essays were reprinted in *The Sound of Mountain Water* (1969).

Stegner died in 1993 as a result of injuries sustained in an auto accident in New Mexico. He left behind a distinguished body of work in both fiction and nonfiction. His best memorial, though, may be the Wallace Stegner Creative Writing Center at Stanford University, which he founded and directed for many years.

Analysis

Wallace Stegner wrote in the great tradition of American realism. Other famous authors of this school were William Dean Howells, Theodore Dreiser, Sherwood Anderson, Stephen Crane, and William Faulkner, to name only a few. The distinguishing feature of realistic fiction is that it deals with ordinary events in the lives of ordinary people; the author's intention is to make his work resemble real life as most people experience it. Plots do not take spectacular turns but evolve slowly, the way life itself evolves. Changes do take place in people's lives, but they take place slowly and without any orderly pattern.

It was appropriate for Stegner to work in the tradition of realism, because it was his lifelong purpose to depict what the American West was really like. For many years, popular fiction had been presenting a lurid picture of the West. The general public imagined a panorama of cowboys and Indians, the U.S. Cavalry riding to the rescue, shootouts on Main Street, masked bandits holding up stagecoaches, cattle stampedes, burning wagon trains, saloons full of drunken men and immoral women, and all the other stereotypes that are still perpetuated in motion pictures and on television. In his famous short story "The Blue Hotel" (1898), Stephen Crane highlighted the contrast between the real West and the Wild West of dime novels; this was what Stegner also wanted to do.

Stegner grew up in the West and knew that, in reality, most of its people were quiet, hardworking pioneers trying to build homes and raise families. These were the people he admired, not legendary figures such as Billy the Kid or Jesse James. Many of Stegner's male characters carried guns, but they could not draw their weapons in a split second or shoot with superhuman accuracy.

The problem with literary realism is that it can be dull, since real life contains few dramatic events. Realism depends on sensitive description and close psychological analysis; the most important events take place inside characters' minds. Stegner was especially interested in how people change. In his novels, these changes may take place over lifetimes; in his short stories, the character changes often take place in a matter of minutes, as in "The Blue-Winged Teal."

Irish novelist James Joyce applied the word "epiphany" to fiction. An epiphany, in this sense, is like a miniature religious experience, a spiritual insight into the true nature of reality that brings about a change of character. These are not necessarily pleasant experiences but can be unpleasant or even terrifying; nevertheless, they are an essential part of growing up. Such epiphanies are integral to many of Stegner's short stories and novels.

In "The Blue-Winged Teal," for example, the whole point of the story is to be found in young Henry Lederer's sudden insight into his father's true nature—and, hence, into his own true nature as his father's son. In Stegner's best-known novel, *Angle of Repose*, the hundreds of pages of narrative lead up to the final epiphany in which the narrator, Lyman Ward, understands his grandparents, their whole generation, their world, and his own nature as their descendant. He understands something that his contemporaries are in danger of forgetting: that it is important to learn to accept life with all of its limitations.

Although Stegner was a contemporary of many of America's most famous authors, including F. Scott Fitzgerald and Ernest Hemingway, he never achieved comparable popular success. His low-key approach to writing was not calculated to attract a mass audience. He supported himself and his family by teaching in colleges and consequently did not feel compelled to sensationalize his material. He is known to connoisseurs of good writing for his sensitive descriptions of people and places as well as for his crystal-clear, unaffected prose style. Readers who are looking for thrills may be disappointed with Stegner's fiction, but readers who are looking for understanding of human nature will find his work satisfying.

Stegner preferred the nineteenth century to the twentieth. He was appalled by the growing scorn of the work ethic, the loss of religious faith, the cynicism about morality, the use of drugs, and the sexual libertinism that he regarded as diseases of the modern world. His interest in the past led him to write history and biography as well as fiction.

Although Stegner is best known as a fiction writer, he left a large body of distinguished nonfiction behind when he died at the age of eighty-four. This versatility is the mark of keen intelligence and dedication to literature. He was also a college professor for much of his life, passing on to younger generations his love of learning, his love of literature, and his love for the American West.

THE BIG ROCK CANDY MOUNTAIN

First published: 1943
Type of work: Novel

A man drags his wife and two sons all over the West in search of riches but ends up penniless and disillusioned.

The Big Rock Candy Mountain was Stegner's first critical and popular success. The title derives from a hobo song of the early 1900's that describes "The Big Rock Candy Mountain" as a utopia where "the handouts grow on bushes."

The book's protagonist, Harry "Bo" Mason, is one of the many dreamers who came West in search of riches. He tries many different occupations but fails to strike it rich. His wife Elsa wants security, respectability, and peace of mind, but she is tied to an incompatible mate. They have two children: Chet, the elder, inherits his father's temperament; Bruce inherits his mother's temperament, and he is considered a sissy by other boys and by his own father.

Bo's best opportunity comes when the Volstead Act introduces Prohibition after World War I. He begins smuggling whiskey across the Canadian border in a car. For a time, he is making considerable money and lavishing it on his family. Then the same thing happens to him that happened repeatedly to freelance entrepreneurs during the growth of the West: A group of better-organized, better-capitalized men drives the independent operators out of business.

Stegner uses a sophisticated format. His story is told from the points of view of all four family members. In the early chapters, the viewpoints of Bo and Elsa are featured, while those of Chet and Bruce become more prominent as the boys grow older. The story covers a period from 1906 to 1942. During that time, the family moves to North Dakota, Washington, Minnesota, Saskatchewan, Utah, and Nevada. Stegner describes the beauties of these places perhaps better than any other writer. He also describes the hardships of existence in regions where summer droughts kill crops and winter blizzards leave whole herds of sheep and cattle dead, standing in their tracks shrouded in ice.

Like most of Stegner's fiction, *The Big Rock Candy Mountain* is autobiographical, and Bruce Mason is a self-portrait. Bo and Elsa die in pursuit of the American Dream, the dream that the new land offers unlimited opportunities to everyone. The trouble is that Bo and his wife have different dreams and are hopelessly incompatible.

At the end of the novel, Bruce, who is now a college graduate, realizes that he must try to reconcile the values he has inherited from both parents. At the end, with both his parents and his older brother dead, Bruce reflects on what their tragedies mean to him:

> Perhaps it took several generations to make a man, perhaps it took several combinations and re-creations of his mother's gentleness and resilience, his father's enormous energy and appetite for the new, a subtle blending of masculine and feminine, selfish and selfless, stubborn and yielding, before a proper man could be fashioned.

THE BLUE-WINGED TEAL

First published: 1950
Type of work: Short story

> A young college student comes home to nurse his dying mother and struggles to cut himself free from a sordid, unhappy past.

Stegner is an acknowledged master of both the novel and short-story forms, and "The Blue-Winged Teal" is often cited as one of his best stories. "The Blue-Winged Teal" fits squarely into the tradition of American realism. It deals with ordinary events among ordinary people.

A young man named Henry Lederer who has returned home from college to be at his dying mother's bedside now feels out of place in his old hometown. College has taught him to value culture and intellectual achievement; his father's ignorant cronies seem gross and absurd. Henry wants to get back to his college environment, but he has no money and is forced to share his father's hotel room and eat at his father's dingy, smelly poolroom. He finds that he despises his father for his lowbrow tastes and immoral behavior. His mother had kept his father on a higher plane, but as soon as his mother dies, his father returns to his old habits. After Henry's mother has been dead for only six weeks, his father is already consorting with loose women; he comes home smelling of cheap perfume.

Henry goes duck hunting and returns with nine ducks of assorted species. Later, one of his father's cronies cooks the ducks for a special feast. One of the ducks is a blue-winged teal; its beauty moves his father to tears, because he remembers how Henry's mother loved those birds.

Henry Lederer experiences an epiphany. He suddenly realizes that his father shares his grief but has a different way of expressing it. Perhaps more important, he realizes that his feelings are not unique but are shared by the whole human race. He realizes that he is young and self-centered; he also realizes that he is surrounded with quiet human suffering that is not often expressed. He becomes a different man as a result of this epiphany; its effect is to release him from psychological captivity in his hometown and to allow him to return to college, where he can pursue his career.

ANGLE OF REPOSE

First published: 1971
Type of work: Novel

A historical novel about a cultured woman with artistic talents who shared her engineer husband's adventures in the West during the period following the Civil War.

Angle of Repose is generally considered to be Stegner's best novel. The narrator, Lyman Ward, a retired history professor, is writing a biography of his grandmother, Susan Burling Ward, and recounting her adventures in the West during the 1870's and 1880's. At the same time, the narrator is recording his own problems as a biographer and as a lonely, divorced retiree. This stylistic device allows Stegner to write about the past in the third person and about the present in the first person.

Stegner based his novel on a collection of letters written by Mary Hallock Foote to a female friend in the East. His sophisticated novel is thus a combination of fact and fiction, of history and biography dramatized by his creative imagination.

Susan is a sensitive woman with artistic talents that find expression in writing, drawing, and painting. She loves culture and refinement and is subjected to a life of hardship and disillusionment when she falls in love with Oliver Ward, a mining engineer who takes her to the West.

Susan's sketches and written descriptions of the West prove to be in demand by Eastern publications. For years, she is the mainstay of the family; her husband, though intelligent and industrious, meets with one failure after another. Stegner describes their life in various mining communities, where Susan bears three children and struggles to make a home.

Susan and Oliver are essentially incompatible. She is verbally expressive while he is taciturn, and she loves refinement and culture while he loves the raw West. Yet they remain together throughout their long lives. Stegner's narrator says that his main purpose in writing Susan's biography is to try to determine why people such as his grandparents stayed married when people of his own time will separate on the merest whim.

Periodically, the narrator breaks into his story to tell about his day-to-day problems. His son thinks that the narrator is too old to be living alone and wants to put him in a nursing home. The young college girl he has hired as a secretary complicates his life with her personal problems, which involve drugs, free sex, and a generally irresponsible lifestyle.

Past and present come together at the end of the novel. The narrator reveals that Oliver develops a serious drinking problem because of his many disappointments in life. This leads to further marital estrangement because Susan had such high moral standards. The narrator has his own drinking problem, which he believes he has inherited from his grandfather.

Finally, the narrator describes his grandmother's illicit love affair with her husband's best friend, who is more sensitive and artistic than Oliver, and how that affair leads to tragedy. She and her lover, Frank Sargent, are so involved in a rendezvous that they do not realize that her five-year-old daughter has wandered off and drowned. Frank is so overwhelmed with remorse that he commits suicide.

Though the narrator's grandparents continue to live together for almost half a century, their relationship remains formal and distant. Stegner's narrator concludes that he is like his grandfather, and he is similarly unable to forgive his own wife, who has also been unfaithful. He chooses to remain alone for the rest of his life.

Summary

Wallace Stegner was born and reared in the West. He loved its landscape and its people. He believed in the traditional American virtues of hard work, integrity and fair play. Although he was as good a writer as any of his more famous contemporaries, he did not achieve spectacular commercial success because he avoided sensationalism. He wrote in the great tradition of American realism and wanted to depict the real West, which was vastly different from the violent West of the popular media. He taught literature and creative writing for much of his life and inspired many young writers.

Bibliography

Arthur, Anthony, ed. *Critical Essays on Wallace Stegner*. Boston: G.K. Hall, 1982.

Eisinger, Chester E. "Twenty Years of Wallace Stegner." *College English* 20 (1958): 110-116.

Foote, Mary Hallock. *A Victorian Gentlewoman in the Far West: The Reminiscences of Mary Hallock Foote*. Edited by Rodman W. Paul. San Marino, Calif.: The Huntington Library, 1972.

Lewis, Merrill, and Lorene Lewis. *Wallace Stegner*. Boise, Idaho: Boise State College, 1972.

Robinson, Forrest Glen, and Margaret G. Robinson. *Wallace Stegner*. Boston: Twayne, 1977.

Stegner, Wallace, and Richard W. Etulain. *Conversations with Wallace Stegner on Western History and Literature*. Rev. ed. Salt Lake City: University of Utah Press, 1990.

_____. *Where the Bluebird Sings to the Lemonade Springs: Living and Writing in the West*. New York: Random House, 1992.

Bill Delaney

GERTRUDE STEIN

Born: February 3, 1874
Allegheny, Pennsylvania
Died: July 27, 1946
Neuilly-sur-Seine, France

Principal Literary Achievement

American expatriate author Stein helped to reshape the sound of American prose.

Biography

Gertrude Stein was born in Allegheny, Pennsylvania, on February 3, 1874, the youngest of five children in a well-to-do Jewish family of German descent. Before she was a year old, her family began a sojourn in Austria and France that would last five years. Stein's early exposure to the sound of English, German, and French may account for her discovery that words possess a weight and shape of their own.

Her childhood and adolescence were spent in Oakland, California, on a ten-acre farm where she grew up close to nature and the simple domestic objects that would make up the vocabulary of much of her later experimental writing. Her formal education was haphazard, but she read the works of William Shakespeare, Mark Twain, and Jules Verne and visited art galleries in San Francisco. The death of her parents by the time she was seventeen led her to form a close bond with her older brother Leo.

When Leo entered Harvard University to study history and esthetics, Gertrude enrolled in Radcliffe College. There she attended the lectures of the philosopher William James and conducted research in automatic writing that later appeared in the *Harvard Psychological Review*. James considered her one of his most brilliant students, and his lectures on the subconscious led her to experiment later with capturing the poetic quality of subconscious speech. After being graduated summa cum laude from Harvard, she enrolled in The Johns Hopkins Medical School to prepare for a career in experimental psychology. After two years, however she grew bored with her medical studies and joined Leo in Paris. Aside from a single visit to America in 1904, she would not return to her native country for thirty years.

Gertrude Stein was twenty-nine when she arrived in Paris in 1903. Over the next forty-three years, she would produce some nine thousand pages of prose portraits, still

lifes, geographies, plays, novels, and operas that would challenge the dominance of plot, character, and formal description in American literature. Her first important book, *Three Lives* (1909), about three working-class servant girls in Baltimore, was printed in a limited edition and admired by a number of appreciative readers. Her next undertaking, *The Making of Americans* (1925), was nearly a thousand pages long and traced the course of history in the lives of two American families.

Living in Paris during the decade when French cubists were transforming the definition of visual art, Stein filled copybook after copybook with sentences that employed words as if they were pieces in a verbal collage. The result was an evocative, nonrepresentational prose that provoked endless ridicule in contemporary reviewers but that continues to fascinate literary scholars to this day.

Gertrude and Leo Stein assembled a select collection of French abstract works. The paintings of Cezanne and Matisse on the walls of the Stein's apartment at 27 rue de Fleurus gave their home the air of a private museum. The expatriate Spanish painter Pablo Picasso was a frequent visitor, and for several months in 1906 he painted Gertrude's portrait while the two discussed the principles of cubism. The result for Stein was a series of word portraits, among them "Matisse" and "Picasso," and *Tender Buttons* (1914), a long cubist work. In *Tender Buttons*, Stein mixed wisdom and nonsense, accident and profundity in a series of meditations on food, rooms, and common household objects: "Celery tastes tastes where in curled lashes and little bits and mostly in remains."

Jealous of his sister's growing reputation, Leo Stein broke off relations and moved to Florence, Italy. His place was taken by Alice B. Toklas, an American from California, who became Gertrude's lifelong companion and private secretary. During World War I, the two women became familiar figures far beyond Paris, as they delivered supplies in a large Ford truck to military hospitals all over France.

Paris by the 1920's was a literary mecca, and the apartment on rue de Fleurus became a gathering place for visiting writers such as Ernest Hemingway, Sherwood Anderson, and F. Scott Fitzgerald, who came to take tea with Toklas and discuss art and life with Stein. Still in her early fifties, with close-cropped hair, Stein was an imposing figure who preferred to dress in simple, homespun clothes. Her favorite topic of discussion concerned how a writer sees and how what is seen can be put down on paper. By this time, her own writing was appearing regularly in small literary magazines, although, outside of certain literary circles, she was more talked about than read. Her name spread throughout the American avant-garde when Ernest Hemingway, in an epigram to his 1927 novel *The Sun Also Rises*, quoted her observation, "You are all a lost generation." When the novel became a best-seller, Stein's remark became the label for an entire postwar generation.

By 1933, when *The Autobiography of Alice B. Toklas* was published, Paris and the "lost generation" had become part of literary nostalgia. There was a hunger on the opposite side of the Atlantic to hear about an earlier Parisian world that had launched modern art and modern literature. Stein's vivid memoir of that time, composed in the voice of her friend and companion, answered a popular need. She wrote the "autobiography" in six weeks, and it was an immediate success. Excerpts appeared in *The Atlantic Monthly*, a hard-cover edition was chosen by the Literary Guild, and *Time* magazine did a cover story on her life and career.

In the following year, Stein and Toklas returned to America after an absence of thirty years. Together they traveled by plane from city to city, as Stein gave lectures to college audiences and submitted to numerous press and radio interviews. Her play *Four Saints in Three Acts* (1934) was produced as an opera with an all-black cast. The First Lady, Eleanor Roosevelt, invited Stein to tea at the White House. Charlie Chaplin met her when she stopped in California. Random House became her publisher and began issuing editions of her more conventional works. Deprived of praise and recognition for two decades, Stein was finally a celebrity in her native country. Awareness of herself as a renowned author with a devoted audience temporarily disturbed her literary concentration, however, and she returned to France with a renewed commitment to carry her verbal explorations even further.

In the decades between World War I and World War II, she produced some of her most notable works. In her own mind, she divided her efforts of these years into "writing" (for a popular audience) and "really writing" (explorations conducted for herself). Her travels were confined to Europe and England. When Germany invaded France in 1939, she and Toklas withdrew to their country home in the Midi and later to a small town on the Swiss border, where the villagers sheltered them as elderly Jewish women during the Nazi occupation. They returned to Paris in late 1944 and opened their home to wandering American soldiers, who saw Stein and her celebrated apartment as a sort of literary shrine. Right up until the end, she continued to write every day with no diminution of her talent. *Brewsie and Willie* (1946) adroitly captured the flavor of GI slang and a new generation's wariness before an America grown powerful and self-satisfied.

Gertrude Stein died of cancer on July 27, 1946, in the American Hospital in Paris. Shortly before she was wheeled into the operating room to undergo an ultimately unsuccessful operation, she was heard to ask, "What is the question?" Receiving no reply, she concluded, "If there is no question then there is no answer." Her companion Alice B. Toklas died twenty-one years later on March 7, 1967.

Analysis

Gertrude Stein believed that the struggle of thought to come to consciousness best revealed the shape and feel of human experience. In a career that spanned thirty-four years, she sought to answer three questions: What is mind? What is writing? How are they connected? Her answers to these questions shattered the conventions of narrative writing and unsettled the reliance of fiction on character, description, and plot.

In her first book, *Three Lives*, about three working-class women in Baltimore, she endeavored to tell a traditional story with a beginning, middle, and end. She discovered, however, that by deliberately misplacing words she could evoke a continuous present in which the characters seemed to unfold before the reader's eyes. One of the book's stories, "Melanctha," was considered an almost perfect example of the modern short story. Typically, though, Stein never repeated the effort; she was not interested in repeating herself. She sought new literary territory that not even she had visited before.

In her next work, *The Making of Americans*, about two American families, she slowly expanded her chronicle until it became a history of the whole of human endeavor. Through repeated rewritings, she discovered that by beginning again and again she could weave the past and future into a continuous present. The book swelled to almost a thousand pages. In the meantime, she began composing word portraits of the people around her, using everything she could collect from their lives. She sought to encompass every fact and detail, until she saw that with enough detail all differences began to blur. Every person was unique and yet not unique.

After her second book, she abandoned traditional subject matter to explore the working of language. Words, she reasoned, were related to each other just as the shapes and forms were related in a cubist canvas. There was no need for words to copy life, since words possessed a life of their own. She shunned ready-made sentences in order to create sentences that no one had heard before.

In Stein's view, words possessed an essential nature that was independent of their use in communication. Describing and explaining belonged to the nineteenth century; as a modernist, she wanted nothing to do with a past obsessed with class divisions, gentility, and linear reality.

She squeezed everything extraneous from her language and wrote in a deliberately primitive style that avoided any hint of history or place. She was not interested in finding her own voice; she wanted to be absent in her writing. She wanted a new prose that reached the limits of purity and innocence. She employed only simple nouns and verbs that had no associations other than their shape and sound on the page. By seeing words, she hoped, people could be made to see writing.

She employed a number of strategies to return words to their original purity. At Radcliffe, she had experimented with automatic writing, and she knew that sentences could be freed from the mind's will. Many people explored automatic writing in the wake of World War I, but Stein would continue her explorations for the rest of her life. Her explorations were not aimless; she wished not to dehumanize language but to free it. Speech, especially American speech, was clear and distinctive, and she looked for ways of catching the rhythm of speech in her sentences. She found that, if she played with the arrangement of words, she could display shades of thought and feeling struggling to be heard. By repeating a phrase over and over in a slightly altered form, she forced the reader to see that rhythm was as much a part of prose as it was of poetry.

Through constant, deliberate repetition, she produced a ballet of words that surveyed everything while staying motionless. Stein demonstrated that prose could achieve a sense of a continuous present and that stories could be told from a central vantage point, without motion and without reliance on plot, character, or scene.

Her modernist explorations did not rely on ancient mythology or obscure academic references but came purely from the senses. Abstract painting taught her to see and write abstractly without reference to past memory or present identity. Flying for the first time in an airplane in 1935 above the Great Plains, she saw that it was the limitless American landscape that allowed Americans to conceive of writing as cubist, without beginning, middle, or end. The geography of her homeland thus allowed her to envision a new kind of writing based solely on design and form.

The results were exciting but also bewildering and boring, and much of her early work was ridiculed and parodied by reviewers. Her most personal work never found a wide audience; the average reader was in a hurry to discover meaning, whereas what Stein offered was design. Each of her sentences was meant to be an object of contemplation.

Stein's writing falls into three groups. In the first are her relatively straightforward narratives and autobiographies: *Three Lives* (1909), *The Autobiography of Alice B. Toklas* (1933), *Everybody's Autobiography* (1937), and *Wars I Have Seen* (1945). In a second group belong her self-explanatory works that describe and defend her method of writing: *Composition as Explanation* (1926), *Lectures in America* (1935); *Narration: Four Lectures* (1935), and *What Are Masterpieces* (1940). The final group consists of her personal explorations of sound and meaning in prose that make up her still lifes, geographies, word portraits, plays, novels, and operas. By the 1930's, she moved easily between all three.

Stein's literary influence was also as a celebrity; her salon in Paris was a meeting place for some of the most creative minds of the twentieth century. One of her earliest friends was the youthful painter Pablo Picasso, whose portrait of her hung above her writing desk. As Picasso's fame spread, so did Stein's; twice she wrote word portraits of him, and eventually she wrote a book for an exhibition of his work at the Museum of Modern Art. In championing modern art, Stein advertised herself. Modernism was the style and subject of her style, and as modernism spread to America after World War I, so did her fame and influence.

Perhaps her greatest influence was upon the prose of others. Many American and European writers sought her advice in the 1920's, but her most eager pupil was Ernest Hemingway. She corrected Hemingway's early manuscripts and urged him to abandon journalism to devote himself to fiction. From her, Hemingway learned the rhythms of modern prose and the truth that could be communicated in simple words. She became his teacher, and the cadence of her repetitive sentences echoes in some of Hemingway's finest writing. The two wrote about different worlds but in a kindred manner. Hers was the domestic world of the kitchen and garden, while his was the self-consciously masculine world of war, hunting, and travel. Later they would feud in public, but their recriminations spoke to the closeness of their creative marriage. If Hemingway is responsible for the new clarity that invaded literature after World War I, then the muted cadences of his teacher can be heard in American writing to this day.

MELANCTHA

First published: 1909
Type of work: Short story

A restless black woman seeks insight into her sensual nature through a series of love affairs.

"Melanctha," the central story in *Three Lives*, is considered one of the most original short stories of the twentieth century. By employing simple words to express complicated thoughts, Stein endowed common people with a complex psychology that earlier writers had given only to characters of high social standing.

"Melanctha" tells the story of Melanctha Herbert, a beautiful light-skinned black women who struggles to comprehend her troubled, passionate nature. Melanctha's language, like her life, moves toward people, then away, then back again, in a spiral of acceptance and rejection.

Melanctha is a victim of her search for excitement and her barely controlled eroticism. In her affair with Jefferson Campbell, a young black doctor called in to attend her dying mother, Melanctha encounters a lover who is her exact opposite. Whereas Melanctha is vibrant, sensual, and committed to living in the present, Jeff Campbell is quiet and thoughtful, a man who recoils from physical passion. The story describes in long stretches of dialogue their tormented debate over the virtues of their respective psychological natures. Slowly, Jeff learns to think less and to feel more deeply, until finally he is able to feel the glory of the physical world. Yet once Melanctha has taught him how to love as she does, she loses interest in him and enters into a series of love affairs that in the end leave her alone facing death in a home for impoverished consumptives.

To counter the bleakness of her tale, Stein invents a glowing, elemental language that evokes an eternal present. Vocabulary is pared to the bone, and syntax and diction are subtly distorted to echo common speech. Phrases are repeated over and over with only minor changes until they assume a hypnotic power. The story is about a love affair and the torture of two people trying to comprehend what they mean to each other. The words they use to explain themselves entrap them. Language as a medium of expression both liberates and obscures emotion. The inner lives of two common people are revealed by the rhythms of their speech but can never be exactly known. Huge psychological spaces are suggested, while the story contains little plot or description. No character is treated as being more important than another. Absent entirely is the socially elevated tone of conventional fiction, and nowhere can the commanding presence of the author be found.

"Melanctha" was a breathtaking advance in short-story writing, but one that Stein never repeated. It was read by few people when it was first published (partly at Stein's expense), but its influence was enormous on such writers as Hemingway, Anderson, and Richard Wright, who borrowed Stein's verbal rhythms to express the inner worlds of black people growing up in Chicago.

PICASSO

First published: 1912
Type of work: Word portrait

The artist Pablo Picasso doggedly struggles to create a new art that can be described but not named.

Stein's word portraits "Matisse" and "Picasso" appeared in a special issue of *Camera Work* in New York City in 1912. The publisher, Alfred Stieglitz, was an accomplished photographer who devoted his life to making photography a creative art. Stieglitz had not quite understood the pieces, which was why he immediately decided to publish them. In doing so, he introduced Stein's writing to America.

Stein was as much a historical figure as a celebrated writer. She and Picasso each created famous portraits of the other. Hers was in words. She had ample time to observe Picasso in the winter of 1906, when she posed for him some eighty times while he struggled to complete his portrait of her. Dissatisfied with his depiction of her head, Picasso departed for Spain. When he returned, he painted it in rapidly. When Stein cut her hair, friends worried that the famous portrait, which hung on the wall of her apartment, no longer resembled her. Picasso's reply was that he had painted Stein as she would come to look.

Stein's description of Picasso employs constant repetition to suggest the presence of someone doggedly moving forward. Picasso is portrayed as being ahead of others, and others are following his example, but he is not aware of his direction, only of the fact that he is moving. Stein's hypnotic, repetitious sentences suggest that Picasso is a man plodding along, his eyes on the work before him, working to bring something out of himself that cannot be described. Stein calls this something "a heavy thing, a solid thing and a complete thing."

She does not dehumanize Picasso, although his drive to paint and his need to paint is shown as almost machinelike. From the outset, she responds to him as a person and singles out his great charm as the hallmark of his nature. In the midst of this charm, she watches as Picasso struggles to bring out of himself something new and meaningful. All of his life, she thinks, something has been coming out of him that is lovely, interesting, disturbing, repellant, and very pretty.

He has always been working and will always be working, she sees. He seems to need to work, and his art is partly a way to satisfy his longing to work. Yet she concludes her portrait of Picasso with the tantalizing thought that, even when he is working hardest, Picasso is never completely at work. She stops just short of saying how significant an ingredient play was to Picasso's art and life.

Later, Stein explained the extreme repetitive style of her portraits as a necessary technique that mimicked the continuous images of the cinema. Through a succession of hypnotic statements, she hoped to erase the distinction between each sentence and to create a continuous thing called a portrait. Like Picasso's early canvases, Stein's portrait of the artist was a thing that might, by degrees, seem new, interesting, disturbing, and very pretty.

COMPOSITION AS EXPLANATION

First published: 1926
Type of work: Essay

The author lectures on the nature of composition, modernism, and the effect of World War I.

Composition as Explanation is an artful blend of literary theory, historical commentary, and personal confession. Delivered originally as a lecture to students at the University of Cambridge and the University of Oxford in 1926, it is one of the first attempts by Stein to explain her method of composition. The essay represents one of the most candid attempts by a writer to communicate the struggle to write to an audience of strangers. As in all of Stein's writing, her sentences refuse to be pinned down and yield new insights with each reading.

The essay begins haltingly, in the manner of a speaker searching for the precise location of her subject. Part of what Stein seeks to communicate, however, is the struggle to give voice to ideas; thus, her sentences echo this struggle. Thoughts are ungraspable, and Stein's halting manner of writing should not be mistaken for clumsiness. To express herself too coherently would be to make the subject of writing too simple and rational. Her words in this essay are best understood if read aloud, since they follow so closely the circular movements of her inner voice. The essential ideas of *Composition as Explanation*, like most of Stein's thinking, rest firmly in common sense and literary experience. Ideas, she suggest, can never be finished, and Stein gets greater range from her thoughts by playing with them, turning them around, and then starting them again from the beginning.

The world does not change, she argues; only the conception of things changes as each generation lives and thinks differently from the previous generation. Nothing changes between generations except the way in which things are seen, and this change leads to new works of art. Artists live on the outer edge of their time, and what they create often seems strange, even ugly, to contemporaries who lag a little behind. After enough time has elapsed for contemplation and study, new works of art are accepted by society, dubbed "classical," and declared to be beautiful. By the time a work of art has become an acknowledged classic, though, some of its thrill has disappeared, since it no longer challenges the viewer. Beauty, Stein argues, is most beautiful when it is new and disturbing. It would be better, she insists, if artists and their audiences could stand together at the same place in time.

Stein believes that artists exist in a continuous present when they write, compose, or paint, since the act of composition can take place only in the present. One result of World War I, she argues, was to push everyone forward in time by almost thirty years. Modernism had started earlier, but the whole world was brought up to the point of modernism by the war, with the result that artists and their contemporaries stood side by side, at the edge of understanding.

After establishing this foundation for her literary theories Stein describes the course of her own career. Although she does not say as much openly, she suggests that her own works, which are considered strange and eccentric by her contemporaries, will some day qualify as classics.

THE AUTOBIOGRAPHY OF ALICE B. TOKLAS

First published: 1933
Type of work: Autobiography

A typical American woman describes artistic life in Paris in the first quarter of the twentieth century.

The Autobiography of Alice B. Toklas is Gertrude Stein's inventive memoir of how she and her Parisian friends must have looked to Alice B. Toklas. The book was an immediate success in America and has remained in print. More conventional than any of Stein's previous books, it described a crucial period in cultural history with a wit, charm, and mock simplicity that disguised the book's brilliant inventiveness.

The subject presented a challenge to Stein's desire to live and write in a "continuous present." Like Picasso, Stein was willing to copy anyone but herself. How, then, was she to produce an autobiography that would be free of her past and of the laws of conventional identity?

Her answer was to write an "autobiography" of someone else and to construct a narrative of constant digression. *The Autobiography of Alice B. Toklas* became the impersonation of an age as seen through the eyes of an ordinary American woman who arrived in Paris in 1907. The years before World War I are described with wit and delight, the war and its aftermath more darkly. Like much of Stein's work, the writing hovers around a constant present by relying on the spoken word. The prose reads like dictation, as though Stein had merely transcribed the lilt and vocabulary of Toklas' voice. Part Stein, part Toklas, the prose is purely American. With its delight in irreverent gossip, the narrative resembles a novel of social history. Only at the end does Toklas reveal the true author, when she remarks that Stein has been threatening to write her autobiography and that this is it. The book thus holds onto a continuous present by ending at the moment of its beginning, as the reader is invited to reread the book as a work by Stein.

Throughout the book, chronology follows curiosity rather than linear time. The section "Gertrude Stein in Paris, 1903-1907" precedes "Gertrude Stein Before She Came to Paris." Although Toklas is seemingly the main character, she disappears on page five and does not reappear for many pages while Stein's story is told.

Indirection is at the heart of every observation. The painter Henri Matisse, for example, is first observed at three removes: Stein quotes a story told by Toklas about the cook Helene's opinion of Matisse's dinner manners. Stein pretends to write about surface details, and yet she succeeds in revealing the nature of life underneath. She constantly digresses, only to return with what she wants to say.

Appraisals of character and talent are delivered from a female viewpoint that has little to do with the male world of professional success, education, and wealth. The long, brilliant section on the leading artists of the day concludes with a series of intimate anecdotes about their wives and mistresses. There is no upstairs or downstairs in Stein's world. Her vision of human personality is bold, irreverent, and thought-provoking. As a work of literary reminiscence, *The Autobiography of Alice B. Toklas* is one of the richest ever written.

Summary

From the time of her arrival in Paris in 1903 until her death in 1946, Gertrude Stein strove to be a central figure in modern literature. She directed a movement that broke with the past and sought fresh forms of literary expression. A bold explorer of prose, she broke away from the nineteenth century's reliance on plot, character, and conventional description to demonstrate how awareness and identity could be evoked through simple words. She deliberately chose an unliterary style and emphasized the power of words by arranging them in unusual ways.

Although her autobiographical works about France are best remembered, Stein left her mark on modern literature through her influence on writers such as Ernest Hemingway and Sherwood Anderson. The cadence and artlessness of much contemporary writing echoes her early experiments in modern prose.

Bibliography

Bridgman, Richard. *Gertrude Stein in Pieces*. New York: Oxford University Press, 1970.

Brinnin, John Malcolm. *The Third Rose: Gertrude Stein and Her World*. Boston: Little, Brown, 1959.

Gallup, Donald, ed. *The Flowers of Friendship: Letters Written to Gertrude Stein*. New York: Alfred A. Knopf, 1953.

Hoffman, Michael J., comp. *Critical Essays on Gertrude Stein*. Boston: G. K. Hall, 1986.

Kellner, Bruce, ed. *A Gertrude Stein Companion: Content with the Example*. New York: Greenwood Press, 1988.

Liston, Maureen R. *Gertrude Stein: An Annotated Critical Bibliography*. Kent, Ohio: Kent State University Press, 1979.

Mellow, James R. *Charmed Circle: Gertrude Stein and Company*. New York: Praeger, 1974.

Rogers, W. G. *When This You See Remember Me: Gertrude Stein in Person*. New York: Rinehart, 1948.

Simon, Linda, ed. *Gertrude Stein: A Composite Portrait*. New York: Avon Books, 1974.

Sutherland, Donald. *Gertrude Stein: A Biography of Her Work*. New Haven: Yale University Press, 1951.

Philip Metcalfe

WILLIAM STYRON

Born: Newport News, Virginia
June 11, 1925

Principal Literary Achievement
An important post-World War II novelist, Styron is considered one of the finest writers to follow in the footsteps of the great Southern writer William Faulkner.

Biography
William Styron was born in Newport News, Virginia, on June 11, 1925, the son of William Clark and Pauline Styron. Styron's roots in the South are deep and can be traced back to the seventeenth century. He grew up steeped in stories of the Civil War and of its battlefields. Reared in Hilton Village, a semirural community several miles from Newport News, he went to segregated schools and lived in a family with black servants. His father worked in shipbuilding in Newport News. His mother, who developed cancer soon after his birth, remained an invalid for eleven years, dying in 1939, after Styron's sophomore year at Morrison High School. Around that time, he published his first story (now lost) in the school newspaper.

Styron was an active student—he was president of his sophomore class and manager of the football team—but his teachers thought he lacked discipline, and he was sent to an Episcopal preparatory school Christchurch, near Urbana, Virginia. In this small school (fifty students), he enjoyed the atmosphere of an encouraging extended family. He wrote for the school newspaper and yearbook, sailed, and played basketball. While he attended chapel every day and church on Sunday, he also took up drinking, one of the traditional activities of a Virginia gentleman.

In 1942, Styron entered Davidson College, a Presbyterian institution near Charlotte, North Carolina. His father thought that the University of Virginia, known for its rowdy drinking parties, would be inappropriate for his son, an indifferent student. Styron joined the college newspaper and literary magazine, and he rid himself of his Tidewater accent after fellow students made fun of it.

At eighteen, Styron joined the Navy expecting to train as an officer, but he was transferred to Duke University. There, he attended classes but was still under military discipline. Duke was a traditional campus, strict about matters of dress, with coeds wearing white gloves on off-campus dates. Again Styron proved a mediocre student, and he was put on active duty by the end of 1944.

After boot camp, Styron performed various duties and spent a few months guarding a prison camp. The dropping of the atomic bombs on Japan spared him the experience of combat, and he returned to the postwar liberated atmosphere of the Duke campus in 1946. In this invigorating environment, he began to develop as a writer of fiction, winning praise from teachers and publishing several stories in the college magazine while also attending writers' conferences.

In 1947, Styron moved to New York, securing a job as an editor at McGraw-Hill, where he read reams of unsolicited manuscripts. As lax an employee as he had been a student, Styron was fired after six months. He provides a vivid portrait of himself as an aspiring writer in the character of Stingo in his novel *Sophie's Choice* (1979). Having taken a writing class at the New School for Social Research taught by Hiram Haydn, a book editor in New York, Styron began to conceive his first novel, *Lie Down in Darkness* (1951). Almost always a slow writer subject to writer's blocks, Styron moved back to Durham for a brief period before finishing the novel in the Flatbush section of Brooklyn and in Valley Cottage, near Nyack, New York.

In 1951, Styron was recalled to active duty in the Marines during the Korean War, and the episode became the basis of his fine novella *The Long March* (1956). His first novel had been hailed by critics, who saw him as the successor to the great Southern novelist William Faulkner. About this time, he also met his future wife, Rose Burgender, and traveled in Europe. He worked on a novella he never completed (about his experiences as a prison guard) and on a novel set in Europe that was eventually published as *Set This House on Fire* (1960).

In 1953, Styron moved to Roxbury, Connecticut. He married Rose Burgender, by whom he had two daughters, Susanna (born in 1955) and Paolo (born in 1958). Active as a reviewer and a superb writer of nonfiction, Styron began work in 1962 on his most controversial novel, *The Confessions of Nat Turner* (1967), which dared to present a slave's experience not only in his own words but also within his consciousness. In spite of fierce attacks, mainly by African American writers, the novel enjoyed enormous critical and popular success, winning Styron the Pulitzer Prize in 1968.

Styron did not publish another novel until *Sophie's Choice* (1979), in which he extended his study of human oppression to the Holocaust—another daring feat of the imagination that again brought him accolades and criticism. He also continued to work on a novel based on his experience in the Marines.

Analysis

Styron is a master of modern literary style. He has been compared to Faulkner because, more than any of his contemporaries, Styron has a feeling for rhythms of language that seem to embody the speech of a whole region, a lush, romantic feeling for nature and for human relationships. Styron is a painstaking writer, often spending a day perfecting a single page. Yet his prose flows so gracefully that his enormous effort usually remains invisible. This is especially true of *Lie Down in Darkness* and *The Confessions of Nat Turner*, both of which appear to be seamless narratives, stories that unfold without a break or flaw in style.

If there is a fault in Styron's style, some critics would say it is his perfectionism. He has been criticized for exercising too much control over his narratives, producing novels that are too meticulous, too polished. This kind of exquisite technique robs his work of a certain rough-edged life, an unruliness that should overtake the writer and ride him, so to speak. Styron's sense of language, in other words, is too precious; it can actually get in the way of the life he is trying to portray. This tendency is perhaps most evident in *The Confessions of Nat Turner*, in which Turner's consciousness is transparently Styron's—that is, Turner is endowed with Styron's gift for language and much of Styron's literary sensibility. Some critics, however, have argued that this is precisely Styron's achievement: endowing characters such as Turner with an integrity and articulateness that is the equal of their author's. From this point of view, Styron's gorgeous vocabulary ennobles his characters and allows them to speak on a higher literary level that is the only way to reveal their full humanity and complexity. There is certainly ample precedent for Styron's sophisticated technique in Faulkner's *As I Lay Dying* (1930), in which the interior monologues use a highly elevated and baroque language to register not merely what the characters are thinking but also what they are as human beings.

Styron is also an excellent observer of social manners. In both his fiction and nonfiction, he is a shrewd reporter, rendering not only the facts of life also but how those facts are received by the senses and turned into feelings. He is a great poet of consciousness who bases his flights of rhetoric on a realistic notation of the data of life.

One of the great themes of Styron's fiction is the South. *Lie Down in Darkness* surveys the modern South by focusing on the life and death of Peyton Loftis, a young woman growing up in a region still recovering from the devastation of the Civil War—psychologically more than physically. The novel suggests that World War I and the "Lost Generation"—those young Americans whose lives were interrupted by war, some of whom stayed in Europe—proved to be a crisis for those who stayed home as well, such as Peyton's father, Milton, whose lack of purpose and hollow life as a Southern gentleman deprive Peyton of basic beliefs, a foundation for her future. She tells her father, in fact, that it is her generation that is lost.

The Confessions of Nat Turner, on the other hand, is Styron's self-confessed attempt to imagine what it must have been like for a slave in Virginia to revolt against his masters. As a descendant of a slave-owning class and as the product of a segregated society, Styron wrote a novel that aimed not only to understand the past but also to effect a kind of reconciliation between the races in the present. His treatment of Nat Turner as a brilliant man, a kind of genius with a gift for language equal to Styron's own, has been perceived by many critics, though by no means all, as a brilliant effort to bridge the gap between past and present. As the African American writer James Baldwin said of the novel, "He has begun the common history—ours."

Sophie's Choice represents a continuation of the themes of *The Confessions of Nat Turner*. The narrator, Stingo, is a white Southerner trying to come to terms with Sophie, a survivor of the Holocaust. The novel contains passages on Southern and

European history, positing a historical identity that is not meant to minimize the differences between cultures but to reveal the overarching experiences, from slavery to the Holocaust, that have shaped the modern world.

Many of Styron's stories have been about survival and suicide. In writing a book about his own suicidal depression, *Darkness Visible* (1992), Styron admits that he did not realize how much this was a pattern in his work, or how drinking has often been a part of this pattern, as it is in the behavior of Milton Loftis, a lawyer with a romantic, literary sensibility similar to Styron's own. Drinking immobilizes Loftis. It eases the pain of his lack of action, the harsh criticisms of his Puritanical wife, and becomes a way to negotiate the boring routines of daily existence. Loftis sees flaws in himself and in his family, but he is fatally blind to what his own daughter needs, because of his adoring, even incestuous, longing for her. Drink becomes the only lubricant that keeps him going. Though Styron has survived and become much more successful than his characters, there is a brooding, depressive sense of existence in his prose, a sense that seems related to his own titanic writer's blocks and his inability to complete work (he has begun and abandoned several novels).

In *This Quiet Dust* (1982) and in *Darkness Visible*, Styron has proven himself a writer of superb nonfiction prose. In both the essay form and the memoir, his precise command of language and his candor make for compelling reading. Perhaps the best example of this is "This Quiet Dust," an account of his trip to survey the site of Nat Turner's rebellion. The essay provides a striking counterpoint to the novel, for the essay reveals not the mind of the slave but the mind of the writer approaching his material, wondering how he can recapture the past and do justice to a figure who has troubled and excited him for more than twenty years.

LIE DOWN IN DARKNESS

First published: 1951
Type of work: Novel

Peyton Loftis' body is brought from New York City to her Virginia home after her suicide, and the story of her life and of her family is told in a series of flashbacks.

Lie Down in Darkness made William Styron's reputation as a novelist. It was a brilliant first novel that showcased a writer in full control of his language, which fit into a perfectly shaped story, beginning on the day Peyton Loftis' body is being returned to her Virginia home. Styron describes the scene, the funeral cortege, and the characters—Peyton's father, Milton, her mother, Helen, and Milton's mistress, Dolly Bonner—who will dominate the story. It is a long day of mourning, yet Styron manages to break up the day with poignant flashbacks that gradually explain the events that led to Peyton's suicide.

Milton is inconsolable over the loss of his daughter. His one hope is that his estranged wife, Helen, will come back to him and repair their relationship, which he now believes is all that he has left in life. Helen does not even want to attend the funeral, let alone readmit Milton into her life. Through a series of flashbacks, it is revealed that Milton had always doted on his daughter and resented his wife's harsh criticism of his drinking, and that Helen has been jealous of Peyton and rejected her in favor of her ailing daughter, Maudie.

Nothing Peyton does seems right in Helen's eyes. When Peyton accidentally drops Maudie, Helen accuses her of doing it deliberately. When a teenage Peyton is given a drink at a party by her father, Helen treats Peyton like a slut and excoriates Milton for turning his daughter into an alcoholic like himself. Although Helen is overly severe, she is largely right about Milton's behavior. Her unbending personality, however, is entirely devoid of humanity.

The novel's climax is reached in a flashback relating the catastrophe of Peyton's wedding. She has been away from home for years, refusing to see her mother, but she is coaxed home by her father. He has stopped drinking and become reconciled with Helen, a development that has come about partly as a result of Maudie's death. The patterns of Peyton's childhood reassert themselves at the wedding—only this time, it is Peyton encouraging her father to drink. She hurts him terribly when she confesses that she thinks he is a jerk and that she has only come home to play a role that will please her parents. She is being honest but very cruel. She has become a rather hopeless figure; she tells her father that she is a part of a lost generation because his generation has provided no substantial legacy, no repository of values that might guide her in a new, uncertain world.

In many ways, the characters of this novel are unpleasant and irredeemable. Yet they do struggle to right themselves, and Styron's deft use of flashbacks, in which the reader's knowledge of the characters increases incrementally, is riveting.

THE CONFESSIONS OF NAT TURNER

First published: 1967
Type of work: Novel

A compelling but controversial first-person narrative of the most successful slave revolt in American history.

When *The Confessions of Nat Turner* first appeared, it was acclaimed as breakthrough both in fiction and in race relations. A white Southerner, steeped in the history of his region, had boldly entered the mind of a black slave, according him the dignity of an articulate voice and making him into a modern hero. Certainly, Styron's Turner is cruel in his taking of close to sixty lives, but he is nevertheless the poet of the aspirations of a people. Early reviews lauded the language and the sympathy with which Styron presented the story.

Soon, though, a group of African American writers attacked the book, accusing Styron of distorting history, of coopting their hero, and of demeaning Turner by endowing him with love for one of his victims, a young white woman. These critics saw Styron as usurping their history much as whites had usurped the labor and the very lives of their ancestors. They rejected the notion that a white Southerner—or any white, for that matter—could fathom the mind of a slave.

Styron defended himself admirably, for he had made a close reading of the historical record and knew exactly where he was taking liberties with history, and he was supported by several historians. Less defensible, or at least problematic, was his decision to endow Turner with a contemporary imagination. Turner does speak in the accents of nineteenth century Virginia, but he thinks very much like Styron. Yet even this seeming defect in the novel may be its major strength. For Styron's point is that Turner was, in many ways, ahead of his time, and that this self-taught slave probably had the mind of a genius who should not be condescended to in language less sophisticated than the writer's own.

Quite aside from this controversy, *The Confessions of Nat Turner* can be read as a tragic love story, of a Nat Turner who learns much from white people even as they oppress him. Styron shows that tenderness was possible between the races even under the regime of slavery—a fact the historian Eugene Genovese has corroborated in his research. By thinking of Turner as his equal, Styron was able to remove the clichés from the presentation of race in fiction. That he touched a nerve in his critics, who violently attacked him, suggests something of the power of that love story and how it might pose a threat to those who doubt the races can reconcile.

SOPHIE'S CHOICE

First published: 1979
Type of work: Novel

Set in post-World War II Brooklyn, *Sophie's Choice* is about the maturing of a young novelist who confronts the Holocaust in his fascination with Sophie, a concentration camp survivor.

Sophie's Choice is Styron's most ambitious novel. It contains the major themes of his previous fiction, embodying his loves of the South and of literature, his experience of war, and his quest to write a major novel summing up the significant issues of his age. His narrator, Stingo, is a callow youth who is living in Brooklyn, as Styron did, trying to write fiction. His sexual experience has been limited, and he finds himself attracted to a beautiful Polish woman, Sophie, the survivor of a concentration camp.

It is 1947, and the incredible suffering of the Holocaust is just beginning to be revealed and understood. The situation becomes complicated for Stingo, who becomes the third member of a triangle when he befriends Sophie's lover, Nathan, who is erratic and paranoic but also charismatic. Nathan flouts propriety, and his radical individualism appeals to the young Stingo, who again like Styron has fared poorly in the bureaucratic publishing world and who is looking for a way to express himself.

Sophie's behavior is puzzling to Stingo; she is passive and willing to let Nathan abuse her. Nathan's cruelty is eventually explained in terms of his drug addiction and mental illness. Similarly, Sophie's willingness to be treated as a victim begins to make sense when Stingo learns of her concentration camp experience—the way she had to make herself available sexually to her captors, and to make her awful choice: surrendering one of her children to the gas ovens.

Sophie is not Jewish. In fact, her father wrote anti-Semitic tracts. Being Polish was enough to send her to the camps. Styron's point is an important one: Millions of non-Jews died in the camps, and the fate of Jew and non-Jew alike is a human tragedy that involves everyone.

Styron's decision to have Stingo narrate the story allows him to deal with the Holocaust sensitively and tactfully. His young alter ego is able to learn gradually about these horrifying events, so that they become a dramatic and believable part of the novel. Yet the narrator alone does not suffice. Styron also includes a narrator who provides essay-like excursions into the history of the Holocaust—a daring and perhaps not always successful addition to the novel.

Sophie's Choice is Styron's darkest vision of the modern world. Sophie and Nathan eventually commit suicide. Her burden of guilt is too great for her to endure life after the war, and Nathan seems to have chosen her for a lover to fulfill his own self-destructive course. What redeems their lives, in a sense, is Stingo's devotion to them, his passion to understand what happened to them and what it means for him. By implication, their story becomes the writer's story, an account of why he writes, and why others should care for lives that end in failure.

Summary

Styron is the poet of human failure. Peyton Loftis kills herself. Nat Turner engages in a suicidal slave revolt. Sophie and Nathan die in a suicide pact. In spite of these depressing stories, Styron's style is uplifting, a beautiful evocation of human beings and settings. Although he himself has been subject to despair, his novels prevail in their sheer artistry. In their graceful language, they suggest that human beings are capable of grace, of a forgiveness beyond guilt. In Styron's novels, there is always the opportunity to communicate and to reconcile human conflicts, even if most such conflicts end badly.

Bibliography

Casciato, Arthur D., and James L. W. West III. *Critical Essays on William Styron.* Boston: G. K. Hall, 1982.

Coale, Samuel. *William Styron Revisited*. Boston: Twayne, 1991.

Crane, John Kenny. *The Root of All Evil: The Thematic Unity of William Styron's Fiction*. Columbia: University of South Carolina Press, 1984.

Fossum, Robert H. *William Styron: A Critical Essay*. Grand Rapids, Mich.: William B. Eerdmans, 1968.

Morris, Robert K., and Irving Malin, eds. *The Achievement of William Styron*. Athens: University of Georgia Press, 1975.

Pearce, Richard. *William Styron*. Minneapolis: University of Minnesota Press, 1971.

Ruderman, Judith. *William Styron*. New York: Frederick Ungar, 1987.

Carl Rollyson

AMY TAN

Born: Oakland, California
February 19, 1952

Principal Literary Achievement

Tan explores the cultural conflict between Chinese and Chinese American generations as well as the tender and difficult relationships between mothers and daughters.

Biography

Amy Tan was the second of three children born to Chinese immigrants John and Daisy Tan. Her father, educated as an electrical engineer in Beijing, became a Baptist minister. Daisy, child of a privileged family, was forced to leave behind three daughters from a previous marriage when she fled Communist troops.

Tan's older brother died in 1967 and her father six months later, both of brain tumors. This began a troubled time for her. At fifteen, she moved to Europe with her mother and younger brother, was arrested for drugs in Switzerland at sixteen, and nearly eloped to Austria with a German army deserter.

Daisy Tan wanted her daughter to be a neurosurgeon and a concert pianist, but Tan felt she could not live up to her mother's expectations. Although her scores were higher in math and science, she left premedical studies to become an English major. In 1974, she earned a master's degree in linguistics from San Jose State University and married tax attorney Lou DeMattei. She began doctoral studies at the University of California at Berkeley but dropped out to become a consultant to programs for disabled children. Later she served as reporter, editor, and publisher for *Emergency Room Reports*.

Tan became a freelance business writer in 1983. She wrote sales manuals and proposals for such firms as American Telephone and Telegraph (AT&T), International Business Machines (IBM), and Apple, and by 1985 was working up to ninety hours a week. Her business writing paid well, and she could choose her projects, but, she has said, "It was death to me spiritually. It was writing that had no meaning to me."

She sought therapy, but she was discouraged when her psychiatrist fell asleep during her sessions. Instead, she decided to cut her work week to fifty hours, study jazz piano, and write fiction in her spare time. She had just read novelist Louise Erdrich's *Love Medicine* (1984), interwoven stories of a Native American family, and was inspired to write her own. At the Squaw Valley Community of Writers fiction workshop, she

met Molly Giles, winner of the Flannery O'Connor Award for fiction. She showed Giles what would become Waverly Jong's story, "Rules of the Game," in *The Joy Luck Club* (1989), and Giles became her mentor.

Tan finished three stories in three years. When *The Joy Luck Club* was sold to Putnam in 1987 on the basis of a proposal and three stories ("Rules of the Game," "Waiting Between the Trees," and "Scar"), Tan closed her business and wrote thirteen more stories in four months. She thought her acceptance was "a token minority thing. I thought they had to fill a quota since there weren't many Chinese-Americans writing."

Like the daughters in her books, Tan was ambivalent about her Chinese background. She contemplated plastic surgery to make herself look more Western, and she did not fully accept her dual culture until 1987, when she and her mother went to China to meet her half-sisters. She has remarked that, "As soon as my feet touched China, I became Chinese."

Writing *The Joy Luck Club* also helped Tan to discover how Chinese she really was. In many respects, it is her family's story. Her mother had formed a Joy Luck Club in China and again in San Francisco. Daisy Tan "was the little girl watching her mother cut a piece of flesh from her arm to make soup, and she was the little girl watching her mother die when she took opium because she had become a third concubine."

Tan's first book was a surprising bestseller in hardcover and paperback. It received the Commonwealth Club Gold Award for Fiction, the Bay Area Book Reviewers Award for Fiction, and the American Library Association Best Book for Young Adults Award and was a finalist for the National Book Award.

For nearly a year, Tan tried to start *The Kitchen God's Wife* (1991). Again her subjects were a Chinese mother and a Chinese American daughter, but this time she focused upon the mother's life in China. The novel received *Booklist*'s editor's choice and was nominated for the Bay Area Book Reviewers award.

The Joy Luck Club was made into a popular movie in 1993. Tan wrote the screenplay with Ron Bass and coproduced the film, directed by Wayne Wang. Her books have been translated into French, German, Italian, Dutch, and Chinese.

Analysis

Tan uses first-person narratives as the basis of both her books. *The Joy Luck Club* was conceived and written as a collection of short stories, but early reviewers began to call it a novel. Her publisher carefully skirted the issue by referring to Tan's "first work of fiction" on the book jacket.

The book is composed of sixteen related stories narrated by three mothers and four daughters. It recalls such loosely structured works as Sherwood Anderson's *Winesburg, Ohio* (1919), William Faulkner's *As I Lay Dying* (1930), and Erdrich's *Love Medicine*, which feature individual narratives that together reflect a culture or a period. Tan organizes *The Joy Luck Club* in terms of the contrast between generations—two sections in the voices of the Chinese-born mothers and two in the voices of their California daughters. The exception is June Woo, whose mother Suyuan, founder of the Joy Luck Club, has just died. June's voice is heard in all four sections of the book.

Tan's second book, *The Kitchen God's Wife*, is structured as a traditional novel, following one major story line. It is narrated by two voices—three chapters by daughter Pearl and all others by mother Winnie Louie, who tells Pearl of her earlier life. This is a book of revelations, illuminated vertically as well as horizontally. Things are never what they seem. When characters think they know the truth, they know only part of it.

In books exploring emotionally intense events, Tan's humor is a pleasant surprise. June, an aspiring child prodigy, takes piano lessons from a deaf teacher. Another family names its four sons Matthew, Mark, Luke, and Bing. Some of the dialogue is priceless: June's mother calls her "a college drop-off," and another mother collects "so-so security." Tan also masters the one-line retort. Learning that Grand Auntie Du is dead at ninety-seven, " 'What was it? . . . A stroke?' " Pearl asks. "'A bus,' my mother said."

A major theme of Tan's work is the conflict between cultures and generations. Of the Chinese women, an extreme example is Winnie Louie's Old Aunt, whose feudal upbringing taught that a woman's eyes should be used for sewing, not reading; ears should listen to orders, not ideas; and lips should only be used to express gratitude or approval. When Winnie's cousin Peanut married a homosexual, her mother-in-law bought her a baby to save face. Their schoolmate, forced to marry a simple-minded man and chided by her unsympathetic mother, hanged herself in despair. Winnie realizes that she has been wrong to hold such women responsible for their troubles, but, she says, "That was how I was raised—never to criticize men or the society they ruled. . . . I could blame only other women who were more afraid than I." Another woman dreams, "In America I will have a daughter just like me. But over there nobody will say her worth is measured by the loudness of her husband's belch."

These are things of which the resentful American daughters have no awareness. They do not understand the intensity of their mothers' need to protect them from life, and they have little sense of their mothers as people. Instead, their mothers seem an embarrassment—stingy, fussy old women. Pearl, in her old bedroom, finds her worn slippers and is impatient that her mother refuses to throw anything away. Later, Winnie, cleaning the same room, takes comfort in these traces of her daughter's childhood.

Tan explores not only the rift between mothers and daughters but also its healing. She believes in the power of love. The daughters have a desperate need to communicate with their mothers and one another that they do not even recognize, and as the barriers to communication begin to crumble, their first tentative steps toward reconciliation promise more.

Tan also examines a deeper question, which she has stated as "what in our life is given to us as fate, and what is given to us as sheer luck of the moment, and what are choices that we make. . . ?" The mothers reared in China were taught to believe in fate and luck. In *The Joy Luck Club*, An-mei Hsu's own mother is the widow of a respected scholar. She is befriended by the Second Wife of a rich man who is attracted to her.

Second Wife arranges the rape of An-mei's mother by this man so that he will take her as a third concubine, since she is now disgraced, and will stop spending so much money in teahouses, leaving more for the wife. When a son is born to An-mei's mother, Second Wife claims the baby as her own. The mother eats poisoned sweet dumplings, telling her daughter, "You see how this life is. You cannot eat enough of this bitterness."

An-mei points out again and again how her unhappy mother had no choice. Yet An-mei has learned from her mother's suicide that choices can be made, and she tries to teach her American daughter, whose marriage is ending, to stand up for herself: "If she doesn't speak, she is making a choice. . . . I know this, because I was . . . taught to desire nothing, to swallow other people's misery, to eat my own bitterness."

The mothers' wisdom and finely drawn characters are revealed in both books by a peeling away of layers, like an onion, down to the unblemished heart. Though the mothers' lives have been harsher, they are incredibly stronger than their uncertain, unhappy daughters. If the mothers were not permitted choices, suggests Tan, perhaps the daughters are weakened by having too many.

Tan employs a world of metaphor and symbolism, especially in *The Joy Luck Club*. A thematic title and vignette introduce each section of that book; for example, "The Twenty-Six Malignant Gates" section alludes to a Chinese book that warns of dangers to children, and here each daughter tells of a problem she faced as a child. In an ironically titled story, "Rice Husband," the shaky marriage of Ying-ying St. Clair's daughter is represented by a wobbly end table, designed by the husband, which is only waiting to collapse. The marriage is further symbolized by the remodeled barn that is the architect couple's new house, furnished in the husband's preferred minimalist style, and pared down and stingy like him. Ying-ying thinks "everything . . . is for looking, not even for good-looking. . . . This is a house that will break into pieces."

THE JOY LUCK CLUB

First published: 1989
Type of work: Short stories

These linked stories reveal the intricate lives and conflicts of four Chinese mothers and their Chinese American daughters.

The Joy Luck Club takes its title from a gathering begun in wartime China by Suyuan Woo, who met with three women in a weekly attempt to maintain their sanity and luck. They prepared special foods and played mah-jongg, even though the city was filled with horror. In 1949, in San Francisco, Suyuan resumed the tradition with three new friends.

One critic has suggested that the book is structured like the four corners of the mah-jongg table at which the women sit, with four stories in each of the book's four sections, and four mother-daughter pairs. In maj-jongg, one critic has noted, "The game starts, always, with the east wind," and June Woo, whose narrative begins and ends the book, sits on the east, taking her dead mother's place. The game ends when one player has a complete hand, and June completes her mother's life and dearest wish when she returns to China, with a ticket paid for by the Joy Luck Club, to meet the two half-sisters her mother was forced to leave behind in her flight.

Recurring motifs link the stories of each mother-daughter pair. The second mother, An-mei Hsu, bears a scar from the spilling of hot soup on her neck as a child, an accident that nearly killed her. She carries a grievous inner scar as well: Her own mother had been banished, her name never spoken. Only later does she understand how her mother dishonored the family by becoming the third concubine of a wealthy married man. Yet when An-mei's grandmother was dying, her mother returned to cut a piece of flesh from her own arm to make a magic healing broth. "This is how a daughter honors her mother," An-mei remembers. "It is *shou* [respect] so deep it is in your bones."

This same mother poisoned herself, timing her death so that her soul would return on the first day of the lunar new year to settle scores with the rich man and Second Wife, ensuring a better future for her children. Dead, she had more power than ever in life.

Lindo Jong, the daughter of peasants, was betrothed at the age of two to her first husband and became a servant in his mother's house until their marriage. Although the family nearly convinced her that a daughter belonged to her mother-in-law and that her husband was a god, Lindo discovered herself on her wedding day: "I was strong. I was pure. I had genuine thoughts inside that no one could see, that no one could ever take away from me."

Thus, Lindo's willful and brilliant American daughter Waverly learns "the art of invisible strength" at six from her mother, who tells her, "Strongest wind cannot be seen." Waverly becomes a chess prodigy, but her early confidence falters as she tries to outwit the mother she fears. The tension between mother and daughter seems strongest with this pair. Waverly wants to become her own person, but her mother wonders, "How can she be her own person? When did I give her up?"

Little Ying-ying St. Clair, daughter of the wealthiest family in Wushi, celebrated the Moon Festival by falling off an excursion boat at night and never found herself again. After an unfortunate first marriage, she lost her "tiger spirit" and became a listless ghost. Motifs of the dark other self, of dissolution and integration, appear in her stories, yet mother-daughter love forms a stronger bond. Ying-ying's daughter struggles to rescue her mother's spirit after the devastating birth of an anacephalic child, and the mother in turn tries to give her daughter courage to break free of an empty marriage: "I will use this sharp pain to penetrate my daughter's tough skin and cut her tiger spirit loose. She will fight me, because this is the nature of two tigers. But I will win and give her my spirit, because this is the way a mother loves her daughter."

In the final section of the book, the mothers connect their past to their daughters' lives and encourage them to be strong. As a Chinese grandmother tells her baby granddaughter, "You must teach my daughter this same lesson. How to lose your innocence but not your hope."

THE KITCHEN GOD'S WIFE

First published: 1991
Type of work: Novel

Winnie Louie recounts her hardships in China and is reconciled with her daughter Pearl.

In *The Kitchen God's Wife*, Auntie Helen confronts her friend Winnie, who has secrets, and Winnie's married daughter Pearl, who has multiple sclerosis but is afraid to face her mother. Helen announces that they must confide in each other or she, who is dying of a "B nine" brain tumor, will tell everything. Winnie agrees and summons her estranged daughter.

Winnie's mother, born into wealth and educated in a missionary school, had met a young revolutionary and threatened to swallow gold if her family did not allow them to marry. Instead, she was made second wife to her grandfather's friend. Winnie remembers living with her mother until she was six, when her mother suddenly died or disappeared; she is never sure which. The child was sent to live with relatives.

After a few years, a young man, Wen Fu, became interested in her cousin Peanut, but Winnie was a better marriage prospect because of her father's wealth, so the Wens chose her. Though she did not love Wen Fu, she hoped for a better life. Instead, the greedy Wen family seized her dowry and sold it or used it for themselves. When Wen Fu began to brutalize and humiliate her, she was not angry: "This is China. A woman had no right to be angry."

In 1937, Wen Fu joined the Kuomintang army under his dead brother's name in order to qualify for an American-staffed flight school. There, Winnie met Helen, wife of another officer. Although popular with other pilots, Wen Fu enjoyed playing sadistic games. He was never injured in their bombing missions because, a coward, he always flew the other way.

As the Japanese army invaded China, pregnant Winnie was sent south to Kunming, where her first child was stillborn. After Wen Fu stole a jeep to impress a woman, he was partially blinded, and she was killed in an accident. From that time, his behavior became even more violent. He destroyed the hospital kitchen with a cleaver. His servant, raped and impregnated, died from a self-induced abortion. Winnie's second baby, brain-damaged by his beatings, was allowed to die. Their son later died of plague.

When World War II was over, they returned to Shanghai, where Winnie's father, a collaborator with the Japanese, was viewed as a traitor. Wen Fu offered to manage his business to protect him, then took control of his money and terrified the household.

Just as Winnie decided to ask her cousin Peanut to help her leave her abusive marriage, she encountered Jimmy Louie, a kind Chinese American officer she had met in Kunming. On a pretext, she escaped her father's house and agreed to stay with Jimmy. In order to divorce Wen Fu, she hired a lawyer, but after his office was vandalized by Wen Fu's thugs, he refused further help.

Wen Fu had Winnie jailed for theft and desertion. Jimmy, who would become her second husband, returned to America because of the scandal and waited for her there. After more than a year, Helen's Auntie Du arranged Winnie's release from prison and helped her to obtain a visa and airline tickets. Wen Fu was tricked into stating publicly that they were divorced so that he could have no further control over her. He returned to rape Winnie at gunpoint before she fled China.

Pearl now realizes that she is probably Wen Fu's daughter, the secret her mother has kept from her. She tells Winnie of her own illness, and Winnie offers hope. She and Helen will go to China to find good medicine for Pearl, for Helen has confessed that she has no brain tumor. She merely pretended to be ill as a way to bring Winnie closer to her daughter.

The Kitchen God is the inhabitant of a small shrine left to Pearl by Grand Auntie Du. He was an unfaithful husband who burned in the fireplace rather than face his good wife. Winnie realizes, "I was like that wife of Kitchen God." She determines to replace his picture with a luckier one. Eventually, she finds a statue of an unnamed goddess for the shrine and names her Lady Sorrowfree, advising Pearl, "She is ready to listen. She understands English. You should tell her everything."

Summary

Amy Tan's books are chiefly concerned with the troubled relationships and the conflicts of love between mothers and daughters who are separated by different cultures as well as by generations. She also covers a wide spectrum of lives and customs of Chinese women up until the postwar Cultural Revolution, and she examines the concepts of fate, luck, and choice. Although Tan does not consider herself a spokesperson for Chinese Americans, her writing has awakened further interest in the Chinese American perspective in American literature.

Bibliography

Chong, Denise. "Emotional Journeys Through East and West." *Quill and Quire* 55, no. 5 (May, 1989): 23.

Schell, Orville. "Your Mother Is in Your Bones." *The New York Times Book Review*, March 19, 1989, 3, 28.

Shear, Walter. "Generational Differences and the Diaspora in *The Joy Luck Club.*" *Critique: Studies in Modern Fiction* 34, no. 3 (Spring, 1993): 193-199.

Tan, Amy. Interview by Barbara Somogyi and David Stanton. *Poets & Writers* 14, no. 5 (September-October, 1991): 24-32

—————. "Lost Lives of Women." *Life* 14 (April, 1991): 90-91.
Wang, Dorothy. "A Game of Show Not Tell." *Newsweek* 113 (April 17, 1989): 68-69.

Joanne McCarthy

JEAN TOOMER

Born: Washington, D. C.
December 26, 1894
Died: Doylestown, Pennsylvania
March 20, 1967

Principal Literary Achievement
Cane, Toomer's unusual experimental novel, is a major product of the Harlem Renaissance of the 1920's, and the poems in it rank among the best African American poetry.

Biography

Nathan Pinchback Toomer (by school age he was known as Eugene Pinchback Toomer) was born in Washington, D.C., on December 26, 1894, the son of Nina Pinchback and Nathan Toomer. Until he was almost eleven, he lived with his maternal grandparents, his father having left the family in 1895. Racially mixed and able to pass as white, the Pinchbacks lived in an affluent white neighborhood, though Toomer's grandfather was well known as a black and briefly had been the governor of Louisiana during Reconstruction. When Nina Toomer remarried (to Archibald Combes, a white man), she and her son moved to New York, where they lived until she died in 1909. Returning to the Pinchbacks, who had experienced financial reversals, teenaged Toomer lived with them and an uncle in a modest black area, attended a black high school, and was faced with confronting the issue of his racial identity. He later wrote that he was "Scotch, Welsh, German, English, French, Dutch, Spanish, with some dark blood." Having lived in both the black and white worlds, for a while he determined to consider himself simply an American, hoping to eschew either racial label.

Between 1914 and 1921, he attended five colleges in three states for brief periods and lived in Chicago, Milwaukee, New York, and Washington. He also changed his name to Jean Toomer, began writing, and in New York came to know such promising young writers as Van Wyck Brooks, Witter Bynner, Waldo Frank, and Edwin Arlington Robinson. While in Washington in 1921, looking after his ailing grandparents and writing full time, he was asked to become temporary principal of the Sparta Agricultural and Industrial Institute, a rural Georgia school for blacks. Whereas his experience in Chicago and Washington served as background for parts of *Cane* (1923), the two months in Sparta introduced Toomer to black life in the South. Its economic

deprivation, spirituality, segregation, and music provided him with the subjects and themes of his major literary work.

He wrote "Bona and Paul," a story in the second section of *Cane*, in 1918 during a stay in Chicago, where the story is set. The other narratives and much of the verse, however, are products of a burst of creativity that began on the train that took him back to Washington from Georgia in November of 1921. A month after his return, he had completed the first draft of "Kabnis" (the third section of the book), which closely reflects his Sparta sojourn. By the end of 1922, he had finished all the pieces that would make up *Cane*, and the book was published in 1923 with a foreward by Waldo Frank, who had become Toomer's close friend and mentor. Despite favorable reviews, only about five hundred copies were sold in 1923; a small second printing was made in 1927. Shortly thereafter, the book went out of print until 1967.

In the aftermath of *Cane*'s publication, Toomer became part of New York City's avant-garde white literary circles, but he objected both to rivalries that prevailed in the fraternity of writers and to attempts to promote him as a black writer. Largely because of these factors, he departed the literary scene by 1925. Though he continued to write, he published over the next four decades only a few short stories, some poetry, a book of maxims and aphorisms, and pamphlets about the Quakers.

Much of *Cane* suggests its author's own uncertainty about his identity (stemming from his mixed racial background and upbringing) and religious beliefs (he commented that he was reared "without benefit of organized religion" but that he "did have religious experiences and . . . did somehow form feelings and notions of God.") Therefore, Toomer was receptive to the philosophy of George Ivanovich Gurdjieff, a Greek-Armenian mystic who taught in Russia until the revolution and then in various Western European cities prior to opening the Institute for the Harmonious Development of Man outside Paris. Central to his teachings was the need to seek a balance of mind, body, and soul through which a person would develop a higher consciousness and achieve his or her maximum potential. Toomer spent the summer of 1924 at Gurdjieff's schools, quickly became a disciple, and during most of the next decade led Gurdjieff groups in New York and Chicago.

Toomer married twice, both times to white women. His first wife was Margery Latimer, a novelist he met while in a Gurdjieff group in Portage, Wisconsin. Within a year, she died in childbirth, though their daughter survived. In 1934, he remarried, to Marjorie Content, an affluent New Yorker active in literary circles. They moved to Doylestown, Pennsylvania, in 1936, where they joined and became active in the Society of Friends, or Quakers. Toomer returned to the Gurdjieff philosophy in the 1950's, but inadequate funds kept him from replicating the Paris institute. Plagued by frail health and alcoholism, he spent much of the last five years of his life in a Doylestown nursing home, where he died on March 30, 1967.

Analysis

Most of the fiction (at least four novels and more than a dozen short stories), drama (about a half-dozen plays), and poetry (more than eighty poems) that Jean Toomer wrote during his lifetime remains in manuscript form, so his public reputation rests almost entirely on one work, *Cane*. Published in 1923, the slim volume includes work in all three genres and is widely recognized as a major product of the Harlem Renaissance, a 1920's flowering of African American art and literature that created intense interest among many white intellectuals.

Cane includes six brief prose cameos, seven stories, and a play, all of which concern African Americans of the time. The book is divided into three sections, the first and last of which are set in rural Georgia; the stories of the middle unit take place in Chicago and Washington, D.C. Between the first two sections, on a separate page, is a picture of an arc that is about one-fourth of a circle. On a page between the second and third parts are two such arcs, leaving an incomplete circle. In a letter to Waldo Frank accompanying the manuscript of *Cane*, Toomer explained the curves: "From three angles, CANE's design is a circle. Aesthetically, from simple forms to complex ones, and back to simple forms. Regionally, from the South up into the North, and back into the South again. Or from the North down into the South and then a return North. . . . Between each of the three sections, a curve. These, to vaguely indicate the design." "Kabnis," the third part of *Cane*, is about a Northern black who goes to the rural South and is unable to adapt. Toomer's explanation of the curves suggests that Kabnis will return to the North. That the circle is left incomplete also points to a continuing alienation between the black cultures of the North and the South, the inability of the old rural and the new urban to reconcile their differences.

In addition to its intrinsic merits, the book is memorable for three reasons. First, Toomer explores aspects of Southern and Northern black life that had not previously been examined in fiction, paying tribute to the past and concurrently showing a race and society in flux. Second, *Cane* as a whole is an exercise in self-discovery. Its sensitive, self-effacing narrator is really the author himself, who is exploring his own ambivalence about his racial identity. Toomer's use of his narrator is similar to Joseph Conrad's use of the character Marlow in much of his fiction. Third, the form of the book is unusual and has been the object of much discussion. Some critics consider it a gathering of fugitives—stories, poems, and a dramatic piece previously published separately in various magazines—that are unified only by recurrent themes and settings. Most, however, label it either as a work that defies standard categorizing or call it an experimental novel, a psychological novel, a poetic novel, or a lyrical novel.

Despite such quibbles over its form, *Cane* is not at all unique. It is similar to James Joyce's *Dubliners* (1914) and Sherwood Anderson's *Winesburg, Ohio* (1919), thematically related story collections that present unified visions of societies, and it also echoes Edgar Lee Masters' *Spoon River Anthology* (1915), a collection of poems that probe the secrets and psyches of a small town's residents. Toomer was familiar with all three works, and he knew and learned from Anderson ("*Winesburg, Ohio* opened my eyes to entirely new possibilities," he wrote). *Cane* and *Winesburg, Ohio* both have narrators who mediate between author and reader, both are made up largely of prose cameos, and both have characters who become "grotesques," in Toomer's case because of the lingering social and psychological effects of slavery.

Distinguishing *Cane* from the other works is the inclusion of poems between and within the stories. Usually folk songs or ballads, the poems reinforce the action and themes of the narratives. Recalling traditional African American music, mainly pre-Civil War slave spirituals, the poems enhance the mood of wistful, even mournful, pastoralism that pervades the book. Toomer believed that spirituals helped slaves to endure their bondage, so their presence in *Cane* gives the book a historical dimension. The poems also provide thematic transition from one narrative to another and heighten the work's impressionistic style, which incorporates myth and symbol. Since Toomer's focus in the novel is on social, racial, and economic problems in both the rural South and urban North of the post-World War I period, he writes both realistically and naturalistically at different times. One critic has described Toomer's style as "a mysterious brand of Southern psychological realism that has been matched only in the best work of William Faulkner." An example of this amalgam of styles is the description of Tom Burwell's lynching in the story "Blood-Burning Moon" (the title of which is taken from a folk song), which is presented both with realistic specificity and in a deliberately ritualistic manner.

"Blood-Burning Moon" and *Cane* as a whole have meaning and significance beyond the author's concerns with racial identity and conflict in the South and North. Most of his men and women, even those who love and are loved, are strangers to those with whom they live. For example, the narrator of "Fern" says, "Men saw her eyes and fooled themselves." The eyes said one thing, but men read another. "They began to leave her, baffled and ashamed," since "men are apt to idolize or fear that which they cannot understand." In "Esther," King Barlo is "slow at understanding." In "Kabnis," the old man who lives below the shop is "a mute John the Baptist of a new religion—or a tongue-tied shadow of an old." In other words, *Cane* also is about people, whatever their race may be, who are unable to communicate even with their own kind.

CANE

First published: 1923
Type of work: Novel

Blacks in the rural South and urban North of the early 1920's confront the difficulties of life in a changing, but still white-dominated, society.

The first part of *Cane* consists of six prose units (only three are fully developed stories) and ten poems that separate them. All are about a segregated South of sugar cane and cotton fields, and women are the main characters in all the narratives. The first, a lyrical two-page sketch, tells of Karintha, who "ripened too soon," and whose languid beauty lures both young and old men despite her passiveness. After giving birth to an illegitimate baby, she abandons it in a sawdust pile at the local mill, sets the mill ablaze, and turns to a life of prostitution. The sadness and futility of two generations of wasted lives are the dominant note here, as in the rest of the narratives.

In the next vignette, Becky is a white woman who violates the social codes by bearing two black sons. Maintained by secret gifts from both races—signs of communal guilt and responsibility—she is a recluse, so the community can publicly deny her existence. When her small cabin burns down one day, she (like Karintha's baby and, in a later story, Tom Burwell) is consumed by fire.

The themes of sexuality, miscegenation, and universal guilt are again merged in "Fern," the story of Fernie Mae Rosen, the illegitimate daughter of a black woman and white Jewish man. A beautiful woman of indifferent sexuality whose "body was tortured with something it could not let out," she is abandoned by her lovers, who nevertheless remain forever under her spell, "vowing to themselves that some day they would do some fine thing for her."

The religious alienation suggested in "Fern" is the thematic core of "Esther," which also dramatizes isolation and frustrated sexuality. When she is nine, introverted Esther becomes infatuated with an itinerant preacher and charlatan, King Barlo. Fourteen years later, when he returns to town, she leaves her parents' home at midnight to search for him. She finds him in a boardinghouse, drunk and with a woman who teases Esther for having a light complexion. "Jeers and hoots pelter bluntly upon her back" as she retreats, bereft of a dream that had sustained her for so long.

Following this story is the poem "Conversion," in which an African deity merges with a "white-faced sardonic god." King Barlo represents this corrupting mix of faiths from two worlds, just as mulatto Esther and Fern suffer from their biracial fusion. Dusk, a recurring descriptive motif in this first section, is a related thematic metaphor for the book as a whole.

"Blood-Burning Moon" is the last and most fully developed story in this section. Tom Burwell, a black laborer in the cane fields, becomes the lover of Louisa, who also is the lover of young Bob Stone, for whose family she works. "Strong as he was with hands upon the ax or plow," Burwell is a gentle introvert and cannot express his feelings for her. Stone, ironically, is a white reflection of Burwell in actions and personality. Their rivalry reaches a climax when Stone goes to the canebrake, where he normally meets Louisa, to confront her with Burwell. A struggle ensues, and Burwell cuts Stone's throat. In retaliation, a white lynch mob, "like ants upon a forage," traps Burwell, takes him to an abandoned cotton factory, and ties him to a stake. While the frightened blacks sneak home and blow out their kerosene lamps, the mob sets Burwell afire. Louisa, in her house, senses his fate; when she looks at the full moon, she sees it as "an evil thing . . . an omen which she must sing to." Thus the first section of the novel ends as it begins, with the immolation of an African American.

Whereas the first unit of *Cane* portrays rural blacks in a South still tied to antebellum mores, the second section shows them trying to cope in the North. It includes seven prose pieces (four of which are developed stories) and five poems. Two impressionistic and symbolic vignettes, "Seventh Street" and "Rhobert," introduce the theme of a white society confining and stifling blacks. In a letter, Toomer described the former story as "The song of a crude new life . . . a new people." The latter presents urban houses as a destructive metaphor, literally burying "banty-bowed, shaky, ricket-legged" Rhobert, whose Northern odyssey in search of opportunity for the family he left behind ends in a lonely death.

"Avey" is the first fully developed narrative in this section. Set in the nation's capital, it echoes tales of the first part, for it too is about a black woman as a remote and indifferent sex object. Avey is graduated from school and becomes a teacher; however, like Karintha and Fern, she turns to prostitution. Though he does not understand her, the immaturely self-centered narrator tries without success to rekindle a boyhood passion for her.

"Theater" also is about unrequited love. Set in a Washington theater during a rehearsal, its main characters are Dorris, a dancer, and John, the manager's brother. Partly because of class differences symbolized by John's fairer skin, nothing comes of their dreams of having an affair, but John also is deterred by his fear that a commitment will compromise his independence. Here, as elsewhere in *Cane*, race and social class inhibit action.

In "Box Seat," too, Dan and Muriel eventually go their separate ways because, by social standards, she is too good for him. Born in a canefield, light-skinned Dan Moore has migrated to Washington, where he is unemployed but hopefully courting Muriel, a teacher. Rejected, he follows her to a theater, where a grotesque exhibition of sparring dwarfs is the feature. The winner sings a song he dedicates to Muriel, a visible presence in her box seat. When he offers her a rose, Muriel at first will not accept it, but she yields to audience pressure, a hypocritical act that ends Dan's passion for her. Serenely tweaking the dwarf's nose, he leaves the theater, "as cool as a green stem that has just shed its flower." Unfulfilled, he nevertheless is a kind of victor; atypical of Toomer's men, Dan no longer is a slave to a woman's "animalism."

In "Harvest Song," the second of two lyrics that follow "Box Seat," a reaper sings not only of his suffering but also of his determined self-control over hunger, thirst, blindness, deafness, and fatigue. "My pain is sweet," he chants, "Sweeter than the oats or wheat or corn." Set as it is between stories that take place in Washington and Chicago, the poem is a wistful glance backward to a pastoral South, where grim deprivation and hardship at least were ameliorated by a successful harvest. Life in the North does not offer any such bounty.

"Bona and Paul" closes the second section. A white woman and a black man, both Southerners, meet in a Chicago physical education school. Paul Johnson, light enough to pass for white, denies that he is black; for Bona Hale, it is what attracts her to him. The climax of the story takes place at the Crimson Gardens, a nightclub featuring black music but patronized by whites. Paul is charmed by this blending of the two races; at the same time, he realizes "that people saw, not attractiveness in his dark skin, but difference." For the first time, he sees himself as he is and is strengthened. Bona also seems invigorated by the experience; as they leave, however, the black doorman leers at them knowingly. Paul pauses and tells him, "Brother, you're wrong." Addressing a fellow black as "brother," Paul has come to terms with his racial identity. Bona disappears, and the story ends. Perhaps she cannot accept Paul's embrace of his blackness; perhaps the knowing, leering look of the doorman makes her realize that she cannot bridge the social gulf of race. As a Southerner, she can cope with ambiguity, but not with certainty. Both characters thus come to a life-altering awareness.

"Kabnis," which makes up the third part of *Cane*, is a closet drama that presents the consequences of a collision between past and present. Ralph Kabnis, a black man of mixed racial heritage, has returned from New York to his native South with an artist's zeal to improve the lot of his people. A self-styled poet, he aims to become their voice. Having accommodated to the conditions under which they live and having come to terms with who they are, however, the black Georgians are indifferent to this savior. They look upon him as a potential troublemaker who could upset a delicate social balance with which they are satisfied.

Kabnis has come to rural Sempter, Georgia, to teach at a black school, but the headmaster soon dismisses him for unspecified reasons. Fred Halsey, a blacksmith, then takes Kabnis on as an apprentice, but he is as inept at this job as he apparently was at teaching. Whereas Halsey, a master artisan, is comfortably secure with his status, Kabnis is "awkward and ludicrous, like a schoolboy in his brother's new overalls."

Halsey cannot help Kabnis. Nor can Lewis, a teacher at the school of whom Halsey says, "He strikes me as knowin a bucketful bout most things." Like Kabnis (and Paul Johnson of "Bona and Paul," and perhaps Toomer himself), Lewis must come to terms with his own ancestry. Unlike Kabnis, he embraces it, a fact demonstrated by his attraction to old Father John, "symbol, flesh, and spirit of the past." When Kabnis rejects the connection by proclaiming, "My ancestors were Southern blue-bloods," Lewis adds, "And black." To Kabnis' response, "Aint much difference between blue an black," Lewis retorts, "Enough to draw a denial from you." The next morning, Halsey's sister Carrie K., "lovely in her fresh energy," with a "calm untested confidence and nascent maternity," tries to help Kabnis climb from a cellar after a night of drinking. When she assures him that she is up to the task, he says, "twont do t lift me bodily. . . . its th soul of me that needs th risin."

By the end of the work, Kabnis has become little more than a childlike scarecrow, assailing Father John and thus rejecting his heritage and sinking to his knees before Carrie K., ashamed and exhausted. In *Essentials: Definitions and Aphorisms*, his 1931 book of maxims, Toomer wrote that "shame of a weakness implies the presence of a strength," so there may be hope for Kabnis after all. At the conclusion of "Kabnis," which also is the end of *Cane*, Toomer writes: "Outside, the sun arises from its cradle in the tree-tops of the forest. Shadows of pines are dreams the sun shakes from its eyes. The sun arises. Gold-glowing child, it steps into the sky and sends a birth-song slanting down gray dust streets and sleepy windows of the southern town." Given the optimistic tone of these final words, and the focus upon Father John and Carrie K., Toomer surely is not as despairing as Kabnis is. Indeed, the young woman and old man likely represent between them the past, present, and future of their race, and Ralph Kabnis may yet find his proper place.

BLUE MERIDIAN

First published: 1936
Type of work: Poem

An optimistic vision of America flourishing from a blending of its many races is the theme of this poem, which Toomer develops in a style recalling Walt Whitman.

While still working on *Cane* in 1920 and 1921, Toomer wrote a 126-line poem he called "The First American," which was published as "Brown River, Smile" in 1932. By that time, he had expanded it considerably, and the 835-line "Blue Meridian" was included in the 1936 anthology *New American Caravan*. Toomer has written of the poem's long gestation period: "Years were to pass . . . before the germ of 'The First American' could grow and ripen and be embodied in 'The Blue Meridian.' " That "germ," according to Toomer, was "that here in America we are in the process of forming a new race, that I was one of the first conscious members of this race. . . ."

Written in free verse, "Blue Meridian" is in the expansive Walt Whitman tradition, with echoes of such poems as "Song of Myself" (1855). More directly, it shows the influence of Hart Crane's longer, loosely connected sequence of poems *The Bridge* (1930), which examines America's past and present and looks ahead to the future. Crane and Toomer, who knew each other, both treat the unifying nature of human experience and Americans' relationship to country and God; in each poem, moreover, the Mississippi River is a central, almost mythic, symbol.

The three parts of Toomer's work open with references to a meridian. First is the Black Meridian, "sleeping on an inland lake." The second section begins with a stanza that tells of the White Meridian "waking on an inland lake." The third unit, consisting of the final twenty-seven lines, serves as a coda, opening with an exuberant stanza about a "*Dynamic atom-aggregate*" Blue Meridian awake and dancing. This progression from slumber to wakefulness parallels what Toomer sees as the American people's increasing awareness of their country's special quality. Tracing the historical development of the nation, he notes that whereas the "great red race was here," "wave after wave," of immigrants came from Europe, islands (Asian and Caribbean), and Africa. The use of the wave image ties in with repeated references to the Mississippi River, which Toomer calls "sister of the Ganges," India's sacred river.

Relevant, too, are the meridians' colors. Disposing of the extremes of black and white, Toomer offers "the high way of the third,/ The man of blue or purple." These are his "new people . . . called Americans." While not denying their "unbroken chain of ancestors," they "outgrow each wider limitation" and grow "towards the universal Human Being." Racial differences no longer will matter; people will be able to aspire without society's hindrance to achieve their desired goals. Optimistic though his vision of the future is, Toomer has no illusions about the journey to the promised land. It will involve, he says, a "struggle through purgatories of many names" and will require help from the "Radiant Incorporeal" or "soul of our universe."

"Blue Meridian" and *Cane* have obvious thematic links, but although the novel concludes on a positive note, the characters are a long way from achieving the "spiritual fusion . . . of racial intermingling" that Toomer claimed to have reached for himself. The sketch of an incomplete circle between the second and third sections of the novel is emblematic of an unattained goal. By contrast, the celebratory optimism of "Blue Meridian" is signaled by its title, for the word "meridian" refers to a complete circle and also can mean the highest point of development, authority, or magnificence.

Summary

Widely praised when published in 1923, *Cane* was not popular, so Jean Toomer probably did not inspire a generation of black writers, as some have suggested. More likely, they simply were influenced by the same white figures (such as Sherwood Anderson and Waldo Frank) to whom he was drawn. His limited influence notwithstanding, he created a masterpiece of American fiction. *Cane* is notable for its unusual form, which incorporates fiction, poetry and drama into a thematically and structurally unified experimental novel. It also stands apart because of Toomer's analysis of the conflicts, hardships, and aspirations of blacks struggling with a legacy of slavery and segregation. He elaborates upon these themes in his epic poem "Blue Meridian," which envisions a future of racial reconciliation and spiritual harmony in what he labels a New America.

Bibliography

Bone, Robert. *Down Home: Origins of the Afro-American Short Story*. New York: Columbia University Press, 1988.

—————. *The Negro Novel in America*. Rev. ed. New Haven, Conn.: Yale University Press, 1965.

Byrd, Rudolph P. *Jean Toomer's Years with Gurdjieff: Portrait of an Artist, 1923-1936*. Athens: University of Georgia Press, 1990.

Durham, Frank, comp. *The Merrill Studies in "Cane."* Columbus, Ohio: Charles E. Merrill, 1971.

Kerman, Cynthia Earl, and Richard Eldridge. *The Lives of Jean Toomer: A Hunger for Wholeness*. Baton Rouge: Louisiana State University Press, 1987.

McKay, Nellie Y. *Jean Toomer, Artist: A Study of His Literary Life and Work, 1894-1936*. Chapel Hill: University of North Carolina Press, 1984.

Toomer, Jean. *The Wayward and the Seeking: A Collection of Writings by Jean Toomer*. Edited by Darwin T. Turner. Washington, D.C.: Howard University Press, 1980.

Gerald H. Strauss

SCOTT TUROW

Born: Chicago, Illinois
April 12, 1949

Principal Literary Achievement

The author of a critically acclaimed memoir about legal education, Turow achieved legendary literary success by reinvigorating the genre of legal suspense.

Biography

Scott Turow was born on April 12, 1949, in Chicago, Illinois, to David D. Turow, a gynecologist, and Rita Pastron Turow, an author of children's books. His early years were spent in that city in what he called a "nouveau-riche Jewish ghetto." When he was thirteen, his family moved to the wealthier and less-ethnic Chicago suburb of Winnetka, Illinois.

In Winnetka, Turow was exposed to what he has called a "quiet current of anti-Semitism" and experienced failure in freshman English at the prestigious New Trier High School. Turow countered with his first literary success, becoming editor of the school newspaper. In the course of this endeavor, he discovered that he could excel in an arena quite apart from that of his ambitious father. He formulated plans to pursue a writing career, sidestepping his parents' wishes for him to become a doctor.

In 1966, Turow entered Amherst College, where, as an English major, he was influenced by Lawrence Durrell's *The Alexandria Quartet* (1962) and Robert Stone's *A Hall of Mirrors* (1967). By the end of his freshman year, he had completed his first novel. The manuscript was rejected by numerous publishers, but a personal response from an editor at Farrar, Straus & Giroux both encouraged him to keep writing and led eventually to a long-term relationship with the publisher.

While still an undergraduate, Turow was also encouraged by the celebrated short-story writer Tillie Olsen and by acceptance of one of his own short stories by the *Transatlantic Review*. After obtaining his B.A. from Amherst in 1970, he accepted a creative writing fellowship at Stanford University. While there, he completed a second novel, which, like the first, was roundly rejected (once again, however, Farrar, Straus & Giroux was encouraging). The plot, centering on a rent strike, seems to have planted the seeds of Turow's interest in the law. After teaching creative writing at Stanford for four years and receiving his M.A., he enrolled at Harvard Law School.

Turow had not, however, abandoned his literary ambitions. Before he entered law

school, his agent negotiated a four-thousand-dollar advance from Putnam Books for a nonfiction account of his first year there. *One L*, published in 1977 just before Turow began his final year of law school, was written in the summer after his first year with the aid of a journal he had kept during the preceding eight months. Although some of Turow's professors and classmates were dismayed by their thinly disguised portraits, *One L* proved to be both a critical and popular success.

After receiving his J.D. in 1978, Turow accepted a position with the United States Attorney for the Northern District of Illinois. Returning to Chicago with his wife, the former Annette Weisberg, an artist, Turow spent eight years in the U.S. Attorney's Office, acting as prosecutor in the highly publicized series of trials known as Operation Greylord, which exposed widespread judicial corruption. During this period, he continued to write, using his half-hour train commute from Wilmette, Illinois, to work on the novel that was to make him a literary phenomenon. *Presumed Innocent* was published by Farrar, Straus & Giroux in 1987, after Turow had taken off the summer of 1986 to complete it. The book made headlines even before publication, largely because of the record sums of money connected with it. Farrar, Straus & Giroux paid Turow an advance of two hundred thousand dollars, the largest the publisher had ever paid for a first novel; Warner Books paid three million dollars for paperback rights, the highest price ever paid for reprint rights to a first novel; and film rights were sold to director Sydney Pollack for one million dollars. The hardback version stayed on the best-seller list for forty-four weeks, the paperback for twenty-nine weeks.

Prior to the publication of *Presumed Innocent*, Turow accepted a partnership position with the large Chicago law firm of Sonnenschein, Carlin, Nath & Rosenthal. During his first year and a half with the firm, he was able to write only from 6:15 to 8:15 a.m. before leaving for his downtown office. In 1988, he reached an agreement that permitted him to spend his mornings at home with his wife and three children, Rachel, Gabriel, and Eve—and with his writing. The first product of this arrangement was a novel centered on both law and family life, *The Burden of Proof*, published in 1990. Like its predecessor, Turow's second novel quickly became a best-seller and brought him great financial rewards. The appearance of a third novel, *Pleading Guilty*, in 1993 was once again evidence of Turow's singular ability to balance his dual careers as novelist and litigator.

Analysis

Scott Turow describes himself as "neurotic," driven to succeed by insecurities that originated in childhood. Despite his accomplishments, he seems to share the sentiments his wife Annette expressed in a 1990 magazine interview, that his astonishing success "is all tenuous . . . not to be trusted." Indeed, even when Turow became a millionaire after publication of *Presumed Innocent*, the couple did not move from the four-bedroom house they bought when Turow was a sixty-thousand-dollar-per-year public prosecutor.

This same driven quality and distrust of success is very much in evidence both in Turow's continued pursuit of demanding dual careers as lawyer and best-selling author and in his literary productions themselves. Indeed, *One L* is itself testimony to Turow's drive and ambition. Not content merely to undertake the daunting task of surviving the first year of Harvard Law School, Turow took on the additional job of writing about it—and himself. The persona he creates for himself in his law-school memoir is not unlike first-year law students everywhere, but the skill with which he conveys his angst about ambition and ethical dilemmas is certainly singular. Moreover, Turow's meditations in *One L* about institutional shortcomings and the corrupting nature of ambition certainly are echoed later on in Rusty Sabich's thoughts on politics and the prosecutor's office in *Presumed Innocent* and in Sandy Stern's reflections on his successful brother-in-law's penchant for corruption in *The Burden of Proof.*

Although all of Turow's works, even *One L*, are fraught with mystery, it is his heroes' respective moral dilemmas that make his books so memorable. For his fictional protagonists, the dilemma always involves the competing demands of family and the law. In part, this dilemma develops out of the demands of a legal career. Rusty Sabich's wife Barbara is alienated and bitter, not only about her husband's affair with a coworker but also about his loyalty to his boss and to his job. Clara Stern is undone by the benign neglect with which she is treated while her litigator husband is developing his practice. Yet it is the philosophical quandaries the lawyer-heroes confront—forcing them to choose between their obligation as officers of the court and their responsibilities toward their families—that lend Turow's novels their resonance.

By way of explaining his phenomenal popularity, Turow himself has pointed out that the duality that characterizes his novels also characterizes American society at the close of the twentieth century. The courtroom has replaced the church as the forum for dealing with the great sociological and philosophical issues of the day, such as abortion and surrogate motherhood. At the same time, Americans are wary of lawyers, who, with their knowledge of "the magic and sacred words," have developed the ability to rationalize the immoral. Such knowledge, in the hands of self-conscious and conscientious individuals such as Rusty Sabich, poses a compelling conundrum, one that is at the center of human experience. It is not too much of a stretch to say that Turow's subject matter is, as William Faulkner characterized his own, "the human heart in conflict with itself."

Turow has said that he feared *Presumed Innocent* would fall between two stools, "too literary for the mystery crowd and too much a mystery to be regarded as a serious novel." Yet critics praised his first novel not only for its suspenseful plot but also for its elegant and philosophical voice. As with *One L*, Turow made good use of what he had experienced firsthand, re-creating the particulars surrounding a murder investigation and trial convincingly out of what he had learned during his career as a prosecutor. What lifts the novel above other courtroom procedurals, however, is in part Turow's choice of the telling detail, which is rendered in nearly poetic terms. For example, the "Dickensian grimness" of the prosecutors' offices is said to make the quality of light there "a kind of yellow fluid, like old shellac." Such fine turns of phrase economically set the mood and grant readers insight into the mindset of Turow's first-person narrator and protagonist. At the same time, the fact that Rusty Sabich sometimes uses vocabulary more reminiscent of Raymond Chandler than Emily Dickinson lets readers know that Turow has not ventured too far afield from his chosen genre.

Reviews of Turow's next book, *The Burden of Proof* were not as uniformly favorable as they had been for *Presumed Innocent*. Some criticized its style as "stodgy"; others likened its plot to Greek tragedy. To be sure, it is a very different book, more a character study of its reserved, superficially stodgy hero and his family than a thriller. The primary attribute it shares with its predecessor, however, is that it is told from the point of view of a lawyer obsessed not so much with solving a mystery but with discovering the truth of his own involvement in an ambiguous death—a truth that no legal proceeding can uncover. As in *Presumed Innocent*, such a truth can only be plumbed by an individual with a philosophical cast of mind and a penchant for self-examination.

In *The Burden of Proof*, Turow once again puts his own legal experiences to good use as background, drawing on his work as a white-collar criminal-defense counsel to create a world in which evil is personified by a wheeler-dealer commodities-firm owner who happens also to be Stern's brother-in-law, Dixon Hartnell. Although Hartnell is involved with Clara's suicide and threatens the stability of Stern's remaining family, he is still a likeable character who practices his own brand of honor; this complex characterization points to Turow's deft hand not only with character delineation but also, once again, to his insight into the ambiguous nature of morality. This insight, which seems to grow out of, even mandate, Turow's dual existence as lawyer and writer is clearly the greatest strength of his books, helping them to rise above the conventions of the legal thriller.

ONE L

First published: 1977
Type of work: Memoir

A student at Harvard University's law school chronicles the turbulent first year of his legal studies.

One L has, for good reason, become required reading for those thinking of entering law school. Having scored in the stratosphere on the Law School Admissions Test, Turow had his choice of law schools, and he chose to enter one of the country's oldest and largest, and arguably the most prestigious, of legal education programs, Harvard Law School. What happened to Turow during his first year there, 1975-1976, is the subject of *One L*, a nonfiction account Turow reconstructed from the diary he kept during eight overwhelming months. While Turow's object is to explore emotions and events that he personally experienced, his meditations on the system of legal education make it clear that these experiences are by no means unique, either to him or to Harvard Law School. The continuing popularity of *One L* attests the universality of its insights.

As more than one reviewer has pointed out, part of the appeal of *One L* is that it reads like a good thriller, as Turow steers the reader through the sustained hysteria leading up to exams and the ensuing race to make Law Review. He relates his own reactions as well as those of his fellow students to the burdensome workload, to the indignities of the fabled Socratic teaching method, and to the ceaseless competition among classmates.

Along the way, he introduces some memorable personalities (Turow made only minor efforts to change names and otherwise to disguise the real-life characters who peopled his first year at law school). The most dominant of these, not unnaturally, are the professors, on whom the students' grades—and, hence, self-definition—depend. Turow's opinion of this small group of individuals evolves; as it does, is it hard for the reader not to speculate as to which professor will emerge as the villain of the piece. Turow does not disappoint: By the end of the book, he has given enough detail about the classroom performance of Professor Perini, who teaches the devilishly hard contracts course, that the reader fully endorses Turow's final judgment that Perini is too much the embodiment of the inhumane aspects of legal training.

In the end, Turow emerges a survivor, a kind of everyman in the rarified atmosphere of Harvard Law School. He does not make Law Review, but his marks are certainly respectable. Most important, he makes it through the trial of the first, formative year in the life of a lawyer with his ethics intact. He has met the enemy, the rapacity and fear inside himself, and he has prevailed.

PRESUMED INNOCENT

First published: 1987
Type of work: Novel

A public prosecutor investigates, then is tried for, the murder of his former colleague and lover.

Presumed Innocent, Turow's first published novel, was an astonishing critical and popular success. In it, he drew upon his own experiences as a prosecutor in the U.S. attorney's Chicago office to draw a detailed and realistic portrait of the world inhabited by his hero, Rusty Sabich, a chief deputy prosecutor in a fictional Midwestern city. The particularity of this world, especially the rendition of the murder trial that is central to the book, accounts in large part for its appeal.

As the novel opens, Sabich's colleague, Carolyn Polhemus, has just been murdered, apparently after she was raped by someone she knew and trusted. The loss is especially jarring for Sabich, who only a few months before had been the victim's lover and, in part because his own marriage is unsatisfactory, is still in love with her. Her murder is also a shock and an embarrassment to Sabich's boss, Raymond Horgan, who is up for reelection. Horgan assigns Sabich to investigate the crime; when Sabich fails to uncover the murderer and Horgan consequently loses the election, Horgan conspires to frame his deputy for the murder.

As in many classic mysteries, nearly any of the characters who people *Presumed Innocent* could have killed Carolyn Polhemus, who was apparently both an unscrupulous prosecutor and a devotee of danger. The final revelation of the killer has frequently been attacked as contrived. Turow, though, has stated, "We talk about literary truths as implausible, fictitious, and yet there is a way in which the mystery novel delivers a truth real life can't deliver." In large part, the truth of *Presumed Innocent* emerges not so much from the trial of Rusty Sabich but from his first-person meditations, which reveal a brooding, philosophical temperament not unlike the author's. What one reviewer saw as flawed storytelling—the fact that "the novel's resolution contains a troubling moral ambiguity"—can also be seen as another of Turow's expert renditions of verisimilitude.

THE BURDEN OF PROOF

First published: 1990
Type of work: Novel

While endeavoring to unravel the mystery surrounding his wife's suicide, a brilliant trial attorney must face his own inadequacies.

The Burden of Proof continues the story of Alejandro "Sandy" Stern, first introduced in *Presumed Innocent* as Rusty Sabich's accomplished defense counsel. Like its predecessor, Turow's second novel opens with a death, the mystery of which is not resolved until story's end. In *The Burden of Proof*, the death is the suicide of Clara, Stern's seemingly constant, reticent wife of thirty-one years. In his effort to unravel the reasons for Clara's death, Stern must look to his own interior landscape rather than to the great world.

Not that *The Burden of Proof* is devoid of action. Clara leaves behind one concrete clue, a note saying only, "Can you forgive me?" Stern quickly discovers that not only had Clara been unfaithful to him but that she had also picked up a venereal disease in the process. What is more, shortly before she killed herself, Clara had written a check to an unknown payee that reduced almost to nothing Stern's prospective inheritance from her estate. As the understated Stern tells an investigating police officer, "Lieutenant, it should be evident that I failed to observe something I should have."

One of the things Stern fails to observe until late in the book is that there is a connection between his wife's suicide and the troubles of his brother-in-law, Dixon Hartnell. Hartnell is the owner of a brokerage house and apparently Stern's most significant client, and throughout the course of *The Burden of Proof* Stern is occupied with defending Hartnell on charges of illegal trading. Exploring Hartnell's defense, Turow provides—as he did in *Presumed Innocent*—interesting insights into legal maneuvering; he also provides less welcome detail about the complexities of commodities trading.

As in his earlier novel, however, the most compelling aspect of *The Burden of Proof* is not solving a mystery so much as it is exploring the psyche and the complex family ties of the hero. This time the tale is not told in first person; although the reader shares Stern's point of view, Turow rightly judged that it would not be fitting to inhabit this character, who is from first to last an outsider, a reserved, formal man, an Argentinean immigrant and a Jew. Some reviewers have quibbled with Turow's endowing his middle-aged, paunchy, balding widower with a reinvigorated sex life, but it is precisely the distance the author keeps from his hero that allows Stern to find love, improbably but touchingly, with the married, pregnant federal prosecutor investigating Hartnell's case. Stern's native reserve also goes a long way toward explaining his sometimes strained relationships with his three children, each of whom has a crucial role to play in the unwinding of Turow's plot.

The Burden of Proof ends, in a sense, where it began, with a death in the family, this time one that ties up all the loose ends. While such a *deus ex machina* can be faulted for being too convenient in resolving a mystery, here it is a suitable end to what might more fittingly be labeled a domestic drama, as signaled by the novel's opening line: "They had been married for thirty-one years, and the following spring full of resolve and a measure of hope, he would marry again."

Summary

Scott Turow's career has been characterized throughout by duality, by his twin vocations as writer and lawyer, by his ambivalent attitude toward his own success at both. His corresponding insight into the ambiguous nature of truth—particularly that of the legal variety—is what powers his work. At a time when lawyers have become the arbiters of moral dilemmas, Turow has done more than any other writer working in the genre of legal suspense to rise above cliché and stereotyping. He explores the protean nature of human experience and the ways in which the law both shapes and contradicts it.

Bibliography

Goldstein, William. "Scott Turow." *Publishers Weekly* 231 (July 10, 1987): 52-53.
Gray, Paul. "Burden of Success." *Time* 135 (June 11, 1990): 68-72.
Gross, Ken, and Barbara Kleban Mills. "Out with Another Blockbuster Novel, Scott Turow is Counting His Blessings—But Cautiously." *People* 33 (June 11, 1990): 57-58.
Shear, Jeff. "A Lawyer Courts Best-Sellerdom." *The New York Times Magazine* 136 (June 7, 1987): 54.

Lisa Paddock

LUIS MIGUEL VALDEZ

Born: Delano, California
June 26, 1940

Principal Literary Achievement
One of the most influential Chicano playwrights of his time, Valdez created a drama dedicated to social progress and to the full exploration of Chicano identity.

Biography

Luis Miguel Valdez was born on June 26, 1940, in Delano, California, the second of ten brothers and sisters. His mother and father were migrant farmworkers, and Luis himself began working in the fields at the age of six. Because his family traveled to the harvests in the San Joaquin Valley, Luis received little uninterrupted schooling.

In an interview, he discussed one significant, and ultimately fortunate, consequence of such a disruptive early life: The family had just finished a cotton harvest; the season had ended, the rains begun, but because their truck had broken down, the family had to stay put. Leaving school one day, Luis realized he had left behind his paper lunch bag, a precious commodity in 1946, given the paper shortages and the family's poverty. When he returned to get it, however, he found his teacher had torn it up. She was using it to make papier-mâché animal masks for the school play. Luis was amazed by the transformation. Although he did not even know what a play was at the time, he decided to try out and was given the leading role as a monkey. The play was about Christmas in the jungle, and the following weeks of colorful preparation were exhilarating. A week before the show was to begin, however, his father got the truck fixed, and the family moved away. Valdez has said of the experience: "That left an unfillable gap, a vacuum I've been pouring myself into ever since."

The pang of that early disappointment sparked a fascination for the theater and a wealth of creative energy that was to bring Valdez remarkable success in the years ahead. Despite his intermittent schooling, Valdez won a scholarship to San Jose State College in 1960. There he studied theater history and developed a lasting enthusiasm for classical Greek and Roman drama. His own work also began to take shape, and his first one-act play, *The Theft*, won a regional playwrighting award. In 1964, he directed his first full-length play, *The Shrunken Head of Pancho Villa*, which audiences greeted warmly.

After receiving a degree in English in 1964, Valdez spent several months traveling

2816

in Cuba before joining the San Francisco Mime Troupe. In 1965, he returned home to Delano and joined the newly formed United Farm Workers Union under the leadership of Cesar Chávez. During this time, Valdez began fully to explore drama as a vehicle for social justice. He developed a form suitable for his migrant-worker audiences: a short skit, or *acto*, designed to inspire Chicanos to political action.

These *actos*, often improvised on flat-bed trucks for workers in the fields, proved so powerful as political weapons that Valdez's life was threatened during the grape strike of 1967. Immensely popular with the workers, the *actos* aroused hostility in the growers, whose exploitative labor practices the plays satirized. Valdez has recalled being "beaten and kicked and jailed. . . . essentially for doing theater." Still, he persisted, and the *actos* gained so much attention that the Teatro Campesino, or Farmworker's Theater, toured the United States performing the works in 1967.

From then on, Valdez's work began to reach increasingly larger audiences. He left the fields late in 1967 for Del Rey, California, where he founded the Centro Campesino Cultural. Between 1969 and 1980, the troupe toured Europe four times and won an Obie Award. Despite such acclaim Valdez remained true to his Chicano, migrant-worker roots. Moving the troupe to Fresno, California, in 1969, Valdez founded an annual Chicano theater festival and began teaching at Fresno State College. As its audience grew, the troupe became more technically sophisticated but continued its efforts to "put the tools of the artist into the hands of the humblest, the working people." The troupe moved in 1971 to rural San Juan Bautista, from which it toured widely among college campuses while remaining deeply involved with the concerns of its own community.

Having spent his entire career well outside mainstream, commercial theater, Valdez decided in 1978 to reach for a still larger audience. The result was *Zoot Suit*, a Broadway-style dance-musical about the Sleepy Lagoon murder trial and the riots that followed in Los Angeles in 1943. Though still quite political, the play succeeds in being genuinely entertaining, particularly in its film adaptation. Like *Zoot Suit*, *Bandido!* (1982) and *"I Don't Have to Show You No Stinking Badges!"* (1986) both reach for more general audiences and explore the Chicano struggle for identity against the limiting stereotypes imposed by an Anglicized history and contemporary American media. Such plays, as well as the successful 1987 film *La Bamba*, which Valdez wrote and directed, speak not only for Chicanos but also to white audiences, forcing them to reexamine their preconceptions about who Chicanos really are. These works also testify to Valdez's extraordinary journey from migrant farmworker to the most vital Chicano voice in American drama.

Analysis

From the earliest and simplest *actos* to the complex sophistication of *"I Don't Have to Show You No Stinking Badges!"* nearly three decades later, Valdez's plays have displayed a remarkable consistency of theme and purpose. Certainly, his work has evolved in scope, depth, and technique, but his basic objectives have remained constant: to expose social injustice, to satirize the oppressors, and to dramatize, in all of its fullness and variety, the struggle to achieve a viable Chicano identity.

Born into a family of migrant farmworkers, Valdez knew firsthand the effects of oppression and exploitation. It was therefore quite natural that his first short plays would deal with the struggles of the farmworkers to unionize. These early *actos* were improvised using a unique collaborative method: Valdez would simply ask striking workers to show what had happened to them during the day. Employing masks or crude signs to indicate different characters—workers, scabs, growers, and so forth—the strikers, under Valdez's direction, produced skits of engaging immediacy, broad humor, and a pointed political message. Their purpose was to raise consciousness, deflate the opposition's authority, and point to a solution. Yet the plays were quite entertaining as well, often transforming and releasing the workers' immediate feelings of fear and frustration through comedy and withering satire.

Though some of the *actos*, such as *Vietnam Campesino* (1970), can seem too bluntly didactic, Valdez learned much from them about making theater a vehicle for inspiring social action. He also sensed, eventually, the need to ground the Chicano experience in something more enduring than immediate political struggle. He returned to the ancient wellsprings of Aztec and Mayan culture to provide such a groundwork for the contemporary Chicano identity.

In his introduction to *Aztlan: An Anthology of Mexican-American Literature* (1972), Valdez frames the problem of Chicano marginalization explicitly:

> His birthright to speak as Man has been forcibly stripped from him. To his conqueror he is patently sub-human, uncivilized, or culturally deprived. The poet in him flounders in a morass of lies and distortions about his conquered people. He loses his identity with mankind, and self-consciously struggles to regain his one-to-one relationship with human existence. It is a long way back. . . . Such is the condition of the Chicano.

That "long way back" took Valdez to pre-Columbian Mexico. What he found there were the achievements of Aztec and Mayan civilization, their astonishing developments in medicine, art, poetry, hygiene, urban planning, and religion, all of which he compares favorably to their European counterparts of the time. To combat the degradation of centuries of Anglo racism, of being seen as "foreigners in the continent of their birth," Valdez wants to reconnect Chicanos to an ancient, proud, and venerable culture. Chicanos must, in his view, revive this connection and rethink their history if they are to maintain an identity in Anglo society.

Valdez attempts this reconnection in a variety of ways. In *Bernabe* (1970), he creates a character, the village lunatic, who physically and metaphorically marries La Tierra (the Earth) and thus reestablishes the Mayan reverence for it. In *Zoot Suit* and *Bandido!*, Valdez reexamines history from the Chicano and Mexican perspective. Thus Tiburcio Vasquez, whom history had portrayed as a mere bandit working the California countryside from 1850 to 1875, becomes in *Bandido!* a revolutionary bent on political rebellion. *Zoot Suit* retrieves for the American conscience an overlooked period of intense racism culminating in the Sleepy Lagoon murder trial and the riots that followed. Both plays try not only to set the record straight but also to discover a source of pride for Chicanos in a history that has been unjustly debased.

The consequence of Chicanos being cut off from the life-giving power of their history and culture is brilliantly dramatized in "*I Don't Have to Show You No Stinking Badges!*", in which Valdez explores the deeply problematic nature of assimilation into Anglo culture. In their desire to fit in with middle-class America, the members of the Villa family find themselves silenced and marginalized. Bit-part actors who rarely receive speaking roles, Buddy and Connie Villa have achieved a comfortable success, but their only connection with their own culture is the stereotyped Mexicans they portray on film. Their son, who enrolled in Harvard Law School at age sixteen, represents the possibility for the epitome of Anglo success. Yet he rebels against this assimilation and drops out of school, only to discover just how rigid the limitations are for Chicanos who reject an Anglo identity.

Stylistically, Valdez is clearly not a realist, though some of his plays—those, for example, depicting actual historical events—employ elements of realism. In all of his plays, however, Valdez takes pains (often in the manner of Bertolt Brecht) to ensure that his audiences never forget that they are watching a play. He does not want to create the illusion of reality or to manipulate the audience into emotional identification with the characters. Plays within plays, characters who speak directly to the audience, radical shifts in time, and many other devices all serve to disrupt the illusion of reality and focus the audience's attention on the artifice before them. Such strategies serve Valdez's purposes well, for he wants audiences to maintain the necessary distance to reflect on the problems that his plays present and to relate them to the world outside the theater. Often the plays are open-ended or have multiple endings, and in this way, too, the audience must actively engage the play and solve it for themselves. These methods do not provide a comfortable or easy theatrical experience, but the rewards of thinking hard about Valdez's plays are indeed worth the effort.

LAS DOS CARAS DEL PATRONCITO

First produced: 1965 (first published, 1971)
Type of work: Play

The boss trades places with one of his farmworkers and discovers how exploited they are.

Las Dos Caras del Patroncito (the two faces of the little boss) typifies, in many ways, Valdez's early *actos*. The piece grew out of a collaborative improvisation during the grape strike of 1965 and dramatized the immediate and intense feelings of its audience. Like all the *actos*, it is brief, direct, didactic, intending not only to express the workers' anger and urge them to join the union but also to satirize the growers and reveal their injustice. The play succeeds brilliantly by enacting a total reversal of what Friedrich Wilhelm Nietzsche termed the master/slave relationship.

The play begins with an undocumented Mexican worker being visited by his *patroncito*, or "little boss," who appears wearing a pig mask and smoking a cigar. Initially, both play their assumed roles of intimidating master and cowering slave to perfection. Soon, though, the patroncito waxes poetic over his Mexicans. Seeing them "barreling down the freeway" makes his "heart feel good; hands on their sombreros, hair flying in the wind, bouncing along happy as babies." " I sure do love my Mexicans," he says. The patroncito reveals a typical condescension, romanticizing the migrant workers' life and regarding them essentially as children. When the farmworker responds by putting his arm around him, however, the patroncito says; "I love 'em about ten feet away from me."

Their conversation takes a peculiar turn as the patroncito verbally coerces the farmworker into agreeing that the workers have it easy, with their "free housing" (labor-camp shacks), "free transportation" (unsafe trucks), and "free food" (beans and tortillas). The boss asserts that he himself suffers all the anxiety that comes from owning a Lincoln Continental, an expensive ranch house, and a wife with expensive tastes. At one point, he asks the farmworker, "Ever write out a check for $12,000?" The audience of migrant workers struggling to raise their wages to two dollars an hour would have felt the irony of such a question; the agony of writing out such a check is not something they would experience any time soon, given their exploited condition.

Yet the *patroncito* actually envies the farmworkers' "freedom" and wishes to trade places. After some coaxing, the farmworker agrees, and the *patroncito* gives him his pig mask, whereupon the power relations between them are reversed. The farmworker now gives the boss a taste of his own medicine. He insults him and proceeds to claim his land, his house, his car, and his wife. The *patroncito* soon realizes that the game has gone too far. He does not want to live himself in the rat-infested shacks he so generously provides for his workers, or ride in his death-trap trucks, or work for such low wages.

By the play's end, the farmworker has so thoroughly abused his *patroncito*, calling him a "spic", "greaseball", and "commie bastard"—all the slurs the workers themselves endured—that the *patroncito* calls for help from union activist Cesar Chávez and screams "huelga" ("strike"). Thus the play brings him full circle from calloused owner to union supporter and suggests that if the oppressors could put themselves in the place of the oppressed, they would see their own injustice.

ZOOT SUIT

First produced: 1978 (first published, 1992)
Type of work: Play

The Sleepy Lagoon murder trial of 1943 shows young Chicanos to be the victims of prejudice.

Zoot Suit, though perhaps Valdez's most commercial play, retains the political spirit of the early *actos* and anticipates the struggle for Chicano identity of Valdez's later works. Because it is a musical, with terrific song and dance throughout, it is his most conventionally entertaining play, but because it dramatizes an overlooked episode in American history that reveals a pervasive racism against Chicanos, it is also one of his most powerful and socially relevant plays.

Set in Los Angeles in the early 1940's, the play centers around the trial and wrongful murder conviction of Henry Reyna and three other Chicano gang members, or "pachucos." Act 1 explores the trial and, through flashback, the violence that leads up to it; act 2 deals with the efforts to appeal the conviction and free the pachucos. Throughout the play, Valdez gives the action an added dimension through the use of two extraordinary devices. One is the mythic figure of El Pachuco. He is larger-than-life, the zoot-suiter par excellence, the embodiment of Chicano pride, machismo, and revolutionary defiance. He dominates the play, though he is seen only by Henry and the audience. Indeed, he may be understood as a layer of Henry's personality externalized, a kind of alter ego who continually advises Henry and comments on, at times even controls, the play. The second device is El Pachuco's counterpart and antagonist, The Press. In *Zoot Suit*, the news media functions as an actual character who symbolizes the racist hysteria of public opinion during World War II. Significantly, it is The Press, rather than a prosecutor, that tries and convicts Henry.

This racist hysteria ("EXTRA! EXTRA!, ZOOT-SUITED GOONS OF SLEEPY LAGOON!. . . . READ ALL ABOUT MEXICAN BABY GANGSTERS!") provides a crucial context for understanding the play. As the United States fought Nazis abroad, it imprisoned Japanese Americans at home, denied African Americans basic human rights, and harassed Mexican Americans in Los Angeles. The irony of Henry's being arrested on trumped-up charges the night before he is to report to the Navy to join the fight against racist Germany is cynically pointed out by El Pachuco, who says that "the mayor of L.A. has declared all-out war on Chicanos." In this climate, racial stereotypes, media-inspired fear, and repressive forces unleashed by war are quite enough to convict the pachucos, even in the absence of any real evidence.

The trial itself is a mockery, a foregone conclusion, and thus Henry finds himself at the mercy of forces he did not create and cannot control. Even those who try to help him—his lawyer, George, and Alice, a reporter from the *Daily People's World*—earn Henry's resentment, for they, too, seem to be controlling his fate. In this sense, El Pachuco represents a compensating fantasy. He is always in control and indeed is able to freeze the action of the play, speak directly to the audience, rerun dialogue, or skip ahead at will. He is a kind of director within the play, and however vulnerable the other young pachucos are, El Pachuco remains invincible. Even when he is tripped and beaten by Marines, he rises up undaunted, clad only in a loincloth, like an Aztec god.

Henry Reyna and the other pachucos are vindicated in the end, winning their appeal and a provisional kind of freedom. Yet Valdez presents multiple endings to Henry's life story. He does so to make the audience see that Henry's character still exists, as do the forces of racism that torment him, and the defiant spirit and cultural pride that will not allow his will to be broken.

I DON'T HAVE TO SHOW YOU NO STINKING BADGES!

First produced: 1986 (first published, 1986)
Type of work: Play

In a rebellious attempt to create his own identity, a young Chicano finds himself trapped by stereotypes.

"*I Don't Have to Show You No Stinking Badges!*" is Valdez's most complex, ambitious, and satisfying play. Satirical, comic, filled with puns and painful insight, the play explores the search for an authentic Chicano identity against the limiting stereotypes and restricted possibilities afforded Mexican Americans in 1980's America.

The play is set in Los Angeles in the home of Connie and Buddy Villa, middle-aged Chicano bit-part actors. The conflict is sparked by the unexpected return of Sonny, their son. Defying his parents' dreams for him, Sonny quits Harvard University Law School and thus forfeits his chance at the kind of Anglo success his parents have not been able to achieve. His return home, with his Chinese American girlfriend, and his announced intention to become an actor, writer, producer, and director—"the newest superstar in Hollywood" and "the next Woody Allen"—creates a crisis in the family that the rest of the play tries to resolve. In a tempestuous family quarrel, Sonny derides his parents' acting; they have made careers playing stereotyped nonspeaking parts as maids, gardeners, bandits, and prostitutes. He proclaims his desire to surpass them. "*I Don't Have to Show You No Stinking Badges!*" then moves to a play within a play. Sonny films his parents and his girlfriend, Anita, but when his parents are called off to a Latino Actors Guild meeting, he decides to act in another way. He takes his father's gun and holds up several fast-food restaurants. The climax of the play occurs when police and news crews arrive at the Villa home; a standoff ensues, replete with gunfire, bullhorns, and live coverage. The play then offers three completely different endings, with Sonny either killing himself, becoming a television director, or returning to Harvard, via spaceship, to finish his law degree.

Valdez gives the play's most compelling theme, the struggle against racial stereotypes to find a viable Chicano identity, a complex and layered treatment. Even the characters' names—Buddy, Connie, and Sonny Villa—suggest a divided identity. "Villa" recalls the Mexican revolutionary Pancho Villa, but their first names are all too typically Anglo. Their cultural frame of reference, moreover, is almost exclusively that of white films and film stars. Throughout the play, they compare themselves and one another to Otto Preminger, Woody Allen, James Bond, Marlon Brando, Al Pacino, and many others. Their understanding of themselves and their world seems to have been defined not by Chicano role models but by Hollywood film stars.

Sonny alone recognizes this problem, and he rebels against it. He sees that his parents' roles as "silent" actors signifies their powerlessness, their marginalized stature in Hollywood, and the invisibility of Chicanos generally. Sonny also understands that by acting the film roles of Mexican stereotypes, his parents have achieved in their private existence nothing more than a "low rated situation comedy" and "a cheap imitation of Anglo life," with a comfortable home, swimming pool, and all the other trappings of middle-class America. Sonny wants no part of it. Yet he knows how limited his options are:

> Here's the main event: the indispensable illiterate cholo gang member-heroin-addict-born-to-lose-image, which I suppose could account for 99% of my future employment in TV land. Just look hostile, dumb, and potentially violent. Preferably with rape on the mind, know what I mean?

Thus Sonny's decision to leave Harvard and create his own films is an attempt to create and control his own identity, not as an imitation Anglo but as a Chicano. For all of his insight and ambition, however, Sonny feels trapped. When his parents abandon his home movie, entitled *Types in Stereo*, Sonny decides to make his acting real. Yet he merely assumes another role, and a stereotypical one at that, of the Chicano bandit. He robs fast-food restaurants, symbols of the emptiness he sees in American life, and thus gives in to the pressures against which he had fought.

The play's multiple endings leave readers and audiences perplexed. Clearly though, Valdez wants audiences to step back and reflect on the relationship between "acting" and reality and to consider the options open, or perhaps closed, to someone like Sonny. Ultimately, the play forces audiences to think deeply about their own stereotypes and to see, in all of its painful complexity, the damage such stereotypes can do.

Summary

Unlike many of his contemporaries who prefer to explore psychological conflicts or the complexities of personal relationships, Luis Valdez has devoted his work to dramatizing social problems. His plays, early and late, expose the injustice endured by Chicanos—not to elicit pity or to portray them as victims, but to focus attention on the forces of oppression and to make Chicanos fully visible in American society. In plays that are satirical, unconventional, unpredictable, painful, and often hilarious, Valdez succeeds in abolishing the stereotypes and showing not only what Chicanos have suffered but also who they really are.

Bibliography

Cizmar, Paula. "Luis Valdez." *Mother Jones* 4 (June, 1979): 47-64.

Eder, Richard. "A Tale of Los Angeles." *The New York Times*, March 25, 1979, p. C13.

Huerta, Jorge A. *Chicano Theater: Themes and Forms*. Ypsilanti, Mich.: Bilingual Press/Editorial Bilingue, 1982.

Shank, Theodore. "A Return to Aztec and Maya Roots." *The Drama Review* 18 (December, 1974) 56-70.

Valdez, Luis. Interview. In *In Their Own Words: Contemporary American Playwrights*, edited by David Savran. New York: Theatre Communications Group, 1988.

John Brehm

MONA VAN DUYN

Born: Waterloo, Iowa
May 9, 1921

Principal Literary Achievement
Van Duyn's examination of everyday experience such as marriage and family relationships has earned her work much critical praise.

Biography
Mona Van Duyn was born in Waterloo, Iowa, on May 9, 1921. She has said that neither of her parents was interested in poetry. She recalls that she read constantly as a child, particularly fairy tales, in spite of the fact that her father would take books out of her hands to urge her to play outdoors. At school, she saw poetry used as a punishment for badly behaved students who had to stay after school to memorize it. Still, she developed an early love for poems. Although her father did not want her to attend college, she was allowed to go (on a scholarship she had won) after carrying out a long campaign of nerves to persuade him. It was only in college, at Iowa State Teachers College (now the University of Northern Iowa), that Van Duyn received encouragement to write. One of her English teachers, Burt Boothe, took her writing seriously, encouraged her to publish, and focused her reading. She received a B.A. in 1942 and an M.A. from the University of Iowa in 1943. In 1943, she married Jarvis A. Thurston, a professor of English.

Van Duyn held several teaching positions from the 1940's to the 1960's, notably at the University of Iowa, the University of Louisville, and Washington University in St. Louis. With her husband, Van Duyn founded and edited *Perspective: A Quarterly of Literature* between 1947 and 1967. She gave up teaching in 1967, saying that teaching took too much of the same energies she needed for writing; she subsequently confined her teaching to summer writing courses. She has also given many poetry readings.

Van Duyn's first book of poems, *Valentines to the Wide World*, was published in 1959. Her second was *A Time of Bees* (1964), followed by *To See, To Take* (1970), *Bedtime Stories* (1972), *Merciful Disguises* (1973), and *Letters from a Father and Other Poems* (1982). All of her work up to *Near Changes: Poems* (1990) has been collected in a volume called *If It Be Not I: Collected Poems 1959-1982*, published in 1993. *Firefall* was also published in 1993.

Recognition for Van Duyn's work has taken the form of several important grants, prizes, and appointments, including service as poetry consultant for the Olin Library Modern Literature Collection at Washington University (where her own papers are housed). She was one of the first five American poets to win a grant from the National Endowment for the Arts (1966), and she has also received a Guggenheim Fellowship (1972). In 1970, she won the prestigious Bollingen Prize for Poetry.

In 1971 *To See, To Take* won the National Book Award. In her acceptance speech, Van Duyn talked about the nature of poetry and the poet's work, saying that in poetry's concern for both sound and sense, it pays tribute to language refined by patterns. Poets inform those patterns with their own voices in an effort to share their experiences with others. To do that requires a caring about others "which is a form of love." Her volume *Near Changes* won the Pulitzer Prize in poetry in 1991.

In 1992, Van Duyn was appointed poet laureate consultant in poetry by the Library of Congress. In an interview, she commented on the position's requirements, saying that her first task was to give a public reading of her work and later a public lecture. Additionally, she hoped to give recognition to young poets by inviting them to read in the Library of Congress' reading series. She noted that her wide experience as a contest judge would prepare her well to make decisions about potential readers' merits. In the same interview, she protested the label "poetess," but she also noted that of the thirty-one poetry consultants named by the Library of Congress before "poet laureate" was added to the title in 1985, only six had been women. She is the first woman to have been named U.S. poet laureate.

In talking about her work habits, Van Duyn has commented that she does extensive revising during the composition of a poem, writing a few lines out in longhand, typing the lines, revising them, and then going on to the next lines. Van Duyn says that she writes only when she has ideas, although she says the system of a daily writing schedule has some appeal for her when ideas seem scarce. By the same token, she no longer relies on feedback from other writers about her work in the way she did as a beginning writer, before she had established her voice.

Analysis

Mona Van Duyn has protested those who apply the label "domestic" to her work, noting that male writers who write about their spouses and the events of their daily lives as often as she does are never labeled that way. In fact, she frequently finds her subjects in literature, including the subject of poetry itself, as well as in history, mythology, and even newspaper items. Nevertheless, her subject matter frequently comes from her daily life, its various events, her family, her travels. At the heart of her achievement is the fact that those domestic events, even those she treats with considerable humor, become metaphors for the complex statements she makes about the world and the place of people in it.

Van Duyn is a formal writer, almost always using rhyme (often slant rhyme) and frequently using regular stanzas. The volume *Firefall* (1993) may serve to illustrate the diversity she achieves. The first poem in the collection, "A Dog Lover's Confession," is prefaced by a lengthy note that identifies it and several other poems in the book as "Minimalist sonnets." She explains that she has kept the Petrarchan or Shakespearean conventions in these works while shortening the conventional ten-syllable line length. She has sometimes also added an extra quatrain. "Miranda Grows Up" works like a sort of inverted Petrarchan sonnet with two-syllable lines, and several similar poems are included in a section called "Minimalist Sonnet Translations of, or Comments on, Poems by Auden, Eliot, Yeats, Frost, Hopkins, Arnold." The collection also contains works in quatrains and other stanza forms, as well as some poems partly in prose.

Rhyme is everywhere in Van Duyn's work. In "Christmas Present for a Poet," for example, she manages to find seventeen rhymes for the word "hornet" (after originally claiming she can find only "hairnet"); they range from "hornat" ("horn at") to "howornate" to "hearnot" to "hernit" (in the phrase "her nit-wit"). The poem is partly a joking apology for a Christmas-gift shirt that made the recipient look like a hornet, but, typically, the work becomes more than that. Van Duyn considers the implications of the golden bars on the dark background to suggest that they are like forms in poetry, like the strands of a hairnet that keep neat what they confine. The shirt was bought as a bargain, she claims, and is not the miraculous weave she would like to have sent, but, like life, it is a bargain of which the best must be made.

Poetry that uses humor and a modest subject to talk about something more serious is typical of Van Duyn. In "Mockingbird Month" (from *Near Changes*), for example, she describes a July in which, apparently ill, she is confined to a house where she spends her time listening to a mockingbird. At first she admires its virtuosity, reads about its abilities to imitate, and notes that it bullies the neighbor's cowardly cat. By the end of the month, however, her feelings have changed. She says the lesson is both for art and art lover: When the bird sings all night, she begins to long for silence, and concludes that she should also husband her own "apprentice words."

In "In Bed with a Book" (from *Near Changes*), Van Duyn uses the detective novel, her favorite sort of escape reading, to talk about death. The first stanza of the poem describes the novel's crimes; bodies are found everywhere. The second stanza asks a serious question—what difference does it make that these dead are denied the joys of human experience? In the third stanza, the speaker notes that all the novel's mysteries will be answered with the detective's solution tomorrow night. Meanwhile, sur-rounded by her loved ones, the speaker is falling asleep, a sleep she calls a "little rehearsal," evidently a rehearsal for the same death that fills the novel.

Van Duyn's work is filled with pictures of family life— an aunt in Texas who describes her apocalyptic religious visions in her chatty letters, a grandmother's series of memories of immigrant life in the Middle West in the late nineteenth century, a speaker's sudden awareness of her love for her husband of many years. By the same token, Van Duyn also makes generous references to the literature of others, to history, and to mythology. Christopher Smart, Alexander Pope, Plato, and Graham Greene all find places in her work, sometimes alongside more immediate references to the speaker's private life.

The nature of love and its place in people's lives is one of Van Duyn's most compelling themes. In "Three Valentines to the Wide World," the title poem of her first collection, an eight-year-old child asks whether God's hobby is love. Van Duyn's later poems repeatedly answer that question affirmatively and suggest that humans are at their best when they too share love, however raggedly they manage to do it. "Quebec Suite" concludes with the speaker identifying the loon, which is lonely in its solitude and spends its days calling across the water to its mate, as her favorite bird. In "The Stream," the speaker recalls her mother, who died a night after she and the daughter had shared a special lunch. Now the speaker knows that she will never be able to talk to her mother about love, that she can no longer be sure even what love is. Yet she knows that although love may be stained by abuse, still, like a narrow underground stream, its existence hidden and even unsuspected, it continues to press its way to the surface.

THREE VALENTINES TO THE WIDE WORLD

First published: 1956
Type of work: Poem

The three parts of this long poem attempt to define the interrelationship between love, beauty, and art.

"Three Valentines to the Wide World" is the first poem in Van Duyn's first book. In looking at the poem's three parts, the reader should remember that a valentine is a short love message, and Van Duyn has addressed these messages to the world, emphasizing in her title the world's vastness.

Part 1 is written in twelve-line stanzas, each stanza composed of three rhymed quatrains. That the rhyme is often slant rhyme (listening is rhymed with chastening, for example) does not diminish its effect.

The first stanza describes an eight-year-old child, awkward and graceless, who stands scratching a scab on her knee. In the second stanza, she asks her profound question without even looking up from her knee: "Mother, is love God's hobby?" The speaker believes that the girl has not yet noticed that suffering and death inhabit the world, that she thinks of God as a gardener who will eventually create new leaves from dead stems. The child receives no answer, and the speaker takes her mind back to her own childhood, when anything seemed possible, including the idea that love that sustains the world. Section 1 ends with a sort of prayer that the child will be able to maintain her sense of a world eternally re-created as she grows into "the grace of her notion."

The second section is composed of seven four-line rhymed stanzas. The tone of this section is more reserved than that of the first; the section forms a sort of meditation on beauty and the function of poetry. The speaker begins by saying that she has never liked landscapes that are huge vistas, the kind one sees from roadside overlooks. They are too divorced from the immediacy of specifics. That loss of awareness of the specific must affect truck drivers, she thinks, as they roll along in a world where everything below the cabs of their trucks must blur into abstraction.

The antidote to this distance is the poem, the speaker says; its function is to create a sort of pressure. "To find some spot on the surface/ and then bear down until the skin can't stand/ the tension and breaks under it. . . ." Only a poem is strong enough to do that, and when it does, the result is both discovery and reminiscence—just what the speaker experienced in the first section. The writer's joy is to use discovery and reminiscence to create, rather like God the gardener.

Section 3 is composed of three eight-line rhyming stanzas and is introduced by a quotation from Geoffrey Chaucer in which the poet says that he cannot bear the beauty of a certain lady's eyes; they will slay him. The speaker here says that, like the lady's eyes, the beauty of earth seems merciless, powerful enough to kill, except when it is tempered by love and art—things in which compassion resides.

LETTERS FROM A FATHER

First published: 1982
Type of work: Poem

These "letters" picture an elderly couple who find solace for their declining health in the pleasure of watching a bird feeder.

The six sections of the title poem of *Letters from a Father* record the slow growth into health and peace of an elderly couple, presumably the speaker's parents, as they find increasing pleasure in a bird feeder the speaker has given them. The voice throughout most of the poem is that of the father. Throughout, the stanzas are composed of rhymed quatrains.

In the first section, the speaker offers a long list of his pains—an ulcerated tooth, pressure sores from a leg brace, a bad prostate gland, and a bad heart. He feels ready to die. His old wife is in even worse shape: She falls down and forgets her medicines; her ankles are swollen, and her bowels are bad. This letter concludes with the old man chastising his daughter for wasting good money on a bird feeder; better to poison the birds and be rid of their diseases and mess, he says.

The next section notes that the daughter has brought her parents a bird feeder of their own— a waste of money, the old man says, since they will surely live no more than a few weeks. Still, he confesses that they are enjoying it. In this section, the old man's physical complaints are still vivid—deafness, a bad heart, and belching—and he has added complaints about the birds. They are not even good for food, like the ones the father used to hunt years ago.

The third section creates a sort of transition; its tone is far more positive than that of the first two. The old man is evidently pleased at the large numbers of birds coming to the feeder, and he asks the daughter for a bird book so that he and "Mother" can identify them. They have even sent "the girl" (evidently a household helper) to buy more feed, although the old man tempers the hopefulness of this remark by noting that she had to go to town anyway (the reader suspects that the father is rationalizing).

In the fourth section, the reader learns that, in their feeding frenzy, some of the birds are flying into the old couple's window and knocking themselves out. The old man recounts how a visitor rescued one unconscious bird and brought it in to be restored by the old man's stroking. His joy in the little bird's recovery is evident. He adds that the bird book has arrived.

The fifth section records the old man's delight in the great variety of birds that frequent the feeder. He has names for all the species and describes their habits with pleasure (reminding the reader of Van Duyn's assertions about the beauty of the specific in "Three Valentines"). He even has a kind word for squirrels. At the end of the section, he notes that he has pulled his ulcerated tooth himself and, despite his predictions, he did not bleed at all.

Section 6 continues to record the old man's newfound joy; moreover, he is full of plans for feeding his birds all summer and next winter, too. Mother is doing well, too. She still forgets her medicine, but her bowels are fine. The old man takes some sly pleasure in noting that he has learned that some birds have three wives.

The last line is in the daughter's voice: "So the world woos its children back for an evening kiss." The kiss is the healing pleasure the old couple take in the specific beauties of the world's birds.

THE STREAM

First published: 1982
Type of work: Poem

Shortly after her mother's death in a nursing home, the speaker reflects on their relationship and compares her mother's love to an underground stream.

"The Stream" is a narrative poem, written in rhymed couplets, which relates the events of the speaker's last four days spent with her mother. The time is three months after the death of the speaker's father; her mother is in a nursing home and hates it. The mother's memory is failing, with the result that, by mistake, she makes a huge effort and dresses herself for a special lunch with her daughter. The lunch is really tomorrow, but the daughter is touched that her frail mother has made so much effort on her own, even fastening to her blouse a pin the daughter once brought her from Madrid.

The daughter has arranged for a special lunch in a lounge in a distant wing of the home, and when they arrive, the mother is uneasy. She does not like it here, she says, and she worries about finding a bathroom if she needs one. Yet when the lunch arrives with its special tablecloth and dishes, she calms herself and enjoys it. She eats more than she has in months, finishes her soup, and eats her own cakes and the daughter's, too, with the daughter feeding her. The daughter remembers that her mother used to like restaurants, although her husband refused to spend the money for them, and that memory, along with her mother's urgent thanks, brings tears to the daughter's eyes.

On their last night together, the daughter helps her mother get ready for bed and watches her go through the rituals of a lifetime—finding the nightgown, washing her face. She looks at the work of age on her mother's body and, as she prepares to leave, tries to reassure her mother that she will call and write; however, she is stopped by tears. Her mother takes the daughter's face in her hands, tells her not to cry, and says that the daughter will never know how much she loves her. At this point, the reader realizes that the relationship between mother and daughter has not been an affectionate one. The speaker's recognition that the mother makes this gesture as if she had done it all her life makes the reader aware that in fact she has not done it. When the daughter says that the statement about love felt true, it is clear that she has not always believed it. The day after the speaker arrives home, the mother dies.

The poem then moves to its central idea: What is love? The speaker compares it to an underground stream, held beneath the surface by pressures no one can understand, perhaps the pressures of the mother's own youth, her parents and husband. Above ground, others would like to locate that stream of love, like dowsers searching for water for a well. Even dowsers, though, are helpless until at last the stream finds its own way to the surface, just as the mother's love was finally articulated when she spoke to her daughter on their last night. It may happen, Van Duyn notes, too slowly, but after sixty years there is a gathering of water at last; to it, the speaker says, she adds her own tears. They are tears of loss and regret, of course, but also tears of love and joy. The combination, Van Duyn implies, is inevitable in this world.

Summary

Mona Van Duyn's poems frequently assert the difficulty of experiencing love in a world where so much goes wrong. Nevertheless, she champions the value of the effort to love, and she implies that art is what helps people to understand love and the world's beauty.

These concerns are linked to Van Duyn's definition of poetry as necessarily involving art and beauty—patterned language, the poet's voice—and the poet's love for those who read the poems. Such affection is betokened by the poet's desire to share meaningful experience with others.

Bibliography

Gordan, Lucy Latane. "Talking with . . . ." *Wilson Library Bulletin* 67 (October, 1992): 28.

Hadas, Rachel. "Serious Poets." Review of *Firefall*, by Mona Van Duyn. *The New York Times Book Review*, July 18, 1993, 11.

Howard, Richard. Review of *Merciful Disguises*, by Mona Van Duyn. *The American Poetry Review* 2 (1973): 9.

Landess, Thomas H. Review of *To See, To Take*. *The Sewanee Review* 81 (Winter, 1972): 137.

Zarin, Cynthia. "Periscope Gaze." Review of *Near Changes*, by Mona Van Duyn. *The New Republic* 203 (December 31, 1990): 36-40.

Ann Garbett

GERALD VIZENOR

Born: Minneapolis, Minnesota
October 22, 1934

Principal Literary Achievement

In poetry and prose, Vizenor has preserved the folkways of the Chippewa Indians, contributing to their trickster tradition while simultaneously highlighting their exploitation by the dominant culture.

Biography

Gerald Robert Vizenor, son of Clement William and LaVerne Peterson Vizenor, is a crossblood member of the Chippewa tribe. Vizenor invented the term "crossblood" to refer to Native Americans of mixed heritage, and he uses the term frequently in his writing. Born in Minneapolis, the author attended New York University after completing three years of military service (1952-1955), part of it served in Japan. After one year at New York University, he transferred to the University of Minnesota, from which he received the bachelor's degree in 1960, following which he pursued graduate study there from 1962 until 1965.

In 1959, Vizenor married Judith Helen Horns, an instructor at the University of Minnesota; they were divorced in 1969. This marriage produced one son, Robert Thomas. Vizenor married Laura Jane Hall in 1981. Immediately before and during his years at the University of Minnesota, he was a group worker and later a corrections agent at penal institutions in Minnesota, where he confronted many of the social tensions that exist between the Native American culture and the dominant culture. These tensions inform much of his writing.

Knowledgeable in a broad range of literature, classical and ethnic, Vizenor gained some of his initial writing experience as a staff writer for the *Minneapolis Tribune*, where he was employed from 1968 until 1970. His books sometimes include items he wrote for the newspaper. In 1971, Vizenor became a trainer of teachers for the Park Rapids Public Schools in Minnesota. He also taught at Lake Forest College and Bemidji State University.

In 1976, Vizenor moved to the University of California at Berkeley, where he was a lecturer until 1980, when he moved to the University of Minnesota as a professor of American Indian studies. By 1987, however, he had returned to the University of California system, this time to the Santa Cruz campus, as a professor of literature and

American Studies. He served in this capacity for several years before returning to Berkeley to assume a position as a professor of ethnic studies.

Vizenor also taught at the University of Tianjin in China. Out of this experience grew his book *Griever: An American Monkey King in China* (1987). This teaching stint in post-Maoist China helped Vizenor to understand, in a more universal light than he had previously attached to them, some of the Native American myths with which he had grown up.

Generally considered the most productive and avant-garde contemporary Native American writer, Vizenor has gained considerable recognition within the more sophisticated circles of the literary establishment. Although his writing is at times diffuse and can be difficult for mainstream American readers to comprehend fully, it remains true to its sources, which is Vizenor's fundamental aim.

Vizenor's screenplay for the short film *Harold of Orange* (1983) won him the Film-in-the-Cities National Award for screenwriting, and the picture was chosen as best film at the San Francisco American Indian Film Festival. Although his first novel, *Darkness in Saint Louis Bearheart* (1973), received meager attention on publication and confounded many of those who did read it, Vizenor's second novel, the more conventional *Griever*, was more widely read and won both the American Book Award of the Before Columbus Foundation and the New York Fiction Collective Prize.

Vizenor's collection of stories *Wordarrows: Indians and Whites in the New Fur Trade* (1978) also helped to secure his literary reputation. Vizenor's *The Trickster of Liberty* (1988), was a biting satire about a huge monument conceived as a Native American counterpart to the Statue of Liberty but abandoned at crotch level. This book, which received widespread attention, struck out at so many of the social ills that affect Native Americans that scarcely any major institution in the dominant culture escaped Vizenor's trenchant invective.

Dedicated to preserving Native American culture through literature, Vizenor helped to found and is general editor of the American Indian Literature and Critical Studies Series of the University of Oklahoma Press. The second offering in the series, Vizenor's *Dead Voices: Natural Agonies in the New World* (1992), reflects the animistic nature of Chippewa mythology and relates to similar animistic cross-currents in other mythologies.

Analysis

Gerald Vizenor, one of the most heterodox and demanding of contemporary writers, consistently produces work that is important for its social commentary (which is usually stinging), for its subtle use of story lines (which are sometimes so subtle as to be almost indiscernible), and for its linguistic invention (which is still in the formative stages). A postmodern, poststructuralist writer, Vizenor does not concentrate much attention on individual characters in his novels. Their motivations and development are secondary to Vizenor's other, more pressing artistic concerns, which have to do with the broader culture and with the conflict between the two major societies upon which his work focuses.

Readers probably absorb Vizenor's novels best if they read them in chronological order. This is partly because characters recur from novel to novel but also, more cogently, because occurrences from the earlier novels are alluded to meaningfully but with little edifying detail in the later novels. Not having read the earlier novels can limit one's comprehension of the later ones.

Having suggested a sequential reading, one can then say that in a novel such as *The Trickster of Liberty* it is not necessary to read the various episodes within the work sequentially. Many of the chapters are independent essays that can be read in any order without reducing the reader's comprehension and appreciation of the work as a whole. These chapters fall within a narrative frame of prologue and epilogue, but the structure reflects a non-western mindset, which the author consciously strives to depict.

The Native American frame of reference is a bewildering one for most members of the dominant culture. Such readers struggle with Vizenor's books until they begin to understand Vizenor conceptually. He does not aim to write Native American stories adapted to the sensibilities of Anglo culture; rather, he attempts to be true to the culture he is depicting and from which he sprang.

Vizenor is not the sort of literary purist who confines his writing to the oral sources through which so much Native American culture has been transmitted and preserved. He uses his extensive literary background to draw upon sources from many ages and from many cultures as he develops his stories. He does so unabashedly and without apology. His writing is much more than a mere extension of the oral tradition of his forefathers.

In conventional American and European literature, actions are expected to result from specific, identifiable sources. In Vizenor's work, however, the causes are often neither articulated nor hinted at, a fact that can create problems for uninitiated readers who approach his novels. The literary reference points on which most readers rely are often missing or, at best, much distorted in Vizenor's writing, as he strives relentlessly and intelligently toward developing new modes of expression.

In his first novel, *Darkness in Saint Louis Bearheart*, Vizenor chooses an apocalyptic setting several decades in the future. Vizenor's cautionary novel foresees the environmental destruction of the United States and, with it, the complete economic collapse of society.

In this first novel, Vizenor displays the extremes of irony of which he is capable and demonstrates as well his considerable gift for satire. He interweaves Native American culture with sociopolitical elements of the dominant society, producing a chilling effect. His biting social satire and keen sensitivity to the contradictions and absurdity of much of contemporary life—particularly when viewed from the Chippewa perspective—continues in his later novels and is most strident, perhaps, in *The Trickster of Liberty*, where the humor has an underlying element of sadness.

Vizenor does not shy away from sexuality or violence in his writing and has been criticized for his concentration on both of these topics. He has confirmed in interviews that he includes violence and sexuality in his work because he believes it is unhealthy to suppress these aspects of the human experience. He claims that to deny violence is to create victims who can be controlled by the symbolic appearance of violence: People cannot fight things that they do not know.

In its presentation of violence, Vizenor's work does not depart significantly from much of the folk literature of the past—the tales of the Brothers Grimm, the Mother Goose rhymes, many of the stories in Greek and Roman mythology. In approaching Vizenor's novels, one must keep in mind the philosophical reasons for the violence that pervades the author's writing.

Judging from some of his public utterances, Vizenor has given considerable thought to developing new ways to work with the English language. He would like to break the bonds of grammatical convention, to imagine ways in which language can be pushed to new extremes. He has experimented with using an intermixture of tribal languages with the English in which he writes. He first attempted such experiments in his collection of stories, *Wordarrows*, with results that left many readers confused and frustrated. In *Griever*, Vizenor introduced elements of Chinese into the mix with moderately successful results, perhaps because *Griever* is structurally a more conventional novel than any of his other work.

In *The Heirs of Columbus*, Vizenor exercised his authorial prerogative to bend history to his own fictional ends, an approach that distressed some of his more literal readers and critics. Vizenor, however, is indisputably daring, interesting, and enticing in everything he writes. If his literary experiments do not always succeed, he must nevertheless be admired for the originality of his attempts.

CROSSBLOODS: BONE COURTS, BINGO, AND OTHER REPORTS

First published: 1990
Type of work: Essays

This collection of essays and articles concentrates on the major issues that confront Native Americans in contemporary America.

Although this volume would have benefited from updating before publication, it is valuable in showing the range of Vizenor's work over a twenty-year span. The pieces included present him as the investigative reporter he was in the early 1970's and as the creative and academic writer he became. The collection is somewhat rag-tag, but it is significant for its illustration of Vizenor's development.

The book is divided into two major sections. The first, "Crossblood Survivance," deals with the problems of those who, like Vizenor, are not pure-blooded. These "crossbloods" constitute the largest group among those who claim to be Native Americans. To survive in their Native American habitat, Vizenor says, these people sell out much that their forbearers held sacred. They redefine treaties, reaching

compromises that promise short-term gains. They are instrumental in bringing gambling to reservations, and they abrogate the hard-won fishing and hunting rights for
which their ancestors fought.

With the money these compromises generate come the problems that accompany
gambling and other easy-money schemes. Vizenor implies that Native Americans are
losing their selfhood or, more accurately, are selling it to the highest bidder. Tribal
pride, once the hallmark of the reservation, is being subordinated to immediate gain.

"Crossbloods and the Chippewa," one of the more current contributions to the
volume, is not tightly structured, yet it focuses compellingly on some of the major
problems that face Native Americans. Not the least of these problems is caused by the
Bureau of Indian Affairs, which exerts pressure to have tribal children attend federal
boarding schools, effectively removing them both from their families and from their
cultures. What is done in the name of education, Vizenor argues, is essentially a form
of tribal genocide imposed by a paternalistic government that thinks it best to
homogenize Native Americans, to draw them into the dominant culture whether they
wish to become a part of it or not.

The second half of this book consists largely of investigative articles written by
Vizenor during his days as a journalist. "Capital Punishment," a detailed report of
Thomas White Hawk's murder of a South Dakota jeweler, shows Vizenor at his
journalistic high point. Yet it might have been desirable for Vizenor to update this
contribution to reflect the commutation of White Hawk's prison sentence and his
reintroduction into the community.

Perhaps the most poignant of the essays in this book is "Bone Courts: The Natural
Rights of Tribal Bones," in which Vizenor writes about a matter that he discusses in
nearly all of his books: the robbing of Indian grave sites in the name of archeology or
anthropology. Vizenor cites Thomas Echo-Hawk, an attorney for the Native American
Rights Fund, who contends that a Native American who desecrates a white person's
grave is imprisoned but that a white person who desecrates a Native American burial
mound wins a doctorate.

THE HEIRS OF COLUMBUS

First published: 1991
Type of work: Novel

   Stone Columbus, who claims direct descent from Christopher Columbus,
attempts to establish a sovereign Native American nation.

Although Gerald Vizenor and his publisher call *The Heirs of Columbus* a novel, it
takes an act of faith to accept it as such. The book, an occasional piece written to mark
the quincentenary of Christopher Columbus' arrival in the New World, is fanciful,
taking great liberties with the facts historians have unearthed. The concept of the book,

nevertheless, is interesting, and the social problems it poses, which are similar to those on which Vizenor has focused in his other writing, are significant. Also important are his use of Native American mythology and his emphasis on the trickster tradition that is a fundamental part of Native American lore.

Stone Columbus is a talk-show host made rich by his floating bingo parlor on the Mississippi River—a riverboat destroyed by fire—whose activities were protected by treaties Stone's forefathers forged with the white invaders of their land. Stone claims direct lineage from Columbus, whom he declares to be a crossblood with Mayan ancestors who visited Europe before Columbus visited the New World.

The line through which Stone claims his lineage begins with Samana, a "hand talker" who was among the first people to greet Columbus when he landed in San Salvador. Samana engages in intercourse with Columbus, who impregnates her. It is through that union that Stone claims his Columbian lineage.

Stone, financially secure and quite well known, attracts around him a band of followers with whom he hopes to establish a Native American nation in the northwestern United States. His followers hope that they can reproduce the healing genes of the Mayan people and use them to save the world from cataclysm. The symbol of Stone's new sovereignty is the half-completed Trickster of Liberty statue, the subject of Vizenor's earlier novel, *The Trickster of Liberty*. Standing in a harbor, visible from toe to crotch—which is where construction terminated—the statue becomes a bitter, mocking emblem of the straits in which Native Americans find themselves.

The great irony of *The Heirs of Columbus* is that the explorer set in motion the forces that landed Native Americans in their present state. Columbus does not emerge from this book as a real character, although Vizenor has researched his material well. Nor is Stone Columbus much more real than his ancestor; rather, he is the symbol of a genocide that a Eurocentric culture has visited upon an indigenous people.

DEAD VOICES: NATURAL AGONIES IN THE NEW WORLD

First published: 1992
Type of work: Novel

Players in a card game actually become the animals depicted on the cards they turn over ritualistically.

White men hear the "dead voices" to which Vizenor refers in his title, the voices of the printed word or carefully prepared lecture. These are the voices not of a ritualistic, story-telling tradition but the desiccated croakings of a literature apart from nature. In this novel, Vizenor focuses on Native Americans who live in urban Oakland, California, rather than on a reservation.

Bagese, a shaman, engages in the tarot-like game of wanaki with the seemingly autobiographical narrator. The game extends from December, 1978, until December, 1979, with a prologue dated February, 1982, and an epilogue dated February, 1992. Vizenor has important things to say; he must say them even at the cost of losing some of his Eurocentric audience. His message becomes a moral imperative.

In wanaki, the participants, over an extended period, turn over cards bearing representations of bears, fleas, squirrels, mantises, crows, and beavers. When a card is turned, a participant becomes the creature on the card; accepting this demands a cognitive leap that people reared outside the Native American tradition cannot comfortably make. The tales that make up this novel—which is perhaps actually more a collection of short fables than a novel—are creation stories. They have to do with the quintessential forces of the universe, but Chippewa forces are far different from those considered quintessential in the Eurocentric world.

Bagese, a "tribal woman who was haunted by stones and mirrors," warns the narrator never to publish the stories in this collection or to reveal the location of her apartment in Oakland. At the end of the year-long wanaki meditation, she disappears without a trace.

Bagese considers the best listeners for her stories to be "shadows, animals, birds, and humans, because their shadows once shared the same stories." This suggestion of intergenerational continuity suggests a Native American concept of reincarnation. Like most of Vizenor's writing, *Dead Voices* is witty, infused with a pervasive humor that distinguishes the author's work from that of such other Native American writers as N. Scott Momaday and Sherman Alexie.

Summary

Gerald Vizenor's work captures the unique spirit of a people who hold a worldview closely attuned to animism. Most Eurocentric people find this worldview incomprehensible; talking stones and plants that react to human commands lie outside their conceptual contexts. Vizenor nevertheless has devoted his life to tapping into this worldview, bent on informing a broad reading public without debasing native materials upon which any legitimate Native American writing is necessarily predicated.

Vizenor tempers his presentations with a sardonic wit and a sometimes raucous humor, both of which help the uninitiated to relate to this literature. His standing as one of the foremost writers of haiku in English helps to explain the sharpness of imagery in much of his prose

Added to his broad and deep understanding of the Native American themes and legends about which he writes is Vizenor's comprehensive understanding of conflict between Native American and the dominant culture. The most prolific—although not the best known—contemporary Native American writer, Vizenor heads the avant-garde of this genre.

Bibliography

Bowers, Neal, and Charles L. P. Silet. "An Interview with Gerald Vizenor." *MELUS* 8 (Spring, 1981): 41-49,

Bruchac, Joseph. *Survival This Way: Interviews with Native American Poets.* Tucson: University of Arizona Press, 1987.

Hochbruck, Wolfgang. "Breaking Away: The Novels of Gerald Vizenor." *World Literature Today* 66 (Spring, 1992): 274-278.

Krupat, Arnold, and Brian Swann, eds. *Recovering the Word: Essays on Native American Literature.* Berkeley: University of California Press, 1987.

Martin, Calvin, ed. *The American Indian and the Problem of History.* New York: Oxford University Press, 1987.

Vizenor, Gerald. *Interior Landscapes: Autobiographical Myths and Metaphors.* Minneapolis: University of Minnesota Press, 1990.

R. Baird Shuman

WENDY WASSERSTEIN

Born: Brooklyn, New York
October 18, 1950

Principal Literary Achievement

As a successful comic playwright, Wasserstein has given voice to the dilemmas and triumphs of modern women.

Biography

Wendy Wasserstein was born in Brooklyn, New York, on October 18, 1950. She was the youngest of the five children of Morris W. Wasserstein, a textile manufacturer, and Lola Scheifer Wasserstein, an amateur dancer, both immigrants from Central Europe. An awkward young girl and a less than elegant dresser, she developed a sense of humor as a survival skill. When she was thirteen, her family moved to the fashionable East Side of Manhattan, where she attended the Calhoun School, an exclusive girl's prep school. In order to be excused from athletics, she wrote the school's musical revue for the mother/daughter luncheons. She also studied at the June Taylor School of Dance and frequently attended Broadway shows.

Wasserstein attended the prestigious Mount Holyoke College, where she studied to be a congressional intern. Her interest in theater, however, was sparked by a summer playwriting course at Smith College and by her junior year excursion at Amherst College, where she participated in theatrical productions. After earning a bachelor of arts degree in history from Mount Holyoke, she received a master of arts in creative writing from the City University of New York, where she studied under novelist Joseph Heller and playwright Israel Horowitz. In 1973, her play *Any Woman Can't*, a satire about a woman whose failure as a tap dancer leads her to marry an egotistical sexist, was produced Off-Broadway at Playwrights Horizons, a theater that would play a significant part in her career.

In 1973, Wasserstein was accepted by both the Columbia School of Business and the Yale University School of Drama, and she chose to attend Yale. While at Yale, she wrote *Happy Birthday, Montpelier Pizz-azz* (1974), a cartoonish caricature of college life focusing on male domination of women, and she collaborated with Christopher Durang on *When Dinah Shore Ruled the Earth* (1975), a parody of beauty contests. These early plays about the suppression of women display an absurdist humor depending on comic caricatures and a broad use of irony.

In her 1975 one-act thesis production at Yale, *Uncommon Women and Others*, her style moved closer to realism. During a summer at the Eugene O'Neill Memorial Theater Center, she expanded the play into a full-length comedy that was eventually produced Off-Broadway in 1977. In 1978, the play appeared on public television. Critics now hailed Wasserstein as a promising new playwright, and her play was produced throughout the country, winning her an Obie Award, a Joseph Jefferson Award, and an Inner Boston's Critics Award.

After adapting John Cheever's short story "The Sorrows of Gin" for a television production on public television, she opened her next play, *Isn't It Romantic*, Off-Broadway in 1981, but critics found the play loosely constructed and full of unnecessary jokes. After seven revisions, she reopened the play in 1983 at Playwrights Horizons, where it achieved critical acclaim and was a box-office success, running for 733 performances.

In 1983, her one-act play *Tender Offer*, about a father who misses his daughter's dance recital, was produced by the Ensemble Studio Theater. In 1986, *The Man in a Case*, her one-act adaptation of an Anton Chekhov short story, was produced by the Acting Company; her 1986 musical *Miami* received only a workshop production. After writing for television and finishing several unproduced screenplays, she rocketed back into national prominence in 1988 with *The Heidi Chronicles*, the play that would establish her as both a noted playwright and a popular success. *The Heidi Chronicles* won the New York Drama Critics Circle Award, the Outer Critics Circle Award and the Drama Desk Award. The play also made Wasserstein the third woman in a decade to win the Pulitzer Prize in drama and the first woman to win a Tony Award for an original drama.

Continuing her success, Wasserstein published a collection of essays, *Bachelor Girls* (1990), and opened *The Sisters Rosensweig* at Lincoln Center in 1992. As both a critical and a box-office success, the play moved to Broadway's Ethel Barrymore Theater and was nominated for a Tony Award.

Analysis

Wendy Wasserstein ventured into playwriting partially because she felt that there was more comedy in her life than on the television situation comedies she saw as a girl. Primarily, though, she began writing plays because she believed that the women in the plays she saw were stereotypes that did not reflect the women that she knew. She set out to write meaningful comedies about women; Wasserstein's plays thus deal primarily with the relationships among intelligent, well-educated, and often highly successful women who are trying to come to terms with both their own identities and society's expectations. In *Uncommon Women and Others*, all the women are graduates of Mount Holyoke college, a prestigious women's college for the academically superior. Harriet in *Isn't It Romantic* is an up-and-coming executive with an M.B.A. from Harvard University, and the protagonist of *The Heidi Chronicles* is an art professor with a degree from Yale. Wasserstein deals with exceptional women.

Wasserstein's exceptional heroines are asked to live up to new expectations for women, but the pressure to be exemplary has left them confused and uncertain about their identity. Much of modern drama focuses on characters who have lost their sense of purpose and cannot figure out who they are or where they belong. Wasserstein works out this theme by exploring the lives of troubled women who are trying to discover what they want in the age of women's liberation. Both Holly in *Uncommon Women and Others* and Janie in *Isn't It Romantic* wish that they were somebody else. Susan in *The Heidi Chronicles* has been so many different people that she does not know who she is anymore.

Outside forces bear down on Wasserstein's heroines as they try to sort out their many choices. They are often torn between their inner yearnings and the many models that are given them by society. Janie and Heidi, like most of Wasserstein's women, are deciding if they want to "have it all" (a husband, children, a career, an active social and community life)—and whether having it all will even make them happy.

Wasserstein's characters are haunted by a sense of loneliness and alienation. In a world of many options, they often do not want to choose, or they become self-absorbed, always questioning their choices. Janie is afraid of living alone, but she feels that she must be true to herself and must not marry a man out of sheer desperation. Heidi, who has fulfilled her potential as a historian of women's art, feels stranded and adopts a child.

The characters in Wasserstein's plays, like those in most modern dramas, are waiting for life to change and for someone or something to transform their world. At a party, Holly says she has two months for something to happen before she goes out in the world; six years later, however, she is still exploring her options. Desperate not to find herself living alone like her mother, Harriet marries the first man that comes along, hoping that he will change her life. Often, fulfillment seems to lie in a distant future. In college, Rita says that she will be amazing by the age of thirty. As time passes and she has still accomplished nothing, she keeps pushing the age of success back. Heidi can only see hope in her daughter's future somewhere in the twenty-first century.

Although Wasserstein deals with the characteristic themes of modern drama, her plays do not display the harsh violence and crude realities of a world gone mad, as many contemporary dramas do. Instead, she creates nostalgic memory plays and romantic comedies focusing on rapidly changing events in which both society and individuals are in a permanent state of transition. Though inwardly confused, her characters are always witty and literate. To break the tension, they play games and act out roles. Frequently, they create romantic fantasies. For example, Heidi and Peter act out a melodramatic romance scene at their first meeting, and Mervyn in *The Sisters Rosensweig* fictionalizes a romantic night of lovemaking out of his past. In Wasserstein's plays, the pain and loneliness of life is broken up by harmless fantasies, and intense emotional confessions are followed by singing and dancing, often to corny romantic and nostalgic music.

Wasserstein's plays are built on episodic scenes that have a cinematic quality. Often she uses framing devices, beginning her dramas in the present and then flashing back to the past, thus juxtaposing present realities with past expectations. Her plots depend less on strong central conflicts than on impressionistic glimpses of characters sorting out their lives. Her dialogue is full of one-liners, witty comebacks, and clever put-downs. Although she employs stereotyped characters, she gives them a sense of believability. Her comedy is often charged with a sense of feeling that either masks the pain that the characters are feeling or helps them to celebrate a moment of joy. Often, tense moments that can turn into nasty confrontation are broken up by humorous lines.

Her satire of modern life may be brittle, but it is rarely caustic. Like her favorite playwright, Anton Chekhov, Wasserstein tries to skirt a fine line between comedy and tragedy. Her Chekhovian characters—wacky, neurotic, but thoroughly human—are lost in their self-reflective worlds, entangled in hopeless relationships, reminiscing about past events, and looking forward to some vague future. As a playwright, Wasserstein is committed without being preachy, serious in her view of the world, but comic in her expression of it.

UNCOMMON WOMEN AND OTHERS

First produced: 1977 (first published, 1978)
Type of work: Play

Amid the social changes of the 1970's, a group of young women express their confusion about their goals in life.

Uncommon Women and Others traces the choices and frustrations of a group of young women attending an exclusive women's college in the early 1970's, a time of social change in which the traditional family expectations for young women were giving way to new possibilities. The women are confused by the options open to them after graduation. The play depends less on plot than on character groupings. The characters form a spectrum of women, with Susie on one end of the spectrum and Carter on the other. Susie is a cheerleader and organizer who, without reflecting on life, bounces through a world of elegant teas, steady boyfriends, and career plans. Carter, on the other hand, is a withdrawn woman who lives solely in the world of the imagination.

Between these two peripheral characters are the five main characters, who are confused about their purposes and goals in life. On one side of the group is Kate, who wants to be a lawyer but feels that such a career choice will compel her to accept a lifetime of boring routines. On the other side is Samantha, a child/woman who will settle for marriage to a man whom she can encourage and stand behind. In the middle is the attractive Muffet, who does not know whether to wait for her prince or to strike out on her own. Balancing Kate and Samantha are two women who do not know what they want. The raunchy Rita does not want to live through a man, nor does she want the business world to transform her into the duplicate of a power-hungry man. The self-conscious Holly, pressured by her parents to lose weight and marry well, keeps postponing her choices.

The drama opens on a reunion of the five women and then flashes back six years to their senior year in college. This device allows for a contrast between the women's present condition and their past expectations. A man's voice representing the male-dominated world spouts ambiguous clichés about the responsibilities of educated women; at the same time, scenes of the women's college gatherings, ranging from formal teas to late-night chats, are depicted onstage. These scenes are punctuated by three rambling and confused monologues delivered by Muffet, Kate, and Holly.

The contrasts in the play's structure are heightened by the contrast in the women and their lives. Samantha is celebrating the birthday of a stuffed animal, while Holly is putting cream into a diaphragm. The women sip sherry and fold their napkins at formal gatherings, then go off and discuss masturbation and the possibilities of male menstruation. These contrasts are further reflected in the women's inner turmoil. Sometimes they are self-assured; at other times, one woman wishes she were like another. These contrasting moods are captured in the play's tone, which balances sensitive moments with sharp comic exchanges.

Although they have seen the frilly world of feminine charm classes come to an end, the women are still baffled six years out of college. Holly is still collecting options that range from having a baby to becoming a birdwatcher, and Rita is waiting until she is forty-five to achieve success. *Uncommon Women and Others* brings to the stage a series of sympathetic and ingratiating young characters, a community of women who can share their emotions, express their insecurities, and play out their fantasies together as they march off into an uncertain future.

THE HEIDI CHRONICLES

First produced: 1988 (first published, 1988)
Type of work: Play

A middle-aged art professor relives the hope and disillusionment of the women's movement.

Wasserstein was inspired to write *The Heidi Chronicles* by the image she had of a woman telling a group of other women how unhappy she feels. The play arose partially out of Wasserstein's anger that the search for personal fulfillment had led to the abandonment both of shared ideals and of a mutual acceptance of different lifestyles. At a crucial moment in the play, Heidi Holland delivers a speech to her prep school alumnae, telling them that she feels stranded. *The Heidi Chronicles*, however, is not an argumentative play; it is a nostalgic journey through one woman's life. The play opens with Heidi's lecture on women's art. Heidi discusses a picture that symbolizes the brevity of youth and life. The picture reminds Heidi of a young girl at a high-school dance who does not know whether to leave or stay and who simply waits for something to happen. In act 2, Heidi, still lecturing, notes that the detached woman in the painting is a spectator, not a participant. Surrounded by flashbacks, these two scenes in the present highlight the play's major themes: the passing away of youthful idealism and the isolating of an outsider who feels increasingly alienated in a changing world.

Heidi's position as an outsider structures almost every scene in the play. The flashbacks begin at a high-school dance in 1965, with Heidi sitting on the side until she meets Peter, who says that if they cannot marry they will still be friends for life. While clinging to the food table at a political gathering, she meets the charismatic Scoop and goes off with him. Later, she accompanies her friend Susan to a women's group. She tries to remain an observer, but she confesses her inability to detach herself from Scoop. As the years flash by, Scoop goes from revolutionary to trendsetter, marrying a woman who cannot compete with him and his career. Susan moves from being a caretaker in a women's commune to working as a fast-talking television producer; her sharing sessions with other women turn into hurried executive lunches.

The play closes with an intermingling of the past and present. The play began with Heidi's meeting with Peter, followed several years later by her meeting with Scoop. The last two scenes follow the same pattern, as the sad and confused Heidi reenacts the two romantic meetings of her youth. The play opens on a nostalgic view of the past and ends with a view of a distant future in which Heidi's adopted daughter will not feel stranded and inferior.

The Heidi Chronicles provides a comic yet wistful view of the passing of a generation. It is a play about the search for identity, the vanishing of ideals, and the effects of isolation and loneliness. It is also a dreamlike play filled with songs of a bygone era, recurring images, and relived moments. Wasserstein is always aware of the history of her generation, a generation caught in the sweep of social change but forever on a journey toward self-discovery.

THE SISTERS ROSENSWEIG

First produced: 1992 (first published, 1993)
Type of work: Play

Three Jewish American sisters examine their lives and explore their future options during a birthday weekend in London.

The Sisters Rosensweig is something of a departure from Wasserstein's earlier dramas. The play takes place in one locale during a single weekend in 1991, at a time when the Soviet Union is dissolving. The action is more limited than in Wasserstein's earlier work; the play, though, is still a series of mixed-up encounters that are held together less by a tight plot than by a series of counterbalancing interactions.

The play follows the structure of Anton Chekhov's famous play, *Tri sestry* (1901; *Three Sisters*, 1920). Like Chekhov's play, it begins with the birthday party of one of the sisters, in this case the fifty-four-year-old Sara Goode. As in *The Three Sisters*, the birthday gifts given are eccentric or inappropriate. Both plays take place not long after the death of a parent who has set goals for the sisters' lives—the father in Chekhov's play and the mother in Wasserstein's. Like Chekhov's play, moreover, Wasserstein's drama is built on a series of arrivals and departures, fanciful monologues, rambling retrospectives, unlikely relationships gone awry, and absurd mishaps occurring at moments of tension. The play captures the Chekhovian view of a society on the brink of change and depicts a group of insecure people who are desperately trying to find a moment of happiness in a world that is falling down around them. Like Chekhov's plays, *The Sisters Rosensweig* mixes comedy with a feeling of sadness and a promise of hope that lies somewhere in the future. Like Wasserstein's own *The Heidi Chronicles*, moreover, the play ends with a mother anticipating a brighter future for her daughter.

The characters in the play are eccentric but believable. Sara Goode, an American Jew living in London, is an executive officer with the European division of a Hong Kong bank. She has one romantic night with Mervyn Kant, a widower who has made his fortune in synthetic furs while retaining his Jewish roots. Pfeni Rosensweig, an international journalist who has set aside her work on the plight of oppressed women to write travelogues, accepts a marriage proposal from Geoffrey Duncan, a flamboyant, bisexual theater director who leaves her for a man. The third sister, Gorgeous Teitelbaum, a forty-six-year-old housewife who has become an amateur psychiatrist on a radio talk show, is taking a group of women from her temple on a tour to see England's crown jewels. Pfeni has seen a relationship slip away, and Gorgeous has to go home to her unemployed husband, who writes mysteries in his basement.

Although the play is set against the backdrop of social and political upheaval, the larger social world is kept at a distance. Characters struggle with their identity, examine their life choices, and try to seize a moment of happiness. After the social activism they saw in *The Heidi Chronicles*, some critics were disappointed that Wasserstein had moved toward traditional drawing-room comedy. *The Sisters Rosensweig*, however, is consistent with her other plays. It is less a play about issues than a play about people.

Summary

Wendy Wasserstein has brought to the stage the hopes and frustrations of modern American women. Her plays are about the quest for identity and the struggle of women to fulfill their personal ambitions without being molded by social pressures; she depicts a generation reflecting on its lost ideals and examining new possibilities. Wasserstein's dramas focus on character instead of plot and are thought-provoking without being preachy, comedic without sacrificing sentiment, and theatrical without losing believability. Critics who favor more revolutionary dramas about women find her plays too traditional and trivializing, but those who champion her works find her stimulating as well as entertaining.

Bibliography

Betsko, Kathleen, and Rachel Koenig. "Wendy Wasserstein." In *Interviews with Contemporary Women Playwrights*. New York: Beech Tree Books, 1987.

Hoban, Phoebe. "The Family Wasserstein." *New York* 26 (January 4, 1993): 32-37.

Hubbard, Kim. "Wendy Wasserstein." *People Weekly* 33 (June 25, 1990): 99-106.

Miller, Judith. "The Secret Wendy Wasserstein." *The New York Times*, October 23, 1992, p. B1.

Rosen, Carol. "An Unconventional Life." *Theater Week* 6 (November 8, 1992): 17-27.

Paul Rosefeldt

JAMES WELCH

Born: Browning, Montana
1940

Principal Literary Achievement

Welch, a novelist and poet of American Indian ancestry, draws his material from Indian experience and history.

Biography

James Welch's father was a Blackfeet Indian; his mother was a member of the Gros Ventre tribe. Browning, Montana, the place of his birth, is the administrative center of the Blackfeet Indian Reservation, and Welch attended school on the Blackfeet and Fort Belknap reservations as a boy.

Although he was not reared in a traditional way, Welch grew up around reservations, listening to stories and absorbing knowledge that would later inform his writing. One example of this can be found in the title of his first book, *Riding the Earthboy Forty* (1971), a collection of poems; the title refers to the fact that, as a youngster, Welch spent time working on a forty-acre field on a ranch owned by neighbors, the Earthboy family. The Earthboy ranch also appears in Welch's second book, *Winter in the Blood* (1974), which opens with a quotation from the title poem of his first book and a description of the "Earthboy place," fictionalized as a cabin near the narrator's home.

Welch studied at the University of Minnesota and Northern Montana College before receiving a bachelor of arts degree from the University of Montana. In an interview, Welch credited Richard Hugo, his writing teacher at the University of Montana, with helping him find his way as a writer. Hugo "opened up a world" to him with some simple advice: "Write about what you know. Where'd you grow up, what was your Indian heritage, what kind of landscape was there?"

While establishing himself as a full-time writer, Welch taught for a while at the University of Montana. He also worked as a laborer, firefighter, and Upward Bound counselor. He served for more than ten years on Montana's state parole board, an experience reflected in his fourth novel, *The Indian Lawyer* (1990), the protagonist of which is a member of the same parole board. Welch has lived for many years with his wife, Lois, on a farm near Missoula, Montana.

Analysis

Welch's situation as a writer is characterized in three lines of his poem "In My First Hard Springtime."

> My horse, Centaur, part cayuse,
> was fast and mad and black. Dandy in flat hat
> and buckskin, I rode the town and called it mine.

The poet's horse has a name imported from Greek mythology, but the animal with the European name is neither white nor assimilated. It is "fast and mad and black" and of Native American ancestry, for it is "part cayuse," a breed developed by Indians.

Welch's ethnic background is Native American but the language he uses and the education that helped him to become a writer are European imports. His writing thus poses a question: Is it possible to do justice to Native American themes using the language of the invasion?

This poem answers by showing a poet proud to "ride the town" outfitted in the clothes of two cultures: European American flat hat, Indian buckskins. In the iconography of the West, "the town" is the definitive European American space, and the townspeople are on top of it. In Welch's poem, the poet is on top. He rides triumphantly, flaunting his Indian heritage, claiming this imported space for himself, reversing the convention that says it is always Europeans who "discover" and claim territory owned by Indians.

Early in his career, Welch stated that he wanted to be known as a poet, not as an "Indian poet." He does believe writers of Indian heritage have some advantages in the presentation of Indian themes. "Whites have to adopt a stance to write about Indian material," he has explained. "For Indian writers that material is much more natural."

Natural or not, Indian themes are challenging for a serious writer. At the time Welch was beginning his career, few literary models were available. Clichés abounded in classical American literature; fantasy Indians such as Henry Wadsworth Longfellow's Hiawatha or James Fenimore Cooper's Uncas reflected the European stereotype of the "noble savage," once described by Welch in an ironic poem as a "mad decaying creep."

The most useful model Welch had to work with was N. Scott Momaday's *House Made of Dawn* (1968), the story of a Pueblo Indian who returns from World War II suffering from culture shock and alcoholism. Complex, severe, and lyrical, this Pulitzer Prize-winning story appeared capable of defining "the Indian novel" for all time.

Welch's first two novels, *Winter in the Blood* and *The Death of Jim Loney* (1979), owe much to Momaday. The protagonists are comparable: alienated Indian men in their early thirties, unable to relate to families, estranged from mainstream and reservation cultures, threatened by alcoholism. Welch's style, especially his restraint and understatement in the presentation of emotionally charged themes, also appears to have been influenced by Momaday.

Welch's third and fourth novels, *Fools Crow* (1986) and *The Indian Lawyer*, move in new directions. *Fools Crow* is a historical novel set in the last days of traditional high plains Indian culture around 1870. *The Indian Lawyer* describes the psychological and social distance that isolates an urban Indian who achieves success in mainstream terms. The protagonist, Sylvester Yellow Calf, is a respected lawyer with a promising future, but his success distances him from his Blackfeet origins, although his background distances him from the white world in which he moves professionally.

From the beginning, however, Welch's writing has had its own complex, often paradoxical character. He uses restraint to show emotion, surrealism to serve the purposes of realism, lyrical nuance to reveal alienation, and ironic humor to develop serious, perhaps tragic, themes. The subtlety of his writing has given rise to a broad range of interpretation. Some critics, focusing on the theme of alienation, see Welch as a grim existentialist. Others, taken by his humor, portray him as a comedian.

In Welch's works, however, humor and seriousness are not mutually exclusive. Welch uses irony to fend off sentimentality. Near the end of *Winter in the Blood*, for example, at the moment when the protagonist achieves an important insight about his Indian heritage, his horse loudly passes gas. This comic "comment" deflates the pathos of a moment of insight, but does not devalue it.

As Welch himself has pointed out, his third novel, *Fools Crow*, provides background for understanding his other books. In *Fools Crow*, the pressure brought to bear on traditional Pikuni (Blackfeet) culture by the white invasion is made starkly clear, but the Pikunis are not glorified, nor are the whites dehumanized. Both cultures appear three-dimensional, as people with families in the background and hopes for the future; Welch presents both groups without moralizing, but he does depict the foibles, weaknesses, and other typically human limitations for all of his characters. Welch's attention to human nuance helps him to present the communal nature of traditional Pikuni society without nostalgia. By showing how each individual is rooted in overlapping social, cultural, and ecological contexts, Welch makes it easier to understand the isolation described in his other books.

Welch uses landscape to illustrate alienation. In his first two novels, the Montana plains appear, in the words of one critic, as a "bleak, vast, nondescript space with a few cheap houses and bars thrown in." *Fools Crow* is set in the same geography but in another world. In the first chapters, when the settlers' influence still seems distant, culture and nature are parts of a single pattern, consisting of story, ritual, and seasonal change. Winter, for example, signifies the return of Cold Maker, the mythological figure who brings the frigid wind from his home in the north. Fearsome but approachable, he was familiar to the Pikuni from appearances in myths and dreams.

When Fast Horse, a young Pikuni, becomes a renegade, severing ties to his immediate and extended tribal family, the traditional world collapses for him, and the land loses familiarity. He finds himself "a solitary figure in the isolation of a vast land." Cold Maker is gone, and Fast Horse has become a stranger in an empty, frozen world. This impersonal, sightless face is the same one that the land turns toward Welch's contemporary protagonists. The nameless cold that haunts them is the "winter in the blood," a season of the soul that yields to no spring or summer.

WINTER IN THE BLOOD

First published: 1974
Type of work: Novel

A contemporary Blackfeet Indian man, haunted by memories of his deceased father and brother, drifts through arbitrary adventures, chancing, finally, upon a living piece of his own history.

Winter in the Blood, Welch's first novel, met with almost unanimous critical acclaim, establishing its author as a major novelist. Narrated by its unnamed protagonist, a thirty-two-year-old Blackfeet Indian man, the story develops in a series of aimless adventures in dusty towns and bars on the edge of the reservation. The narrator, searching half-heartedly for the girlfriend who has run off with his rifle and electric razor, appears only marginally interested in his own actions. His father and brother, the only people with whom he had ever been close, are both dead, but their absence is more present to him than the world around him. By reliving the painful memories of their deaths, the narrator begins to come to terms with their absence. The novel's ending is ambivalent about the protagonist's future, but he appears to be moving to take control of his life.

The book's central theme is alienation. The narrator, whose namelessness underscores his estrangement, describes himself as a "servant to a memory of death." Indeed, memories of death are the only events in which he fully participates: First Raise, his father, frozen on his way home from Dodson, where he drank with the white ranchers and made them laugh; Mose, his brother, killed in an automobile accident while herding cattle.

An estranged protagonist preoccupied with death, dusty towns set against a bleak and endless landscape—all this sounds like a Montana version of the alienated, half-real, half-surreal worlds portrayed by Albert Camus and Franz Kafka. There is, however, a starkly lyrical element in Welch's language that sets his work apart from the tradition of European surrealism. The landscape may be harsh and distant, but it is not without grace or voice. Detached as he is, the narrator is still aware of the vastness of the land. He is close, so to speak, to its distance. When the night sky clears, he wonders about the stars: "One looked at them with the feeling that he might not be seeing them, but rather obscure points of white that defied distance, were both years and inches from his nose."

The ghosts and memories that haunt the land allow an echo of familiarity, a slight intimacy so fragile that it can only tolerate oblique, ironic reference, as in the case of the vanishing fish. The muddy river that runs past the narrator's home belongs to an ecology that has as much difficulty sustaining natural life as the narrator's psychological environment has in sustaining emotional life. The fish, trucked in by "the men from the fish department," simply disappear, until, finally, the men from the fish department disappear too. Still, the narrator goes to the river and fishes. He catches nothing, but when he loses his lure to a fallen tree, the landscape responds: A magpie squawks "from deep in the woods on the other side of the river."

Nature may be losing its ability to nurture, but it is not totally witless. It has preserved a sense of irony. The comic comment of the narrator's horse passing gas as the narrator achieves new insight into his heritage is a similar example.

The narrator's relationship to his home is similarly complex. It is a place to which he returns, though he feels only emptiness toward the people who live there: mother, grandmother, girlfriend. "None of them counted; not one meant anything to me." Here, too, Welch uses irony to indicate a dimension of awareness in the narrator's consciousness that belies the layered indifference. The narrator remembers that his grandmother, too infirm to move out of her rocking chair, saw only the ancient tribal enemy in his Cree girlfriend and spent days plotting to murder her with a paring knife concealed in her stocking. The girlfriend, oblivious to the old woman's scheming, spent her time reading film magazines and imagining that she looked like Raquel Welch.

The scene is ludicrous, but the author is not ridiculing these people. Along with senility, the scene reveals the old woman's fierceness of spirit and rootedness in tradition. Despite her physical incapacity, she has a power and presence lacking in the younger woman.

The narrator takes several steps toward reclaiming his Blackfeet heritage, but each such step is interwoven with ironic and realistic elements that dispel both nostalgia for the past and unguarded optimism for the future. He discovers who his grandfather was and learns more about his grandmother's courage, but the same discovery reveals the harsh treatment she received in the traditional Blackfeet culture.

In one of the book's closing moments, the narrator throws himself into a furious, mock-epic struggle to rescue a cow stuck in a mudhole. The cow is rescued. Despite its muddy, slapstick qualities, this gesture of involvement indicates a shift away from the old habit of indifference. This bit of progress has its price: the narrator's old horse, the last living tie to the time when his father and brother were living, succumbs. Perhaps the connection was no longer necessary.

THE DEATH OF JIM LONEY

First published: 1979
Type of work: Novel

A half-breed living in a small Montana town finds both strands of his ancestry inaccessible and brings about his own death.

The theme and setting of Welch's second novel, *The Death of Jim Loney*, are similar to those of his first, Loney is a thirty-five-year-old half-breed living in Harlem, a small

Montana town near the reservation. The differences between Loney and the narrator of *Winter in the Blood*, however, are considerable. The earlier book's narrator lives on the reservation and visits the towns. Jim Loney resides in town and visits the reservation but he is not at home anywhere. He is a "breed," half non-Indian, half non-white, neither here nor there. His Indian mother is absent, perhaps insane; his white father is physically present in Harlem, near enough for Loney to know he is "the worst sort of dirt."

Even more than *Winter in the Blood*, this is the story of absolute isolation. Even the protagonist's name is a play on "lone" and "lonely," a fact underscored by his nickname, "The Lone Ranger." The narrator of *Winter in the Blood* felt nothing for the people in his home, but at least there was a place called home. The relationships seemed empty but still carried memories. The narrator lived in the past, but this was more livable than anything available to Jim Loney.

Loney and his sister, Kate, were abandoned by their mother as infants. Their father, now a sixty-two-year-old barfly living on pasteurized cheese and scrounged beer, abandoned them as children. Kate has made a career in education and wants to bring Loney to Washington, D.C., to live with her. Loney's girlfriend, Rhea, a teacher from a wealthy family in Dallas, dreams of escaping with him to Seattle.

Kate, determined and competent, sees the extent of Loney's danger more clearly than Rhea, but Kate has clamped down her own emotional life as the price of her own survival. Rhea feels Loney's vulnerability, but she is out of her depth, lacking the experience to see the implications. "Oh, you're so lucky to have two sets of ancestors," she exclaims. "You can be Indian one day and white the next."

Loney takes some steps toward uncovering his past, but his two sets of inaccessible ancestry add up to nothing he can start from or move toward. The two strands of his past haunt him in memories and dreams he cannot penetrate: an ominous bible verse from Loney's European American side ("Turn away from man in whose nostrils is breath, for of what account is he?") and daily visions of a dark bird, which Loney thinks must be something "sent by my mother's people."

Death finds its occasion when the dynamic between Loney and a hunting companion generates an accidental shooting. The companion, a childhood acquaintance, now an economically successful, assimilated Indian who learned ranching from "white men from down the valley," is killed. Loney did not act intentionally, but he feels that the intention was near him. He claims responsibility in order to stage his own execution at the hands of the reservation police.

FOOLS CROW

First published: 1986
Type of work: Novel

A historical novel about an isolated band of Pikuni (Blackfeet) Indians in the twilight of traditional high plains Indian culture.

Welch's first two novels focused on one character and fragments of immediate families. *Fools Crow*, however, is as much about the protagonist's extended family, band, and tribe as about the protagonist himself. Yet the author has not abandoned one theme for another, replacing alienation with community; rather, he continues to work the same theme turned inside out. The interrelatedness shown in this narrative makes it possible to understand the isolation of the first two novels. Mainstream readers tend to see individualism and a certain amount of isolation as normal. This book makes it clear that American Indians are coming from a different experience.

As the story begins, the main character is an uncertain adolescent named White Man's Dog who has no standing among his people. He conducts himself well on a horse-stealing raid against the Crow tribe, and he gains a new name, Fools Crow, and growing status as a healer and leader.

To this extent, *Fools Crow* is a traditional *Bildungsroman*, a story of transition from youth to adulthood. Yet this story is exceptional in that as the protagonist grows, his world contracts, collapsed by white encroachment, smallpox, and repeating rifles. Survivors are left sorting through the traditional ways of thinking and healing, looking for explanations that still make sense.

Several options are shown. One Pikuni chief, Heavy Runner, chooses assimilation. He allows his desire to do what is best for his people to deceive him into believing that the whites, too, want the best for them. Owl Child, on the other hand, leads a renegade group of young Pikuni men who plunder, rob, and murder. Their actions provide the soldiers with a convenient justification for a brutal massacre.

Fools Crow and his father reject both these options. Heavy Runner's way is based on self-deception, Owl Child's on self-destruction. Owl Child's renegades break ties with family and tribe, become dependent on the plunder they take, and fight among themselves. Despite their talk of driving out the whites, they come increasingly to reflect, in appearance and behavior, the norms of the culture they hate.

Owl Child and his followers are the nineteenth century ancestors of Welch's twentieth century protagonists. Fools Crow has a vision in which he sees Pikuni children "quiet and huddled together, alone and foreign in their own country." It is easy to imagine a young Jim Loney or the narrator of *Winter in the Blood* standing among them.

Fools Crow hopes that the Pikunis will find a way that leads further than assimilation or suicidal resistance. Is this possible? The novel ends on a somber but resolute note: "Burdened with the knowledge of his people, their lives and the lives of their children, he knew they would survive, for they were the chosen ones."

Summary

James Welch is a major writer who draws his material from his Native American heritage. The central theme of his work is alienation, one that has been a preoccupation of modern literatures from all over the world. Restrained and understated, Welch's style develops ideas through attention to detail and nuance in a way that is often lyrical. His work sometimes exposes the surreal in the conventional, but it always serves the larger goal of breaking through stereotype, nostalgia, romanticism, and other falsehoods of conventional vision to discover human realities.

Bibliography

Allen, Paula Gunn. "A Stranger in My Own Life: Alienation in American Indian Prose and Poetry." *MELUS* 7, no. 2 (1980): 3-19.

Horton, Andrew. "The Bitter Humor of *Winter in the Blood*." *American Indian Quarterly* 4 (May, 1978): 131-139.

Kiely, Robert. Review of *The Death of Jim Loney*, by James Welch. *The New York Times Book Review*, November 4, 1979, 14.

Lincoln, Kenneth. "Back-Tracking James Welch." *MELUS* 6, no. 1 (Spring, 1979): 23-40.

Velie, Alan R. "Blackfeet Surrealism: The Poetry of James Welch." In *Four American Indian Literary Masters*. Norman: University of Oklahoma Press, 1982.

Welch, James. "I Just Kept My Eyes Open: An Interview with James Welch." In *Survival This Way*, edited by Joseph Bruchac. Tucson: University of Arizona Press, 1987.

Wild, Peter. *James Welch*. Boise, Idaho: Boise State University, 1983.

Ted William Dreier

AUGUST WILSON

Born: Pittsburgh, Pennsylvania
April 27, 1945

Principal Literary Achievement

Wilson's award-winning plays, which have earned him acclaim as one of the leading playwrights of his time, offer a portrait of the black experience in twentieth century America.

Biography

August Wilson was born in Pittsburgh, Pennsylvania, in 1945. The son of a white father who was rarely present and a black mother who struggled to rear her six children on welfare and the meager income from janitorial jobs, Wilson learned firsthand about the hardships and prejudice facing blacks in American society. When the family moved to a predominantly white neighborhood, bricks were thrown through their windows, and Wilson's schools days at Central Catholic High School were marked by racial epithets left scrawled on his desk. Young August nevertheless received a sense of pride and self-esteem from his mother, a proud, determined woman who insisted that her children spend time reading each day.

Wilson's formal schooling ended in the ninth grade. Refusing to believe that a well-researched and footnoted paper that Wilson submitted could be his own work, his teacher gave him a failing grade. Wilson tore up the paper and never returned to school, choosing instead to educate himself at the local public library, where he read extensively on a wide range of subjects. There, he discovered for the first time the works of black authors such as Langston Hughes, Ralph Ellison, and Richard Wright.

Wilson's teenage years were also a time of great anger and frustration, which found occasional release in outbursts of rage as he and his friends smashed the black lawn jockeys they found in front of white homes. During the 1960's, he joined several Black Power organizations, and for many years he adopted a militant stance toward society's racial injustices. He supported himself during this period with a brief stint in the Army and by working as a short-order cook and a stock clerk. A keen observer of the world around him, he also began storing up the details of life in the black community that would later find their way into his plays.

Wilson's career as a writer began almost by chance when he was twenty. His older sister paid him twenty dollars to write a college term paper for her, and he used the

money to buy himself a used typewriter. Still supporting himself with odd jobs, Wilson began writing poetry and became associated with the Black Arts movement in Pittsburgh. In 1968, he and playwright Rob Penny founded the Black Horizon Theater, where he worked as a producer and director. Wilson began writing one-act plays in the early 1970's, but it was not until he had moved to St. Paul, Minnesota, in 1978 that he began work on his first full-length play, *Jitney* (1979), the first entry in his ambitious cycle of dramas about African American life in the twentieth century. It was also during this period that Wilson met and married his second wife, Judy Oliver. An earlier marriage had produced a daughter, Sakina.

In 1979, Wilson began submitting plays to the O'Neill National Playwrights Conference. When his first four submissions were rejected—the conference rejected *Jitney* twice—Wilson found himself reassessing his previous efforts and embarking on a new project that would test the true depth of his writing talents. The result, *Ma Rainey's Black Bottom*, was accepted by the O'Neill Conference and given a staged reading in 1982. It was there that Wilson met the conference's artistic director, Lloyd Richards. A powerful force within the American theater community, Richards was for many years the dean of the Yale University School of Drama and the director of the school's acclaimed repertory theater, as well as the first African American ever to direct a play on Broadway. Their meeting led to an ongoing collaboration between writer and director that would contribute greatly to Wilson's subsequent work.

At Richard's urging, Wilson applied for and received numerous grants and fellowships that allowed him to concentrate his efforts solely on his writing. Wilson's plays have had their original stagings under Richards' direction at the Yale Repertory Theater before moving on to other regional theaters and to Broadway. *Ma Rainey's Black Bottom* opened on Broadway in 1984 and received the New York Drama Critics Circle Award, and Wilson followed it in 1987 with *Fences*, which received four Tony Awards, the Drama Critics Circle Award, the first American Theater Critics Association New Play Award, and the Pulitzer Prize in drama. *Fences* was followed by *Joe Turner's Come and Gone* in 1988 and *The Piano Lesson* in 1990, both of which received the Critics Circle Award. *The Piano Lesson* also brought Wilson his second Pulitzer Prize. The Broadway opening of *Two Trains Running*, which received the Critics Circle Award and the American Theater Critics Association New Play Award, occurred in 1992.

Analysis

Since he first gained recognition with the Broadway production of *Ma Rainey's Black Bottom* in 1984, August Wilson has been hailed by critics as one of the most important writers to appear in the American theater in the latter half of the twentieth century. His work has received numerous awards, including two Pulitzer Prizes, and Wilson himself has been the recipient of several grants and fellowships, including the McKnight Fellowship in Playwriting, the Whiting Writer's Award, and Bush, Rockefeller, and Guggenheim fellowships. He has been hailed by *The New York Times* as "the theater's most astonishing writing discovery in this decade" and by William A.

Henry III, the theater critic for *Time*, as "certainly the most important voice to emerge in the Eighties, maybe the most important in the last thirty years or so."

What Wilson has brought to the American theater is a fresh perspective on a subject he knows intimately: the lives of African Americans struggling to survive in a society riddled with prejudice and hatred. Declaring that "language is the secret to a race," Wilson gives voice in his plays to the rhythms, cadences, and phrasings heard in the homes and on the streets of the black community, bringing to life characters whose experiences have previously been given little exposure outside of that community. From Troy Maxon in *Fences*, who opposes his son's athletic scholarship because he believes it will lead only to disappointment, to Levee, the jazz musician in *Ma Rainey's Black Bottom* who sells the rights to his music to a white recording company, to Hambone in *Two Trains Running*, who has been driven to the point of madness by his obsessive quest for the ham he is owed in payment by a white employer, Wilson's characters capture the pain and struggle of the African American experience with a complexity and power that transform everyday life into compelling drama.

Wilson believes firmly that the road to empowerment for African Americans must include a willingness to embrace their heritage and draw on the sense of history it provides. He urges black America to study its complex legacy, from the culture of Africa itself through slavery, segregation, and the Civil Rights movement, and search there for the examples of courage and endurance that lie at the heart of any people's sense of pride and self-awareness. In a 1987 interview, Wilson said, "Blacks in America want to forget about slavery—the stigma, the shame. That's the wrong move. If you can't be who you are, who can you be? How can you know what to do? We have our history. We have our book, which is the blues. And we forget it all."

As a playwright, Wilson has set out to explore African American history in all of its diversity through dramatic means. Beginning with his earliest full-length play, *Jitney*, he embarked on an ambitious cycle of plays, each set in a different decade, focusing on different aspects of the black experience in the twentieth century. The plays have not been written in chronological order; *Jitney*, although the first written, is set in the 1970's. *Jitney* concerns Pittsburgh's black jitney bus drivers, who created jobs for themselves by driving fares into black neighborhoods where white cab drivers refused to go. *Ma Rainey's Black Bottom* is set in a 1920's Chicago recording studio, where a great blues singer is working in a setting rife with racial tensions. *Fences*, the next play in the cycle, depicts the conflicts within a black family in the 1950's as a father and son clash over the son's future. *Joe Turner's Come and Gone* is set in 1911 and tells the story of a man who has made his way to Pittsburgh after enduring years of illegal enforced servitude in the South. *The Piano Lesson* takes place in the 1930's and focuses on the Charles family and their conflict over a piano that represents their family's heritage. *Two Trains Running* is set in a Pittsburgh restaurant and explores the lives of urban blacks amid the turmoil of the 1960's.

These plays examine widely differing facets of the black experience, yet similar themes and messages run throughout all of them: the destructive results of racial discrimination, the need for courage, determination, and pride in the face of the staggering legacy of black history, and an appreciation for black culture itself—both artistic and social—as a means of survival. Wilson's characters are frequently flawed and always complex, their individual personalities shaped by the experiences that have made up their lives. Their despair and hardships can be traced to the crushing denial of their worth by the dominant white society, and their salvation comes only through self-reliance and self-acceptance. In many of Wilson's plays, rage and frustration that remain unresolved are often turned not on whites but on other blacks, perpetuating the destructive cycle.

Like all great writers, Wilson has himself been influenced by other artists whose work he admires. His early influences included the poets Dylan Thomas and John Berryman as well as writer Ralph Ellison, author of *Invisible Man* (1952). He names as his principal inspirations a quartet he terms "my four B's": playwright Amiri Baraka, the Argentinian writer Jorge Luis Borges, the artist Romare Bearden, whose paintings inspired both *Joe Turner's Come and Gone* and *The Piano Lesson*, and, heading the list, the blues.

MA RAINEY'S BLACK BOTTOM

First produced: 1984 (first published, 1985)
Type of work: Play

A group of blues musicians in the 1920's deal with the effects of racial injustice.

Ma Rainey's Black Bottom was the first of August Wilson's plays to win wide acclaim, and it remains among his finest work. Set in a recording studio in the 1920's, the story takes place over the course of an afternoon, as a group of musicians and the legendary blues singer Ma Rainey record several songs. Much of the play takes the form of discussions and arguments among the four musicians, each of whom brings his own perspective to questions of prejudice and the problems facing blacks in American society. Toledo, a thoughtful, serious man, speaks of racial pride and the need for self-determination. Cutler places his trust in religion. Slow Drag is uncomplicated and unwilling to question his lot too deeply. Levee believes that his musical talent will bring him respect and power. Ma Rainey herself is outspoken, demanding, and well aware that she will be tolerated only as long as her records make money for her white producers.

Ma Rainey's Black Bottom contains many of the themes that run throughout Wilson's subsequent work: the devastating effects of racial discrimination, the callous indifference with which white society has traditionally regarded black Americans, and the idea that the key to black self-reliance and salvation lies in developing a sense of heritage and history. The play's central message is contained in a comment made by Toledo: "As long as the colored man look to white folks to put the crown on what he say . . . as long as he looks to white folks for approval . . . then he ain't never gonna find out who he is and what he's about. He's just gonna be about what white folks want him to be about."

Ma Rainey is as aware as Toledo of the harsh realities of black life in American society, commenting that "they don't care nothing about me. All they want is my voice." Fiercely determined to play her hand well for as long as it lasts, she demands star treatment and respect from her producers, knowing that it will end when her popularity wanes.

For Toledo and Levee, however, Toledo's words will have tragic repercussions. As Levee sees his dreams of fame and success dissolve into the reality of the producer's offer to pay him five dollars per song to "take them off your hands," his anger turns to murderous rage against Toledo, who has accidentally stepped on his shoe. The opening Levee thought he saw in the white power structure was an illusion, and it is Toledo who pays the price for his despair.

FENCES

First produced: 1985 (first published, 1985)
Type of work: Play

A black family is torn apart by the father's adultery and his refusal to let his son accept a football scholarship.

August Wilson received his first Pulitzer Prize for *Fences*, which also won several Tony Awards during its Broadway run. The powerful family drama is set during the 1950's, when the first hints of change in race relations often gave rise to generational conflicts between hopeful young blacks and their wary, experience-scarred parents. The play was inspired by Wilson's memories of his own stepfather, a onetime high school football player who had hoped to win an athletic scholarship and study medicine only to find that no college in Pittsburgh would give a scholarship to a black player.

In *Fences*, Wilson's stepfather becomes Troy Maxson, a proud, hard-working garbage man who once played baseball in the Negro Leagues. Embittered by the disappointments of his own life, Troy refuses to believe that times have changed when his son, Cory, is offered a football scholarship. Certain that athletics hold no hope of a better life for his son, Troy refuses to sign the necessary papers, effectively denying Cory his chance at a college education. Troy also deeply angers his wife when she learns that he has fathered a child by another woman, an act that destroys the bond that has held the couple together throughout their bleak life together.

At the heart of the play's father/son conflict is an unbridgeable disparity between Troy and Cory's abilities to believe that society can indeed change in its treatment of black Americans. Although Troy's unbending harshness often casts him in an unsympathetic light, Wilson grounds his character's personality in the frustrations and injustices that have shaped the course of his life. Cory is unable to understand the full impact of the events that have influenced his father's attitudes, and the two men ultimately engage in a showdown that destroys their relationship.

Fences is also a story about relationships between husbands and wives, and in Rose Maxson, Wilson has created one of his strongest female characters. Rose's rage at her husband's betrayal, her articulate refusal to accept his justifications as valid, and her painful decision to rear Troy's illegitimate daughter as her own all mark her as a complex and remarkable character. Wilson's plays are notable for the powerful voice given to black women as well as black men, and nowhere is this more in evidence than in the compassionate, impassioned characterization of Rose. Her words speak for a generation of black women, just as her husband's life embodies the hardships faced by black men.

THE PIANO LESSON

First produced: 1987 (first published, 1990)
Type of work: Play

A brother and sister argue over a family heirloom, a piano that represents their heritage as the descendants of slaves.

The Piano Lesson brought August Wilson his second Pulitzer Prize in drama and, like *Fences*, its subject is a family conflict. The story is set in 1930's Pittsburgh, where Doaker Charles lives with his niece, Berniece, and her young daughter, Maretha. The arrival of Berniece's brother, Boy Willie, from Mississippi sets the plot in motion, as Boy Willie declares his intention of selling a piano that holds a unique place in the family's history. Originally owned by a man named Sutter, who had received it in payment for Doaker's grandmother and father, the piano was carved by Doaker's grandfather with scenes depicting the family's life in slavery. Berniece refuses to part with such a powerful symbol of her family's terrible history, while Boy Willie hopes to earn enough from the sale to buy Sutter's land from his descendants.

At the center of the pair's disagreement is the issue of confronting rather than rejecting the African American heritage of slavery. For Berniece, the piano is a source of strength; it reminds her of the courage and endurance shown by her ancestors, and she believes that selling the piano would be a denial of that history. Boy Willie believes in looking only to the future, and he cannot understand his sister's refusal to part with the instrument.

An unexpected dimension is added to the story with Berniece and Doaker's declarations that they have seen the ghost of Sutter's grandson, whom Berniece believes Boy Willie murdered in order to get his land. The ghost is a very real presence in the play; Wilson is not afraid to incorporate aspects of the supernatural in his work and has also done so in *Joe Turner's Come and Gone*. In both plays, phenomena that might be dismissed as fantastic are embraced as an outgrowth of African culture and are incorporated into the story in imaginative and effective ways. *The Piano Lesson*'s dramatic conflict is resolved when Boy Willie does battle with the ghost as Berniece draws on the power of the piano itself to exorcise the spirit. The action is both dramatically compelling and a stunning symbolic evocation of the power that black history can bring to those who embrace it.

Summary

August Wilson's groundbreaking cycle of plays chronicling the black experience in the twentieth century has brought a vital new voice to the American theater. The stories he tells and the complex characters he creates offer powerful dramatic portraits of lives that have often been marginalized or forgotten altogether. Believing that only by embracing their history can African Americans find a true sense of their heritage, Wilson draws on important periods in black history as background material for his plays. His poetic explorations of African American lives and culture embody the sentiment he once expressed in an interview: "Claim what is yours."

Bibliography

Brown, Chip. "The Light in August." *Esquire*, April, 1989, 116-125.
Freedman, Samuel G. "A Voice from the Streets." *The New York Times Magazine* 136 (March 15, 1987): 36.
Gussow, Mel. "Fine-Tuning *The Piano Lesson*." *The New York Times Magazine* 138 (September 10, 1989): 18.
Migler, Rachel. "An Elegant Duet." *Gentlemen's Quarterly*, April, 1990, 114-118.
Poinsett, Alex. "August Wilson." *Ebony*, November, 1987, 68-71.
Staples, Brent. "August Wilson." *Essence*, August, 1987, 51-54.
Wilson, August. "How to Write a Play Like August Wilson." *The New York Times*, March 10, 1991, p. H5.

Janet Lorenz

LANFORD WILSON

Born: Lebanon, Missouri
April 13, 1937

Principal Literary Achievement
One of the most prolific and accessible of major contemporary American dramatists, Wilson successfully bridges the distance between repertory, regional, Off-Broadway, and Broadway theater.

Biography
Lanford Wilson was born on April 13, 1937, in Lebanon, Missouri, a locale he would later use as the setting for his cycle of plays about the mythical Talley family. When he was five years old, his parents divorced, and his mother took him to live in Springfield, Missouri; the search to establish a relationship with an absent father would constitute an important motif in a number of his plays, most notably the autobiographical memory play *Lemon Sky* (1970) and *Redwood Curtain* (1992), in which a half-Vietnamese girl tracks down her American father. When Wilson's mother remarried in 1948, the family moved to a farm in Ozark, Missouri. While a high-school student there in the mid-1950's, Wilson received his formative experiences in the theater, acting the role of the narrator Tom in a production of Tennessee Williams's *The Glass Menagerie* (1944) and attending a production of Arthur Miller's *Death of a Salesman* (1949) at Southwest Missouri State College.

In 1956, Wilson traveled to California for an unsuccessful reunion with his biological father. While there, he studied art history at San Diego State College, claiming it made him aware of "what our heritage was, and what we are doing to it," which becomes a pivotal concern in several works, particularly *The Mound Builders* (1975). In the late 1950's, Wilson, by then an artist working for an advertising firm in the Midwest, enrolled in a playwriting class offered by the University of Chicago and began working in the one-act form. He moved to the Greenwich Village section of New York in 1962 and, early the following year, saw a production of an absurdist work by Eugéne Ionesco at the Off-Off-Broadway Caffe Cino; the play's blend of the funny and the serious had a profound effect on the young playwright. Over the next few years, Caffe Cino and Ellen Stewart's La Mama Experimental Theater Club would provide a hospitable home for many of Wilson's short works, including *The Madness of Lady Bright* (1964), which dramatizes the descent of an aging homosexual queen

into insanity and remains an impressive contribution to the development of a gay theater, and *The Rimers of Eldritch* (1966), which might be seen as Wilson's dark version of Thornton Wilder's *Our Town* (1938). His first full-length work, *Balm in Gilead*, focusing like many of his plays on society's down-and-outers, opened in 1965.

With dissections of two marriages, a troubled interracial one in *The Gingham Dog* (1968) and a middle-aged disillusioned one in *Serenading Louie* (1970), Wilson branched out into regional theaters, a movement then burgeoning in importance for developing playwrights. In 1969, Wilson and three others, including the director Marshall Mason, organized the Circle Repertory Company, which became the home for the premiere productions of virtually all of Wilson's plays. His *The Hot l Baltimore* (1973) captivated audiences for more than a thousand performances and won for Wilson his first New York Drama Critics Circle Award for Best American Play. Wilson's later plays continued to open at Circle Repertory or regional theaters, eventually moving on to Broadway; *Angels Fall* (1982), for example, began at the New World Festival in Miami, while *Burn This* (1987) was first seen at the Mark Taper Forum in Los Angeles. He continued to garner accolades and awards, including a Pulitzer Prize in drama for *Talley's Folly*. As befits an artist for whom the image of the garden—either lost or restored—is a potent symbol and for whom the preservation of the past is an overriding concern, Wilson's hobby is tending the gardens around his restored house in Sag Harbor, Long Island.

Analysis

Although Lanford Wilson has often been spoken of as a distinctively Midwestern playwright in the tradition of William Inge, he is by no means a narrow regionalist. His canvas is all of America, rural and urban, East and West as well as Midwest, with characters from every socioeconomic strata. Of his first half-dozen long plays, only *The Rimers of Eldritch* occurs in a small town. Reminiscent of the Welsh poet Dylan Thomas' *Under Milk Wood* (1954), Wilson's play tells of the murder of the village idiot/outsider Skelly as he tries to prevent a rape. Wilson's town of Eldritch shares more in common with the poet Edgar Lee Masters' Spoon River than it does with *Our Town*'s pristine Grovers' Corners, since Eldritch contains small-town narrowness, repression, and hypocrisy. The symbolic hoarfrost (rime) blights all, and the ritual killing of the scapegoat accomplishes no regenerative purpose.

The Rimers of Eldritch, a threnody for voices, is as much readers' theater as traditional play. It employs several techniques that Wilson uses in other works from the same period: a montage or collage structure, featuring multiple protagonists involved in simultaneous actions; direct address, monologues, and overlapping voices; and an almost cinematic use of lighting to achieve effects analogous to film close-ups and fade-outs. Such devices appear again in *Balm in Gilead* and *The Hot l Baltimore*, both of which are set in urban places—a corner lunchroom and a hotel lobby—that should be sanctuaries fostering a sense of community and belonging but that are instead peopled by society's outcasts and underclass: prostitutes and pimps, drunks and drug dealers, the lost and lonely and dislocated. Wilson, a former graphic artist, is especially adept at handling theater space; more than anything, it is the setting of *The Hot l Baltimore* that establishes the link between Wilson and the Russian master Anton Chekhov.

The locale of *The Hot l Baltimore* is the lobby of a once-elegant railroad hotel now ready for the wrecker's ball; Wilson comments that "the theater, evanescent itself, and for all we do perhaps disappearing here, seems the ideal place for the representation of the impermanence of our architecture," thus cluing the reader into change and decay as central motifs. The play's action occurs on Memorial Day and builds on the dichotomy between past and present, permanence and progress, and, as in Chekhov, culture and materialism, beauty and use. The characters decry the diminishing countryside, the decline of the railroads, and the environmental pollution destroying the land—all effects of the greedy "vultures" who glorify financial gain. Even though Wilson's language may lack the elegiac poeticism of some other literary descendants of Chekhov, such as Tennessee Williams, in his use of place as symbol to convey meaning visually, as well as in his recurrent emphasis on the rape of culture and civilization by an amoral business class, Wilson remains the chief Chekhovian dramatist writing in contemporary America—as David Storey is in Great Britain.

The Chekhovian patterns also adumbrate other works in the Wilson canon: These include *Fifth of July* (1978), in which a family faces the prospect of seeing its ancestral home bought for use as a recording studio and its land turned into an airstrip; and *Redwood Curtain*, in which a family always careful to balance its business dealings with the need to preserve the environment is powerless to resist the huge conglomerate that will cut down the ancient trees—a direct allusion to Chekhov's *Vishnyovy Sad* (1904; *The Cherry Orchard*, 1908). As in Chekhov's play, the destruction of the forest is linked with the disintegration and dispersal of the family unit: Trees hacked off at the ground are like a family denied its collective memory, left with no sense of rootedness or identity. Although Wilson does not push as incessantly as does Arthur Miller the notion of the debasement of the American Dream by the drive for unlimited success through competition and aggression, this criticism remains implicit in his Chekhov-like questioning of what has been sacrificed or lost in order to achieve material gain.

An integral part of the formulation of the American Dream has always been the promise of a New Eden, the restored garden to the West. The California in Wilson's *Lemon Sky*, however, is a sterile wasteland, both environmentally and emotionally, where nothing is "naturally" green; rather, everything is autumnal, "umber, amber, olive, sienna, ocher, orange." While gardens, literal and symbolic, proliferate in Wilson's work, they are just as likely to be dying out (as in *The Hot l Baltimore* and *Redwood Curtain*) as growing or thriving (as in *Fifth of July*). When the garden is healthy, it is usually because an artist tends and nurtures it. Even the creative imagination itself seems to atrophy when cut off from garden places. Artists and artist figures—often estranged from their fathers—abound in Wilson's plays. In *Lemon Sky* an adolescent writer-son is rejected by a long-lost father who suspects him of homosexuality. In *Burn This*, a choreographer learns that the creative process necessarily involves drawing upon personal experience; eradicating the line between life and art can give rise to a representation that somehow mysteriously transcends life. In *Redwood Curtain*, a young pianist who discovers her identity through music expresses disillusionment with a public increasingly lacking any interest in art.

In the apocalyptic *Angels Fall*, set in a Southwestern mission church under threat of radioactive fallout in a postnuclear "garden" surrounded by a uranium mine, a reactor, and a missile base, the concept of artist expands to include all who recognize their vocation—be they teachers, painters, priests, doctors, or athletes; once one hears the call and decides "what manner of persons who ought to be," then "magic . . . happens and you know who you are." Each of these characters, in the face of the pervasive danger of annihilation, goes forth from this temporary sanctuary committed to doing his or her work in a perilous world. If the determination to work that one finds at the end of a Chekhov play sometimes seems but a hollow response to fear of facing the void, when such a determination occurs in Wilson (for example in *Angels Fall* or in *Fifth of July*), it reflects instead a hard-won resolve, a positive renewal of oneself to active fellowship in the community of humankind.

THE MOUND BUILDERS

First produced: 1975 (first published, 1976)
Type of work: Play

An archeological dig pits scientists against land developers, uncovering not only a primitive god-mask but also human greed, jealousy, and violence.

The most complex treatment of Wilson's themes appears in *The Mount Builders*, probably his most impressive achievement. The action occurs in "the mind's eye" of Professor August Howe, who recalls an archeological dig he led the preceding summer in southern Illinois that unearthed an ancient burial ground of the Temple Mound People. Howe (accompanied by his wife Cynthia and their daughter) and his young assistant Dan Loggins (accompanied by his pregnant wife Jean) come into conflict with the owner of the property and his twenty-five-year-old son Chad, who hope to make a great deal of money by selling the land for a vacation resort. Chad, who is carrying on an affair with Cynthia Howe, had saved Dan from drowning the summer before but now tries unsuccessfully to lure Jean away from him. Thwarted both personally in his desire for Jean and financially because laws prevent developing the property, Chad eventually kills Dan, bulldozes the excavation, and kills himself, leaving the god-king mask to be reburied by the mythic flood waters.

Wilson's dramaturgy in this memory play approximates that of Williams in *The Glass Menagerie*; the playing area might be seen as August's mind, with the slides of the precious artifacts that are projected onto the back wall prompting his remembrances. The central conflict is between the preservation of a culture, on the one hand,

and commercial progress on the other; between a past age of poetry and a present age of facts. The scientists stand poised between commercial promoters and creative artisans, capable of bending either way. Whereas the ancient tribe sought its immortality through gorgeous works used in rituals, contemporary humans seek theirs through material gain. When Dan holds the death mask from the god-king "up to his face, and almost inadvertently it stays in place," it is perhaps an act of hubris, revealing his lack of sufficient awe for the primitive culture and leading unwittingly to his death at the hands of the sexually jealous and money-crazed Chad.

The contemporary artist who arrives in this Midwestern "garden of the gods" is Howe's sister Delia. The author of one successful novel, she has been unable to summon up the creativity necessary to produce a second book. The source of her writing block was the death of her father and her separation from the paternal home. If the heritage of the past, whether childhood home or ancient burial site, serves as a creative spur to the artist, then once these places are lost or defiled, judged as worthless or anachronistic except when exploited for profit, all that remains is "syllables, not sense." Lack of adequate respect for the past results in a present beset by greed and violence and a decline into savagery.

FIFTH OF JULY

First produced: 1978 (first published, 1978)
Type of work: Play

Three generations of a family and four friends from the Vietnam era gather to replay the past and decide on a direction for the future.

The first of Wilson's plays about the Talley family, *Fifth of July* explores two of the playwright's favorite preoccupations: the need to preserve the past in order to live humanely in the present and the importance to both self and society of embracing one's vocation. Although *Fifth of July* is an ensemble piece with several protagonists, the focal character is Kenny Tally, who arrived back from Vietnam with five citations for bravery but without any legs. It is 1977, and Kenny is determined not to return to his calling as a high-school teacher. Feeling discomfort over coming home alive, if maimed, from the war, Kenny senses the invisibility imposed upon veterans of an unpopular cause when others refuse to look at them out of shame or guilt. Joining Kenny at the family homestead are his Aunt Sally Friedman, who has come back to spread the ashes of her deceased husband Matt (the story of their courtship is later told in the 1979 play *Talley's Folly*), Kenny's sister June, a flower-child from the 1960's, and June's daughter, Shirley, an aspiring writer. Also visiting are John Landis, a record promoter who wants to buy the Talley property, and his wife Gwen; they had attended the University of California at Berkeley with Kenny and June but had deliberately gone to Europe without Kenny, leaving him behind to be drafted.

Tending the grounds of the Talley home has been Jed, Kenny's homosexual lover. Jed has gradually been replanting the property in the manner of a traditional English garden that will take years to mature; recently, he has rediscovered a lost rose that once again will be propagated at Sissinghurst Castle in England, "the greatest rose garden in the world." Jed, in his planting of the garden and his caring for and loving the disabled Ken, is the new Adam who inspires a sense of purpose and restores a feeling of community after the fall.

Both Sally, a representative of the oldest generation of Talleys onstage, and Shirley, a member of the family's youngest generation, join Kenny in resisting the lure of spatial dislocation to answer instead the pull of the ancestral home. If necessary, Sally herself will buy the Talley place so that it will not go out of family control and become a cement airstrip, especially now that she and Jed have spread Matt's ashes among the roses. While Shirley commits the younger generation to renewing the Talley clan, Kenny—once he has learned how to understand the virtually unintelligible speech of his young half-cousin through creatively having the boy record a story—overcomes the temptation to give up teaching and recommits himself to his "mission" in life. On all levels—the archetypal, the natural, the familial, and the individual—the movement of *Fifth of July* is thus from despair and death to renewal and rebirth.

TALLEY'S FOLLY

First produced: 1979 (first published, 1979)
Type of work: Play

Two misfits approaching middle age discover they are made for each other, and they pledge love and commitment despite the opposition of a prejudiced family.

Set on July 4, 1944, *Talley's Folly* concerns two characters who are revealed largely through exposition and lengthy monologues: Sally Talley, a nurse headed for self-imposed spinsterhood, and Matt Friedman, a liberal Jewish accountant fond of using comedy routines to mask his vulnerability. The "folly" of the play's title and the locale for the action is a boathouse that Sally's Uncle Everett constructed in place of a gazebo he had hoped to build. Wilson opens the play using a Wilder-like frame, with Matt as narrator/stage manager conspiratorially explaining to the audience that they are about to witness a "once-upon-a-time" romance that could happen only in the theater.

When Matt narrates the history of his family—of a Prussian father and Ukrainian mother "indefinitely detained" by the Germans in World War I; of a Latvian sister tortured by the French so their father would divulge information he never had; and of himself, born in Lithuania and arriving as a refugee with his uncle from Norway via Caracas—he distances the painful story by narrating it in the third person. Because of his wandering family's past, Matt considers himself non-nationalistic, feeling little allegiance to any political cause or "ism." Although he escaped the draft because of his age, he is not unaffected by the war (which, he believes, governments deliberately prolong for economic stability). Uncertain that there will ever be a time after this war, he refuses to bring another child into the world "to be killed for political purposes," and thus he hesitates to marry Sally.

Sally yearns on this Independence Day to break free from a restrictive family that is anti-liberal, anti-Semitic, and anti-German—and, therefore, anti-Matt. Yet political, religious, and racial intolerance are not all that prevent her marriage. Years before, she was engaged to her high-school sweetheart; their marriage portended a merger of two prominent families, but her father committed suicide during the Depression. Finally, she reveals to Matt (and to the audience waiting to hear her secret) that an illness has left her sterile. Once her misconception that Matt is only claiming that he would never father a child in order to spare her the burden of not being able to give him one is cleared away, these two can come together.

The boathouse "folly" has always been, for Sally, a green world, a place of escape and magic. Matt and Sally leave the boathouse to return to a family and a community unprepared to accept them and ready to ostracize them, just as Matt, the stage manager again at plays' end, sends the audience out from the theater exactly ninety-seven minutes later into their own imperfect world. A dissonance exists between what Matt calls the "waltz" or "valentine" of this fairy tale the audience has been watching and the prejudice that pervades their world. Sally Talley's own folly, shared by Matt, is the courage to choose love in spite of the world's unwillingness to dissolve barriers of class, nationality, politics, and religion.

Summary

Partly because Lanford Wilson has chosen to premiere his plays at Circle Repertory or in regional theaters, he has seldom attracted the sustained media attention accorded such contemporaries as David Rabe, Sam Shepard, and David Mamet. Yet his works are among the most distinctively American dramas of the last quarter of the twentieth century. For Wilson's emphases closely reflect issues at the heart of the nation's survival: tolerance for the have-nots and outsiders; respect for the multicultural heritage of the past; the need to preserve beauty in the face of technological advance; the value of work in defining one's self; and the importance of community for instilling a sense of belonging and rootedness.

Bibliography

Barnett, Gene A. *Lanford Wilson*. Boston: Twayne, 1987.

Busby, Mark. *Lanford Wilson*. Boise, Idaho: Boise State University, 1987.

Dasgupta, Gautam. "Lanford Wilson." In *American Playwrights: A Critical Survey*, edited by Bonnie Marranca and Gautam Dasgupta. New York: Drama Book Specialists, 1981.

Herman, William. *Understanding Contemporary American Drama.* Columbia: University of South Carolina Press, 1987.

Jacobi, Martin J. "The Comic of Lanford Wilson." *Studies in the Literary Imagination* 21 (Fall, 1988): 119-134.

Schvey, Henry I. "Images of the Past in the Plays of Lanford Wilson." In *Essays on Contemporary American Drama.* edited by Hedwig Bok and Albert Wertheim. Munich: Max Huber Verlag, 1981.

Witham, Barry B. "Images of America: Wilson, Weller, and Horovitz." *Theatre Journal* 34 (May, 1982): 223-232.

Thomas P. Adler

JAMES WRIGHT

Born: Martins Ferry, Ohio
December 13, 1927
Died: New York, New York
March 25, 1980

Principal Literary Achievement

One of the most admired and widely read poets of his generation, Wright was particularly noted for his formal dexterity, grace of phrasing, and humane themes.

Biography

James Arlington Wright was born and reared in Martins Ferry, Ohio, near Wheeling, West Virginia, a small town on the Ohio River that provides the setting and background for a number of his poems. Following high school, he served for three years in the U.S. Army in the aftermath of World War II, returning to attend Kenyon College in Ohio, where he began writing poetry. Upon graduation he spent a year in Austria as a Fulbright Fellow and then entered graduate school at the University of Washington, where he obtained both M.A. and Ph.D. degrees.

He began teaching at the University of Minnesota in 1957, later moving to Macalaster College in St. Paul. Yale University Press in 1957 published his first book, *The Green Wall*, in its Yale Younger Poets Series, a remarkable achievement for a writer still in graduate school. The volume received positive reviews, especially for its skillful versification and formal facility. A second book, *Saint Judas*, appeared in 1959, when Wright also completed his Ph.D. dissertation; this volume, too, gained critical applause. These first two books are noteworthy in that some of Wright's best-known and most often reprinted pieces appeared in them, particularly "Arrangements with Earth for Three Dead Friends," "A Winter Day in Ohio," and "The Alarm." These books also established Wright's characteristic settings and themes—notably of loneliness alienation; these remained constants throughout his career.

During his Minnesota period, Wright came in contact with the poet and editor Robert Bly, who had a significant influence on him. Bly had remained largely aloof from the formalist-traditionalist schools that had dominated poetry during the first half of the century. He advocated instead an intuitive, subjective approach that sought for elemental responses and their expressive equivalents rather than abstract formal patterns and rhetorical cleverness. This movement, eventually called the "deep image"

school of the 1960's and 1970's, had special affinities with the highly subjective, language-distorting work of the central American writers Pablo Neruda and César Vallejo, who were in turn strongly influenced by Spanish Surrealism and Futurism. Although Wright later denied that Bly had been more than a catalyst to an internal process already begun, these forces combined to modify Wright's style extensively. His next book, *The Branch Will Not Break* (1963), shows the extent of the change.

This change was pivotal in Wright's career; it turned him in the direction in which he would find his characteristic voice. His earlier poems were directed toward realizing a fine exterior beauty, toward shaping exquisite verbal structures—poems as works of art, to which the poet was largely subordinate. They are mainly poems of the mind. The newer poems come from the heart; they attempt literally to put feelings into words, almost as if they are just in the act of becoming aware of themselves.

As if to symbolize his development, Wright moved at this time from the Midwest to become a professor at the City University of New York, where he remained for the rest of his life. While there he published *Shall We Gather at the River* in 1968; in that volume, he carries the personalization of his poetry one step further. Wright forces his readers to look at aspects of their civilization that are typically ignored and compels them to recognize neglected parts of humanity.

Wright's larger poems—both the Wright "New Poems" included in *Collected Poems* (1971) and those gathered in *Two Citizens* (1973) (which he later repudiated), *Moments of the Italian Summer* (1976), *To a Blossoming Pear Tree* (1977), *The Temple in Nimes* (1982), and *This Journey* (1982)—move back to a more affirmative position, yet they do not abandon Martins Ferry and his typical subjects. An extended visit to Europe, especially Italy, opened a remarkable new vein, meditations on monuments of antiquity, especially in contrast with modern behavior. These show, at times, a rare geniality. While working on these materials, he contracted cancer and died on March 25, 1980, at the age of fifty-two.

Analysis

James Wright proceeded through three rather distinct phases in his poetic career, in all of which he produced work so commendable that he is considered one of the half-dozen best poets of his generation. He is also one of a few poets to have gathered a kind of popular following. For several years after his death, a group of devotees met annually in Martins Ferry on the anniversary to hold a memorial reading and reminisce about his life and work.

His first phase persists through the early volumes *The Green Wall* and *Saint Judas*. The poems of this period are very much in the style fashionable at mid-century: composed in strict formal patterns, witty and ironic in tone, integrating a battery of rhetorical devices into a fused, weighty whole. The poems had substance; they were made objects, conspicuous for the fineness of their finish. In keeping with the dictum that the poet should incorporate as much of his poetic heritage as he could, they reflected, drew on, and added to the long, unbroken line of English poetry. Wright's background and education suited him well for this kind of work. At mid-century,

American sympathies were stridently pro-British; the country had fought two wars to rescue and preserve the British cultural heritage. Furthermore, although Wright came from a working-class background, his education reinforced traditional British values. Kenyon College sponsored *The Kenyon Review*, one of the most influential literary quarterlies of the time—and one particularly associated with the dissemination of the New Criticism, which emphasized the idea of the poem as a cultural object. Further, Wright earned a Ph.D. in English literature with a dissertation on Charles Dickens. He was steeped in British culture.

Thus, many of these poems are conventional. Yet this does not mean that they are negligible; several are among the finest of the period. "Arrangements with Earth for Three Dead Friends," for example, is so good as to be almost timeless. For a variety of reasons, however, Wright came to feel that this approach to poetry was limited; intellectualism and formalism had not cornered the market. This opened his second phase, which appears full-blown in *The Branch Will Not Break*. The change is much less thematic than stylistic. Wright's characteristic attitudes and motifs persist; he remains the poet of the downtrodden in mind and body, the castaways of society, the commonplace victims trapped in the poor streets. The subjects—the natural and human victims of a vicious society—remain constant, but the difference of orientation makes them seem more personal. Wright had always concerned himself with loneliness, despair, and death, but he had seemed to escape from them in his poems. The new poems make the loss felt.

In this respect, he shares the capacity of Walt Whitman for sympathizing with the great unwashed multitudes; he seems uniquely able to tune in to the secret loneliness, the inward emptiness, the gut-filling sense of loss that allow all of humanity to relate to the concept of Everyman and his fate. Yet, Wright's formal strategy has been transformed. In place of the highly wrought verbal textures and patterns of his earlier verse, Wright turns to a poetry that speaks simply, in relaxed breaths, from the heart. If the earlier poems were perceptions turned to elegant filigree and lace, these are states of feeling just finding their first stage of articulation into words and images.

One celebrated poem that reveals this is "Autumn Begins in Martins Ferry, Ohio." In it, Wright brilliantly contrasts the empty lives of three varieties of fathers with the superficially highlighted ones of their adolescent sons. The lives of the fathers are over; all that is left for them is to dream about the heroism they have become too old to enact. At the same time, their football-player sons sacrifice their bodies in the vain—or at best temporary—quest of athletic glory. The conjunction is a compounding of futility; yet this is the best that can be hoped for in these degenerate times. In this poem, Wright creates a delicate equilibrium between the objective and the subjective, the head and the heart.

Wright's next volume, *Shall We Gather at the River*, carries the negativism of his new vision to extreme points, opening up a third phase. It seems almost as if once the poet began listening to the murmurs of his heart, he found it impossible to exercise restraint. The book as a result is a gallery of monologues and portraits of people broken by the world. In "Before a Cashier's Window in a Department Store," for example, he creates the state of mind of a derelict standing on the street staring at a cashier and manager in a store filled with merchandise completely irrelevant to his state of need. They ignore him, of course; worse than negligible in their world, he feels their glances pass through him, as if he were dead. He likens himself to corpses picked over on a battlefield, an image that sums up the dominant feeling of the volume. Even when he works in regular stanzaic patterns, harking back to his beginnings, his vision remains desolate, inconsolable—as in "Two Postures Beside a Fire," in which he returns to his boyhood home to spend an evening with his father and discovers that he brings nothing that can lighten the life of the aged man.

The emotional desolation of the speakers of these poems is palpable, to the extent that the book has been referred to by several critics as painful, even unbearably so. The pain comes from Wright's uncanny ability to create images of those broken by the ruthless strains of modern life—in his phrase, of "the poor washed up by the Chicago winter." The book offers little respite from the unrelenting disclosure of suffering. Yet it does provide a kind of relief. For these are powerful poems; Wright sometimes penetrates the heart of despair and catches the anguish residing there.

THE GREEN WALL

First published: 1967
Type of work: Poems

Wright's first book of poems demonstrates sophisticated command of formal design, delicate phrasing, and evocative images, especially of death and suffering.

A first book of poetry usually lays a mere foundation; with *The Green Wall*, James Wright built an entire structure for a poetic career. Moreover, since several of these poems continue to be anthologized half a century after composition, they continue to constitute a significant part of his achievement. In these poems, Wright displays an unusual sureness of touch, as if he had always known what his themes were going to be and had only waited for the right opportunity. "The Fishermen," for example, juxtaposes the carefree carelessness of two young men drinking beer by the oceanside with the chronic, age-old sadness of old men fishing there. By bringing these images together, Wright manages to fuse them, to show their essential identity: They are two stages of the male experience. Then he extends the fusion; men have always been like this, and in drawing near the sea, they near their primordial roots. The sea is their end, the natural entity they will join after death, just as it had been their beginning.

This theme of the community of all living things in death permeates the book. It reappears in "On the Skeleton of a Hound," in which the speaker pays homage to the spirit now absent, but remembered in and with, a dog's bones. Over the skeleton, the speaker conjures up the memory of how the animal's being flamed over the woods. Before leaving, he scatters the bones to the woods, even heaving the skull over a tree—not in disrespect, but as a reconsecrating act; he is returning the bones to the care of the Earth. It will handle them properly, remaking them into part of the eternal community.

"Three Steps to the Graveyard" could stand as the distilled center of the book. The "three steps" are actually three stages of visitation, three arcs that constitute a circle in life, all commemorating death. The speaker records three visits, once in the spring; once in summer with his father, which somehow becomes the end of the year; once at the end of autumn. In spring, the father shelters the boy, but then leaves him in darkness and "bare shade." In autumn, everything, even the field mice, tremble in anticipation. The three steps span life, bringing it to death, as is fitting. This theme culminates in "Arrangements with Earth for Three Dead Friends," Wright's most famous poem. In it, Wright manages to evade a usually fatal trap: He dares to write about the death of children. For centuries, conventional poetic wisdom has held that such topics are poison; it is impossible to write about them, without becoming hopelessly sentimental—what the eighteenth century poet Alexander Pope called "bathetic." Wright, though, creates a masterpiece. Moreover, he does it in exactly the way his seventeenth century predecessor Ben Jonson did—by so formalizing his treatment that the poem takes on the impersonal objectivity of a carving in stone. The restraint is managed so delicately that it turns a personal grief into a tribute of felt beauty, the enduring note of this volume.

SAINT JUDAS

First published: 1959
Type of work: Poems

In this collection, Wright consolidates the gains of his earlier work, expands into the region of love, and deepens his vision of the omnipresence of death.

The title figure of *Saint Judas*, the paradox of the consecrated villain, reflects much of the spirit of this book. The poems are arranged in three sections, which at first do not seem to have much connection: "Lunar Changes," "A Sequence of Love Poems," and "The Part Nearest Home." Yet they ultimately disclose continuity, both internally and with Wright's previous work. Formally and thematically, the links to the past are quite clear. Wright is still working primarily with traditional formal patterns, still approaching poetry as if it consisted of art objects carved carefully by the artist out of all the resources of language. His subjects remain death, loss, the suffering intrinsic to life, and the way these experiences bind all life into a single sheaf.

Near the end of "Lunar Changes," one poem, "The Revelation," provides a key. The speaker is meditating about his dead father, recalling how anger continues to divide them. But even as he feels the anger rising again, a beam of moonlight illuminates a vision of his father weeping and reaching out to him. As they embrace, formerly barren apple boughs shed petals. Love can overcome even the separation of death; through love, death can be a solvent for life, unifying all living things in its embrace. Death may even be necessary for the existence of love.

This bridges into "A Sequence of Love Poems," which needs the title, because otherwise few readers would identify these as such. "In Shame and Humiliation," for example, is overtly about the distinctly human act of cursing, especially the way in which males define themselves by that act. "A Breath of Air" similarly seems a lissome mood piece, but its connection to love seems tenuous. Eventually, Wright instills his point: These are love poems not because they celebrate love—though some do, in quite unconventional ways—but because they create the possibility of love. They record stages of self-awareness that must precede love. Thus "A Girl Walking into a Shadow" creates a sympathetic projection of a girl barely noticed in passing and shows that this act of imaginative identification is itself an act of love, one that further qualifies the speaker for loving.

"The Part Nearest Home" returns to the familiar territory of Wright's home themes. It includes work on death-row inmates, funerals, visits to his father's grave, all integrated under the signs of the community of the living and the dead. The sonnet "Saint Judas" acts as centerpiece for the set. It is a stunning evocation of a ready-made image perfect for Wright: the villain in spite of himself, the man who betrays Christ because he is doing God a kindness. This Judas brings about the death of Christ, to be sure, but he does it as an act of love, because it will make salvation possible for men, otherwise desolate. Wright sets up a striking scenario to reveal this aspect of Judas and fit him into his vision of the relation of death and love. He presents Judas as on his way to kill himself when he finds a man being beaten by thieves. Immediately, he leaves his business to rescue the victim. Judas, in other words, becomes the Good Samaritan, the figure Christ himself set up as the ideal Christian. Yet—and this is vintage Wright—he also presents Judas as becoming aware that not even this act of charity can remove his guilt. The book is complex, but it deepens Wright's vision.

THE BRANCH WILL NOT BREAK

First published: 1963
Type of work: Poems

In this volume, Wright turns to simpler, more personal forms and to a more uncompromising vision of the sufferings generated by human indifference.

The very title of *The Branch Will Not Break* seems to disclose the spiritual and emotional state Wright had reached at the time it was published. He had been confronting the strains and stresses of modern life throughout his career. Now he was making a statement of his fitness: Whatever the pressure, he could stand up to it, as if determined to prove that his central theme of the coexistence of death and life, suffering and love, were more than just a pious hope.

Recognizing this has led many critics to misemphasize the impact of some aspects of these poems. By consensus, these works show the solidification of Wright's despair before the absolute bleakness of his defining work, *Shall We Gather at the River*. Yet there is more wit, vitality, humor, and variety in this book than that judgment would indicate.

These poems are much less formal than Wright's earlier work, and much more personal and intimate; the voice speaks from within rather than assuming a public posture. There is less apparent artifice and polish, more spontaneity, more emphasis on the words of the heart. "Autumn Begins in Martins Ferry, Ohio," for example, has nothing like the strict stanzaic forms characteristic of his poems. The lines are arbitrary, broken apparently according to whim; they suggest the almost inarticulate murmurings that proceed just beyond the range of conscious recognition. They also re-create the scene in graphic detail, neatly conflating the dreams of two generations, the older people caught in the act of deflecting their hopes to their offspring, the younger ones oblivious of any frame of reference more encompassing than daily frivolity. Overriding all, however, is the idea that both generations are more profoundly interconnected than they realize, and that this interconnection foreshadows the path of salvation.

The volume contains several masterpieces, but "A Blessing" would outshine galaxies. In apparently effortless breath-units, Wright depicts an encounter between two travelers and two wild ponies. The lines ripple, as if imitating the movements of the horses. Wright fuses the horses' dancing, the excited breathing of the men, and the pacing of the lines into the same rhythm, so that all become part of the whole. The poem becomes an act of communion. Wright catches the rapt commingling of the speaker with the animals through direct description; it comes as no surprise when he likens the filly's ear with the "skin over a girl's wrist" or expresses his desire to embrace her. This merely anticipates the final transformation, which then appears simply natural: The poet offers to leave his body—which in the poem he has already done—and realizes that if he does, it will put forth blossoms. Wright has used this image before, to symbolize his reconciliation with his dead father; here, he signifies his fusion with the natural universe.

Summary

By all measures, James Wright deserves his ranking as one of the foremost American poets of the middle century. Among his peers, he alone is honored by annual convocations in his name held by common readers. He will long be remembered for his heart-wrenching realizations of animals, children, and familiar but rarely perceived states of mind.

Bibliography

Elkins, Andrew. *The Poetry of James Wright*. Tuscaloosa: University of Alabama Press, 1991.

Smith, Dave, ed. *The Pure Clear Word: Essays on the Poetry of James Wright*. Urbana: University of Illinois Press, 1982.

Stein, Kevin. *James Wright: The Poetry of a Grown Man*. Athens: Ohio University Press, 1989.

Wright, James. *Collected Prose*. Edited by Anne Wright. Ann Arbor: University of Michigan Press, 1983.

——————, and Annie Wright. *The Summers of James and Annie Wright: Sketches and Mosaics*. New York: Sheep Meadows Press, 1981.

James Livingston

JAY WRIGHT

Born: Albuquerque, New Mexico
May 25, 1934 or 1935

Principal Literary Achievement

By incorporating cross-cultural themes into his poetry about the African American experience, Wright has distinguished himself from other contemporary black writers.

Biography

Jay Wright was born on May 25, in either 1934 or 1935 in Albuquerque, New Mexico to Leona Dailey, a Virginian of black and Native American heritage, and George Murphy, an African American from Santa Rosa, New Mexico, who claimed to be of Cherokee and Irish descent. Soon after Jay's birth, his father, a construction worker and handyman, adopted the name Mercer Murphy Wright and relocated to California. Jay lived with his mother until he was three years old, when she gave her son to a black Albuquerque couple, Frankie and Daisy Faucett, who were known for taking in children. The Faucetts were a religious couple, and they exposed Wright to African American church tradition while he lived in their home.

Wright attended the Albuquerque public schools until he was in his early teens, when he went to live with his father and later his stepmother in San Pedro, California. During his high-school years, he began to play organized baseball, and upon graduation worked as a minor-league catcher for several California teams. During those years, he also learned to play the bass guitar, and this interest in music later led him to explore rhythm and style. Wright joined the Army in 1954 and served in the medical corps until 1957; he was stationed in Germany, and he took the opportunity to travel widely throughout Europe, where he encountered a variety of cultural traditions.

A year after he returned to the United States, he enrolled at the University of California at Berkeley, where he studied comparative literature. He received his B.A. in 1961, and the next fall attended Union Theological Seminary in New York City on a Rockefeller grant. He left Union in 1962 and began graduate study in literature at Rutgers University, taking a brief leave to teach English and history at the Butler Institute in Guadalajara, Mexico.

Returning to Rutgers in 1965, he spent the next three years there, completing all the requirements for the doctoral degree except the dissertation, and received an M.A.

degree in 1966. While studying at Rutgers, he lived and worked in Harlem, where he met other African American writers, including Larry Neal and Amiri Baraka, who were also exploring black tradition. In 1967, he was awarded a National Council on the Arts grant to further his studies. That same year, his early poems were published in a chapbook, *Death as History*.

In 1968, he married Lois Silber, and the couple moved to Mexico. They lived briefly in Guadalajara and then in Jalapa, where they stayed until 1971. During this time, Wright occasionally returned to the United States, spending brief periods as a writer-in-residence at Tougaloo College in Mississippi in 1968 and Talladega College in Alabama in 1969-1970. Beginning in 1970, he wrote plays on a Hodder Fellowship at Princeton University. In 1971, Wright's second book of poetry, *The Homecoming Singer*, was published. Appearing at the height of interest in contemporary black writing, the book received considerable critical acclaim.

In 1971, the couple left for Scotland, where Wright spent the next two years as a fellow at Dundee University. Returning to the United States, they lived in New Hampshire on and off from 1973 to 1978. In 1975, Wright began teaching at Yale University, where he remained until 1979. During this period, Wright published three books of poetry, all of which refine the mythology and continue the autobiographical themes he began in the early books. In these books, he also synthesizes the results of his studies in African, Hispanic, and Native American cultures. *Soothsayers and Omens* and *Dimensions of History* both appeared in 1976, *The Double Invention of Komo* in 1980.

In 1979, Wright settled in New Hampshire and began teaching at Dartmouth College; he has also taught at the Universities of Utah, Kentucky, and North Carolina. He has traveled extensively throughout the Americas and Europe, and with a writers' group, he visited the People's Republic of China in 1988. In the 1980's, Princeton University Press published three more books of his poetry: *Explications Interpretations* in 1984, *Selected Poems of Jay Wright* in 1987, and *Elaine's Book* in 1988. *Boleros* appeared in 1991.

Wright is also the author of several one-act plays based on African myths, including *Balloons* (1968), *The Adoration of Fire* (1983), and *The Death and Return of Paul Batuata* (1985). His full-length plays include a *Death as History* (1967) and *The Hunt and Double Night of the Wood* (1968). In the 1960's, a Berkeley, California, radio station performed a number of his dramatic works. His poetry has appeared in numerous periodicals and anthologies, including *Black World*, *Evergreen Review*, *New American Review*, *New Black Voices*, *The Nation*, and the *Yale Review*. The fall 1983 issue of *Callaloo* is devoted to his writings.

Analysis

In a 1983 interview, Jay Wright stated, "For me, multi-cultural is the fundamental process of human history." In this respect he differs from such other African American writers of his generation as Amiri Baraka, who in the late 1960's and early 1970's favored a black cultural nationalism. Wright looks for his spiritual roots not only in

African traditions but also in the linkages between these and other cultural traditions of the West and East. This quest for intellectual and spiritual identity extends throughout his poetic career. It is his main theme.

In the earlier poetry, Wright uses conventional English autobiographical poetic narrative. As his search expands to the myths and traditions of other cultures, he integrates styles and allusions from these cultures into the poems. Some, because they use obscure references and rhythms, are difficult. These techniques, however, enhance the thematic material and emphasize the complex relationship between the African American present and past.

Wright is well prepared to take on such a complicated task. Of African, Irish, and Native American descent himself, he grew up in the Southwestern and Western United States. Later in his life, he traveled throughout Europe and lived in the East and in Mexico. In college, he studied comparative literature and became well versed in the traditions and mythologies of Western Europe, Africa, North and South America, the Caribbean, and Asia. Few writers have such an extensive background to contemplate cross-cultural themes as does Wright.

Readers get their first real glimpse of Wright's magnitude in *Soothsayers and Omens*, where he looks for his personal roots in African tradition and culture. Poems such as "Sources" use both West African and pre-Columbian mythologies. Two poems about the eighteenth century African American scientist Benjamin Banneker integrate elements of Dogon theology, an African ritual he also works into many of his later poems. *The Dimensions of History*, however, is the book in which Wright fully explores the idea that all cultural traditions are part of the African American cultural heritage and collective memory. The book is arranged in the format of an initiation ritual involving separation, transition, and reincorporation. Wright delves into cultural traditions throughout time and space and explores how, in each myth, the dead relate to the living.

This awareness that the dead have something to say to the living propels Wright on his quest to find spiritual order personally and collectively. Many of his earlier poems in *The Homecoming Singer* (1971) examine the relationship between his ancestors and himself, between his biological father and his foster father. He also grounds his search in the Southwestern places of his early childhood as he explores Native American mythology. In "An Invitation to Madison County," he looks to the South for a sense of community with black tradition. In "The Albuquerque Graveyard," he tries to find answers to his personal past by contemplating his dead relatives.

He also searches for his place in a collective past. His long book-length poem *The Double Invention of Komo* is based on a male initiation ceremony of the Komo society of the Bambara tribe. Poetically describing this ritual, which has 266 signs relating to gods, enables Wright to synthesize its elements and values with other patterns he has found during his quest, thus making him individually a part of a collective community of like spirits. Feeling a part of a cosmology, he has the security to venture further into the unknown. The alienation he expresses in his earlier work is gone; by understanding the complexities of his past, he has regained his identity and come to realize his authentic cultural and spiritual heritage.

Wright uses more challenging references as he delves deeper into his quest and discovers cultural linkages. In "Homecoming," from *Soothsayers and Omens*, Wright intersperses quotations from Dante with images from West African mythology. Later poems become even more complex. In the second part of *Dimensions of History*, Wright mixes allusions to Aztec, Egyptian, Mayan, Incaic, Arabic, Christian, Yoruba, Akan, Dogon, and Bambara mythologies.

Wright also incorporates rhythms from other cultures. He believes that a poem ought to employ the rhythm of the culture it portrays. In *Explications/Interpretations*, he makes poetic use of the beat of African American music. In "Twenty-Two Tremblings of the Postulant" ("Improvisations Surrounding the Body"), he arranges a complex blues structure into twenty-two stanzas; each corresponds not only to a part of the body but also to a specific musical chord. This interest in music corresponds to Wright's search for forms that embody the rhythms of all African American cultural groups.

In Wright's poetry, music and dance forms open the way to understanding not only the African cultural heritage but also many other traditions. By recording his search for knowledge throughout cultures, Wright is unique in uncovering the links between cultures. These links imply kinship, and despite the difficulty of some of the poems, Wright's explorations, built around the single theme of self-discovery, represent a unique perspective in African American literature.

AN INVITATION TO MADISON COUNTY

First published: 1971
Type of work: Poem

Searching for his identity, the African American poet discovers links to his own past in the traditions of a black family in rural Mississippi.

"An Invitation to Madison County" comes from *The Homecoming Singer*, Jay Wright's second book of poetry. In many poems in this work, he portrays places he has lived or visited. He uses these autobiographical materials as springboards from which to launch his search for identity. "An Invitation to Madison County" relates his experiences in rural Mississippi when he toured the South on a fellowship in the 1960's. When he first arrives, the poet feels alienated. At the end of the poem, however, he visualizes a common tradition as he begins to communicate with a rural black family.

The first three stanzas express the tension the poet feels in Mississippi, far away from the familiar environment of New York City. He is anxious, trying to write in his "southern journal," but "can't get down the apprehension,/ the strangeness, the uncertainty" that he feels in the small town. He envisions Southern white racism, but nothing happens: "No one has asked me to move over/ for a small parade of pale women,/ or called me nigger, or asked me where I'm from." His host picks him up at the airport, and they drive silently through the quiet streets. He is still apprehensive as they approach the small college campus, that, like the poet, seems alien to the environment. Even the conversations of young students and instructors do not break the invisible wall surrounding him; he still feels "not totally out of Harlem." He wonders how he will let his hosts know that he does not want to listen to pleasantries but rather wants them to teach him something about what it means to be black.

His anxiety begins to dissipate in the next three stanzas, after he meets a young girl who "knows that I can read" and who simply accepts him for what he is. Chatting naturally about the land and her life, she takes him to her home, "a shack dominated by an old stove." He meets her mother, who treats him as she would any stranger, politely but warily. Despite her dismissal, he stays. After watching him sniff the food and observe her nine-year-old son, the woman senses that he is searching for something. She is right. He is fantasizing about how she is preparing her son to go to the big city and perhaps meet someone like him, a poet "who will tell him all about the city," and who will understand the boy because he understands his background. The poet, though, does not yet understand these people and their cultural link to himself, so he is "still not here,/ still can't ask an easy question." He cannot tell the family why he is here or speak of his preconceived notions about the South.

In the last three stanzas, the poet begins to get beyond his own feelings. He places himself "in Madison County,/ where you buy your clothes, your bread,/ your very life, from hardline politicians." He sees the road, the escape route to the city, where uncertainty lies. He puts himself in their place, "listening for your apprehension,/ standing at the window in different shadows," and finally perceives some of their feelings.

Seeing the similarity of their tensions and fears to his own prepares him to understand what happens when the father comes home from work in the field to have a meal. With only a nod, the man surveys his home and everyone in it, and performs the daily ritual: "His wife goes in, comes out with a spoon,/ hands it to you with a gracious little nod,/ and says, 'Such as. . .'" With this phrase, the poet realizes the sense of community for which he has come. He recalls hearing the phrase from his own mother when she invited anyone in to eat, from black waitresses in the Southwest, and from people in the Harlem ghetto, "when people, who have only themselves to give,/ offer you their meal."

Throughout his poetic career, Wright returns many times to such places as Mississippi to record the experiences that have given him clues to his identity as an African American. Yet his alienation not only from white society but also from the more conventionally rebellious posture of black artists pushes him to explore cultural traditions other than African that eventually will provide spiritual and intellectual answers to his questions.

THE ALBUQUERQUE GRAVEYARD

First published: 1976
Type of work: Poem

Discovering his past enables the poet to see himself as part of an order rather than as an isolated alienated individual.

"The Albuquerque Graveyard" comes from the middle section of Wright's third book, *Soothsayers and Omens*, a volume that marks his first steps toward defining a spiritual order and his place in it. In these poems, Wright explores African creation myths that have become a part of the cross-cultural collective memory. Using this new perspective, he revisits the Mexico and New Mexico of his earlier work.

"The Albuquerque Graveyard" is typical of the transitional poems in the second and third parts of the four-part volume. In it, the poet returns to a cemetery he has visited many times, but this time with a new challenge: understanding himself in the context of past generations of African Americans.

He begins the poem by commenting about the difficulty of getting to the cemetery: "It would be easier/ to bury our dead/ at the corner lot"; that way, he would not have to get up before dawn and take several buses. The search follows a familiar routine. On the way to the rear of the cemetery, he passes the opulent graves of white people and remarks that "the pattern of the place is clear to me."

The poet articulates what that pattern means in the next four lines: "I am going back/ to the Black limbo,/ an unwritten history/ of our own tensions." He refers not only to the cemetery's physical layout but also to an historical pattern. In the poem, "limbo" has two meanings: Blacks are in limbo, an area of uncertainty and neglect where their struggles have not been articulated; moreover, they must consciously maintain a tense balance, as a person does when doing the limbo, the dance created on the crowded slave ships. The poet wants to write the history that has been forgotten and to unwrite that which has been done in error. He wants to solidify the place of the African American—the dead as well as the living—in Western culture.

The poet sees the cemetery's occupants lying "in a hierarchy of small defeats." He stops by individual graves and recalls the people buried there: a man who saved pictures of the actor and singer Paul Robeson and who dreamed of acting the part of the heroic Othello; a woman who taught him to spell so that he would become the writer she could never be. Yet the memories of these "small heroes" bother him, because he cannot put them and himself in a larger, more significant context.

He ends the poem by describing the uneasy search for his relatives, the "simple mounds I call my own." He finds them, drops his flowers on the graves, and heads for home. He confronts his relatives' graves still feeling alienated. The experience of connecting with his personal past is pivotal in Wright's poetic development, however;

it paves the way for his process of conversion by enabling him to see himself as an integral part of an order in the world rather than an unconnected life.

CODA

First published: 1991
Type of work: Poem

To live an authentic life, a person must understand spiritual connections between past and present.

"Coda" is the last poem in Wright's collection *Boleros*, a book he dedicated to his wife Lois. Like a coda that ends a musical composition by summarizing main themes and variations, the poem forms a definitive ending to a volume in which Wright continues his spiritual and intellectual quest. This quest takes many biographical and mythological forms. He tells of places he has lived both physically, such as Mexico, and spiritually such as India. He reinvents stories and explores new poetic forms. In "Coda," Wright uses meter and rhyme reminiscent of the bolero dance, with its triple meter and staccato endings. He uses an open stanza form, incorporating lines from popular Latin American songs into an English-language environment. The form of the poem thus enhances its content, which concerns the search for culture cross-currents.

"Coda" is a good example of Wright's continuing effort to transform language and cultural visions into new forms that emphasize themes from the body of his poetry. The three stanzas all use eight lines, with a conventional paired rhyme scheme. A refrain, repeated three times at the end, finishes the poem. Allusions to Latin American culture deepen the density of the poetic context. Poems such as "Coda" challenge the reader to enter the world of an original poet who is continuing his quest for identity.

Summary

In his introduction to *Selected Poems of Jay Wright* (1987), the critic Robert Stepto stated that Wright's distinction as a poet is that he explores not only American patterns of community and history but also the larger body of transatlantic traditions. In doing so, Wright "enables us to imagine that breaking the vessels of the past is more an act of uncovering than of sheer destruction, and that we need not necessarily choose between an intellectual and a spiritual life, for both can still be had."

Wright's poetry is a record of his quest to understand personally and collectively the patterns of both these lives and the relationships between them. His cross-cultural approach to his quest makes him one of the most original voices in contemporary literature.

Bibliography

Callaloo 6 (Fall, 1983). Special issue on Jay Wright.

Harris, Wilson. *The Womb of Space: The Cross-Cultural Imagination*. Westport, Conn.: Greenwood Press, 1983.

Kutzinski, Vera M. *Against the American Grain: Myth and History in William Carlos Williams, Jay Wright, and Nicolás Guillén*. Baltimore: The Johns Hopkins University Press, 1987.

Stepto, Robert. "After Modernism, After Hibernation: Michael Harper, Robert Hayden, and Jay Wright." In *Chant of Saints: A Gathering of Afro-American Literature, Arts, and Scholarship*, edited by Michael S. Harper and Robert Stepto. Urbana: University of Illinois Press, 1979.

_____. Introduction to *Selected Poems of Jay Wright*. Princeton, N.J.: Princeton University Press, 1987.

Louise M. Stone

AUTHOR INDEX

AUTHOR INDEX

AUTHOR INDEX

AUTHOR INDEX

SALINGER, J. D.
Catcher in the Rye, The, **5**-1803
Franny and Zooey, **5**-1805
"Perfect Day for Bananafish, A," **5**-1806
SANDBURG, CARL
"Chicago," **5**-1813
"Grass," **5**-1814
SAROYAN, WILLIAM
"Daring Young Man on the Flying
Trapeze, The," **5**-1825
Human Comedy, The, **5**-1821
"Man with the Heart in the Highlands,
The," **5**-1826
Time of Your Life, The, **5**-1823
SARTON, MAY
As We Are Now, **8**-2703
"Gestalt at Sixty," **8**-2704
Journal of a Solitude, **8**-2702
SEXTON, ANNE
"All My Pretty Ones," **8**-2713
"Starry Night, The," **8**-2712
"With Mercy for the Greedy," **8**-2714
SHANGE, NTOZAKE
Betsey Brown, **5**-1838
For Colored Girls . . . , **5**-1833
Photograph, A, **5**-1835
Sassafrass, Cypress, and Indigo, **5**-1836
SHEPARD, SAM
Buried Child, **5**-1848
Fool for Love, **5**-1851
Geography of a Horse Dreamer, **5**-1847
La Turista, **5**-1845
Tooth of Crime, The, **5**-1846
True West, **5**-1850
SILKO, LESLIE MARMON
Ceremony, **5**-1858
Storyteller, **5**-1859
SIMON, NEIL
Barefoot in the Park, **5**-1866
Brighton Beach Memoirs, **5**-1871
Last of the Red Hot Lovers, **5**-1869
Odd Couple, The, **5**-1868
SMILEY, JANE
Age of Grief, The, **8**-2720
Ordinary Love and Good Will, **8**-2721
Thousand Acres, A, **8**-2723

SMITH, LULA CARSON. *See*
McCULLERS, CARSON.
SNYDER, GARY
"Bath, The," **5**-1883
Earth House Hold, **5**-1879
"Regarding Wave," **5**-1881
"Riprap," **5**-1880
SONG, CATHY
"Heaven," **8**-2732
"Pale Arrangement of Hands, A," **8**-2731
"Picture Bride," **8**-2730
SOTO, GARY
"Black Hair," **8**-2740
"Chuy," **8**-2739
"Elements of San Joaquin, The," **8**-2738
STAFFORD, JEAN
Boston Adventure, **8**-2746
Catherine Wheel, The, **8**-2747
"Healthiest Girl in Town, The," **8**-2749
STAFFORD, WILLIAM
"It's All Right," **8**-2758
"Things I Learned Last Week," **8**-2756
"Traveling Through the Dark," **8**-2755
STEGNER, WALLACE
Angle of Repose, **8**-2766
Big Rock Candy Mountain, The, **8**-2764
"Blue-Winged Teal, The," **8**-2765
STEIN, GERTRUDE
Autobiography of Alice B. Toklas, The,
8-2777
Composition as Explanation, **8**-2776
"Melanctha," **8**-2774
"Picasso," **8**-2775
STEINBECK, JOHN
Cannery Row, **6**-1894
East of Eden, **6**-1897
Grapes of Wrath, The, **6**-1893
Of Mice and Men, **6**-1890
Pearl, The, **6**-1896
Red Pony, The, **6**-1892
STEVENS, WALLACE
"Anecdote of the Jar," **6**-1906
"Chocorua to Its Neighbor," **6**-1911
"Emperor of Ice-Cream, The," **6**-1908
"Idea of Order at Key West, The," **6**-1909
"Of Modern Poetry," **6**-1910

CLV

AUTHOR INDEX

TITLE INDEX

TITLE INDEX

TITLE INDEX

TITLE INDEX

"Structure of Rime, The" (Duncan) **2**-596

Studs Lonigan: A trilogy. *See* Judgment Day, Young Lonigan, *and* The Young Manhood of Studs Lonigan.

"Sudden Trip Home in the Spring, A" (Walker) **6**-2036

Suddenly Last Summer (Williams, T.) **6**-2148

Sula (Morrison) **4**-1432

Sum of All Fears, The (Clancy) **7**-2327

Summer and Smoke (Williams, T.) **6**-2144

Sun Also Rises, The (Hemingway) **3**-902

"Sun-Down Poem." *See* "Crossing Brooklyn Ferry."

"Sunday Morning" (Stevens) **6**-1904

Sunlight Dialogues, The (Gardner) **2**-747

Suttree (McCarthy, C.) **4**-1199

"Swimmer" (Cheever) **1**-382

Tales of the South Pacific (Michener) **4**-1353

Talley's Folley (Wilson, L.) **8**-2876

Tamar (Jeffers) **3**-1009

Taming the Star Runner (Hinton) **3**-930

Tatlin! (Davenport) **7**-2343

"Tea at the Palaz of Hoon" (Stevens) **6**-1907

Teaching a Stone to Talk (Dillard) **2**-546

"Teeth Mother Naked at Last, The" (Bly) **1**-221

Tehanu: The Last Book of Earthsea (Le Guin) **3**-1127

"Tell Me a Riddle" (Olsen) **5**-1551

"Tell-Tale Heart, The" (Poe) **5**-1646

Tender Is the Night (Fitzgerald) **2**-689

Terms of Endearment (McMurtry) **4**-1258

"Territory" (Leavitt) **7**-2572

Tex (Hinton) **3**-929

That Was Then, This Is Now (Hinton) **3**-926

Their Eyes Were Watching God (Hurston) **3**-961

Theophilus North (Wilder) **6**-2132

"There's a certain Slant of light." *See* Poem 258.

"Theresa's Friends" (Creeley) **2**-451

Thin Man, The (Hammett) **2**-818

"Things I Learned Last Week" (Stafford, W.) **8**-2756

Third Life of Grange Copeland, The (Walker) **6**-2031

This Side of Paradise (Fitzgerald) **2**-684

Thomas and Beulah (Dove) **7**-2352

"Those Weary Blues" (Hughes) **3**-951

Thousand Acres, A (Smiley) **8**-2723

Three Farmers on Their Way to a Dance (Powers, R.) **8**-2684

"Three Valentines to the Wide World" (Van Duyn) **8**-2831

Through the Ivory Gates (Dove) **7**-2354

"Time of Friendship, The" (Bowles) **1**-236

Time of Your Life, The (Saroyan) **5**-1823

"Time-Travel" (Olds) **8**-2658

Tiny Alice (Albee) **1**-39

"To a Little Girl, One Year Old, in a Ruined Fortress" (Warren) **6**-2047

"To Build a Fire" (London) **3**-1152

To Kill a Mockingbird (Lee) **3**-1116

"To the Film Industry in Crisis" (O'Hara) **8**-2649

Tobacco Road (Caldwell) **1**-316

Tooth of Crime, The (Shepard) **5**-1846

Tracks (Erdrich) **2**-653

"Tract" (Williams) **6**-2158

"Tradition and the Individual Talent" (Eliot) **2**-616

"Traveling Through the Dark" (Stafford, W.) **8**-2755

"Tree at My Window" (Frost) **2**-724

Tribute to the Angels, The. *See* Trilogy.

Trilogy (H. D.) **3**-858

Tripmaster Monkey (Kingston) **3**-1091

Triton (Delany) **2**-472

"Trolling for Blues" (Wilbur) **6**-2121

Tropic of Cancer (Miller, H.) **4**-1379

Tropic of Capricorn (Miller, H.) **4**-1380

Trout Fishing in America (Brautigan) **1**-273

True Grit (Portis) **5**-1670

"True Import of Present Dialogue, Black vs. Negro, The" (Giovanni) **2**-782

True West (Shepard) **5**-1850

Turista, La (Shepard) **5**-1845

Turn of the Screw, The (James) **3**-997

Two for the Seesaw (Gibson) **2**-761

Typee (Melville) **4**-1326

TITLE INDEX

CULTURAL INDEX

African American Writers

CULTURAL INDEX

Asian American Writers

European American Writers

CULTURAL INDEX

CULTURAL INDEX

CULTURAL INDEX

CULTURAL INDEX

CULTURAL INDEX

CULTURAL INDEX

CULTURAL INDEX

Jewish American Writers

Latino Writers

Native American Writers

CULTURAL INDEX

INDEX OF WOMEN WRITERS